THE
Six O'Clock
Scramble
MEAL PLANNER

A Year of Quick, Delicious Meals to
Help You Prevent and Manage Diabetes

AVIVA GOLDFARB

American
Diabetes
Association®

Director, Book Publishing, Abe Ogden; Managing Editor, Project Manager, Rebekah Renshaw; Acquisitions Editor, Victor Van Beuren; Production Manager, Melissa Sprott; Composition, pixiedesign, llc; Cover Design, Jody Billert, Design Literate Studio; Photography, Renée Comet, Linda Wolpert; Printer, RR Donnelley.

Printed in the United States of America
1 3 5 7 9 10 8 6 4 2

The suggestions and information contained in this publication are generally consistent with the *Standards of Medical Care in Diabetes* and other policies of the American Diabetes Association, but they do not represent the policy or position of the Association or any of its boards or committees. Reasonable steps have been taken to ensure the accuracy of the information presented. However, the American Diabetes Association cannot ensure the safety or efficacy of any product or service described in this publication. Individuals are advised to consult a physician or other appropriate health care professional before undertaking any diet or exercise program or taking any medication referred to in this publication. Professionals must use and apply their own professional judgment, experience, and training and should not rely solely on the information contained in this publication before prescribing any diet, exercise, or medication. The American Diabetes Association—its officers, directors, employees, volunteers, and members—assumes no responsibility or liability for personal or other injury, loss, or damage that may result from the suggestions or information in this publication.

⊚ The paper in this publication meets the requirements of the ANSI Standard Z39.48-1992 (permanence of paper).

ADA titles may be purchased for business or promotional use or for special sales. To purchase more than 50 copies of this book at a discount, or for custom editions of this book with your logo, contact the American Diabetes Association at the address below or at booksales@diabetes.org.

American Diabetes Association
1701 North Beauregard Street
Alexandria, Virginia 22311

Library of Congress Cataloging-in-Publication Data

Names: Goldfarb, Aviva.
Title: The six o'clock scramble meal planner / Aviva Goldfarb.
Other titles: 6 o'clock scramble meal planner
Description: Alexandria : American Diabetes Association, 2016. | Includes index.
Identifiers: LCCN 2015047905 | ISBN 9781580405676 (pbk. : alk. paper)
Subjects: LCSH: Diabetes--Diet therapy--Recipes. | LCGFT: Cookbooks.
Classification: LCC RC662 .G5984 2016 | DDC 641.5/6314--dc23 LC record available at http://lccn.loc.gov/2015047905

CONTENTS

Cilantro Lime Shrimp
SIDE DISHES: Buckwheat; Steamed Broccoli with Lemon-Pepper Seasoning

page
254

For the tens of thousands of hard-working, loving, Six O'Clock Scrambling moms and dads who believe in the power of family dinners, and who plan, shop, and chop to make it happen week after week.

Spaghetti with Creamy Avocado Pesto and Roasted Tomatoes

SIDE DISHES: Roasted Brussel Sprouts

page
358

Acknowledgments

One of the things I love most about food is the way it brings us together in pleasurable shared experiences. Before I began developing recipes and writing cookbooks, I was in the political world in Washington, DC. I tired of the endless partisan fighting and longed to do something with my professional life that unified people and improved their lives more directly.

With food and recipes, we share, we include, and we nourish each other. The most divisive issue we usually face when it comes to recipes is whether we love or loathe cilantro or papaya (I love the first and loathe the second).

When I make a new recipe, I can't wait to tell other people about it. When I hear about or see a picture of a dish someone else made, I get excited to try it, maybe put my own twist on it, and then of course, serve it to my family and friends. For me, cooking is a nurturing collaboration of effort and experiences.

Any collection of recipes is a team effort. I am grateful to the people who shared their recipes with me and who tested and critiqued my recipes, improving them in the process. I am also grateful to YOU for choosing to cook and serve these recipes to the people you care about.

Because it's a weekly meal planner, this book is about three times as long as most cookbooks and putting it together took massive effort. In particular, I want to thank my do-everything colleague Betsy Goldstein for helping me create the weekly meal plans and keep this massive project on track, always with good humor and keen attention to detail. Special thanks to food photographers Renee Comet, Linda Wolpert, and Kirsten Wisniakowski for their beautiful photographs of the dishes and to food stylist Lisa Cherkasky for making them look so appetizing. I am grateful to Kathryn Spindel, whose recipe edits keep us on our toes (and often make us giggle). Thank you to my slow cooker guru Marla Kostis for converting so many of my recipes for the slow cooker. I so appreciate the guidance and support of Abraham Ogden, Rebekah Renshaw, Katie Curran, and Samantha Boyd at the American Diabetes Association, and to Bonnie Benwick at *The Washington Post* for letting me share many of my recipes with the readers of their incomparable Food section, which brought my work to the attention of the ADA.

Many people contributed recipes or ideas that inspired me. I am grateful to Shawn Askew, Joy Bauer, Dara Baylinson, Nancy Bolen, Hillary Bratton, Melissa Clark, Chef Ann Cooper, Alice Currah, Melissa d'Arabian, Christine Dallaire, Laurie David, Jolynn Dellinger, Kristen Donoghue, Gretchen Douglas, Marilyn Emery, Debbie Firestone, April Fulton, Carla Geovanis, Sharon Hauer Gill, Jennifer Grosman, Jennifer Gross, Jessica Honigberg, Michele Houghton, Julia Jayne, Alison Kavanaugh, Susan Levy, Jenny Lim, Michelle Mainelli, Larry McCleary, Laurie McLean, Jessica McMaken, Megan Miller, Sena Murphy, Karen Murray, Anne O'Neill, Jill Rabach, Robin Robertson, Jeanne Rossomme, Molly Rubel, Traci Sara, Esther Schrader, Stephanie Witt Sedgwick, Katherine

Newell Smith, Lizzy Smith, Ailea Sneller, Molly Thompson, Kim Tilley, Kirstin Uhrenholdt, Jenna Weber, Amanda Wendt, Ames Williford, and Will Witkop, who shared their creations and even tolerated my alterations and adaptations of them. I so appreciate my online food community of writers, bloggers, and cooks who keep me motivated during the 6:00 "scramble" and are always generous with their suggestions, especially Olga Berman, Monica Bhide, Laura Kumin, Kristin O'Keefe, Amy Riolo, and Robyn Webb.

Recipes that come out perfectly in our kitchens don't always translate from our written versions to someone else's table, and that's crucial to discern before we share them widely or publish them. A humongous cheer for The Six O'Clock Scramble recipe testers: Elena Berzon-Ezzell, Nancy Bolen, Amy Cherwin, Kathryn Howell Dalton, Marilyn Emery, Debbie Falkow, Debbie Firestone, Mareesa Frederick, Kim Freeman, Jennifer Grosman, Leanne Guido, Kim Jackson, Gina Jermakowicz, Melinda Kelley, Greg Kershner, Randi Abramowitz Kottler, Bob Loeb, Jamila Mergerson, Samantha McKenzie, Anne O'Neill, Ashley Parkinson, Krysta Pascuzzo, Alexandra Taylor, Maxine Silverman, Sandra Simmons, Ailea Sneller, Amy Stanley, Nikki Wolf, Sally Ashe Wood, and Bobbi Woods, who bravely try my recipes before they are published and so eloquently share their feedback and suggestions, and are always kind, even when recipes don't quite work.

All my heart goes to my three most important recipe testers, Andrew, Solomon, and Celia. Seldom do you cringe anymore when I tell you what's for dinner: You gamely taste all my kitchen concoctions, no matter how strange, and only rarely get up to make yourself nachos or cereal instead. Watching your tastes and personalities develop at the dinner table over the last 18 years has been my greatest joy. Thank you for making dinnertime my favorite time of day.

I hope you and your family enjoy the recipes and they help you savor some new healthy flavors and foods. For printable versions of the grocery lists and other resources, please visit **TheScramble.com/Diabetes**, and share your feedback and recipe suggestions with me at **aviva@thescramble.com**.

Warmly,
Aviva

Introduction

Are You Ready To Live Longer, Feel Better, and Save up to 5 Hours and $133 each Week?

An astounding fact—if we stay on the same trajectory, by 2050, 1 in 3 Americans will have diabetes or pre-diabetes. Chances are there's someone you love who lives with this challenging disease. In fact, if you are reading this cookbook, there's a good chance it's you or someone in your immediate family. If you have just been diagnosed, you are now probably in the most stressful phase of diabetes: trying to figure out how to change your life to manage the disease without giving up all the foods you love, and how to get healthier, feel better, and live longer, without turning your whole life upside down.

The good news is that diabetes is very manageable for most people, and a diabetes-friendly diet can be incredibly delicious and easy to prepare. With the changes you'll make in your diet, you will likely start to feel better in countless ways—you'll lose some weight if you need to, have more energy, and even feel more nourished than with your prior way of eating. While a diabetes diagnosis is never welcome news, it can also give you an opportunity to adopt a healthier diet and lifestyle, something you've likely been wanting to do but haven't made a priority until now. Doing this can not only improve your diabetes prognosis and reduce or eliminate your need for medication, but it can also improve your heart health, increase your longevity, and improve your quality of life.

But making changes isn't always fun or easy at first. That's why I'm so glad you're holding this book! For 18 years, I've been helping people enjoy family dinners while saving time and money, and eating healthier, more interesting, and more flavorful meals. Through The Six O'Clock Scramble, my meal planning website, and my cookbooks, I've helped nearly 100,000 people enjoy more healthy, homemade meals by giving them: 1) fast and easy recipes that work with our busy lifestyles; and 2) weekly meal plans with grocery lists so they can shop just once a week and waste less food.

My grandfather Isadore Shlensky had diabetes. I have early memories of watching him give himself insulin shots in his stomach. (Maybe that's where my fear of needles developed!) As a child, I couldn't imagine having to give myself shots every day. More recently, Grandpa Ise's daughter, my beloved Aunt Gerry, was diagnosed with diabetes. So far she has been able to manage her condition with medicine and some lifestyle changes. I want to do what I can to help people avoid diabetes or live better with this tough, yet treatable disease.

While I'm no expert in diabetes, I have become an expert in healthy cooking and eating over the course of my 18 years of developing and sharing healthy recipes, including writing four cookbooks. That's why I've teamed up with the American Diabetes Association, the country's leading resource for people and families living with diabetes, to write *The Six O'Clock Scramble Meal Planner* for people with diabetes and pre-diabetes.

Dinnertime, Unscrambled

The Six O'Clock Scramble Meal Planner takes the stress and guesswork out of planning your dinners, whether you are cooking for 1, 2, or your whole family, including kids:

- Recipes are organized by season and by week to give you variety throughout your week and your year.

- Each weekly meal plan comes with an accompanying organized grocery list so you can shop for all the meals at once, saving time, money, and effort.

- All recipes take 30 minutes or less of actual prep time, which means you can get a healthy, flavorful dinner on the table with very little time and effort.

- Each recipe is paired with one or two easy side dishes so you have a complete meal ready at the same time.

- Many of the recipes can be prepared in the slow cooker, saving even more time and effort.

- Throughout the book, you'll find helpful tips to make cooking and shopping easier, save time and money, and reduce waste.

- If you are a more adventurous eater, each recipe has suggestions for boosting the flavor with interesting spices, sauces, or add-ins.

- Throughout the book, you'll find easy recipes for making delicious salad dressings, snacks, and dips, items that are too often expensive, salty, and filled with unnecessary chemicals and ingredients.

- You'll also get healthy breakfast, lunch, snack, and dessert ideas to keep your energy and your mood up throughout the day.

Sometimes making healthy changes takes a little getting used to. Throughout my many years publishing and sharing recipes, I've been flooded with notes from people who couldn't believe how much they and their families were enjoying these healthier, easier meals, and how much better they were feeling by making and enjoying these recipes with their families.

So pick your season, pick your week, or just turn to week 1 and dive in, and begin shopping and cooking these easy, delicious meals for your family. Within two weeks, you'll probably wonder how you ever lived without *The Six O'Clock Scramble Meal Planner*.

I want to hear from you about your experience with *The Six O'Clock Scramble Meal Planner*, and hope this book helps you make positive transformations in your family and your health— send me a note at **aviva@thescramble.com** or visit me at **TheScramble.com/Diabetes** or on Facebook at **facebook.com/thesixoclockscramble** or on Twitter at **Twitter.com/thescramble**.

In the meantime, if you need more healthy menu planning guidance and recipes, plus the flexibility to customize your weekly plans, please sign up for a free trial of *The Six O'Clock Scramble Meal Planner*. It offers healthy recipes with complete nutritional information to continue your journey—and your family's— toward a healthier, longer, and more enjoyable life. Start your free meal planning trial at **TheScramble.com/Diabetes**.

page 28

Honey-Dijon Chicken
SIDE DISHES: Red Potatoes Tossed with Fresh Herbs; Zucchini Fries

Cajun Fish Sandwiches with Crunchy Slaw
SIDE DISH: Lightly Buttered Corn

page
30

♉ SPRING

SPRING

Asian Chicken Fritters (1)
SIDE DISH: Steamed Edamame (1a)

Grilled Salmon with Fresh Herb Pesto (2)
SIDE DISH: Grilled or Broiled Asparagus (2a)

Crispy Taco Tumblers (3)
SIDE DISH: Guacamole with Carrots (3a); Fruity Swirl Smoothies (3b)

Rigatoni with Mushrooms, Marsala, and Mascarpone (4)
SIDE DISH: Orange Slices (4a)

Spinach & Quinoa Salad with Cashews and Cranberries (5)
SIDE DISH: Dinner Rolls (5a)

SHOPPING LIST

PRODUCE
1 pound **baby carrots or large carrots** (3a)
10 **scallions** (1)(5)
1 large **yellow onion** (4)
6 ounces **baby spinach** (5)
1/4 cup **fresh dill** (5)
1/2 cup **fresh mint leaves** (5)
1/4 cup **fresh herbs** (basil, cilantro, parsley, or chives) (2)
1 pound **asparagus** (2a)
1 pound sliced **cremini mushrooms** (4)
2–3 **avocados** (3a)
1–1 1/2 **lemons** (2)(5)
1/2 **lime** (3a)
3–6 **oranges** (4a)
2/3 cup **blueberries, fresh or frozen** (3b)
1 **banana** (3b)
2 2/3 cups **mango, fresh or frozen** (3b)

MEAT AND FISH
1 pound **boneless, skinless chicken breasts** (1)
1–1 1/2 pounds **salmon (preferably wild Alaskan) or halibut fillet** (2)
1 pound **lean ground turkey or beef** (3)

SHELVED ITEMS

1 package **whole-wheat dinner rolls** (5a)

1 cup **quinoa** (5)

16 ounces **whole-wheat rigatoni noodles** (4)

1/2 cup **salsa** (3)

2 tablespoons **Asian sweet chili sauce or teriyaki sauce** (1)*

1/4 cup **Marsala wine** (4)

15 ounces canned **kidney beans** (3)

8 ounces **diced water chestnuts** (1)

1/2 cup **dried cranberries** (preferably naturally sweetened) (5)

1 1/2 tablespoons **pine nuts** (2)

1 cup **cashews** (5)

SPICES

1/2 teaspoon **salt** (2)(3a)

3/8–1/2 teaspoon **kosher salt** (1a)(2a)

1/4 teaspoon **salt-free lemon pepper seasoning** (2a)

1 teaspoon **dried thyme** (4)

5/8 teaspoon **black pepper** (1)(2)

1/2 teaspoon **ground ginger** (1)

3/4 teaspoon **garlic powder** (1)(3a)

STAPLES

2 tablespoons + 1/4 cup **extra-virgin olive oil** (2a)(4)(5)

2 1/3 tablespoons **vegetable oil** (2)

3 tablespoons **canola or vegetable oil** (1)

1/4 cup + 2 tablespoons **reduced-sodium soy sauce** (use wheat/gluten-free if needed) (1)(4)

1 teaspoon **honey** (2)

1 **egg** (1)

1 1/2 teaspoons **minced garlic** (2a)(4)

1/4 cup **flour** (use wheat/gluten-free if needed) (1)

REFRIGERATED/FROZEN

1/3 cup **shredded cheddar cheese** (3)

1/2 cup **crumbled reduced-fat feta or goat cheese** (5)

1/4 cup **grated Parmesan cheese** (4)*

1/4 cup **mascarpone** (4)

1 1/3 cups **nonfat vanilla yogurt** (3b)

1/2 cup **sour cream** (3)*

2 cups **orange juice** (3b)

16 **egg roll wrappers** (sold frozen or refrigerated) (3)

3/4 cup **frozen corn kernels** (3)

1 1/2 pounds **edamame (Japanese soybeans, sold frozen) or frozen peas** (1a)

Get free, printable versions of the shopping lists from this book at TheScramble.com/diabetes.

*optional ingredients

SPRING WEEK 1 • 3

These crispy little cuties, from former Six O'Clock Scramble intern Molly Rubel, are so much fun to make and eat. You can eat them on buns if you prefer, but we like them best dipped in a little Asian sweet chili sauce, duck sauce, or spicy mustard. Serve the fritters with Steamed Edamame.

Asian Chicken Fritters

PREP: 15 MINUTES • **COOK:** 20 MINUTES • **SERVES:** 6 • **SERVING SIZE:** 2 FRITTERS

1 pound boneless, skinless chicken breasts, cut into 1/4–1/2-inch chunks

1 (8-ounce) can diced water chestnuts, drained and chopped into 1/4–1/2-inch chunks

6 scallions, dark and light green parts, thinly sliced

1 egg, lightly beaten

1/4 cup flour

1/4 cup reduced-sodium soy sauce (use wheat/gluten-free, if needed)

1/2 teaspoon garlic powder (look for salt-free variety)

1/2 teaspoon black pepper

1/2 teaspoon ground ginger

3 tablespoons canola or vegetable oil

DO AHEAD OR DELEGATE: Cut the chicken, chop the water chestnuts, slice the scallions, beat and refrigerate the egg, combine the dry spices with the flour, make and refrigerate the fritter batter.

1. Preheat the oven to 400°F. Line a baking sheet with a silicone mat or nonstick cooking spray. In a large bowl, combine all the ingredients except the oil.

2. Heat a large skillet over medium-high heat (a cast iron skillet works especially well for even browning) and add half the oil. When it is hot, scoop the chicken mixture into the skillet (an ice cream scoop works well for even fritters), making sure not to crowd the pan—you might even want to use two large skillets, or cook them in two batches, using the remaining oil for the second batch.

3. Fry the fritters without moving them until they are golden brown, about 3 minutes per side, and transfer them to the baking sheet. Bake the fritters until they are cooked through, 6–8 minutes. (Meanwhile, prepare the edamame.) Serve immediately.

FLAVOR BOOSTER
Add 2 tablespoons Asian sweet chili sauce or teriyaki sauce to the batter and increase the garlic powder and the ground ginger to 3/4 teaspoon each.

Steamed Edamame (Japanese Soybeans)

SERVES: 6 • **SERVING SIZE:** 1 CUP

1 1/2 pounds edamame (Japanese soybeans, sold frozen) or frozen peas
1/8 teaspoon kosher salt (optional)

1. Prepare the edamame according to the package directions. Sprinkle the cooked edamame with kosher salt, if desired.

TIP
You may notice that I suggest using a silicone mat in some of my recipes. The reason I like them is that they are an effective calorie-free (and Earth-friendly) alternative to nonstick cooking spray, foil, or parchment paper when baking. They are reliably nonstick and are oven-safe to 475°F.

NUTRITIONAL INFORMATION | ASIAN CHICKEN FRITTERS:

EXCHANGES / CHOICES:
1/2 Starch; 1 Nonstarchy Vegetable; 2 Protein, lean; 1 Fat

Calories: 210; Calories from Fat: 90; Total Fat: 10 g; Saturated Fat: 1.3 g; Trans Fat: 0 g; Cholesterol: 75 mg; Sodium: 425 mg; Potassium: 260 mg; Total Carbohydrate: 10 g; Dietary Fiber: 2 g; Sugar: 1 g; Protein: 19 g; Phosphorus: 165 mg

NUTRITIONAL INFORMATION | EDAMAME:

EXCHANGES / CHOICES:
2 Nonstarchy Vegetable; 1 Protein, lean; 1 Fat

Calories: 140; Calories from Fat: 55; Total Fat: 6 g; Saturated Fat: 0.7 g; Trans Fat: 0 g; Cholesterol: 75 mg; Sodium: 5 mg; Potassium: 495 mg; Total Carbohydrate: 11 g; Dietary Fiber: 6 g; Sugar: 2 g; Protein: 12 g; Phosphorus: 190 mg

Use your favorite herbs to create a fresh-tasting sauce for grilled fish. (You can leave the sauce off the fish for picky eaters, but our kids like it.) For the sauce, you can use only basil or cilantro, or add other fresh herbs you have in your garden or refrigerator. Serve with Grilled Asparagus.

Grilled Salmon with Fresh Herb Pesto

PREP + COOK: 25 MINUTES • **SERVES:** 4 • **SERVING SIZE:** 4 OUNCES SALMON + 2 TABLESPOONS PESTO

1 pound salmon (preferably wild Alaskan) or halibut fillet

2 1/3 tablespoons vegetable oil, divided use

1/4 teaspoon salt

1/8 teaspoon black pepper

1/4 cup fresh herbs, including any combination of basil, cilantro, parsley, or chives, coarsely chopped

1 tablespoon water

1/2 lemon, juice only (about 2 tablespoons)

1 1/2 tablespoons pine nuts

1 teaspoon honey

DO AHEAD OR DELEGATE: Make and refrigerate the pesto.

1. Preheat the grill to medium-high heat. Brush the top and sides of the salmon (or halibut) with 1 teaspoon of oil and season with salt and pepper. In a blender or food processor, puree the herbs, 2 tablespoons oil, the water, lemon juice, pine nuts, and honey. Transfer the mixture to a small serving bowl.

2. (Start the asparagus now, if you are serving it.) Grill the fish skin side down on top of aluminum foil or a grilling tray for about 10 minutes without flipping it, until it flakes easily and is no longer dark pink in the middle. (Alternatively, bake the fish in the oven at 400°F for 12–15 minutes until it is cooked through.) When the fish is done, slide a thin spatula between the fish and the skin, allowing the skin to stick to the foil or tray, and transfer the fish to a serving plate. Serve the fish topped with the herb pesto.

SLOW COOKER DIRECTIONS: Place the salmon on a piece of aluminum foil, brush the flesh with oil and sprinkle with salt and pepper. Fold the foil over the salmon to make a packet. (If your piece of salmon is larger than your slow cooker, cut it to fit, and place each piece on its own individual packet.) Cook on low for 6–8 hours or on high for 3–4 hours, until the salmon is done. Remove it from the foil and top it with the pesto to serve. (Slow cooker cooking times may vary—get to know your slow cooker and, if necessary, adjust cooking times accordingly.)

FLAVOR BOOSTER
Stir 1/2 teaspoon lemon zest into the pesto.

Grilled Asparagus

SERVES: 4 • **SERVING SIZE:** 3–5 SPEARS (1/4 RECIPE)

1 pound asparagus
1 tablespoon extra-virgin olive oil
1/2 teaspoon minced garlic (about 1 clove)
1/4 teaspoon kosher salt
1/4 teaspoon salt-free lemon-pepper seasoning

1. Preheat the grill or broiler. Trim the ends of the asparagus spears and lay them in a flat dish. In a small bowl, combine the olive oil, garlic, salt, and lemon-pepper seasoning. Drizzle the oil mixture over the asparagus and stir them to coat. Grill them on a vegetable or fish grilling tray or broil them on a baking sheet for 10–15 minutes, flipping once, until they are tender and starting to brown.

NUTRITIONAL INFORMATION | SALMON WITH FRESH HERB PESTO:

EXCHANGES / CHOICES:
3 Protein, lean; 3 Fat

Calories: 265; Calories from Fat: 160; Total Fat: 18 g;
Saturated Fat: 2.5 g; Trans Fat: 0 g; Cholesterol: 65 mg;
Sodium: 225 mg; Potassium: 455 mg; Total Carbohydrate: 3 g;
Dietary Fiber: 0 g; Sugar: 2 g; Protein: 23 g; Phosphorus: 330 mg

NUTRITIONAL INFORMATION | GRILLED ASPARAGUS:

EXCHANGES / CHOICES:
1 Nonstarchy Vegetable; 1/2 Fat

Calories: 45; Calories from Fat: 30; Total Fat: 3.5 g;
Saturated Fat: 0.5 g; Trans Fat: 0 g; Cholesterol: 0 mg;
Sodium: 120 mg; Potassium: 145 mg; Total Carbohydrate: 3 g;
Dietary Fiber: 2 g; Sugar: 1 g; Protein: 2 g; Phosphorus: 40 mg

TIP

Try to avoid grocery shopping when you're hungry. A recent study published by the *Journal of the American Medical Association* determined that skipping a meal before heading to the market can lead shoppers to purchase 31 percent more high-calorie foods. Late afternoon shoppers also bought fewer low-calorie foods relative to their overall purchase than those who shopped after lunch on a full stomach.

My friend and hostess extraordinaire Katherine Newell Smith described these taco cups to me as a fun party snack, but seeing as we have a lot more family dinners than parties, I decided to make them a festive meal instead. It's always fun to have a meal that we can eat with our hands. Using meatless crumbles cuts the calories and fat and increases the fiber, and it's amazingly reminiscent of real meat. Serve with Guacamole with Carrots and Fruity Swirl Smoothies.

Crispy Taco Tumblers

PREP + COOK: 30 MINUTES • **SERVES:** 8 • **SERVING SIZE:** 2 TACO CUPS

1 pound lean ground turkey

15 ounces canned kidney beans, drained and rinsed (or 1 1/2 cups cooked)

1/2 cup salsa, plus more for serving, any variety (I used salsa verde)

3/4 cup frozen corn kernels

16 (7-inch square) egg roll wrappers (sold frozen or refrigerated)

1/3 cup shredded cheddar cheese

1/2 cup sour cream, for serving (optional)

FLAVOR BOOSTER
Use spicy salsa, sharp cheddar or pepper jack cheese, and/or sprinkle a little hot sauce on each cup before serving.

DO AHEAD OR DELEGATE: Trim the egg roll wrappers as directed and refrigerate. Shred the cheese, if necessary, and refrigerate.

1. Preheat the oven to 400°F. Meanwhile, in a nonstick skillet over medium-low heat, combine the meat, beans, and salsa and cook until bubbling. (Note: if you are using meat rather than meatless crumbles, cook the meat first, drain if necessary, and add the beans and salsa when the meat is just cooked through, and cook for another minute or two to warm through.) Stir in the corn and remove it from the heat.

2. Using kitchen scissors, cut off the corners of the egg roll wrappers so they are circles instead of squares (this makes them easier to stuff into the muffin cups with room for the filling). Press each egg roll wrapper into a muffin cup, leaving as much space in the middle of the cup as possible. Spray the surface of each cup with nonstick cooking spray (this isn't necessary if you don't like to use it, but it makes them crispier) and bake them for 5 minutes until they start to turn golden brown on the edges. (Meanwhile, make the guacamole, if you are serving it.)

3. Spoon the taco mixture into each of the cups to fill them most of the way, and top each with about 1 teaspoon of cheese. Bake for 5 minutes or until the cheese is melted and the shells are golden. (Meanwhile, prepare the smoothies, if you are serving them.) Serve immediately, topped with guacamole, salsa, and/or sour cream, if desired.

Guacamole with Carrots

PREP: 10 MINUTES • **SERVES:** 8
SERVING SIZE: 2 TABLESPOONS GUACAMOLE AND 1/2 CUP CARROTS

2 avocados
1/2 lime, juice only (about 1 tablespoon)
1/4 teaspoon salt
1/4 teaspoon garlic powder
1 pound baby carrots, or large carrots cut into sticks

1. Mash the flesh of the avocados with the lime juice. Add the salt and garlic powder. Serve with the carrots.

Fruity Swirl Smoothies

SERVES: 8 • **SERVING SIZE:** 1 CUP

2 cups orange juice
1 1/3 cups nonfat vanilla yogurt
2 2/3 cups mango (frozen works well)
2/3 cup blueberries (frozen work well)
1 banana, peeled

1. In a blender, combine the juice, yogurt, mango, blueberries, and banana. Add 1 cup of ice cubes if desired, especially if you used fresh rather than frozen fruit. Blend on high speed for 30–60 seconds until smooth.

TIP

Here's how food photographer Linda Wolpert makes the taco cups so pretty: When looking at the circular egg roll wrap, imagine that it is divided into four pie pieces. Bring each of the corners of the pie pieces up to the middle to make a flower.

NUTRITIONAL INFORMATION | CRISPY TACO TUMBLERS:

EXCHANGES / CHOICES:
2 1/2 Starch; 2 Protein, lean

Calories: 295; Calories from Fat: 65; Total Fat: 7 g;
Saturated Fat: 2.4 g; Trans Fat: 0.1 g; Cholesterol: 50 mg;
Sodium: 425 mg; Potassium: 370 mg; Total Carbohydrate: 37 g;
Dietary Fiber: 4 g; Sugar: 2 g; Protein: 20 g; Phosphorus: 230 mg

NUTRITIONAL INFORMATION | GUACAMOLE WITH CARROTS:

EXCHANGES / CHOICES:
2 Nonstarchy Vegetable; 1 Fat

Calories: 85; Calories from Fat: 55; Total Fat: 6 g;
Saturated Fat: 0.8 g; Trans Fat: 0 g; Cholesterol: 0 mg;
Sodium: 115 mg; Potassium: 365 mg; Total Carbohydrate: 9 g;
Dietary Fiber: 4 g; Sugar: 3 g; Protein: 1 g; Phosphorus: 40 mg

NUTRITIONAL INFORMATION | FRUITY SWIRL SMOOTHIES:

EXCHANGES / CHOICES:
1 1/2 Fruit

Calories: 100; Calories from Fat: 5; Total Fat: 0.5 g;
Saturated Fat: 0.1 g; Trans Fat: 0 g; Cholesterol: 0 mg;
Sodium: 20 mg; Potassium: 345 mg; Total Carbohydrate: 24 g;
Dietary Fiber: 2 g; Sugar: 19 g; Protein: 2 g; Phosphorus: 55 mg

Even if you're not the biggest fan of mushrooms, you might not be able to resist them once they're simmered with garlic, soy sauce, and Marsala wine. Serve with Orange Slices.

Rigatoni with Mushrooms, Marsala, and Mascarpone

PREP + COOK: 30 MINUTES • **SERVES:** 9 • **SERVING SIZE:** 1 1/3 CUPS

16 ounces whole-wheat rigatoni

1 tablespoon extra-virgin olive oil

1 pound sliced cremini mushrooms, or use button mushrooms, or half of each

1 large yellow onion, diced

1 teaspoon minced garlic, (about 2 cloves)

1 teaspoon dried thyme, or use 2 teaspoons fresh

2 tablespoons reduced-sodium soy sauce (use wheat/gluten-free if needed)

1/4 cup Marsala wine, or use sherry or white wine (if you don't cook with wine use 1/4 cup chicken or vegetable broth and 1 tablespoon balsamic vinegar)

1/4 cup mascarpone, or use cream cheese, crème fraiche, or 2–3 tablespoons olive oil for a dairy-free version

1/4 cup grated Parmesan cheese, for serving

DO AHEAD OR DELEGATE: Cook the pasta and toss it with a little oil to prevent sticking, dice the onion, peel the garlic, slice the mushrooms, grate the Parmesan cheese, if necessary, or fully prepare and refrigerate the dish.

1. Cook the rigatoni in salted water according to the package directions until it is al dente. Meanwhile, heat a large heavy skillet over medium heat and add the oil. When it is hot, add the mushrooms, onions, garlic, and thyme, and sauté them until the mushrooms darken and the onions are translucent, 8–10 minutes. Add the soy sauce and wine and simmer it for 5–7 more minutes, stirring occasionally, until the pasta is done and the liquid in the mushrooms is reduced by about half. (Meanwhile, slice the oranges, if you are serving them.)

2. Drain the noodles, allowing some liquid to cling to them, return them to the pot, and stir in the mascarpone until it melts. Top with the mushrooms and onions and serve immediately, topped with the Parmesan cheese at the table, if desired, or refrigerate for up to 3 days.

SLOW COOKER DIRECTIONS: Combine the mushrooms, onions, garlic, thyme, soy sauce, and wine in the slow cooker, and cook on low for 6–10 hours. Add the mascarpone 15 minutes before serving, and stir to melt. Serve it over cooked pasta and topped with Parmesan cheese, if desired. (Slow cooker cooking times may vary—get to know your slow cooker and, if necessary, adjust cooking times accordingly.)

Orange Slices

SERVES: 8 • **SERVING SIZE:** 1/2 ORANGE

4 medium oranges

1. Cut the oranges into wedges for serving.

FLAVOR BOOSTER

Use extra minced garlic and top the pasta with freshly ground black pepper.

TIP

Wondering what to do with leftover mascarpone? Try spreading it on toast or a baked pizza crust and drizzling it with honey and black pepper, or stirring it into mashed potatoes.

NUTRITIONAL INFORMATION | RIGATONI WITH MUSHROOMS, MARSALA, AND MASCARPONE:

EXCHANGES / CHOICES:
2 1/2 Starch; 1 Nonstarchy Vegetable; 1 Fat

Calories: 260; Calories from Fat: 55; Total Fat: 6 g;
Saturated Fat: 2.5 g; Trans Fat: 0.1 g; Cholesterol: 10 mg;
Sodium: 185 mg; Potassium: 395 mg; Total Carbohydrate: 44 g;
Dietary Fiber: 6 g; Sugar: 4 g; Protein: 10 g; Phosphorus: 225 mg

NUTRITIONAL INFORMATION | ORANGE SLICES:

EXCHANGES / CHOICES:
1/2 Fruit

Calories: 35; Calories from Fat: 0; Total Fat: 0.0 g;
Saturated Fat: 0 g; Trans Fat: 0 g; Cholesterol: 0 mg;
Sodium: 0 mg; Potassium: 140 mg; Total Carbohydrate: 9 g;
Dietary Fiber: 2 g; Sugar: 7 g; Protein: 1 g; Phosphorus: 10 mg

Have you tried quinoa yet? If not, I recommend it! Nutritionally it's a powerhouse, it has a pleasing texture and unlike many whole grains it cooks as quickly as white rice. Six O'Clock Scramble member Julia Jayne sent me a wonderful recipe for her spinach and quinoa salad recipe that inspired my own version. Serve with Whole-Wheat Dinner Rolls.

Spinach & Quinoa Salad with Toasted Cashews and Dried Cranberries

PREP + COOK: 25 MINUTES • **SERVES:** 6 • **SERVING SIZE:** 1 1/2 CUPS SALAD + 1 1/3 TABLESPOONS DRESSING

1 cup quinoa, preferably red or tricolor

1/2–1 lemon, juice only (1/4 cup)

1/4 cup extra-virgin olive oil (preferably something light and fruity, if you have it)

1 teaspoon dried dill or 1/4 cup fresh dill, finely chopped

6 ounces baby spinach, sliced into thin strips (about 6 cups)

1/3 cup scallions, dark and light green parts, thinly sliced (about 4 scallions)

1/2 cup fresh mint leaves, chopped

1 cup cashews, lightly toasted, coarsely chopped, or use toasted pumpkin seeds for a nut-free alternative

1/2 cup dried cranberries

1/2 cup crumbled reduced-fat feta or goat cheese

DO AHEAD OR DELEGATE: Cook the quinoa, prepare the dressing, slice the spinach and the scallions, and toast and chop the cashews.

1. Cook the quinoa according to package directions (this can be done up to 2 days in advance).

2. In a measuring cup or medium bowl, combine the lemon juice, olive oil, and dried dill, if using it (if using fresh dill, add it with the remaining salad ingredients). (Meanwhile, warm the rolls, if you are serving them.)

3. In a large bowl, combine the remaining ingredients, except the cheese. Stir in the cooked quinoa and the dressing, then gently fold in the cheese. Season with salt and pepper to taste. Serve immediately or refrigerate for up to 3 days.

FLAVOR BOOSTER
Add 1 tablespoon seasoned rice vinegar and/or 1 teaspoon honey to the salad dressing.

Whole-Wheat Dinner Rolls

SERVES: 6 • **SERVING SIZE:** 1 ROLL

6 whole-wheat dinner rolls

1. Warm the dinner rolls in a 300°F oven for 5 minutes.

TIP

You can toast cashews in a toaster or conventional oven. Preheat the oven to 350°F, and spread the cashews on a baking sheet. Bake them for 10–15 minutes or until they are golden brown, stirring occasionally. For a quicker method, use the stovetop. Spread the nuts evenly in a skillet and heat them over medium heat for about 5 minutes or until golden and fragrant. Make sure to stir or shake the nuts while cooking them to keep them from burning.

NUTRITIONAL INFORMATION | SPINACH AND QUINOA SALAD WITH TOASTED CASHEWS AND DRIED CRANBERRIES (ANALYSIS FOR SALAD ONLY):

EXCHANGES / CHOICES:
1 1/2 Starch; 1/2 Fruit; 1/2 Carbohydrate; 1 Protein, lean; 2 Fat

Calories: 310; Calories from Fat: 125; Total Fat: 14 g;
Saturated Fat: 3.2 g; Trans Fat: 0 g; Cholesterol: 5 mg;
Sodium: 175 mg; Potassium: 540 mg; Total Carbohydrate: 38 g;
Dietary Fiber: 5 g; Sugar: 10 g; Protein: 12 g; Phosphorus: 345 mg

(ANALYSIS FOR DRESSING ONLY):

EXCHANGES / CHOICES:
2 Fat

Calories: 80; Calories from Fat: 80; Total Fat: 9 g;
Saturated Fat: 1.2 g; Trans Fat: 0 g; Cholesterol: 0 mg;
Sodium: 0 mg; Potassium: 10 mg; Total Carbohydrate: 1 g;
Dietary Fiber: 0 g; Sugar: 0 g; Protein: 0 g; Phosphorus: 0 mg

NUTRITIONAL INFORMATION | WHOLE-WHEAT DINNER ROLLS:

EXCHANGES / CHOICES:
1 Starch

Calories: 95; Calories from Fat: 15; Total Fat: 1.5 g;
Saturated Fat: 0.3 g; Trans Fat: 0 g; Cholesterol: 0 mg;
Sodium: 145 mg; Potassium: 100 mg; Total Carbohydrate: 18 g;
Dietary Fiber: 3 g; Sugar: 3 g; Protein: 3 g; Phosphorus: 80 mg

SPRING WEEK 2

Carpool Chicken (1)
SIDE DISH: Whole-Wheat Couscous (1a)

Rockfish with Tomatoes and Herbs Baked in a Foil Packet (2)
SIDE DISH: Steamed Broccoli Tossed with Olive Oil and Grated Parmesan Cheese (2a)

Texas Hero (a.k.a. The Davey Crockett) (3)
SIDE DISH: Fruit Cones (3a)

Farfalle with Artichoke Hearts, Baby Spinach, and Lemon Ricotta (4)
SIDE DISH: Roasted Fennel Bulbs (4a)

Creamy Corn and Potato Chowder (5)
SIDE DISH: Green Salad with Shredded Red Cabbage, Blue Cheese, and Walnuts (5a)

SHOPPING LIST

- -

🥕 PRODUCE
1 **carrot** (3)

1 **shallot** (4)

1/2 **yellow onion** (3)

2 **small yellow onions** (1)(5)

1 1/2 **red or orange bell peppers** (1)(5)

1 **yellow bell pepper** (1)

6–8 stalks **celery** (3)(5)

1 large **tomato** (2)

4 cups **lettuce, any variety** (5a)

6 ounces **baby spinach** (4)

1/2 cup **red or purple cabbage** (5a)

3 cloves **garlic** (2)

3–4 **fennel bulbs** (4a)

1 pound **broccoli** (2a)

1 **zucchini or yellow squash** (1)

1 small **russet potato** (5)

1/2 **lemon** (4)

2 cups **fresh seasonal fruit** (3a)

🍖 MEAT AND FISH
1 1/2–2 pounds **boneless, skinless chicken breasts** (1)

1 pound **ground turkey, beef, vegetarian ground meat, or canned kidney beans** (3)

3–4 **rockfish fillets, or other thin white fillets** (about 1 pound) (2)

SHELVED ITEMS

8 **whole-wheat buns** (use wheat/gluten-free buns if needed) (3)

1–2 cups **whole-wheat or regular couscous** (1a)

16 ounces **whole-wheat farfalle noodles** (use wheat/gluten-free if needed) (4)

15 ounces **no-salt-added tomato sauce** (3)

3 cups **reduced-sodium chicken or vegetable broth** (5)

15 ounces **canned kidney beans** (3)

14 ounces **canned artichoke hearts** (4)

8 **ice cream cones** (3a)

3 tablespoons **walnut pieces** (5a)

SPICES

1–1 1/4 teaspoons **salt** (2)(4)(5)

1/4 teaspoon **kosher salt** (4a)

1 **bay leaf** (5)

1 1/2 teaspoons **dried oregano** (1)(4)

1/2 teaspoon **dried parsley or basil** (1)

1 1/2 teaspoons **dried thyme** (2)(5)

1/2–3/4 teaspoon **black pepper** (2)(4)(5)

1/4 teaspoon **garlic powder** (1)

STAPLES

1 1/2 teaspoons **unsalted butter** (2)

2 tablespoons **trans fat-free tub-style margarine or butter** (5)

6 tablespoons **extra-virgin olive oil** (2)(2a)(4)(4a)

1 tablespoon **white wine vinegar** (2)

8 ounces **balsamic vinaigrette dressing** (1)

2 tablespoons **ketchup** (3)

2 tablespoons **Worcestershire sauce** (3)

8 dashes **hot pepper sauce, such as Tabasco** (3)*

1 tablespoon **brown sugar** (3)

4 teaspoons **honey or pure maple syrup** (3a)*

1/2 cup **1% milk** (5)

3 tablespoons **flour** (use wheat/gluten-free if needed) (5)

REFRIGERATED/FROZEN

1 1/2 tablespoons **crumbled blue cheese or Gorgonzola** (5a)

1 tablespoon **grated Parmesan cheese** (2a)

1 cup **nonfat ricotta cheese** (4)

1 cup **fat-free vanilla yogurt** (3a)

2 cups **corn kernels, frozen or fresh** (5)

Get free, printable versions of the shopping lists from this book at **TheScramble.com/diabetes**.

*optional ingredients

SPRING WEEK 2 • **15**

This moist and colorful chicken, suggested by Six O'Clock Scramble member Jessica McMaken, is a snap to throw together on a busy night. You can get it ready hours before dinner, and refrigerate it until it's time to bake. Use any vegetables you like instead of those I've suggested, such as asparagus, artichoke hearts, or potatoes. Serve with Whole-Wheat Couscous.

Carpool Chicken

MARINATE: 60 MINUTES • **PREP:** 15 MINUTES • **COOK:** 30 MINUTES • **SERVES:** 8 • **SERVING SIZE:** 1 1/2 CUPS

1 1/2 pounds boneless, skinless chicken breasts, cut into 1-inch pieces, or use shrimp or extra-firm tofu packed in water

1 red or orange bell pepper, diced

1 yellow bell pepper, diced

1 zucchini or yellow squash, diced

1 small yellow onion, chopped

1/2 teaspoon dried oregano

1/2 teaspoon dried parsley or basil

1/4 teaspoon garlic powder

ORANGE BALSAMIC VINAIGRETTE

1 /4 cup olive oil

1/8 cup orange juice

1/8 cup balsamic vinegar

1 tablespoon Dijon mustard

DO AHEAD OR DELEGATE: Cut and refrigerate the chicken, dice the bell peppers, the squash, and the onion, prepare the salad dressing, combine the dry seasonings, combine all the ingredients and refrigerate.

1. Preheat the oven to 350°F. Put the diced chicken and vegetables in a 9 × 13-inch baking dish. Mix together the Orange Balsamic Vinaigrette ingredients and drizzle the dressing and spices over everything and gently stir it to coat evenly. (Refrigerate for 1–24 hours, if desired, or bake immediately.)

2. Bake for 30 minutes, stirring once after 20 minutes, until the chicken is cooked through. (Meanwhile, prepare the couscous, if you are serving it.) Serve immediately or refrigerate for up to 3 days.

FLAVOR BOOSTER
Stir in a handful of fresh basil or other fresh herbs once the chicken has cooked. Season with freshly ground black pepper and top the dish with freshly grated Parmesan cheese.

Whole-Wheat Couscous

SERVES: 8 • **SERVING SIZE:** 2/3 CUP

1 1/2 cups whole-wheat or regular couscous

1. Prepare the couscous according to package directions, using water or broth for the liquid. For even more flavor, stir fresh herbs, toasted pine nuts or slivered almonds, and/or dried cranberries or currants into the hot couscous.

NUTRITIONAL INFORMATION | CARPOOL CHICKEN (ANALYSIS FOR CHICKEN AND DRESSING):

EXCHANGES / CHOICES:
1 Nonstarchy Vegetable; 2 Protein, lean; 1 Fat

Calories: 185; Calories from Fat: 80; Total Fat: 9 g;
Saturated Fat: 1.5 g; Trans Fat: 0 g; Cholesterol: 50 mg;
Sodium: 95 mg; Potassium: 325 mg; Total Carbohydrate: 6 g;
Dietary Fiber: 1 g; Sugar: 3 g; Protein: 19 g; Phosphorus: 160 mg

(ANALYSIS FOR ORANGE BALSAMIC VINAIGRETTE DRESSING ONLY):

EXCHANGES / CHOICES:
1 Fat

Calories: 60; Calories from Fat: 55; Total Fat: 6 g;
Saturated Fat: 0.8 g; Trans Fat: 0 g; Cholesterol: 0 mg;
Sodium: 40 mg; Potassium: 15 mg; Total Carbohydrate: 1 g;
Dietary Fiber: 0 g; Sugar: 1 g; Protein: 0 g; Phosphorus: 0 mg

NUTRITIONAL INFORMATION | WHOLE-WHEAT COUSCOUS:

EXCHANGES / CHOICES:
1 1/2 Starch

Calories: 105; Calories from Fat: 5; Total Fat: 0.5 g;
Saturated Fat: 0 g; Trans Fat: 0 g; Cholesterol: 0 mg;
Sodium: 0 mg; Potassium: 60 mg; Total Carbohydrate: 24 g;
Dietary Fiber: 4 g; Sugar: 0 g; Protein: 4 g; Phosphorus: 20 mg

TIP

As is the case with many meats, the longer this recipe marinates, the more flavorful it becomes. I have prepared this dish right after my kids have walked out the door for school in the morning. By the time I bake it at dinnertime, it has soaked up so much flavor from the dressing and herbs.

Making fish in a packet keeps it so moist and flavorful. This version, suggested by Scramble member Sharon Hauer Gill, has simple flavors and takes just a few minutes to prepare. Sharon uses parchment paper to make hers, but I find foil much easier to wrap tightly around the fish. Serve with Steamed Broccoli Tossed with Olive Oil and Grated Parmesan Cheese.

Rockfish with Tomatoes and Herbs Baked in a Foil Packet

PREP + COOK: 20 MINUTES • **SERVES:** 4 • **SERVING SIZE:** 2/3 PACKET

2 teaspoons extra-virgin olive oil

3 cloves garlic, chopped

1 large tomato, diced (about 2 cups)

1 tablespoon white wine vinegar

1 pound rockfish fillets, or other thin white fillets (3–4 fillets)

1 teaspoon dried thyme, or use fresh thyme leaves

1 1/2 teaspoons unsalted butter, chopped

1/2 teaspoon salt, or to taste

1/8 teaspoon black pepper, or more to taste

DO AHEAD OR DELEGATE: Peel and chop the garlic, dice the tomato.

1. Preheat the oven to 450°F (or heat the grill to medium-high). Heat the oil over medium heat in a small skillet, add the garlic, and cook until it is fragrant and just starting to turn golden, about 1 minute. Remove from the heat. Meanwhile, combine the tomatoes and vinegar in a bowl.

2. Lay each fillet in the middle of its own large square of heavy-duty foil (about 12–15 inches), top each fillet with 1/3 or 1/4 of the garlic (depending on how many fillets you have), the tomato and vinegar mixture, thyme, and butter, and season everything with salt and pepper. Wrap the foil into an airtight packet around the fish and tomatoes, folding and sealing the edges, and put the packets in a large glass or ceramic baking dish (unless you are grilling them). Bake (or grill) them for 10 minutes until the fish flakes easily with a fork. (Meanwhile, make the broccoli, if you are serving it.) Carefully open the packets, transfer the fish to a serving platter, and serve immediately.

FLAVOR BOOSTER
Add 1 teaspoon capers or diced olives to each packet.

Steamed Broccoli Tossed with Olive Oil and Grated Parmesan Cheese

SERVES: 4 • **SERVING SIZE:** 5 SPEARS

1 pound broccoli (tough bottoms cut off), cut into 20 spears
1 tablespoon extra-virgin olive oil
1 tablespoon grated Parmesan cheese

1. Steam the broccoli spears until tender, about 7–10 minutes. Drain the broccoli and toss immediately with the oil and cheese.

TIP

While standard foil works just fine, when making foil packets, I find that heavy-duty foil works best for me. It's sturdier and thicker than the standard foil. Just remember to rinse and recycle the foil after using it!

NUTRITIONAL INFORMATION | ROCKFISH WITH TOMATOES AND HERBS BAKED IN A FOIL PACKET:

EXCHANGES / CHOICES:
1 Nonstarchy Vegetable; 3 Protein, lean

Calories: 155; Calories from Fat: 45; Total Fat: 5 g;
Saturated Fat: 1.6 g; Trans Fat: 0.1 g; Cholesterol: 60 mg;
Sodium: 380 mg; Potassium: 665 mg; Total Carbohydrate: 4 g;
Dietary Fiber: 1 g; Sugar: 2 g; Protein: 22 g; Phosphorus: 260 mg

NUTRITIONAL INFORMATION | STEAMED BROCCOLI TOSSED WITH OLIVE OIL AND GRATED PARMESAN CHEESE:

EXCHANGES / CHOICES:
1 Nonstarchy Vegetable; 1 Fat

Calories: 65; Calories from Fat: 35; Total Fat: 4 g;
Saturated Fat: 0.7 g; Trans Fat: 0 g; Cholesterol: 0 mg;
Sodium: 50 mg; Potassium: 290 mg; Total Carbohydrate: 6 g;
Dietary Fiber: 2 g; Sugar: 2 g; Protein: 3 g; Phosphorus: 70 mg

These sandwiches are reminiscent of the Sloppy Joes many of us enjoyed as kids. I've updated our moms' version by using lower-fat ground turkey, adding some healthy veggies to the sauce, and serving them on whole-grain rolls. The finer you dice the carrots and peppers, the less likely your kids will be able to detect them. Serve with Fruit Cones for dessert.

Texas Hero (a.k.a. The Davy Crockett)

PREP + COOK: 25 MINUTES • **SERVES:** 8 • **SERVING SIZE:** 1 SANDWICH WITH 1/8 OF THE FILLING

1 pound lean ground turkey, beef, vegetarian ground meat, or canned kidney beans

1/2 yellow onion, finely diced

2 stalks celery, finely diced

1 carrot, finely diced

15 ounces no-added-salt tomato sauce

1 tablespoon brown sugar

2 tablespoons Worcestershire sauce

15 ounces canned kidney beans, drained and rinsed

2 tablespoons ketchup

8 whole-wheat buns

DO AHEAD OR DELEGATE: Dice the onion, celery, and carrot.

1. In a large skillet over medium heat, brown the meat in its own juices until it is almost cooked through. (If you are using vegetarian ground "meat" or an extra can of beans, add it after the tomato sauce instead.) Drain off the excess liquid, if necessary, and add the diced vegetables to the skillet. (Heat 1 tablespoon olive oil in the pan first, if using vegetarian ground "meat" or beans.)

2. Sauté the mixture for 2 more minutes and add all the remaining ingredients, except the buns. Bring to a boil, reduce the heat, cover the skillet, and simmer for about 15 minutes until the vegetables are tender. (Meanwhile, dice the fruit for the Fruit Cones, if you are serving them.) At this point you can refrigerate the meal for up to 3 days, freeze it for up to 3 months, or proceed to the next step.

3. To serve the sandwiches, toast the buns lightly and fill each one with a large spoonful of the meat mixture.

SLOW COOKER DIRECTIONS: No need to brown the meat. Simply put all the ingredients except the buns in the slow cooker and cook on low for 8–10 hours or on high for 4–6 hours. Serve as directed.

FLAVOR BOOSTER

Add 1 teaspoon chili powder to the skillet with the vegetables and use hot pepper sauce (try chipotle-flavored Tabasco!) on the sandwiches.

Fruit Cones

SERVES: 8 • **SERVING SIZE:** 1 CONE

2 cups fat-free yogurt, vanilla or another flavor of your choosing

8 ice cream cones, or use waffle bowls

4 cups fresh fruit, like blueberries, bananas, strawberries, and kiwi, diced

1. Spoon 1/4 cup of the yogurt into each ice cream cone or waffle bowl. Top each cone with 1/3–1/2 cup of the fruit.

TIP

For a long time I thought of celery as a vegetable that added crunch and color to recipes but didn't have a ton of nutritional value. However, I recently learned that celery contains a nutrient called luteolin, which has anti-inflammatory properties and may help prevent the buildup of plaque in the brain that can contribute to Alzheimer's disease.

NUTRITIONAL INFORMATION | TEXAS HERO:

EXCHANGES / CHOICES:
2 Starch; 2 Nonstarchy Vegetable; 2 Protein, lean

Calories: 290; Calories from Fat: 55; Total Fat: 6 g;
Saturated Fat: 1.6 g; Trans Fat: 0.1 g; Cholesterol: 45 mg;
Sodium: 395 mg; Potassium: 695 mg; Total Carbohydrate: 40 g;
Dietary Fiber: 8 g; Sugar: 10 g; Protein: 19 g; Phosphorus: 280 mg

NUTRITIONAL INFORMATION | FRUIT CONES:

EXCHANGES / CHOICES:
1/2 Fruit; 1/2 Milk, fat-free; 1/2 Carbohydrate

Calories: 115; Calories from Fat: 10; Total Fat: 1 g;
Saturated Fat: 0.2 g; Trans Fat: 0 g; Cholesterol: 0 mg;
Sodium: 60 mg; Potassium: 275 mg; Total Carbohydrate: 26 g;
Dietary Fiber: 2 g; Sugar: 13 g; Protein: 3 g; Phosphorus: 80 mg

Our kids really enjoyed this dinner, although it's sophisticated enough to serve to adults at a dinner party. Serve with Roasted Fennel Bulbs.

Farfalle with Artichoke Hearts, Baby Spinach, and Lemon Ricotta

PREP + COOK: 30 MINUTES • **SERVES:** 9 • **SERVING SIZE:** 1 1/3 CUPS

16 ounces whole-wheat farfalle (butterfly-shaped) noodles

3 tablespoons extra-virgin olive oil

1 shallot, finely chopped

1 teaspoon dried oregano

14 ounces canned artichoke hearts, drained and quartered

1/2 lemon, juice only (about 2 tablespoons, plus 2 teaspoons zest)

6 ounces baby spinach

1 cup nonfat ricotta cheese

1/4–1/2 teaspoon salt

1/8 teaspoon black pepper

DO AHEAD OR DELEGATE: Chop the shallot, drain and quarter the artichoke hearts, and juice the lemon.

1. (Start the fennel first, if you are serving it.) Cook the pasta in salted water until it is al dente. When it is almost done, scoop out 1/2 cup of the cooking water and set it aside.

2. Once the pasta goes into the water, heat a large skillet over medium heat and add the oil. When the oil is hot, add the shallots and sauté them until they are soft, about 3 minutes. Add the oregano, artichoke hearts, and lemon juice, and cook for about 2 minutes until the artichokes are heated through. Stir in the spinach, cover, and cook until the spinach is wilted, about 2 minutes. Reduce the heat to medium-low, stir in the ricotta, reserved pasta cooking water, lemon zest, salt, and pepper, and cook until creamy. Pour the sauce over the warm pasta and serve immediately.

FLAVOR BOOSTER
Sprinkle some crushed red pepper flakes or freshly ground black pepper over the finished dish.

Roasted Fennel Bulbs

SERVES: 9 • **SERVING SIZE:** 1/3 BULB

3–4 fennel bulbs, cut into 6 equal parts
1 tablespoon extra-virgin olive oil
1/4 teaspoon kosher salt

1. Preheat the oven to 400°F. Trim off the fronds (everything above the bulb) and cut the fennel bulbs into 6 equal parts. Toss them with the olive oil to coat them, put them on a baking sheet, sprinkle them with the salt, and bake. After 20 minutes, flip the fennel and cook it for an additional 15–20 minutes until the edges are browned and the centers are soft.

TIP

It can be challenging to remember to scoop some of the cooking water from your pasta pot before draining the pasta. When I need to do this for a recipe, I put a measuring cup right by the pot or in my colander. That way I can't miss it when I go to drain the pasta.

NUTRITIONAL INFORMATION | FARFALLE WITH ARTICHOKE HEARTS, BABY SPINACH, AND LEMON RICOTTA:

EXCHANGES / CHOICES:
2 1/2 Starch; 1 Nonstarchy Vegetable; 1 Protein, lean

Calories: 260; Calories from Fat: 45; Total Fat: 5 g;
Saturated Fat: 0.8 g; Trans Fat: 0 g; Cholesterol: 10 mg;
Sodium: 205 mg; Potassium: 335 mg; Total Carbohydrate: 44 g;
Dietary Fiber: 7 g; Sugar: 3 g; Protein: 13 g; Phosphorus: 210 mg

NUTRITIONAL INFORMATION | ROASTED FENNEL BULBS:

EXCHANGES / CHOICES:
1 Nonstarchy Vegetable

Calories: 30; Calories from Fat: 15; Total Fat: 1.5 g;
Saturated Fat: 0.2 g; Trans Fat: 0 g; Cholesterol: 0 mg;
Sodium: 80 mg; Potassium: 215 mg; Total Carbohydrate: 4 g;
Dietary Fiber: 2 g; Sugar: 1 g; Protein: 1 g; Phosphorus: 25 mg

This satisfying chowder can really be enjoyed in any season. You can add a cup of cooked and diced or shredded chicken or a can of baby clams if you prefer, but we like it best just like this. Serve with Green Salad with Shredded Red Cabbage, Blue Cheese, and Walnuts.

Creamy Corn and Potato Chowder

PREP: 20 MINUTES • **COOK:** 20 MINUTES • **SERVES:** 4 • **SERVING SIZE:** 2 CUPS

2 tablespoons trans fat-free tub-style margarine or butter

1 small yellow onion, finely chopped

4–6 stalks celery, thinly sliced (1 cup total), cut the stalks in half lengthwise first if they are very wide

1/2 red or orange bell pepper, finely chopped

1/2 teaspoon dried thyme

1 bay leaf

3 tablespoons flour

2 cups reduced-sodium chicken or vegetable broth

1 small russet (baking) potato, cut into 1/2-inch pieces

2 cups corn kernels, frozen or fresh

1 1/2 cups 1% milk

1/8 teaspoon salt

1/4–1/2 teaspoon black pepper, to taste

DO AHEAD OR DELEGATE: Chop the onion and the bell pepper, slice the celery, cut the potato and store covered with water to prevent browning, or fully prepare and refrigerate the soup.

1. In a medium saucepan, melt the margarine over medium heat. Add the onions, celery, bell peppers, thyme, and bay leaf and sauté until the vegetables are slightly softened, about 5 minutes. Add the flour and stir continuously until it is absorbed.

2. Add the broth and bring to a boil, stirring occasionally. Add the potatoes and corn, return to a boil, reduce the heat and simmer the soup, uncovered, stirring occasionally, for about 15 minutes or until the potatoes are fork tender. (Meanwhile, prepare the salad, if you are serving it.)

3. Stir in the milk, salt, and pepper, and remove the bay leaf. Serve the soup immediately or refrigerate it for up to 3 days.

SLOW COOKER DIRECTIONS: Whisk the flour and milk in the slow cooker until smooth. Add the remaining ingredients, and cook on low for 8–10 hours or on high for 4–5 hours. (Slow cooker cooking times may vary—get to know your slow cooker and, if necessary, adjust cooking times accordingly.)

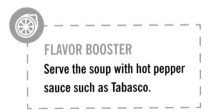

FLAVOR BOOSTER
Serve the soup with hot pepper sauce such as Tabasco.

Green Salad with Shredded Red Cabbage, Blue Cheese, and Walnuts

SERVES: 4 • **SERVING SIZE:** 1 CUP

4 cups lettuce, any kind, chopped or torn
1/2 cup red cabbage, thinly sliced
1 1/2 tablespoons crumbled blue cheese or Gorgonzola cheese
3 tablespoons walnut pieces, chopped
1/4 cup Orange Balsamic Vinaigrette Dressing (page 16)

1. In a large bowl, combine the lettuce, cabbage, blue cheese, walnuts, and balsamic vinaigrette or salad dressing of your choice.

NUTRITIONAL INFORMATION | CREAMY CORN AND POTATO CHOWDER:

EXCHANGES / CHOICES:
1 1/2 Starch; 1/2 Milk, fat-free; 1 Nonstarchy Vegetable; 1/2 Fat

Calories: 205; Calories from Fat: 55; Total Fat: 6 g;
Saturated Fat: 1.9 g; Trans Fat: 0 g; Cholesterol: 5 mg;
Sodium: 435 mg; Potassium: 635 mg; Total Carbohydrate: 33 g;
Dietary Fiber: 4 g; Sugar: 10 g; Protein: 8 g; Phosphorus: 195 mg

NUTRITIONAL INFORMATION | GREEN SALAD WITH SHREDDED RED CABBAGE, BLUE CHEESE, AND WALNUTS (ANALYSIS FOR SALAD ONLY):

EXCHANGES / CHOICES:
1 Nonstarchy Vegetable; 2 Fat

Calories: 105; Calories from Fat: 80; Total Fat: 9 g;
Saturated Fat: 1.6 g; Trans Fat: 0 g; Cholesterol: 0 mg;
Sodium: 85 mg; Potassium: 145 mg; Total Carbohydrate: 4 g;
Dietary Fiber: 1 g; Sugar: 2 g; Protein: 2 g; Phosphorus: 45 mg

TIP

If you're someone who often peels their fruits and vegetables (like potatoes and apples), consider eating the skins. In addition to being full of vitamins and minerals, the peel has fiber, which moves quickly through your digestive tract and has been linked to decreased risk of colon cancer.

SPRING

WEEK 3

Honey-Dijon Chicken (1)
SIDE DISH: Red Potatoes Tossed with Fresh Herbs (1a); Zucchini Fries (1b)

Cajun Fish Sandwiches with Crunchy Slaw (2)
SIDE DISH: Lightly Buttered Corn (2a)

Golden Tofu with Snow Peas (3)
SIDE DISH: Brown Rice (3a)

Spicy Bulgur Pilaf with Spinach and Tomatoes (4)
SIDE DISH: Applesauce with Cinnamon and Granola (4a)

No-Chicken Noodle Soup (5)
SIDE DISH: Green Salad with Red Bell Peppers, Goat Cheese, and Pecans (5a)

SHOPPING LIST

PRODUCE
4 **carrots** (5)
1 teaspoon **fresh chives** (1a)
2 1/2 **yellow onions** (3)(4)(5)
1/2 **red bell pepper** (5a)
1 **red or yellow bell pepper** (3)
4 stalks **celery** (5)
6 cups **lettuce, any variety** (5a)
6–9 ounces **baby spinach** (4)
12 ounces **bagged coleslaw or broccoli slaw** (2)
2 teaspoons **fresh ginger** (3)
1 teaspoon **fresh rosemary** (1a)
1 teaspoon **fresh thyme** (1a)
2 **zucchini** (1b)
1 pound **red potatoes** (1a)
1 cup **snow peas** (3)
1/4 **lime** (2a)*

MEAT AND FISH
4 **boneless, skinless chicken cutlets or chicken breasts** (1)
1 pound **flounder, catfish, tilapia, or other thin white fish fillets** (2)

SHELVED ITEMS

4 **whole-wheat buns** (2)

1 1/2 cups **quick-cooking brown rice or regular white rice** (3a)

1 cup **bulgur wheat** (4)

2 cups **fine egg noodles** (5)

1/4 cup **panko breadcrumbs** (use wheat/gluten-free if needed) (1b)

3/4 cup **low-fat granola or muesli** (4a)

3/4 cup **marinara or pizza sauce** (1b)

14 1/2 ounces **canned petite diced tomatoes with green chilies** (or without green chilies if you don't like spicy food) (4)

1 1/2 cups + 64 ounces **low-sodium chicken or vegetable broth** (4)(5)

1 tablespoon **apple cider vinegar** (2)

1 tablespoon **rice wine or mirin** (3)

15 ounces **canned chickpeas** (garbanzo beans) (4)

3 cups **unsweetened applesauce** (4a)

2 tablespoons **pecans** (5a)

SPICES

1 1/4 teaspoons **salt** (1)(1a)(1b)(2)(5)

1 teaspoon **dried oregano** (1b)

1 teaspoon **dried basil** (1b)

1 teaspoon **dried thyme** (5)

1/2 teaspoon **black pepper** (1)(2)(5)

1/2 teaspoon **ground cinnamon** (4a)

1/4 teaspoon **allspice** (4)

1/4 teaspoon **ground cumin** (4)

1/2 teaspoon **paprika** (1)

2 teaspoons **Cajun or Old Bay seasoning** (2)

STAPLES

3 teaspoons + 1 tablespoon **butter** (2)(2a)(5)

1 tablespoon **trans fat-free margarine or butter** (1)

4 tablespoons **extra-virgin olive oil** (1a)(2)(4)(5)

2 tablespoons **vegetable oil** (3)

1/4 cup **reduced-fat mayonnaise** (2)

1/4 cup **vinaigrette dressing** (5a)

5 tablespoons **honey-Dijon mustard** (use wheat/gluten-free if needed) (1)

2 tablespoons **reduced-sodium soy sauce or tamari** (use wheat/gluten- free if needed) (3)

REFRIGERATED/FROZEN

2 tablespoons **goat or feta cheese, crumbled** (5a)

1 tablespoon **grated Parmesan cheese** (1b)

1 teaspoon **sugar** (3)

1/2 tablespoon **honey** (2)

3 **eggs** (1b)(2)

4 teaspoons **minced garlic** (3)(4)(5)

1 cup **flour** (use wheat/gluten-free if needed) (1)(2)

1/4 cup **breadcrumbs** (use wheat/gluten-free if needed) (1)

1/4 cup **cornmeal** (1b)

1 pound **extra-firm tofu packed in water** (or use boneless chicken breasts) (3)

16 ounces **frozen corn kernels** (2a)

Get free, printable versions of the shopping lists from this book at TheScramble.com/diabetes.

*optional ingredients

SPRING WEEK 3 • 27

Originally suggested by our friend Kristen Donoghue, this simple chicken has been a popular and kid-friendly Scramble recipe for years. Serve with Red Potatoes Tossed with Fresh Herbs and Zucchini Fries.

Honey-Dijon Chicken

PREP + COOK: 30 MINUTES • **SERVES:** 4 • **SERVING SIZE:** 1 BREAST (ABOUT 3 OUNCES COOKED)

4 boneless, skinless chicken cutlets or chicken breasts

5 tablespoons honey-Dijon mustard

1 tablespoon water

1/8 teaspoon salt

1/8 teaspoon black pepper

1/4 cup breadcrumbs

1/4 cup flour

1/2 teaspoon paprika

1 tablespoon trans fat-free margarine or butter

DO AHEAD OR DELEGATE: Prepare both the honey-mustard and the breadcrumb mixtures.

1. (Start the zucchini and the potatoes first). Preheat the oven to 425°F. Line a baking sheet with foil and spray with nonstick cooking spray. If you aren't using chicken cutlets, cover the chicken breasts with plastic wrap and pound them with a mallet to uniform thickness (about 1/2 inch). This is important so they cook quickly and evenly.

2. In a shallow bowl or plate, combine the honey-Dijon mustard, water, salt, and pepper. In another shallow bowl or plate, combine the breadcrumbs, flour, and paprika. Coat both sides of the chicken with the mustard mixture, then the breadcrumb mixture, and place on the baking sheet.

3. Melt the butter or margarine in the microwave (about 30 seconds on high) or on the stovetop, and drizzle it over the chicken. Bake the chicken for 10–15 minutes, without flipping it, until the chicken is lightly browned and no longer pink inside the thickest part.

FLAVOR BOOSTER

Stir 1/2 teaspoon dry mustard powder or 1 teaspoon Chinese spicy mustard into the honey-mustard mixture. Serve the chicken with additional honey-mustard sauce (combine 2 parts mustard to 1 part honey).

TIP

You may find that the mustard mixture adheres to the chicken breasts more easily if you pat the chicken breasts lightly with a paper towel to get rid of any excess moisture.

NUTRITIONAL INFORMATION | HONEY-DIJON CHICKEN:

EXCHANGES / CHOICES:
1 Carbohydrate; 3 Protein, lean

Calories: 215; Calories from Fat: 55; Total Fat: 6 g;
Saturated Fat: 1.4 g; Trans Fat: 0 g; Cholesterol: 65 mg;
Sodium: 410 mg; Potassium: 255 mg; Total Carbohydrate: 15 g;
Dietary Fiber: 1 g; Sugar: 1 g; Protein: 26 g; Phosphorus: 220 mg

NUTRITIONAL INFORMATION | RED POTATOES TOSSED WITH FRESH HERBS:

EXCHANGES / CHOICES:
1 1/2 Starch; 1/2 Fat

Calories: 125; Calories from Fat: 30; Total Fat: 3.5 g;
Saturated Fat: 0.5 g; Trans Fat: 0 g; Cholesterol: 0 mg;
Sodium: 150 mg; Potassium: 425 mg; Total Carbohydrate: 22 g;
Dietary Fiber: 2 g; Sugar: 1 g; Protein: 2 g; Phosphorus: 50 mg

NUTRITIONAL INFORMATION | ZUCCHINI FRIES:

EXCHANGES / CHOICES:
1 Carbohydrate; 1 Nonstarchy Vegetable; 1/2 Fat

Calories: 110; Calories from Fat: 20; Total Fat: 2 g;
Saturated Fat: 0.6 g; Trans Fat: 0 g; Cholesterol: 0 mg;
Sodium: 240 mg; Potassium: 445 mg; Total Carbohydrate: 18 g;
Dietary Fiber: 3 g; Sugar: 6 g; Protein: 5 g; Phosphorus: 75 mg

SIDE DISHES

- -

Red Potatoes Tossed with Fresh Herbs

SERVES: 4 • **SERVING SIZE:** 4 OUNCES

1 pound red potatoes

1 tablespoon extra-virgin olive oil

1/4 teaspoon salt

1 teaspoon fresh thyme, leaves only

1 teaspoon fresh rosemary, chopped

1 teaspoon fresh chives, finely chopped

1. Boil the potatoes in salted water for 15–20 minutes until they are fork tender. Drain then cut them in halves or quarters, and toss in a serving bowl with the oil, salt, thyme, rosemary, and chives, or fresh herbs of your choice.

Zucchini Fries

SERVES: 4 • **SERVING SIZE:** 6 FRIES

2 zucchini

2 eggs, whites only

1/4 cup panko breadcrumbs

1/4 cup cornmeal

1 tablespoon grated Parmesan cheese

1 teaspoon dried oregano

1 teaspoon dried basil

3/4 cup marinara or pizza sauce

1. Heat the oven to 425°F. Spray a large baking sheet with nonstick cooking spray. Cut the ends off the zucchini and slice in quarters lengthwise (so you have 8 long strips), then cut each strip into 3 shorter pieces.

2. Beat the egg whites in a shallow bowl until they are frothy. In another shallow bowl, combine the panko, cornmeal, cheese, oregano, and basil. Dip each zucchini strip into the egg whites, then into the panko mixture. Place them on the baking sheet, spray the tops with nonstick cooking spray, and bake for 20 minutes, flipping once, until they are browned. Serve with marinara sauce.

These sandwiches, suggested by longtime Six O'Clock Scramble member Molly Thompson, are fun to make and even more fun to eat. If you are really short on time buy pre-made coleslaw instead of using the recipe below. Serve with Lightly Buttered Corn.

Cajun Fish Sandwiches with Crunchy Slaw

PREP + COOK: 30 MINUTES • **SERVES:** 4 • **SERVING SIZE:** 1 FISH SANDWICH

1/2 (12-ounce) bag coleslaw or broccoli slaw, or shred 3 cups of cabbage, carrots, and/or broccoli stems

2 tablespoons reduced-fat mayonnaise

1 tablespoon apple cider vinegar

1/2 tablespoon honey

1/16 teaspoon salt

1/16 teaspoon black pepper

3/4 cup flour

2 teaspoons Cajun or Old Bay seasoning

1 egg

2 teaspoons butter

1 tablespoon extra-virgin olive oil

1 pound flounder, catfish, tilapia, or other thin white fish fillets, cut into 4 even pieces

4 whole-wheat buns

DO AHEAD OR DELEGATE: Make and refrigerate the coleslaw, combine the flour and the Cajun or Old Bay seasoning, and beat and refrigerate the egg.

1. In a medium serving bowl, combine the slaw, mayonnaise, vinegar, honey, salt, and pepper. Set it aside. (If possible, make this up to 24 hours in advance and refrigerate it until you are ready to serve. Mix it well before serving.)

2. In a shallow dish or bowl, combine the flour and Cajun or Old Bay seasoning. In another shallow bowl, beat the egg.

3. In a large heavy skillet (a cast iron pan works great for this), heat the butter and oil over medium heat until it is bubbling.

4. Dip the fish pieces in the flour mixture to coat them. Dip them in the egg, letting the excess drip back into the bowl. Dip them back into the flour mixture to recoat. (Make the corn now, if you are serving it.) Cook the fish until it is nicely browned and crispy, about 2–3 minutes per side. Remove the fish to a plate.

5. Toast the buns. Serve the fish inside the buns and topped with the slaw.

FLAVOR BOOSTER
Serve the sandwiches topped with barbecue sauce or your favorite sandwich spread. Finely grate 1/4 onion into the coleslaw.

Lightly Buttered Corn

SERVES: 4 • **SERVING SIZE:** 2/3 CUP

1 pound frozen corn kernels

1 teaspoon butter

1/2 lime, juice only (optional)

1. Steam the corn in the microwave or on the stovetop for 3–5 minutes (we like it a little undercooked so it doesn't get chewy). Toss the hot corn with the butter and fresh lime juice, if desired.

TIP

Don't let your apple cider vinegar languish in your pantry! It's a fabulous addition to salad dressings, marinades, and chutneys, and can perk up sautéed greens.

NUTRITIONAL INFORMATION | CAJUN FISH SANDWICHES WITH CRUNCHY SLAW:

EXCHANGES / CHOICES:
2 Starch; 3 Protein, lean; 1 Fat

Calories: 350; Calories from Fat: 110; Total Fat: 12 g; Saturated Fat: 3 g; Trans Fat: 0.1 g; Cholesterol: 115 mg; Sodium: 440 mg; Potassium: 560 mg; Total Carbohydrate: 34 g; Dietary Fiber: 4 g; Sugar: 6 g; Protein: 27 g; Phosphorus: 390 mg

NUTRITIONAL INFORMATION | LIGHTLY BUTTERED CORN:

EXCHANGES / CHOICES:
1 1/2 Starch

Calories: 100; Calories from Fat: 15; Total Fat: 1.5 g; Saturated Fat: 0.7 g; Trans Fat: 0 g; Cholesterol: 5 mg; Sodium: 10 mg; Potassium: 265 mg; Total Carbohydrate: 22 g; Dietary Fiber: 3 g; Sugar: 3 g; Protein: 3 g; Phosphorus: 90 mg

I first made this dish the night after we had a heavy, salty meal at a Chinese restaurant and decided that homemade Chinese-style food is much more satisfying, can be just as quick, and is definitely less expensive. Serve with Brown Rice.

Golden Tofu with Snow Peas

PREP + COOK: 30 MINUTES • **SERVES:** 4 • **SERVING SIZE:** 1 1/2 CUPS

1 pound extra-firm tofu packed in water, (or use boneless chicken breasts, diced, or large shrimp)

2 tablespoons vegetable oil, divided use

2 tablespoons reduced-sodium soy sauce or tamari (use wheat/gluten-free if needed)

1 tablespoon rice wine or mirin

1 teaspoon sugar

1/2 yellow onion, cut into thin strips (quarter the onion top to bottom first)

1 cup snow peas, cut lengthwise into matchsticks

1 red or yellow bell pepper, cut into matchsticks

1 chunk (1-inch) ginger root, peeled and minced (2 teaspoons ginger)

1 teaspoon minced garlic, (about 2 cloves)

DO AHEAD OR DELEGATE: Cut the tofu, onion, snow peas, and bell pepper, prepare the sauce, peel and mince the ginger and garlic.

1. Cut the tofu in half crosswise and wrap both halves in a clean absorbent dish towel for at least 10 minutes, and up to 12 hours (you can leave it on the counter, rather than refrigerate it). When you are ready to cook it, cut the tofu into 1/2-inch cubes.

2. Heat 1 tablespoon oil in a large nonstick skillet over medium heat. Cook the tofu, turning every few minutes, until it is completely golden, about 15 minutes (if you are using shrimp or diced chicken, sauté until cooked through). Remove the tofu from the pan and set it aside. (Meanwhile, start the rice, if you are serving it.)

3. In a small bowl, combine the soy sauce, rice wine, and sugar to make the sauce.

4. Add the remaining oil to the skillet, and stir-fry the onions for about 2 minutes until they just start to brown. Add the snow peas, peppers, ginger, and garlic and stir-fry for about 2 more minutes until the vegetables are tender-crisp. Pour the sauce over the vegetables and stir-fry for 1 minute. Mix in the tofu. Serve immediately or refrigerate it for up to 3 days.

FLAVOR BOOSTER
Use a little extra ginger and garlic and serve the dish with Asian chili garlic sauce or other hot sauce.

Brown Rice

SERVES: 4 • **SERVING SIZE:** 1/2 CUP

1 1/2 cups quick-cooking brown rice

1. Prepare the rice according to package directions.

NUTRITIONAL INFORMATION | GOLDEN TOFU (OR CHICKEN) WITH SNOW PEAS:

EXCHANGES / CHOICES:
1/2 Carbohydrate; 1 Nonstarchy Vegetable; 1 Protein, medium fat; 1 1/2 Fat

Calories: 215; Calories from Fat: 125; Total Fat: 14 g;
Saturated Fat: 1.2 g; Trans Fat: 0 g; Cholesterol: 0 mg;
Sodium: 290 mg; Potassium: 325 mg; Total Carbohydrate: 11 g;
Dietary Fiber: 2 g; Sugar: 5 g; Protein: 13 g; Phosphorus: 195 mg

NUTRITIONAL INFORMATION | BROWN RICE:

EXCHANGES / CHOICES:
1 1/2 Starch

Calories: 115; Calories from Fat: 10; Total Fat: 1 g;
Saturated Fat: 0.2 g; Trans Fat: 0 g; Cholesterol: 0 mg;
Sodium: 5 mg; Potassium: 45 mg; Total Carbohydrate: 24 g;
Dietary Fiber: 2 g; Sugar: 0 g; Protein: 3 g; Phosphorus: 85 mg

TIP

Tamari is a type of soy sauce that is slightly thicker and darker in color than ordinary soy sauce. It also has a deeper, richer flavor than its lighter counterpart and is often wheat-free.

Scramble member Gretchen Douglas invented this recipe when she was cleaning out her fridge at the end of the week. The result is a super-healthy recipe that is steeped with flavor. Serve with Applesauce with Cinnamon and Granola.

Spicy Bulgur Pilaf with Spinach and Tomatoes

PREP: 20 MINUTES • **COOK:** 15 MINUTES • **SERVES:** 6 • **SERVING SIZE:** 1 1/2 CUPS

1 tablespoon extra-virgin olive oil

1 yellow onion, diced

1 teaspoon minced garlic (about 2 cloves)

1/4 teaspoon allspice

1/4 teaspoon ground cumin

6–9 ounces baby spinach

14 1/2 ounces canned petite diced tomatoes with green chilies (or without green chilies for a milder flavor), with liquid

1 1/2 cups reduced-sodium chicken or vegetable broth

1 cup bulgur wheat

15 ounces canned chickpeas (garbanzo beans), drained and rinsed

DO AHEAD OR DELEGATE: Dice the onion and peel the garlic.

1. In a medium or large stockpot, heat the oil over medium heat. Add the onions, garlic, allspice, and cumin, and sauté until the onions are very soft, about 10 minutes. Add the spinach to the pot, cover, and cook for 2–3 minutes until it wilts. Add the tomatoes with their liquid, the broth, and the bulgur, and mix well. Bring to a boil, cover, and simmer for 15 minutes, or until the bulgur is tender and most of the liquid is absorbed.

2. Stir in the chickpeas and serve immediately or refrigerate it for up to 3 days.

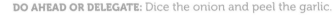

FLAVOR BOOSTER
Squeeze fresh lemon over the dish and stir in fresh chopped lemon zest and parsley.

Applesauce with Cinnamon and Granola

SERVES: 4
SERVING SIZE: 1/2 CUP APPLESAUCE + 2 TABLESPOONS GRANOLA

3 cups unsweetened applesauce

1/2 teaspoon ground cinnamon

3/4 cup low-fat granola or muesli

1. In each small bowl, top 1/2 cup applesauce with a sprinkle of cinnamon and 2 tablespoons of granola or muesli.

TIP

Best known as an ingredient in tabouli salad, bulgur wheat is a high-fiber grain that can be used in place of rice, couscous, or other similar grains. Bulgur can come in a variety of sizes so be sure to check the package for the appropriate cooking time.

NUTRITIONAL INFORMATION | SPICY BULGUR PILAF WITH SPINACH AND TOMATOES:

EXCHANGES / CHOICES:
2 Starch; 1 Nonstarchy Vegetable; 1/2 Fat

Calories: 215; Calories from Fat: 35; Total Fat: 4 g;
Saturated Fat: 0.5 g; Trans Fat: 0 g; Cholesterol: 0 mg;
Sodium: 430 mg; Potassium: 505 mg; Total Carbohydrate: 39 g;
Dietary Fiber: 10 g; Sugar: 6 g; Protein: 10 g; Phosphorus: 150 mg

NUTRITIONAL INFORMATION | APPLESAUCE WITH CINNAMON AND GRANOLA:

EXCHANGES / CHOICES:
1/2 Starch; 1 Fruit

Calories: 100; Calories from Fat: 10; Total Fat: 1 g;
Saturated Fat: 0.1 g; Trans Fat: 0 g; Cholesterol: 0 mg;
Sodium: 35 mg; Potassium: 120 mg; Total Carbohydrate: 24 g;
Dietary Fiber: 2 g; Sugar: 14 g; Protein: 2 g; Phosphorus: 35 mg

My daughter Celia has always loved chicken noodle soup. Now that she's a vegetarian I wanted to come up with a way for her to still enjoy it. It turns out that chicken really isn't essential to a great tasting "chicken" soup—in fact, I think the celery and garlic are where much of the flavor resides. This recipe makes a very noodley soup. If you want more broth and fewer noodles, use just 1–1 1/2 cups of the noodles. Serve with Green Salad with Red Bell Peppers, Goat Cheese, and Pecans and Whole-Grain Bread.

No-Chicken Noodle Soup

PREP + COOK: 30 MINUTES • **SERVES:** 6 • **SERVING SIZE:** 2 CUPS

1 1/2 teaspoons butter

1 tablespoon extra-virgin olive oil

1 yellow onion, diced

2 teaspoons minced garlic (3–4 cloves)

4 stalks celery, sliced (use the leaves, too)

4 carrots, sliced

1 teaspoon dried thyme

64 ounces low-sodium chicken or vegetable broth

4 ounces of drained extra-firm tofu, cubed

2 cups fine egg noodles

DO AHEAD OR DELEGATE: Dice the onion, peel the garlic, slice the celery and the carrots, and dice the tofu.

1. Heat a stockpot over medium heat, add the butter and oil, and when the butter melts, add the onions, garlic, celery, and carrots. Sauté until the onions are tender and translucent, 8–10 minutes. (Meanwhile, prepare the salad, and warm the bread, if you are serving them.)

2. Stir in the thyme, then add the broth and bring to a boil. Add the tofu and noodles and cook until the noodles are just tender, about 4 minutes if you are using fine egg noodles. Season with pepper to taste, and serve immediately.

SLOW COOKER DIRECTIONS: Add all ingredients except the tofu and noodles to the slow cooker, and cook on low for 8–10 hours or on high for 3–4 hours. Thirty minutes before serving, add the tofu and noodles and turn the slow cooker to high for the final 30 minutes of cooking. (Slow cooker cooking times may vary—get to know your slow cooker and, if necessary, adjust cooking times accordingly.)

FLAVOR BOOSTER
Add 2–3 tablespoons of chopped fresh parsley with the broth. Add up to 1/2 teaspoon salt, if desired.

Green Salad with Red Bell Peppers, Goat Cheese, and Pecans

SERVES: 6 • **SERVING SIZE:** 1 1/2 CUPS

6 cups lettuce, chopped or torn

1/2 red bell pepper, diced

2 tablespoons goat or feta cheese, crumbled

2 tablespoons pecans

1/4 cup Orange Balsamic Vinaigrette (page 98) or dressing of your choice

1. In a large salad bowl, combine the lettuce, bell peppers, cheese, and pecans. Toss thoroughly with the vinaigrette or salad dressing of your choice.

Whole-Grain Bread

SERVES: 6 • **SERVING SIZE:** 1 SLICE (1 OUNCE)

6 slices whole-grain bread

1. Warm the bread in a 300°F oven for 5–8 minutes, if desired.

NUTRITIONAL INFORMATION | NO-CHICKEN NOODLE SOUP:

EXCHANGES / CHOICES:
1 Starch; 2 Nonstarchy Vegetable; 1 Fat

Calories: 175; Calories from Fat: 45; Total Fat: 5 g;
Saturated Fat: 1.7 g; Trans Fat: 0 g; Cholesterol: 25 mg;
Sodium: 185 mg; Potassium: 580 mg; Total Carbohydrate: 23 g;
Dietary Fiber: 3 g; Sugar: 5 g; Protein: 9 g; Phosphorus: 140 mg

NUTRITIONAL INFORMATION | GREEN SALAD WITH RED BELL PEPPERS, GOAT CHEESE, AND PECANS:

EXCHANGES / CHOICES:
1 Nonstarchy Vegetable; 1 1/2 Fat

Calories: 85; Calories from Fat: 65; Total Fat: 7 g;
Saturated Fat: 1.8 g; Trans Fat: 0 g; Cholesterol: 5 mg;
Sodium: 50 mg; Potassium: 125 mg; Total Carbohydrate: 4 g;
Dietary Fiber: 1 g; Sugar: 2 g; Protein: 2 g; Phosphorus: 55 mg

NUTRITIONAL INFORMATION | WHOLE-GRAIN BREAD:

EXCHANGES / CHOICES:
1 Starch

Calories: 70; Calories from Fat: 10; Total Fat: 1 g;
Saturated Fat: 0.2 g; Trans Fat: 0 g; Cholesterol: 0 mg;
Sodium: 125 mg; Potassium: 70 mg; Total Carbohydrate: 12 g;
Dietary Fiber: 2 g; Sugar: 1 g; Protein: 3 g; Phosphorus: 60 mg

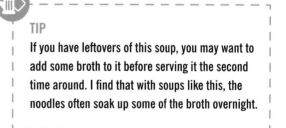

TIP

If you have leftovers of this soup, you may want to add some broth to it before serving it the second time around. I find that with soups like this, the noodles often soak up some of the broth overnight.

SPRING

WEEK 4

Savory Spice-Rubbed Strip Steak with Cinnamon Apples (1)
SIDE DISH: Red or Orange Bell Peppers with Light Ranch Dressing (1a)

Garlic Crusted Shrimp with Cherry Tomatoes (2)
SIDE DISH: Buckwheat (Kasha) (2a)

Potato, Spinach, and Garlic Soup with Sausage (3)
SIDE DISH: Whole-Wheat Crackers (3a); Green Salad with Sliced Onions, Parmesan Cheese, and Dried Cranberries (3b)

Grilled Portobello Mushroom Fajitas (4)
SIDE DISH: Mangos (4a)

Asian Edamame and Brown Rice Salad with Avocado (5)
SIDE DISH: Hard-Boiled Eggs (5a)

SHOPPING LIST

🥕 PRODUCE

3 **carrots** (5)
3 **scallions** (5)
1 large **yellow onion** (4)
1/4 **yellow or red onion** (3b)
3 **red or orange bell peppers** (1a)
2 **green bell peppers** (4)
1 cup **cherry tomatoes** (2)
6 cups **lettuce, any variety** (3b)
6 ounces **baby spinach** (3)
3 tablespoons **fresh flat-leaf parsley** (2)
1 teaspoon **fresh or dried rosemary** (3)
6 medium **red potatoes** (3)
6 ounces **portobello mushroom caps** (4)
1 **avocado** (5)
1 **lime** (5)
2 **mangos** (4a)
6 small **red apples** (1)

🍖 MEAT AND FISH

1 pound large **shrimp, peeled and deveined** (preferably U.S. or Canadian farmed or wild shrimp) (2)

1 1/2 pounds **lean New York strip or top loin steaks** (1)

8 ounces **precooked turkey, chicken, or meatless sausage**, any flavor (use wheat/gluten-free if needed) (3)

SHELVED ITEMS

3/4 cup **brown rice** (quick-cooking or traditional) (5)

1–2 cups **buckwheat** (2a)

6 medium **whole-wheat tortillas** (soft taco size) (4)

64 ounces **low-sodium chicken or vegetable broth** (3)

6 tablespoons **salsa** (4)*

2 teaspoons **sweet Asian chili sauce** (5)

1 teaspoon **sriracha hot chili sauce** (5)

6 tablespoons **light ranch dressing** or other dip (1a)

1 tablespoon **rice wine vinegar** (5)

2 teaspoons **toasted sesame oil** (5)

2 tablespoons **dried cranberries or cherries** (3b)

1/4 cup **dried cranberries** (preferably naturally sweetened) (5)

12 **whole-wheat crackers** (3a)

SPICES

1 1/4 teaspoons **salt** (1)(2)(4)

1 teaspoon **dried oregano** (1)

1/4 teaspoon **cayenne pepper** (1)

7/8 teaspoon **black pepper** (1)(2)(3)

1/2 teaspoon **ground coriander** (1)

1 teaspoon **ground cumin** (1)

1/2 teaspoon **curry powder** (5a)*

1 tablespoon **chili powder** (4)

1/2 teaspoon **paprika** (5a)*

STAPLES

1 teaspoon **butter** (2)

2 1/2 tablespoons + 1/4 cup **extra-virgin olive oil** (2)(3)(4)

1/8 cup **balsamic vinegar** (4)

1/4 cup **vinaigrette dressing** (3b)

1 tablespoon **reduced-sodium soy sauce** (use wheat/gluten-free if needed) (5)

6 **eggs** (5a)

2 tablespoons + 1 1/2 teaspoons **minced garlic** (2)(3)(4)

1/4 cup **panko or traditional breadcrumbs** (use wheat/gluten-free if needed) (2)

REFRIGERATED/FROZEN

1/4 cup **crumbled goat or feta cheese** (4)

4 tablespoons + 1/4 cup **grated Parmesan cheese** (2)(3)(3b)

6 tablespoons **fat-free sour cream** (4)*

12 ounces **frozen shelled edamame** (5)

Get free, printable versions of the shopping lists from this book at TheScramble.com/diabetes.

*optional ingredients

SPRING WEEK 4 • 39

A fabulous spice rub can really liven up the flavor of grilled meats. My son, Solomon, my husband, Andrew, and I found this flavor so appealing that we didn't even need to dip the steak in any sauce, though some may prefer to dip theirs in ketchup. Serve with Bell Peppers with Light Ranch Dressing.

Savory Spice-Rubbed Strip Steak with Cinnamon Apples

PREP + COOK: 25 MINUTES • **SERVES:** 6 • **SERVING SIZE:** 3 OUNCES + 1 SMALL APPLE

1 teaspoon dried oregano

1 teaspoon ground cumin

1/2 teaspoon ground coriander

1/2 teaspoon salt

1/4 teaspoon black pepper

1/4 teaspoon cayenne pepper, or use 1/2 teaspoon chili powder if cayenne is too spicy

1 1/2 pounds lean New York strip or top loin steaks

6 small (4 ounce) red apples, sliced and sprinkled with cinnamon

DO AHEAD OR DELEGATE: Prepare the spice rub, rub it on the steak, and refrigerate, or fully prepare and refrigerate the steak.

1. Preheat the grill to medium-high heat (or you can cook the steaks indoors on a cast iron skillet over medium-high heat). In a small bowl, combine all of the spices, and sprinkle and rub the mixture over both sides of the steaks. (Leave one steak plain or very lightly seasoned if you have picky eaters.)

2. When the grill is hot, cook the steaks for 3–5 minutes per side, depending on how well done you like them. (Meanwhile, slice the apples, if you are serving them.) Slice the steak into thin strips and serve with the cinnamon apples. Serve immediately or refrigerate for up to 3 days.

FLAVOR BOOSTER

Use both cayenne and chili powder for the spice rub. Serve the steak with lime wedges.

Bell Peppers with Light Ranch Dressing

SERVES: 6 • **SERVING SIZE:** 1/2 PEPPER + 1 TABLESPOON DRESSING

3 medium red or orange bell peppers

6 tablespoons light ranch dressing

1. Seed and thinly slice the bell peppers and serve with the dressing or dip of your choice.

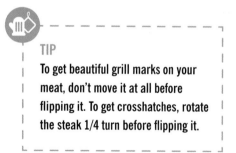

TIP

To get beautiful grill marks on your meat, don't move it at all before flipping it. To get crosshatches, rotate the steak 1/4 turn before flipping it.

NUTRITIONAL INFORMATION | SAVORY SPICE-RUBBED STRIP STEAK WITH CINNAMON APPLES:

EXCHANGES / CHOICES:
1 Fruit; 4 Protein, lean

Calories: 230; Calories from Fat: 55; Total Fat: 6 g;
Saturated Fat: 2.5 g; Trans Fat: 0.4 g; Cholesterol: 80 mg;
Sodium: 250 mg; Potassium: 465 mg; Total Carbohydrate: 15 g;
Dietary Fiber: 3 g; Sugar: 11 g; Protein: 28 g; Phosphorus: 265 mg

NUTRITIONAL INFORMATION | BELL PEPPERS WITH LIGHT RANCH DRESSING:

EXCHANGES / CHOICES:
1 Nonstarchy Vegetable; 1 Fat

Calories: 65; Calories from Fat: 30; Total Fat: 3.5 g;
Saturated Fat: 0.5 g; Trans Fat: 0 g; Cholesterol: 0 mg;
Sodium: 150 mg; Potassium: 175 mg; Total Carbohydrate: 6 g;
Dietary Fiber: 2 g; Sugar: 4 g; Protein: 1 g; Phosphorus: 50 mg

This delectable Italian-style shrimp takes just minutes to whip up (as long as you purchase the shrimp already peeled and deveined), but it's not short on flavor. The shrimp would also be delightful on top of angel hair noodles. Serve with Buckwheat (Kasha).

Garlic Crusted Shrimp with Cherry Tomatoes

PREP + COOK: 15 MINUTES • **SERVES:** 4 • **SERVING SIZE:** 1 CUP

1/4 cup panko or traditional breadcrumbs

1 teaspoon butter

1 tablespoon extra-virgin olive oil

1 pound large peeled and deveined shrimp, fresh (never frozen), if possible

1 tablespoon minced garlic, (4–6 cloves)

1 cup halved and seeded cherry tomatoes (use your thumb to poke the seeds out of the halves)

1/8 teaspoon black pepper, or to taste

3 tablespoons fresh flat-leaf parsley, chopped, or use basil

2 tablespoons grated Parmesan cheese

DO AHEAD OR DELEGATE: Toast the breadcrumbs, thaw the shrimp, if necessary, peel the garlic, halve the tomatoes, and combine the parsley and the panko.

1. (Start the buckwheat first, if you are serving it.) Toast the breadcrumbs in a dry heavy skillet until they are golden brown.

2. Meanwhile, in a large heavy skillet, heat the butter and oil over medium heat. When the butter is bubbling, add the shrimp in a single layer and sauté for about 2 minutes per side until they are pink and opaque throughout.

3. Add the garlic, tomatoes, and pepper, and cook everything for 2–3 more minutes, until the tomatoes start to soften. Stir in the parsley (or basil), panko, Parmesan cheese, and toss until the shrimp and tomatoes are nicely coated. Serve immediately.

SLOW COOKER DIRECTIONS: Melt the butter. Combine the butter, oil, shrimp, garlic, tomatoes, and pepper in the slow cooker, and toss to combine. Cook on low for 1 1/2–2 1/2 hours, until the shrimp are opaque. About 5 to 10 minutes before serving, add the parsley and toasted panko or breadcrumbs to the slow cooker, and toss to combine. (Slow cooker cooking times may vary—get to know your slow cooker and, if necessary, adjust cooking times accordingly.)

FLAVOR BOOSTER
Sprinkle some red pepper flakes in with the parsley and panko and/or squeeze a little fresh lemon juice over the finished dish.

Buckwheat (Kasha)

SERVES: 4 • **SERVING SIZE:** 3/4 CUP

1 cup uncooked buckwheat (kasha)

1. Prepare the buckwheat (kasha) according to the package directions, using 2 cups of water or reduced-sodium vegetable or chicken broth.

TIP

Dry the shrimp thoroughly with cloth or paper towels so they can get a nice sear in the pan, rather than getting watery.

NUTRITIONAL INFORMATION | GARLIC CRUSTED SHRIMP WITH CHERRY TOMATOES:

EXCHANGES / CHOICES:
1/2 Carbohydrate; 3 Protein, lean

Calories: 170; Calories from Fat: 45; Total Fat: 5 g;
Saturated Fat: 1.5 g; Trans Fat: 0 g; Cholesterol: 195 mg;
Sodium: 165 mg; Potassium: 385 mg; Total Carbohydrate: 6 g;
Dietary Fiber: 1 g; Sugar: 1 g; Protein: 26 g; Phosphorus: 270 mg

NUTRITIONAL INFORMATION | BUCKWHEAT:

EXCHANGES / CHOICES:
1 1/2 Starch

Calories: 95; Calories from Fat: 5; Total Fat: 0.5 g;
Saturated Fat: 0.1 g; Trans Fat: 0 g; Cholesterol: 0 mg;
Sodium: 0 mg; Potassium: 90 mg; Total Carbohydrate: 21 g;
Dietary Fiber: 3 g; Sugar: 1 g; Protein: 4 g; Phosphorus: 75 mg

Six O'Clock Scramble member Laurie McLean suggested this filling soup. It's quite adaptable—for example, you may want to use mushrooms instead of sausage, or stir in a can of diced tomatoes or white beans. Serve with Green Salad with Sliced Onions, Parmesan Cheese, and Dried Cranberries, and with Whole-Wheat Crackers.

Potato, Spinach, and Garlic Soup with Sausage

PREP: 10 MINUTES • **COOK:** 35 MINUTES • **SERVES:** 6 • **SERVING SIZE:** 2 CUPS

1 1/2 tablespoons extra-virgin olive oil

1 1/2 pounds red potatoes (about 6 medium potatoes), diced

1 teaspoon fresh or dried rosemary

1 tablespoon minced garlic (4–6 cloves)

8 ounces precooked chicken, turkey or meatless sausage, or mushrooms, diced

64 ounces low-sodium chicken or vegetable broth

6 ounces baby spinach

1/2 teaspoon black pepper, or to taste

1/4 cup grated Parmesan cheese, for serving

DO AHEAD OR DELEGATE: Dice the potatoes and sausage, peel the garlic, and grate the cheese, if necessary.

1. In a large stockpot or Dutch oven, heat the oil over medium heat. Add the potatoes, rosemary, garlic, and sausage and cook, stirring frequently, so the potatoes don't stick to the pot, for about 15 minutes, until the sausage is browned. (Meanwhile, make the salad, if you are serving it.)

2. Add the broth to the pot, raise the heat to bring the soup to the boil, partially cover, and simmer, stirring occasionally, for about 20 minutes, until the potatoes are fork tender.

3. Stir in the spinach and pepper. Serve immediately, topped with the Parmesan cheese, or refrigerate for up to 3 days.

SLOW COOKER DIRECTIONS: Place all ingredients except the cheese in the slow cooker and cook on low for 7–12 hours or on high for 4–5 hours. Top with the cheese at the table. (Slow cooker cooking times may vary—get to know your slow cooker and, if necessary, adjust cooking times accordingly.)

FLAVOR BOOSTER
Use spicy sausage and serve the soup at the table with hot pepper sauce, such as Tabasco.

Whole-Wheat Crackers

SERVES: 6 • **SERVING SIZE:** 2 CRACKERS

12 whole-wheat crackers, such as Finn Crisp or Ak-Mak

1. Serve with the soup and salad.

Green Salad with Sliced Onions, Parmesan Cheese, and Dried Cranberries

SERVES: 6 • **SERVING SIZE:** 1 CUP

6 cups lettuce, chopped

1/4 yellow or red onion, sliced

2 tablespoons grated Parmesan cheese

2 tablespoons dried cranberries or cherries

1/4 cup Orange Balsamic Vinaigrette (page 16)

1. Combine the lettuce, onions, Parmesan cheese, and cranberries. Toss the salad with the dressing, to taste.

NUTRITIONAL INFORMATION | POTATO, SPINACH, AND GARLIC SOUP WITH SAUSAGE:

EXCHANGES / CHOICES:
1 1/2 Starch; 1/2 Carbohydrate; 1 Protein, lean; 1 Fat

Calories: 235; Calories from Fat: 70; Total Fat: 8 g;
Saturated Fat: 2.4 g; Trans Fat: 0 g; Cholesterol: 35 mg;
Sodium: 375 mg; Potassium: 1085 mg; Total Carbohydrate: 29 g;
Dietary Fiber: 3 g; Sugar: 4 g; Protein: 13 g; Phosphorus: 215 mg

NUTRITIONAL INFORMATION | WHOLE-WHEAT CRACKERS:

EXCHANGES / CHOICES:
1/2 Starch

Calories: 45; Calories from Fat: 10; Total Fat: 1 g;
Saturated Fat: 0.1 g; Trans Fat: 0 g; Cholesterol: 0 mg;
Sodium: 90 mg; Potassium: 40 mg; Total Carbohydrate: 8 g;
Dietary Fiber: 2 g; Sugar: 0 g; Protein: 2 g; Phosphorus: 40 mg

NUTRITIONAL INFORMATION | GREEN SALAD WITH SLICED ONIONS, PARMESAN CHEESE, AND DRIED CRANBERRIES:

EXCHANGES / CHOICES:
1/2 Carbohydrate; 1/2 Fat

Calories: 65; Calories from Fat: 40; Total Fat: 4.5 g;
Saturated Fat: 0.8 g; Trans Fat: 0 g; Cholesterol: 0 mg;
Sodium: 55 mg; Potassium: 100 mg; Total Carbohydrate: 5 g;
Dietary Fiber: 1 g; Sugar: 4 g; Protein: 1 g; Phosphorus: 25 mg

Portobello mushrooms are a meaty vegetable and, just like beef or chicken, they take well to marinades and grilling. (However, if you don't want to grill them, these would be equally good cooked in a cast iron skillet.) Serve with Mangos.

Grilled Portobello Mushroom Fajitas

MARINATE: 30 MINUTES • **PREP:** 15 MINUTES • **COOK:** 20 MINUTES • **SERVES:** 6 • **SERVING SIZE:** 1 FAJITA

6 ounces portobello mushroom caps, sliced, or use 3/4–1 pound boneless, skinless chicken breasts

1 large yellow onion, halved top to bottom and thinly sliced

2 green bell peppers, thinly sliced

1/4 cup extra-virgin olive oil

1/8 cup balsamic vinegar

1 tablespoon chili powder

1/2 teaspoon salt

1 1/2 teaspoons minced garlic (about 3 cloves)

6 medium whole-wheat tortillas

1/4 cup crumbled goat or feta cheese

6 tablespoons fat-free sour cream, for serving

6 tablespoons salsa, for serving

DO AHEAD OR DELEGATE: Make the marinade and slice and marinate the mushrooms, onion, and peppers.

1. Put the mushrooms, onions, and peppers in a large resealable bag. Combine the oil, vinegar, chili powder, salt, and garlic, and add to the bag with the vegetables. Massage the vegetables gently to coat well with the marinade. Refrigerate for at least 30 minutes and up to 48 hours.

2. Preheat the grill to medium-high heat. Spray a vegetable grilling tray or a piece of foil with nonstick cooking spray, or brush it with a little vegetable oil, and heat it on the grill. Drain the vegetables in a colander and transfer to the grilling tray. Grill with the cover closed for about 15 minutes, flipping once, until they are tender and partially browned but not charred. (Meanwhile, slice the mangos, if you are serving them.)

3. Heat the tortillas in the microwave or on a hot skillet for 30 seconds to 1 minute so they are soft and warm. Place about 1/2 cup of the vegetables in the center of each tortilla, top with about 2 teaspoons cheese, and about 1 tablespoon each sour cream and/or salsa, if desired. Fold the bottoms up and the sides in and serve immediately.

SLOW COOKER DIRECTIONS: No need to marinate the vegetables in advance. Place the mushrooms, onions, and peppers in the slow cooker. Combine the oil, vinegar, chili powder, salt, and garlic, and pour over the vegetables, stirring to combine. Cook on low for 6–10 hours or on high for 2–3 hours, then assemble and serve with warmed tortillas as directed. (Slow cooker cooking times may vary—get to know your slow cooker and, if necessary, adjust cooking times accordingly.)

Mangos

SERVES: 6 • **SERVING SIZE:** 1/2 CUP

2 large mangos, peeled and sliced, or use frozen mango chunks or sliced peaches

1. To slice a mango, stand it on its end and slice each of the halves off as close to the oblong pit as possible. Using a small, sharp knife, score the flesh into strips or squares, turn the skin inside out, and cut the flesh off the peel.

FLAVOR BOOSTER

Double the chili powder and/or serve the fajitas with spicy salsa.

TIP

For a gluten-free alternative, use corn tortillas in place of whole-wheat tortillas.

NUTRITIONAL INFORMATION | GRILLED PORTOBELLO MUSHROOM FAJITAS:

EXCHANGES / CHOICES:
1 1/2 Starch; 2 Nonstarchy Vegetable; 2 Fat

Calories: 250; Calories from Fat: 100; Total Fat: 11 g;
Saturated Fat: 2.7 g; Trans Fat: 0 g; Cholesterol: 10 mg;
Sodium: 425 mg; Potassium: 425 mg; Total Carbohydrate: 32 g;
Dietary Fiber: 5 g; Sugar: 6 g; Protein: 7 g; Phosphorus: 265 mg

NUTRITIONAL INFORMATION | MANGOS:

EXCHANGES / CHOICES:
1 Fruit

Calories: 55; Calories from Fat: 0; Total Fat: 0 g;
Saturated Fat: 0.1 g; Trans Fat: 0 g; Cholesterol: 0 mg;
Sodium: 0 mg; Potassium: 155 mg; Total Carbohydrate: 14 g;
Dietary Fiber: 1 g; Sugar: 12 g; Protein: 1 g; Phosphorus: 15 mg

Your family will be super-charged after eating this sweet and tangy nutritious rice salad, inspired by a recipe from Today Show nutrition expert Joy Bauer. If you can't find shelled edamame you can use frozen peas instead. Serve with Hard-Boiled Eggs.

Asian Edamame and Brown Rice Salad

PREP + COOK: 30 MINUTES • **SERVES:** 6 • **SERVING SIZE:** 1 1/4 CUPS

3/4 cup brown rice

12 ounces frozen shelled edamame (about 2 1/2 cups), or use frozen peas

3 carrots, diced into 1/2-inch pieces

3 scallions, dark and light green parts, thinly sliced

1/4 cup dried cranberries

1 lime, juice only, about 2 tablespoons

1 tablespoon reduced-sodium soy sauce (use wheat/gluten-free if needed)

1 tablespoon rice wine vinegar

2 teaspoons toasted sesame oil

2 teaspoons sweet Asian chili sauce, or substitute mango chutney or apricot jam

1 teaspoon sriracha hot chili sauce, or use Tabasco

1 avocado, peeled and diced

DO AHEAD OR DELEGATE: Cook the rice and the edamame, dice the carrots, slice the scallions, juice the lime, and prepare the salad dressing, or fully prepare and refrigerate the salad.

1. (Start the eggs first, if you are serving them.) Prepare the rice and edamame according to the package directions and drain the edamame.

2. In a large bowl, combine the rice, edamame, carrots, scallions, and dried cranberries.

3. In a small bowl, whisk together the lime juice, soy sauce, vinegar, oil, and sweet and hot chili sauces. Pour the dressing over the salad and gently stir in the avocado. The salad can be chilled for up to 2 days before serving, but add the avocado just before serving.

FLAVOR BOOSTER
Serve with extra sweet and hot chili sauce and with extra soy sauce. Cook the rice in 1/2 water and 1/2 light coconut milk.

Hard-Boiled Eggs

SERVES: 6 • **SERVING SIZE:** 1 EGG

6 eggs
1/2 teaspoon paprika (optional)
1/2 teaspoon curry powder (optional)

1. In a medium saucepan, cover the eggs in cold water and bring the water to a boil. When the water boils, turn off the heat, cover the pot, and let the eggs sit in the hot water for 15 minutes (no peeking). Transfer the eggs to a bowl of ice water, then peel them, starting by cracking the skinny pointed end and peeling down from there. Sprinkle with a bit of paprika or curry powder, if desired.

TIP

To finely dice a carrot, cut it in half to create two shorter pieces, then cut each half lengthwise down the middle, and set the flat sides down on a cutting board. Cut those quarters into 2 or 3 long pieces, depending on the carrot's size, and chop the long pieces into smaller dice.

NUTRITIONAL INFORMATION | ASIAN EDAMAME AND BROWN RICE SALAD:

EXCHANGES / CHOICES:
1 1/2 Starch; 1/2 Fruit; 1 Nonstarchy Vegetable; 1 1/2 Fat

Calories: 245; Calories from Fat: 80; Total Fat: 9 g; Saturated Fat: 1.3 g; Trans Fat: 0 g; Cholesterol: 0 mg; Sodium: 155 mg; Potassium: 535 mg; Total Carbohydrate: 35 g; Dietary Fiber: 8 g; Sugar: 7 g; Protein: 9 g; Phosphorus: 190 mg

NUTRITIONAL INFORMATION | HARD-BOILED EGGS:

EXCHANGES / CHOICES:
1 Protein, medium fat

Calories: 70; Calories from Fat: 45; Total Fat: 5 g; Saturated Fat: 1.6 g; Trans Fat: 0 g; Cholesterol: 185 mg; Sodium: 70 mg; Potassium: 70 mg; Total Carbohydrate: 0 g; Dietary Fiber: 0 g; Sugar: 0 g; Protein: 6 g; Phosphorus: 100 mg

SPRING

WEEK 5

Orange Chicken and Vegetable Stir-Fry (1)
SIDE DISH: Brown Rice (1a)

Tangy Tuna and White Bean Salad Wraps (2)
SIDE DISH: Honeydew Melon (2a)

Scrambalaya (Cajun Jambalaya with Smoked Ham) (3)
SIDE DISH: Green Salad with Celery, Walnuts, and Feta Cheese (3a)

Italian Shells with Fresh Mozzarella, Sundried Tomatoes, and Spinach (4)
SIDE DISH: Green Beans with Mustard-Lemon Sauce (4a)

North African Shakshuka (Love Shack-shuka) (5)
SIDE DISH: Indian naan, Middle Eastern Flatbread, or Pita (5a)

SHOPPING LIST

PRODUCE

2 **carrots** (1)
1 1/2 medium **yellow onions** (1)(3)
1 large **yellow onion** (5)
1 **green bell pepper** (3)
7–8 stalks **celery** (2)(3)(3a)
1 **tomato** (2)*
1 head **iceberg or romaine lettuce** (3a)
6–9 ounces **baby spinach** (4)
5 cloves **garlic** (1)(5)
1 teaspoon **fresh ginger** (1)
1/2 cup **fresh basil** (4)
1 1/2 cups **fresh flat-leaf Italian parsley** (2)(4)
1 head **broccoli** (1)
1 pound **green beans** (4a)
1 1/4 **lemons** (2)(4a)
1–2 **oranges** (1)
1 **honeydew melon or cantaloupe** (2a)
1 medium **zucchini** (5)
28 ounces **whole plum tomatoes** (5)
1/4 cup **fresh cilantro** (5)

MEAT AND FISH

1 pound **boneless, skinless chicken breasts** (1)
12 ounces **lower-sodium, lean smoked ham, turkey kielbasa, or vegetarian sausage** (use wheat/gluten-free if needed) (3)

SHELVED ITEMS

1 cup **quick-cooking brown rice** (1a)

2 cups **white rice** (3)

16 ounces **medium whole-wheat shell pasta** (4)

6 **whole-wheat or spinach wraps** (2)

1/4 cup **julienne-cut sundried tomatoes** (4)

32 ounces **low-sodium chicken or vegetable broth** (3)

2 tablespoons **rice vinegar** (1)

2/3 tablespoon **oyster or hoisin sauce** (1)

15 ounces **canned white beans** (2)

10 ounces **chunk light tuna** (2)

2 tablespoons **walnuts** (3a)

4 pieces **Indian naan, Middle Eastern flatbread, or pita** (5a)

SPICES

1/2 teaspoon **salt** (2)(5)

3 **bay leaves** (3)

1/2 teaspoon **dried thyme** (3)

1/4 teaspoon **dried thyme or herbes de Provence** (3a)

1/4 teaspoon **crushed red pepper flakes** (4)

5/8–1 1/8 teaspoons **black pepper** (2)(3)(5)

1/2 teaspoon **ground cumin** (3)

1 teaspoon **dry mustard** (3)

1 teaspoon **ground cumin** (5)

1 teaspoon **ground paprika** (5)

1/8–1/4 teaspoon **cayenne** (5)

STAPLES

4 teaspoons **butter** (4a)

2 tablespoons + 1/4 cup **extra-virgin olive oil** (3)(3a)(5)

1 tablespoon **vegetable or canola oil** (1)

1/8 cup **red wine vinegar** (3a)

2 tablespoons **mayonnaise** (2)

2 1/2 teaspoons **Dijon mustard** (use wheat/gluten-free if needed) (3a)(4a)

1 2/3 tablespoons **reduced-sodium soy sauce** (use wheat/gluten-free if needed) (1)

1/2 tablespoon **pure maple syrup** (3a)

1 tablespoon **honey** (1)

2 tablespoons **cornstarch** (1)

8 **eggs** (5)

REFRIGERATED/FROZEN

2 tablespoons **crumbled feta cheese** (3a)(5)

1 cup **marinated mozzarella balls** (4)

Get free, printable versions of the shopping lists from this book at **TheScramble.com/diabetes**.

*optional ingredients

SPRING WEEK 5 • 51

Alice Currah, the talented photographer and cook behind the popular blog Savory Sweet Life, was also my co-contributor at PBS Parents Kitchen Explorers, where she shared her fabulous recipe for Orange Chicken. I've adapted it here so you can try it, too. You can experiment with other vegetables instead of the broccoli and carrots, like green beans, celery, mushrooms, snap peas, etc., just keep the total measurement to about 5 cups of vegetables. Serve with Brown Rice.

Orange Chicken and Vegetable Stir-Fry

PREP + COOK: 30 MINUTES • **SERVES:** 4 • **SERVING SIZE:** 1 1/2 CUPS

1–2 oranges, juice and zest (1/2 cup juice and 1 tablespoon zest)

2 cloves garlic, chopped

1 2/3 tablespoons reduced-sodium soy sauce (use wheat/gluten-free if needed)

2 tablespoons rice vinegar

2/3 tablespoon oyster or hoisin sauce

1 tablespoon honey

1 teaspoon fresh ginger, peeled and minced, or use 1/4 teaspoon ground ginger

1 pound boneless, skinless chicken breasts, cut into bite-sized pieces

2 tablespoons cornstarch

1 tablespoon vegetable or canola oil

1/2 yellow onion, diced

1 head broccoli (1 pound), cut into small florets

2 carrots, sliced

1 tablespoon water

DO AHEAD OR DELEGATE: Combine and refrigerate the ingredients for the sauce, cut and refrigerate the chicken, dice the onion, cut the broccoli, and slice the carrots.

1. (Start the rice first, if you are serving it.) In a blender, combine the orange juice and zest, garlic, soy sauce, vinegar, oyster or hoisin sauce, honey, and ginger and puree until smooth. Transfer the sauce to a large nonstick skillet, bring it to a low boil, and simmer, stirring occasionally, for about 5 minutes until it thickens. Pour the sauce into a measuring cup or bowl, and rinse and dry the skillet.

2. In a medium bowl, toss the chicken and the cornstarch until the chicken is fully coated.

3. Heat the oil in the skillet over medium-high heat, add the chicken and onions, and stir-fry until the chicken is almost cooked through, 3–4 minutes. Add the broccoli, carrots, and water, and stir-fry everything for about 3 minutes until the broccoli is bright green. Add the sauce and continue cooking for 1 minute until the sauce is heated through. Serve immediately over steamed rice, if desired.

FLAVOR BOOSTER
Add 1/4–1/2 teaspoon crushed red pepper flakes to the pan with the chicken and onions. Serve with fresh lime wedges.

Brown Rice

SERVES: 4 • **SERVING SIZE:** 1/2 CUP

1 cup quick-cooking brown rice

1. Prepare the rice according to package directions.

TIP

Coating the chicken with cornstarch helps give it a brown and crispy crust and helps to thicken the sauce.

NUTRITIONAL INFORMATION | ORANGE CHICKEN AND VEGETABLE STIR-FRY:

EXCHANGES / CHOICES:
1 Carbohydrate; 2 Nonstarchy Vegetable; 3 Protein, lean

Calories: 255; Calories from Fat: 65; Total Fat: 7 g;
Saturated Fat: 1.1 g; Trans Fat: 0 g; Cholesterol: 65 mg;
Sodium: 400 mg; Potassium: 645 mg; Total Carbohydrate: 22 g;
Dietary Fiber: 4 g; Sugar: 11 g; Protein: 28 g; Phosphorus: 255 mg

NUTRITIONAL INFORMATION | BROWN RICE:

EXCHANGES / CHOICES:
1 1/2 Starch

Calories: 115; Calories from Fat: 10; Total Fat: 1 g;
Saturated Fat: 0.2 g; Trans Fat: 0 g; Cholesterol: 0 mg;
Sodium: 5 mg; Potassium: 45 mg; Total Carbohydrate: 24 g;
Dietary Fiber: 2 g; Sugar: 0 g; Protein: 3 g; Phosphorus: 85 mg

I made this salad for a quick and healthy weekend lunch for my husband Andrew and me, but it also makes a super easy weeknight dinner recipe, especially for a warm evening when you don't want to heat up the oven. You can also serve the salad over greens or wrap it in lettuce leaves. Serve with Honeydew Melon.

Tangy Tuna and White Bean Salad Wraps

PREP + COOK: 15 MINUTES • **SERVES:** 6 • **SERVING SIZE:** 1 WRAP

10 ounces chunk light tuna, drained (we love Wild Planet sustainable tuna)

2 stalks celery, halved lengthwise and thinly sliced

2 tablespoons mayonnaise

1 lemon, use all the juice and some of the zest

15 ounces canned cannellini or white kidney beans, drained and rinsed

1/2 cup fresh parsley, finely chopped, or use 1 teaspoon dried Italian seasoning

1/8 teaspoon salt, or to taste

1/8 teaspoon black pepper, or to taste

6 whole-wheat tortillas or spinach wraps

1 tomato, chopped (optional)

DO AHEAD OR DELEGATE: Halve and slice the celery, juice and zest the lemon, chop the parsley and the tomato, if using, or fully prepare and refrigerate the tuna salad.

1. (Dice the melon first, if you are serving it.) In a mixing bowl, flake the tuna and mix in the celery, mayonnaise, and lemon juice. Gently stir in the beans, parsley, salt, and pepper. At this point, you can proceed or refrigerate the mixture for up to 3 days.

2. Warm the tortillas in the microwave to soften and put a scoop of the salad in the middle, top with some tomatoes, if desired, and wrap them up burrito-style.

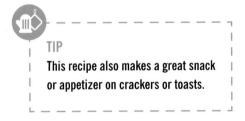

TIP
This recipe also makes a great snack or appetizer on crackers or toasts.

Honeydew Melon

SERVES: 6 • **SERVING SIZE:** 1 CUP

1 honeydew melon

1. Peel and dice the honeydew. If the melon needs extra flavor, sprinkle it with a teaspoon of superfine sugar and fresh lemon or lime juice.

FLAVOR BOOSTER

Add 1 tablespoon capers or chopped green olives and/or 1–2 tablespoons finely chopped red onion or add a squeeze of sriracha to the wrap.

NUTRITIONAL INFORMATION | TANGY TUNA AND WHITE BEAN SALAD WRAPS:

EXCHANGES / CHOICES:
1 1/2 Starch; 1 Protein, lean; 1 Fat

Calories: 210; Calories from Fat: 65; Total Fat: 7 g;
Saturated Fat: 2 g; Trans Fat: 0 g; Cholesterol: 20 mg;
Sodium: 415 mg; Potassium: 410 mg; Total Carbohydrate: 23 g;
Dietary Fiber: 6 g; Sugar: 1 g; Protein: 15 g; Phosphorus: 225 mg

NUTRITIONAL INFORMATION | HONEYDEW MELON:

EXCHANGES / CHOICES:
1 Fruit

Calories: 60; Calories from Fat: 0; Total Fat: 0 g;
Saturated Fat: 0.1 g; Trans Fat: 0 g; Cholesterol: 0 mg;
Sodium: 30 mg; Potassium: 380 mg; Total Carbohydrate: 15 g;
Dietary Fiber: 1 g; Sugar: 14 g; Protein: 1 g; Phosphorus: 20 mg

My friend and colleague Jeanne Rossomme used to live in New Orleans, where she learned to make this zesty jambalaya. She calls it Poor Man's Jambalaya because it's not as meaty as other versions. Serve with Green Salad with Celery, Walnuts, and Feta Cheese.

Scrambalaya (Cajun Jambalaya with Smoked Ham)

PREP: 25 MINUTES • **COOK:** 20 MINUTES • **SERVES:** 8 • **SERVING SIZE:** 1 1/2 CUPS

2 tablespoons extra-virgin olive oil

12 ounces lower-sodium lean smoked ham, turkey kielbasa, or vegetarian sausage, diced into 1/4-inch pieces

3 bay leaves

1/2–1 teaspoon black pepper, to taste (depending on your tolerance for spiciness)

1 teaspoon dry mustard

1/2 teaspoon ground cumin

1/2 teaspoon dried thyme

1 medium yellow onion, chopped

3–4 stalks celery, chopped (1 1/2 cups)

1 green bell pepper, chopped

2 cups white rice, uncooked

32 ounces low-sodium chicken or vegetable broth

DO AHEAD OR DELEGATE: Dice the ham or sausage, combine the dry seasonings, chop the onion, the celery, and the bell pepper, or fully prepare and refrigerate or freeze the dish.

1. In a large stockpot, heat the oil over medium-high heat. Add the ham or sausage and cook for about 5 minutes until nicely browned. (If you have picky eaters, remove some of the ham/sausage to serve to them separately before proceeding with the recipe.)

2. Add the remaining ingredients, except the rice and broth, and sauté for about 10 more minutes until the vegetables soften, stirring occasionally. Add the rice and stir frequently for about 3 minutes to coat. Add the broth and simmer, uncovered, for about 20 minutes until the rice is tender to the bite, stirring occasionally, and making sure to scrape the bottom of the pot so the rice doesn't stick. (Meanwhile, make the salad, if you are serving it.)

3. Turn off the heat, cover the pot, and let the flavors meld until you are ready to dig in. Remove the bay leaves before serving. You can make this up to 2 days in advance, or freeze for up to 3 months.

SLOW COOKER DIRECTIONS: Rub the inside of a slow cooker with the oil, then place all remaining ingredients in the slow cooker. Cook on high for 2 hours, then check rice for doneness. If rice is not completely softened, cook for 30 more minutes. Alternatively, place all remaining ingredients except the rice in the slow cooker and cook on low for 4 hours. Add the rice and cook 1 1/2 hours more, checking for doneness as above. (If substituting brown rice for white, increase cooking time by 30 minutes.) (Slow cooker cooking times may vary—get to know your slow cooker and, if necessary, adjust cooking times accordingly.)

FLAVOR BOOSTER

Use 1 teaspoon black pepper and serve with hot pepper sauce, such as Tabasco.

Green Salad with Celery, Walnuts, and Feta Cheese

SERVES: 8 • **SERVING SIZE:** 1 CUP

1 head iceberg or romaine lettuce, chopped (about 8 cups)

2 stalks celery, sliced

2 tablespoons walnuts, chopped

2 tablespoons crumbled feta cheese

2 tablespoons extra-virgin olive oil

1 tablespoon red wine vinegar

1/2 tablespoon pure maple syrup

1/2 teaspoon Dijon mustard (use wheat/gluten-free if needed)

1/4 teaspoon dried thyme or herbes de Provence

1. Combine the lettuce, celery, walnuts, and feta cheese. Toss the salad with 2–4 tablespoons homemade maple-Dijon dressing.

2. **To make the maple-Dijon dressing:** whisk together the oil, vinegar, maple syrup, mustard, and dried thyme or herbes de Provence. Refrigerate any extra dressing for up to 2 weeks.

TIP

If you're inspired, you can get really creative with the meat you put into jambalaya. In addition to ham, some people incorporate chicken, shrimp, or even alligator (!) into this dish.

NUTRITIONAL INFORMATION | SCRAMBALAYA:

EXCHANGES / CHOICES:
2 1/2 Starch; 1 Nonstarchy Vegetable; 1 Protein, lean

Calories: 270; Calories from Fat: 40; Total Fat: 4.5 g;
Saturated Fat: 0.9 g; Trans Fat: 0 g; Cholesterol: 20 mg;
Sodium: 410 mg; Potassium: 355 mg; Total Carbohydrate: 42 g;
Dietary Fiber: 2 g; Sugar: 3 g; Protein: 13 g; Phosphorus: 165 mg

NUTRITIONAL INFORMATION | GREEN SALAD WITH CELERY, WALNUTS, AND FETA CHEESE:

EXCHANGES / CHOICES:
1 Nonstarchy Vegetable; 1 Fat

Calories: 60; Calories from Fat: 45; Total Fat: 5 g;
Saturated Fat: 1 g; Trans Fat: 0 g; Cholesterol: 0 mg;
Sodium: 50 mg; Potassium: 145 mg; Total Carbohydrate: 3 g;
Dietary Fiber: 1 g; Sugar: 2 g; Protein: 1 g; Phosphorus: 30 mg

This homey Italian-style dish is sure to make your whole family happy. If you can't find marinated mozzarella balls, plain fresh mozzarella will still be delicious. Serve with Green Beans with Mustard-Lemon Sauce.

Italian Shells with Fresh Mozzarella, Sundried Tomatoes, and Spinach

PREP + COOK: 30 MINUTES • **SERVES:** 8 • **SERVING SIZE:** 1 1/2 CUPS

16 ounces medium whole-wheat shell pasta

1/4 cup julienne-cut sundried tomatoes, not packed in oil

1/4 teaspoon crushed red pepper flakes

1 cup marinated mozzarella balls + 1/4 cup of their oil

1/2 cup fresh basil, or more to taste

1/2 cup fresh flat-leaf parsley, or more to taste

6–9 ounces baby spinach

DO AHEAD OR DELEGATE: Cook the pasta and store it tossed with a little oil to prevent sticking. Cut the sundried tomatoes, chop the parsley, chop and refrigerate the mozzarella, or fully prepare and refrigerate the dish.

1. Prepare the shells according to the package directions. (Start the green beans, if you are serving them.)

2. Meanwhile, in a large serving bowl, combine the sundried tomatoes and the crushed red pepper flakes with 1/4 cup of the oil from the mozzarella (if using water-packed mozzarella, use your own olive oil instead).

3. Coarsely chop the fresh herbs and mozzarella and set them aside.

4. One minute before the pasta is fully cooked, add the spinach to the boiling water. Drain the spinach and the shells and add them to the serving bowl. Toss in the fresh herbs, allow the noodles to cool for about 2 minutes, and toss in the cheese (otherwise it will melt and become stringy). Serve immediately, or refrigerate it for up to 3 days.

FLAVOR BOOSTER
Double the amount of crushed red pepper flakes, or sprinkle some extra on the finished dish along with a splash of balsamic vinegar or fresh lemon juice.

Green Beans with Mustard-Lemon Sauce

SERVES: 8 • **SERVING SIZE:** 1/2 CUP

1 pound green beans

2 teaspoons butter

2 teaspoons Dijon mustard

1/4 lemon, juice only

1. Trim the green beans and cut them in half crosswise. In a medium saucepan, bring 1/2 inch of water to a boil. Add the green beans, cover, reduce the heat, and steam for 6–8 minutes until they reach desired tenderness. Drain and return beans to the pot. Stir in the butter, mustard, and lemon juice.

TIP

If your sundried tomatoes are very hard, soak them in warm water for 10 minutes or longer before adding them.

NUTRITIONAL INFORMATION | ITALIAN SHELLS WITH FRESH MOZZARELLA, SUNDRIED TOMATOES, AND SPINACH:

EXCHANGES / CHOICES:
3 Starch; 1 Protein, lean; 1 1/2 Fat

Calories: 330; Calories from Fat: 110; Total Fat: 12 g;
Saturated Fat: 3.7 g; Trans Fat: 0 g; Cholesterol: 15 mg;
Sodium: 135 mg; Potassium: 335 mg; Total Carbohydrate: 45 g;
Dietary Fiber: 6 g; Sugar: 3 g; Protein: 13 g; Phosphorus: 240 mg

NUTRITIONAL INFORMATION | GREEN BEANS WITH MUSTARD-LEMON SAUCE:

EXCHANGES / CHOICES:
1 Nonstarchy Vegetable

Calories: 25; Calories from Fat: 10; Total Fat: 1 g;
Saturated Fat: 0.6 g; Trans Fat: 0 g; Cholesterol: 5 mg;
Sodium: 40 mg; Potassium: 75 mg; Total Carbohydrate: 4 g;
Dietary Fiber: 2 g; Sugar: 1 g; Protein: 1 g; Phosphorus: 15 mg

I adapted this delicious recipe from Melissa Clark's version in The New York Times. Instead of zucchini, you can use bell peppers or eggplant. Shakshuka is a popular breakfast in North Africa and the Middle East. Since we hardly ever have time for a breakfast that takes 30 minutes, I'm a big fan of breakfast for dinner, especially when it's one as flavorful and savory as this. Serve with Indian Naan, Middle Eastern Flatbread, or Pita Bread.

North African Shakshuka (Love Shack-shuka)

PREP + COOK: 30 MINUTES • **SERVES:** 8 • **SERVING SIZE:** 1 CUP

2 tablespoons extra-virgin olive oil

1 large yellow onion, halved and thinly sliced

1 medium zucchini, halved and thinly sliced

3 garlic cloves, thinly sliced

1 teaspoon ground cumin

1 teaspoon paprika

1/8–1/4 teaspoon cayenne, to taste

28 ounces whole plum tomatoes with their juices, coarsely chopped

1/2 teaspoon salt

1/4 teaspoon black pepper

2 ounces feta cheese, crumbled (about 1 cup)

8 eggs

1/4 cup fresh cilantro or basil, chopped, for serving

DO AHEAD OR DELEGATE: Halve and slice the onion and zucchini, slice the garlic, combine the dry spices, chop the tomatoes, or fully prepare the recipe without the eggs and refrigerate or freeze it.

1. Preheat oven to 375°F.

2. Heat the oil in a large heavy skillet, preferably cast iron, over medium heat. Add the onions and zucchini, and sauté for 8–10 minutes until tender. Add the garlic and cook for 1 minute, then add the cumin, paprika, and cayenne, and cook for 1 more minute.

3. Add the tomatoes, salt, and pepper and simmer until the tomatoes have thickened, about 10 minutes. Stir in the cheese.

4. Gently crack the eggs into the skillet, spreading them evenly over the tomatoes. Season with a pinch of coarse salt, if desired. Transfer the skillet to the oven and bake until eggs are just set, 7–8 minutes (they will continue to cook for a couple of minutes after you remove them from the oven). Sprinkle with the fresh herbs and serve immediately.

FLAVOR BOOSTER
Use smoked paprika instead of regular paprika.
Serve with hot pepper sauce such as Tabasco, sriracha, or harissa, if you have it.

Indian Naan, Middle Eastern Flatbread, or Pita Bread

SERVES: 4 • **SERVING SIZE:** 3 1/4 INCH SQUARE

4 pieces Indian naan, Middle Eastern flatbread, or pita

1. Warm the bread either in the microwave for about 1 minute or wrapped in foil in the oven at 300°F for 8–10 minutes.

TIP

This is a recipe that can be doubled or tripled and frozen in portions. Just remove it from the freezer the night or morning before you plan to eat it to let it thaw. Then heat it on the stove or in the microwave and poach the eggs. Voilà—quick, easy, and healthful.

NUTRITIONAL INFORMATION | NORTH AFRICAN SHAKSHUKA:

EXCHANGES / CHOICES:
2 Nonstarchy Vegetable; 1 Protein, medium fat; 1 Fat

Calories: 160; Calories from Fat: 90; Total Fat: 10 g;
Saturated Fat: 3.2 g; Trans Fat: 0.1 g; Cholesterol: 190 mg;
Sodium: 315 mg; Potassium: 490 mg; Total Carbohydrate: 10 g;
Dietary Fiber: 3 g; Sugar: 5 g; Protein: 9 g; Phosphorus: 175 mg

NUTRITIONAL INFORMATION | INDIAN NAAN:

EXCHANGES / CHOICES:
1 Starch

Calories: 90; Calories from Fat: 20; Total Fat: 2.5 g;
Saturated Fat: 0.3 g; Trans Fat: 0 g; Cholesterol: 10 mg;
Sodium: 110 mg; Potassium: 45 mg; Total Carbohydrate: 15 g;
Dietary Fiber: 1 g; Sugar: 1 g; Protein: 3 g; Phosphorus: 35 mg

SPRING (WEEK 6)

Caesar Salad with Chicken (1)
SIDE DISH: Sourdough Bread (1a)

Tender Fish and Tomato Curry (2)
SIDE DISH: Punjabi-Style Potatoes (2a)

Savory Korean Vegetable Pancakes (3)
SIDE DISH: Asian Cucumber Salad (3a)

Bowties with Sage and Sausage (4)
SIDE DISH: Spinach Salad with Diced Oranges and Sliced Red Onion (4a)

Zucchini, White Bean, and Tomato Gratin (5)
SIDE DISH: Bulgur Wheat (5a)

SHOPPING LIST

- -

🥕 PRODUCE
1 **carrot** (3)
11 **scallions** (3)
3 **yellow onions** (2)(4)(5)
1 **small yellow onion** (2a)
1/2 **red onion** (4a)
1 **jalapeño pepper** (2a)
2 stalks **celery** (2)
1 1/3 **tomatoes** (2)(2a)
1 head **romaine lettuce** (1)
24 ounces **baby spinach** (4a)
3 cloves **garlic** (5)
2 teaspoons **fresh ginger** (2a)
10 fresh **sage leaves** (4)
4 **zucchini** (3)(5)
2 **cucumbers** (3a)
1 pound **red potatoes** (2a)
1/2 **lemon** (1)
2 **oranges** (4a)

🍖 MEAT AND FISH
1–1 1/2 pounds **boneless, skinless chicken breasts or meatless chicken strips or patties** (1)

1 pound **catfish or other thick white fish fillet** (2)

12 ounces **sweet Italian chicken sausage** (use wheat/gluten-free if needed) (4)

🫙 SHELVED ITEMS

1 loaf **sourdough bread** (1)(1a)

1 1/2 cups **bulgur wheat or use quick-cooking brown rice** (5a)

3 cups **low-sodium chicken or vegetable broth** (5a)

1 tablespoon + 2 teaspoons **rice vinegar** (3)(3a)

1/2 cup **red wine** (4)

16 ounces **whole-wheat bowtie pasta (farfalle)** (use wheat/gluten-free if needed) (4)

15 ounces **canned cannellini beans** (also called white kidney beans) (5)

43 ounces **diced tomatoes** (4)(5)

2 cups **low-sodium vegetable juice** such as V8 (2)

1/2 teaspoon **anchovy paste** (1)

🧂 SPICES

1 1/2 teaspoons **salt** (1)(2)(2a)(3)(4)(5)

1/4 teaspoon **kosher salt** (1)

1/2 teaspoon **dried basil** (5)

1/2 teaspoon **dried thyme** (5)

3/8 teaspoon **black pepper** (2)(4)

1 teaspoon **garam masala** (an Indian spice blend) (2a)

1 2/3 teaspoons **curry powder** (2)(2a)

1/8 teaspoon **garlic powder** (1)

1 tablespoon **toasted sesame seeds** (3a)

🫙 STAPLES

6–7 tablespoons + 8 teaspoons **extra-virgin olive oil** (1)(2)(4)(5)

2 teaspoons + 1/4 cup **canola or vegetable oil** (2a)(3)

2 tablespoons **reduced-fat mayonnaise** (1)

1/4 cup **vinaigrette dressing** (4a)

4 1/4 tablespoons **reduced-sodium soy sauce** (use wheat/gluten-free if needed) (3)(3a)

1 teaspoon **Worcestershire sauce** (1)

2 teaspoons **sugar** (3)(3a)

2 **eggs** (3)

1 1/2 teaspoons **minced garlic** (1)(2a)

2 cups **all-purpose flour** (use wheat/gluten-free if needed) (3)

1/4 cup **seasoned panko or breadcrumbs** (5)

❄️ REFRIGERATED/FROZEN

1/2 cup **shredded Parmesan cheese** (1)

1 cup **grated Parmesan cheese** (4)(5)

Get free, printable versions of the shopping lists from this book at **TheScramble.com/diabetes**.

*optional ingredients

SPRING WEEK 6 • **63**

This is one of my kids' favorite meals. Adapt the recipe to suit your family's palate, using meatless chicken strips or patties, shrimp, or chickpeas instead of the chicken. Serve with Sourdough Bread.

Caesar Salad with Chicken

PREP + COOK: 30 MINUTES • **SERVES:** 6 • **SERVING SIZE:** 2 CUPS SALAD + 1 TABLESPOON DRESSING

1 pound boneless, skinless chicken breasts or meatless chicken strips or patties

4 tablespoons extra-virgin olive oil, divided use

1/4 teaspoon salt

1/8 teaspoon garlic powder

CROUTONS

1 loaf sourdough bread (use 2 slices for the croutons and serve the rest as the side dish)

1/4 teaspoon kosher salt

CAESAR DRESSING

2 tablespoons reduced-fat mayonnaise

1/2 teaspoon minced garlic (about 1 clove)

1/2 lemon, juice only (about 2 tablespoons)

1 teaspoon Worcestershire sauce

1/2 teaspoon anchovy paste, or use mashed capers or seasoned soybean paste

1 head romaine lettuce, chopped or ripped into bite-sized pieces (8–10 cups)

1/2 cup shredded Parmesan cheese

DO AHEAD OR DELEGATE: Cut the chicken into strips and refrigerate, cook and refrigerate the chicken, make the croutons, and make and refrigerate the dressing.

1. Preheat the oven or toaster oven to 400°F.

2. Cut each chicken breast crosswise into thin strips. Place the chicken in a flat dish, drizzle with 1 tablespoon oil, salt, and garlic powder, and flip the chicken several times to coat. Heat a large nonstick skillet over medium heat. Sauté the chicken, turning occasionally, until it is cooked through, about 5–7 minutes. (Set some cooked chicken aside for non-salad eaters, if necessary.)

3. **To make the croutons**, cut two slices of the bread into 1/2-inch cubes. In a medium bowl, toss the bread cubes with 1 tablespoon oil and the kosher salt. Place them on a baking sheet in a single layer and bake for 3–5 minutes, until they are slightly crisp and lightly browned. Watch them carefully so they don't burn. Set them aside. (After the croutons are prepared, reduce the temperature of the oven to 300°F to warm the remainder of the bread, if desired.)

4. **To make the dressing**, thoroughly whisk together the mayonnaise, 2 tablespoons oil, garlic, lemon juice, Worcestershire sauce, and anchovy paste.

5. Just before serving, toss the lettuce, cheese, chicken, croutons, and dressing (you may not need to use all the dressing) in a large salad bowl, and serve with the warmed bread, if desired.

NUTRITIONAL INFORMATION | CAESAR SALAD WITH CHICKEN (ANALYSIS FOR SALAD ONLY):

EXCHANGES / CHOICES:
1/2 Carbohydrate; 3 Protein, lean

Calories: 180; Calories from Fat: 70; Total Fat: 8 g;
Saturated Fat: 1.8 g; Trans Fat: 0 g; Cholesterol: 45 mg;
Sodium: 325 mg; Potassium: 305 mg; Total Carbohydrate: 8 g;
Dietary Fiber: 2 g; Sugar: 1 g; Protein: 19 g; Phosphorus: 170 mg

(ANALYSIS FOR CAESAR DRESSING ONLY):

EXCHANGES / CHOICES:
1 1/2 Fat

Calories: 75; Calories from Fat: 70; Total Fat: 8 g;
Saturated Fat: 1.2 g; Trans Fat: 0 g; Cholesterol: 0 mg;
Sodium: 60 mg; Potassium: 15 mg; Total Carbohydrate: 1 g;
Dietary Fiber: 0 g; Sugar: 0 g; Protein: 0 g; Phosphorus: 0 mg

NUTRITIONAL INFORMATION | SOURDOUGH BREAD:

EXCHANGES / CHOICES:
1 Starch

Calories: 80; Calories from Fat: 5; Total Fat: 0.5 g;
Saturated Fat: 0.1 g; Trans Fat: 0 g; Cholesterol: 0 mg;
Sodium: 145 mg; Potassium: 35 mg; Total Carbohydrate: 16 g;
Dietary Fiber: 1 g; Sugar: 1 g; Protein: 3 g; Phosphorus: 30 mg

SIDE DISH

Sourdough Bread

SERVES: 4 • **SERVING SIZE:** 1 SLICE

Remaining sourdough bread from main dish

1. Slice and serve with the salad.

FLAVOR BOOSTER
Add plenty of freshly ground black pepper and use aged Parmesan cheese.

TIP
Don't throw away those heels of bread that are languishing in your fridge or your bread box! Instead, throw them in a food processor to create breadcrumbs. You can then freeze them and use as needed to bread chicken or fish.

This was a bit of a desperation dinner, as we had just returned from a trip, so the refrigerator was nearly bare, though I had managed to stop at the fish market. The fish and vegetables turned out tender and delicious and it was definitely a recipe worth sharing. Serve with Punjabi-Style Potatoes.

Tender Fish and Tomato Curry

PREP + COOK: 30 MINUTES • **SERVES:** 4 • **SERVING SIZE:** 4 OUNCES FISH + 3/4 CUP SAUCE

1 tablespoon extra-virgin olive oil

1 yellow onion, halved top to bottom and thinly sliced

2 stalks celery, thinly sliced

1 teaspoon curry powder

2 cups low-sodium vegetable juice

1 tomato, diced

1 pound catfish or other thick white fish fillet, cut into 1-inch chunks

1/4 teaspoon salt, or to taste

1/4 teaspoon black pepper, or to taste

DO AHEAD OR DELEGATE: Slice the onion and the celery, dice the tomato, and cut the fish into chunks and refrigerate.

1. (Start the potatoes first, if you are serving them.) In a Dutch oven or deep skillet, heat the oil over medium to medium-high heat. Add the onions and celery and sauté, stirring often, until tender, about 7 minutes.

2. Stir in the curry powder for about 30 seconds, and then add the vegetable juice and the tomatoes. When it starts to bubble gently, stir in the fish and keep it at a simmer for about 7 minutes until the fish is cooked through. Season with salt and pepper.

SLOW COOKER DIRECTIONS: Add all ingredients to the slow cooker and cook on low for 4–5 hours, or on high for 2–2 1/2 hours. (Slow cooker cooking times may vary—get to know your slow cooker and, if necessary, adjust cooking times accordingly.)

FLAVOR BOOSTER

Double the curry powder and use spicy V8, or serve the stew with hot pepper sauce, such as Tabasco. Serve with fresh lemon or lime wedges.

TIP

If you are watching your waistline, eat foods that require a little effort and can't be mindlessly popped into your mouth. Some great examples are pistachio nuts or peanuts in the shell, and fruits like oranges and grapefruits that require peeling.

Punjabi-Style Potatoes

SERVES: 4 • **SERVING SIZE:** 1 CUP

4 teaspoons canola or vegetable oil

1/2 small yellow onion, finely diced

2 teaspoons fresh ginger

1 teaspoon minced garlic

1 small jalapeño pepper, seeded and finely diced

2/3 teaspoon curry powder

2/3 teaspoon garam masala (an Indian spice blend)

1/3 tomato, chopped

1 pound red potatoes, chopped

1/3 teaspoon salt

2/3 cup warm water

1. Heat a large heavy skillet over medium heat, and add the oil. When it is hot, add the onions, and when they start to brown, add the ginger, garlic, jalapeño, curry powder, and garam masala. Cook for 2 more minutes, then stir in the tomatoes.

2. Add the potatoes and salt and stir to coat them. Add the water, bring to a boil, cover, and reduce the heat to simmer for 15 minutes.

3. Uncover and simmer for 10 more minutes or until most of the liquid is absorbed and the potatoes are very tender. Serve immediately.

NUTRITIONAL INFORMATION | TENDER FISH AND TOMATO CURRY:

EXCHANGES / CHOICES:
2 Nonstarchy Vegetable; 2 Protein, lean; 1 1/2 Fat

Calories: 230; Calories from Fat: 100; Total Fat: 11 g;
Saturated Fat: 2.1 g; Trans Fat: 0.1 g; Cholesterol: 65 mg;
Sodium: 360 mg; Potassium: 825 mg; Total Carbohydrate: 11 g;
Dietary Fiber: 3 g; Sugar: 7 g; Protein: 21 g; Phosphorus: 300 mg

NUTRITIONAL INFORMATION | PUNJABI-STYLE POTATOES:

EXCHANGES / CHOICES:
1 1/2 Starch; 1 Nonstarchy Vegetable; 1/2 Fat

Calories: 155; Calories from Fat: 45; Total Fat: 5 g;
Saturated Fat: 0.4 g; Trans Fat: 0 g; Cholesterol: 0 mg;
Sodium: 200 mg; Potassium: 540 mg; Total Carbohydrate: 26 g;
Dietary Fiber: 3 g; Sugar: 3 g; Protein: 3 g; Phosphorus: 70 mg

When my family went to a Korean restaurant in Rockville, Maryland, I fell in love with these savory vegetable pancakes. I recreated them at home and hope you find them as delightful as we did. Serve with Asian Cucumber Salad.

Savory Korean Vegetable Pancakes

PREP: 15 MINUTES • **COOK:** 30 MINUTES • **SERVES:** 6 • **SERVING SIZE:** 1 PANCAKE

2 cups all-purpose flour

1/4 teaspoon salt

2 eggs

2 cups water

1/4 cup canola or vegetable oil, divided use

11 scallions, thinly sliced (dark and light green parts), divided use

1 carrot, grated

1 zucchini, grated

3 1/4 tablespoons reduced-sodium soy sauce (use wheat/gluten-free if needed)

1 teaspoon sugar

1 tablespoon rice vinegar

DO AHEAD OR DELEGATE: Whisk together the eggs, water, and oil and refrigerate, slice the scallions, grate the carrot and the zucchini, and make the sauce.

1. Preheat the oven to 300°F.

2. Combine the flour and salt in a large mixing bowl. In a medium bowl, whisk together the eggs, water, and 1 tablespoon of the oil. Whisk the liquid mixture into the flour mixture until smooth. Stir in 10 of the scallions (reserve 1 for the dipping sauce), the carrots, and the zucchini.

3. In a small serving bowl, combine the soy sauce, sugar, vinegar and 1 scallion. Set aside.

4. In a large nonstick skillet, heat 1 tablespoon oil over medium to medium-high heat. (For faster preparation, use 2 skillets so you can cook 2 pancakes at once.) When it is very hot, ladle about 1/6 of the batter (or about 1 1/4 cups) into the pan, spreading it quickly with the bottom of the ladle to get it as smooth and thin as possible. Cook until the bottom is browned, about 3–4 minutes, then flip and cook on the other side. (Meanwhile, prepare the salad, if you are serving it.) Remove the pancake and transfer it to a baking sheet in the oven to keep warm. Continue with remaining batter, adding 1 teaspoon or so of oil to the pan as needed.

5. Cut each pancake into 6 wedges and serve with the dipping sauce.

Asian Cucumber Salad

SERVES: 6 • **SERVING SIZE:** 2/3 CUP

1 tablespoon reduced-sodium soy sauce (use wheat/gluten-free if needed)

2 teaspoons rice vinegar

1 teaspoon sugar

2 cucumbers, peeled, seeded, and diced

1 tablespoon toasted sesame seeds

1. In a medium bowl whisk together the soy sauce, vinegar, and sugar. Add the cucumbers and toss thoroughly. Top with the sesame seeds. Serve immediately or refrigerate for up to 3 days.

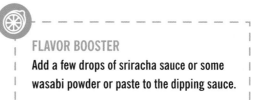

FLAVOR BOOSTER

Add a few drops of sriracha sauce or some wasabi powder or paste to the dipping sauce.

TIP

If you are grating just 1 or 2 carrots, a hand or standing grater works well. While holding the carrot firmly, rub the carrot down the side of the grater. Just watch your fingers so you don't cut them when the carrot gets small. If you have a large quantity of carrots that need to be grated, you may want to pull out your food processor, if you have one, as this will significantly speed up the task.

NUTRITIONAL INFORMATION | SAVORY KOREAN VEGETABLE PANCAKES:

EXCHANGES / CHOICES:
2 Starch; 1 Nonstarchy Vegetable; 1 Protein, lean; 1 1/2 Fat

Calories: 285; Calories from Fat: 100; Total Fat: 11 g;
Saturated Fat: 1.3 g; Trans Fat: 0 g; Cholesterol: 60 mg;
Sodium: 435 mg; Potassium: 275 mg; Total Carbohydrate: 38 g;
Dietary Fiber: 3 g; Sugar: 3 g; Protein: 8 g; Phosphorus: 115 mg

NUTRITIONAL INFORMATION | ASIAN CUCUMBER SALAD:

EXCHANGES / CHOICES:
Free food

Calories: 20; Calories from Fat: 10; Total Fat: 1 g;
Saturated Fat: 0.1 g; Trans Fat: 0 g; Cholesterol: 0 mg;
Sodium: 95 mg; Potassium: 85 mg; Total Carbohydrate: 3 g;
Dietary Fiber: 1 g; Sugar: 2 g; Protein: 1 g; Phosphorus: 25 mg

Six O'Clock Scramble member Alison Kavanaugh sent me one of her family's favorite recipes that she also likes to deliver to friends when they have a new baby. My family loved it, too, especially topped with freshly grated Parmesan cheese. Serve with Spinach Salad with Diced Oranges and Sliced Red Onion.

Bowties with Sage and Sausage

PREP + COOK: 30 MINUTES • **SERVES:** 9 • **SERVING SIZE:** 1 3/4 CUPS

16 ounces whole-wheat bowtie or farfalle pasta

1 tablespoon extra-virgin olive oil

1 yellow onion, chopped

10 fresh sage leaves, chopped

12 ounces sweet Italian chicken sausage, or use meatless sausage, thinly sliced

1/2 cup red wine (don't use cooking wine), or use 1/4 cup chicken broth and 1 tablespoon red wine vinegar

28 ounces diced tomatoes, or use 2 pounds fresh diced tomatoes, with their liquid

1/8 teaspoon salt, or to taste

1/8 teaspoon black pepper, or to taste

1/2 cup grated Parmesan cheese, or to taste

DO AHEAD OR DELEGATE: Cook the pasta and store tossed with a little oil to prevent sticking, chop the onion and the sage, slice and refrigerate the sausage, or fully prepare and refrigerate the dish.

1. Cook the pasta according to the package directions and drain.

2. Meanwhile, heat the oil in a large skillet over medium heat. Add the onions, sage, and sausage and cook until the onions are softened and the sage and sausage are browned, 8–10 minutes. Add the wine and stir, loosening up any browned bits from the bottom of the pan.

3. Add the tomatoes and simmer for 15–20 minutes, or longer if time allows, stirring occasionally. (Meanwhile, prepare the salad, if you are serving it.) Season with salt and pepper, to taste, and serve immediately, topped with the cheese, or refrigerate for up to 2 days.

SLOW COOKER DIRECTIONS: Combine all ingredients, except the pasta and cheese in the slow cooker, and cook on low for 8–10 hours or on high for 4–5 hours. Serve over cooked pasta and topped with the cheese. (Slow cooker cooking times may vary—get to know your slow cooker and, if necessary, adjust cooking times accordingly.)

Spinach Salad with Diced Oranges and Sliced Red Onion

SERVES: 9 • **SERVING SIZE:** 2 CUPS

24 ounces baby spinach

2 medium oranges, peeled and diced (reserve juice to add to salad dressing)

1/2 red onion, thinly sliced

9 tablespoons Orange Balsamic Vinaigrette Dressing (page 16)

1. In a large salad bowl, toss the spinach with the oranges, onion, and vinaigrette dressing to taste.

FLAVOR BOOSTER
Add a pinch of red pepper flakes to the skillet with the sausage mixture.

NUTRITIONAL INFORMATION | BOWTIES WITH SAGE AND SAUSAGE:

EXCHANGES / CHOICES:
2 1/2 Starch; 1 Nonstarchy Vegetable; 1 Protein, lean; 1/2 Fat

Calories: 290; Calories from Fat: 65; Total Fat: 7 g;
Saturated Fat: 1.9 g; Trans Fat: 0 g; Cholesterol: 30 mg;
Sodium: 440 mg; Potassium: 360 mg; Total Carbohydrate: 44 g;
Dietary Fiber: 8 g; Sugar: 4 g; Protein: 17 g; Phosphorus: 250 mg

NUTRITIONAL INFORMATION | SPINACH SALAD WITH DICED ORANGES AND SLICED RED ONION:

EXCHANGES / CHOICES:
1/2 Carbohydrate; 1 Fat

Calories: 95; Calories from Fat: 55; Total Fat: 6 g;
Saturated Fat: 0.9 g; Trans Fat: 0 g; Cholesterol: 0 mg;
Sodium: 100 mg; Potassium: 510 mg; Total Carbohydrate: 9 g;
Dietary Fiber: 3 g; Sugar: 5 g; Protein: 3 g; Phosphorus: 45 mg

This colorful and versatile recipe comes from Dara Baylinson of Potomac, Maryland, who says it's one of the few vegetarian recipes that she makes that her children love. It can also be served as a hearty side dish for company. Serve with Bulgur Wheat.

Zucchini, White Bean, and Tomato Gratin

PREP: 25 MINUTES • **COOK:** 15 MINUTES • **SERVES:** 6 • **SERVING SIZE:** 1 3/4 CUPS

8 teaspoons extra-virgin olive oil, divided use

1 yellow onion, chopped

3 cloves garlic, chopped

1/2 teaspoon dried thyme, or 1 1/2 teaspoons fresh thyme

1/2 teaspoon dried basil, or 4 leaves fresh basil, chopped

3 zucchini, quartered lengthwise and chopped (6–7 cups total)

15 ounces diced tomatoes, with their liquid

15 ounces canned cannellini beans (also called white kidney beans), drained and rinsed

1/4 teaspoon salt, or to taste

1/2 cup grated Parmesan cheese

1/4 cup seasoned panko or breadcrumbs

DO AHEAD OR DELEGATE: Chop the onion and the zucchini, peel and chop the garlic, make the breadcrumb mixture, or fully assemble and refrigerate the casserole

1. Preheat the oven to 400°F and spray a 2-quart baking dish with nonstick cooking spray.

2. In a large heavy skillet, heat 2 tablespoons oil over medium to medium-high heat and sauté the onions, garlic, thyme, and basil for 1 minute until the garlic is fragrant. Add the zucchini and sauté with the onions for about 10 minutes until both are tender and the onions are starting to brown. Add the tomatoes, beans, and salt to the skillet, bring the mixture to a low boil, and simmer, covered, for 5 minutes, stirring occasionally.

3. Meanwhile, in a large measuring cup or medium bowl, combine the cheese, panko or breadcrumbs, and 2 teaspoons oil.

4. Smooth the zucchini mixture into the casserole dish. (At this point you can refrigerate the casserole and the cheese mixtures separately for up to 24 hours, if desired.)

5. When ready to cook, top the casserole evenly with the cheese mixture. Transfer to the oven and bake for 10–15 minutes until the topping is browned. (Meanwhile, make bulgur wheat, if you are serving it.) If necessary, put the casserole under the broiler for a minute to finish browning the topping. Serve immediately.

FLAVOR BOOSTER

Serve with black pepper and extra Parmesan cheese.

SLOW COOKER DIRECTIONS: Prepare the topping as directed. Combine everything except the topping in the slow cooker, then spread the topping as directed. Cook on low for 6–8 hours, or on high for 3–4 hours. (Slow cooker cooking times may vary—get to know your slow cooker and, if necessary, adjust cooking times accordingly.)

Bulgur Wheat

SERVES: 6 • **SERVING SIZE:** 3/4 CUP

1 1/2 cups bulgur wheat

3 cups low-sodium chicken or vegetable broth, or use water or combination of water and broth

1. In a medium saucepan, combine the bulgur wheat and the broth or combination of broth and water. Bring to a boil, cover, and simmer for 15 minutes until tender.

TIP

Tomatoes are a great source of vitamin C and lycopene, both of which are good for your skin. No need to worry if you're eating the canned variety as opposed to fresh—canned tomatoes are cooked, and our bodies actually have an easier time absorbing lycopene from cooked tomatoes.

NUTRITIONAL INFORMATION | ZUCCHINI, WHITE BEAN, AND TOMATO GRATIN:

EXCHANGES / CHOICES:
1 Starch; 1 Nonstarchy Vegetable; 1 Protein, lean; 1 Fat

Calories: 180; Calories from Fat: 70; Total Fat: 8 g;
Saturated Fat: 1.9 g; Trans Fat: 0 g; Cholesterol: 5 mg;
Sodium: 350 mg; Potassium: 670 mg; Total Carbohydrate: 21 g;
Dietary Fiber: 5 g; Sugar: 5 g; Protein: 8 g; Phosphorus: 170 mg

NUTRITIONAL INFORMATION | BULGUR WHEAT:

EXCHANGES / CHOICES:
2 Starch

Calories: 145; Calories from Fat: 5; Total Fat: 0.5 g;
Saturated Fat: 0.2 g; Trans Fat: 0 g; Cholesterol: 0 mg;
Sodium: 50 mg; Potassium: 260 mg; Total Carbohydrate: 31 g;
Dietary Fiber: 7 g; Sugar: 0 g; Protein: 6 g; Phosphorus: 135 mg

SPRING

WEEK 7

Grilled Chicken Breasts with Cajun Rub (1)
SIDE DISH: Light Potato Salad (1a); Strawberries (1b)

Baked Salmon with Zucchini, Red Onions, and Dill (2)
SIDE DISH: Baked Asparagus (2a); Whole-Grain Bread (2b)

California Taco Salad (3)
SIDE DISH: Corn or Whole-Wheat Tortillas (3a)

Tortellini Soup with Spinach and Tomatoes (4)
SIDE DISH: Green Salad with Apples, Gorgonzola Cheese, and Pecans (4a)

Savory Sesame Tofu (5)
SIDE DISH: Steamed Rice and Peas (5a)

SHOPPING LIST

PRODUCE

1/4 **white onion** (1a)

1/4 **red onion** (2)

1 small head **iceberg or romaine lettuce** (3)

1 head **lettuce, any variety** (4a)

3 cups **baby spinach** (4)

2 tablespoons **fresh dill** (2)

1/2–1 cup **fresh flat-leaf parsley or cilantro** (1a)

1 **zucchini** (2)

1 1/2 pounds **asparagus** (2a)

1 1/2–2 pounds **Yukon Gold or white potatoes** (1a)

1 **avocado** (3)

1 1/4 **lemons** (2)(2a)

1 1/2 **limes** (1a)(3)

1 pound **strawberries** (1b)

1 **red apple**, such as Gala or Fuji (4a)

1 **mango** (3)

MEAT AND FISH

2 pounds **boneless, skinless chicken breasts** (1)

1/2 pound **cooked and shredded chicken breast** (3)*

1 pound **salmon fillet**, preferably wild Alaskan salmon (2)

🗄 SHELVED ITEMS

1 cup **quick-cooking brown rice or regular white rice** (5a)

1 cup **tortilla chips or corn kernels** (3)

6 **corn or whole-wheat tortillas** (3a)

15 ounces **no-salt-added diced tomatoes** (4)

32 ounces **low-sodium chicken or vegetable broth** (4)

1 cup **salsa** (3)*

1 teaspoon **chili-garlic sauce or sriracha** (5)*

1 tablespoon **rice vinegar** (5)

1/2 cup **barbecue sauce** (1)*

15 ounces **canned black or red beans** (3)

1/2 cup **sliced black olives** (3)

2 tablespoons **pecans** (4a)

4 slices **whole-grain bread** (2b)

🧂 SPICES

3/4 teaspooon **salt** (1a)(2)(5a)

1/4 teaspoon **kosher salt** (2a)

3/4 teaspoon **garlic salt** (1)

1/4–1/2 teaspoon **salt-free lemon pepper seasoning** (2a)*

1 1/2 teaspoons **dried oregano** (1)(4)

1/2 teaspoon **dried basil** (4)

1 teaspoon **dried thyme** (1)

1/4–1/2 teaspoon **cayenne pepper** (1)

1/2 teaspoon **black pepper** (2)(2a)(4)

1/4 teaspoon **ground ginger** (5)

1 teaspoon **garlic powder** (1)

2 tablespoons **paprika** (1)

1 teaspoon **toasted sesame seeds** (5)

🫙 STAPLES

5 tablespoons **extra-virgin olive oil** (1a)(2)(2a)(4)

1 tablespoon **sesame oil** (5)

2 tablespoons **reduced-fat mayonnaise** (1a)

3/4 cup **vinaigrette dressing** (3)(4a)

2 tablespoons + 2 teaspoons **reduced-sodium soy sauce** (use wheat/gluten-free if needed) (5)(5a)

1 tablespoon **pure maple syrup** (5)

2 1/2 teaspoons **minced garlic** (1a)(4)(5)

🍦 REFRIGERATED/FROZEN

2 tablespoons **crumbled Gorgonzola or blue cheese** (4a)

1/2 cup **shredded reduced-fat Monterey Jack cheese** (3)

1/4 cup **grated Parmesan cheese** (4)

1 cup **nonfat sour cream** (3)*

16 ounces **extra-firm tofu packed in water** (5)

9 ounces **whole-wheat or regular cheese tortellini** (4)

2/3 cup **frozen peas** (5a)

Get free, printable versions of the shopping lists from this book at **TheScramble.com/diabetes**.

*optional ingredients

I love the color and the burst of flavor that this deep red seasoning gives to grilled chicken (this seasoning blend would also be delicious on fish, pork, or tofu). You may want to make extra seasoning blend to save for future recipes, or even to give as a gift. Serve with Light Potato Salad and Strawberries.

Grilled Chicken Breasts with Cajun Rub

MARINATE: 30 MINUTES • **PREP + COOK:** 20 MINUTES • **SERVES:** 6 • **SERVING SIZE:** 4 1/3 OUNCES EACH

2 tablespoons paprika

3/4 teaspoon garlic salt, or use regular salt

1 teaspoon garlic powder

1/4–1/2 teaspoon cayenne pepper, to taste

1 teaspoon dried thyme

1 teaspoon dried oregano

2 pounds boneless, skinless chicken breasts, or use pork tenderloin or firm fish fillets

1/2 cup barbecue sauce, for serving (optional)

DO AHEAD OR DELEGATE: Make the spice blend, rub the chicken with the spices and refrigerate, or fully prepare and refrigerate the chicken.

1. In a small bowl, combine all of the spices. Rub the mixture over the surfaces of the chicken. If time allows, cover the chicken and refrigerate for at least 30 minutes and up to 24 hours to increase the flavor.

2. (Start the potato salad now, if you are serving it.) Preheat the grill to medium-high heat (about 400°F on a gas grill). (Alternatively you can cook the chicken in a grill pan or a cast iron skillet with 1 tablespoon olive or vegetable oil in the pan.) Rub the grates of your grill with a paper towel dipped in vegetable oil (use tongs, rather than your fingers) before grilling the meat to keep it from sticking.

3. Cook the chicken without moving it for about 5 minutes per side, until it has nice grill marks on the outside and is cooked through. Slice the chicken into thick slices and serve immediately, with the barbecue sauce, if desired, or refrigerate for up to 3 days.

FLAVOR BOOSTER
Use the optional barbeque sauce or some hot sauce, double the garlic powder and/or cayenne pepper in the spice mixture.

TIP
Give your metabolism a boost—eating lean protein like chicken can use seven times more energy to digest than something high in carbohydrates or fats.

Light Potato Salad

SERVES: 6 • **SERVING SIZE:** 1/2 CUP

1 1/2–2 pounds Yukon Gold or white potatoes, peeled and chopped into 1-inch pieces

2 tablespoons extra-virgin olive oil

2 tablespoons reduced-fat mayonnaise

1/2 teaspoon minced garlic (about 1 clove)

1/4 teaspoon salt

1 lime, juice only (about 2 tablespoons)

1/4 white onion, finely diced (about 1 cup)

1/2–1 cup fresh parsley or cilantro, finely chopped, to taste

1. Boil the potatoes in lightly salted water for 15 minutes, or until fork tender. In a large serving bowl, whisk together the oil, mayonnaise, garlic, salt, and lime juice. Add the cooked potatoes, the onions, and the parsley or cilantro. Toss thoroughly and chill until ready to serve.

Strawberries

SERVES: 6 • **SERVING SIZE:** 2/3 CUP SLICED BERRIES

1 1/2 pounds strawberries

1. Slice berries and serve.

NUTRITIONAL INFORMATION | GRILLED CHICKEN BREASTS WITH CAJUN RUB:

EXCHANGES / CHOICES:
4 Protein, lean

Calories: 180; Calories from Fat: 35; Total Fat: 4 g;
Saturated Fat: 1.1 g; Trans Fat: 0 g; Cholesterol: 90 mg;
Sodium: 240 mg; Potassium: 325 mg; Total Carbohydrate: 2 g;
Dietary Fiber: 1 g; Sugar: 0 g; Protein: 32 g; Phosphorus: 245 mg

NUTRITIONAL INFORMATION | LIGHT POTATO SALAD:

EXCHANGES / CHOICES:
1 1/2 Starch; 1 Fat

Calories: 145; Calories from Fat: 55; Total Fat: 6 g;
Saturated Fat: 0.8 g; Trans Fat: 0 g; Cholesterol: 0 mg;
Sodium: 180 mg; Potassium: 370 mg; Total Carbohydrate: 22 g;
Dietary Fiber: 2 g; Sugar: 3 g; Protein: 2 g; Phosphorus: 50 mg

NUTRITIONAL INFORMATION | STRAWBERRIES:

EXCHANGES / CHOICES:
1/2 Fruit

Calories: 35; Calories from Fat: 0; Total Fat: 0 g;
Saturated Fat: 0 g; Trans Fat: 0 g; Cholesterol: 0 mg;
Sodium: 0 mg; Potassium: 165 mg; Total Carbohydrate: 8 g;
Dietary Fiber: 2 g; Sugar: 5 g; Protein: 1 g; Phosphorus: 25 mg

I love when we can make a dish that has our vegetables and protein in the same pan so they can all cook together. The salmon is so moist when cooked this way, but the zucchini stays tender-crisp. If you like zucchini more on the tender side then slice it extra thin (you might even like to use extra zucchini and onions if your family members are big fans). Serve with Whole-Grain Bread and Baked Asparagus.

Baked Salmon with Zucchini, Red Onions, and Dill

PREP + COOK: 30 MINUTES • **SERVES:** 4 • **SERVING SIZE:** 4 OUNCES + 2 TABLESPOONS SAUCE

1 pound salmon fillet, preferably wild
   Alaskan salmon

1 zucchini, halved lengthwise and sliced

1/4 red onion, thinly sliced, or more to taste

2 tablespoons fresh dill, chopped, or use
   1 teaspoon dried

1 tablespoon extra-virgin olive oil

1 lemon

1/4 teaspoon salt

1/8 teaspoon black pepper

DO AHEAD OR DELEGATE: Slice the zucchini and the onion, chop the dill if using fresh, or fully assemble and refrigerate the dish for up to 12 hours before baking.

1. Preheat the oven to 400°F.

2. Spray a 9 × 13-inch glass or ceramic baking dish with nonstick cooking spray and put the salmon in the center. Spread the vegetables around the fish, and top everything with the dill, oil, and juice of half the lemon. Thinly slice the other half lemon and spread it around the dish. Season the fish and vegetables with the salt and pepper.

3. Bake, uncovered, for 20 minutes. (Meanwhile, prepare the asparagus and warm the bread, if you are serving them.) Remove the salmon from the oven and serve immediately.

SLOW COOKER DIRECTIONS: Combine all ingredients except the salmon in the slow cooker and cook on low for 6–7 hours or on high for 3 hours. Place the salmon on top of the vegetables and top with additional salt, pepper, dill, and lemon juice if desired. Cook for 1 more hour on high or 2 more hours on low, until the salmon flakes easily with a fork (length of cooking will also depend on thickness of fish). (Slow cooker cooking times may vary—get to know your slow cooker and, if necessary, adjust cooking times accordingly.)

FLAVOR BOOSTER
Add 1–2 cloves of sliced garlic to the vegetables before baking.

NUTRITIONAL INFORMATION | BAKED SALMON WITH ZUCCHINI,
RED ONIONS, AND DILL:

EXCHANGES / CHOICES:
1 Nonstarchy Vegetable; 3 Protein, lean; 1 Fat

Calories: 210; Calories from Fat: 100; Total Fat: 11 g;
Saturated Fat: 2.3 g; Trans Fat: 0 g; Cholesterol: 65 mg;
Sodium: 230 mg; Potassium: 590 mg; Total Carbohydrate: 5 g;
Dietary Fiber: 1 g; Sugar: 2 g; Protein: 24 g; Phosphorus: 335 mg

NUTRITIONAL INFORMATION | BAKED ASPARAGUS:

EXCHANGES / CHOICES:
1 Nonstarchy Vegetable; 1/2 Fat

Calories: 50; Calories from Fat: 30; Total Fat: 3.5 g;
Saturated Fat: 0.5 g; Trans Fat: 0 g; Cholesterol: 0 mg;
Sodium: 130 mg; Potassium: 190 mg; Total Carbohydrate: 4 g;
Dietary Fiber: 2 g; Sugar: 1 g; Protein: 2 g; Phosphorus: 45 mg

NUTRITIONAL INFORMATION | WHOLE-GRAIN BREAD:

EXCHANGES / CHOICES:
1 Starch

Calories: 70; Calories from Fat: 10; Total Fat: 1 g;
Saturated Fat: 0.2 g; Trans Fat: 0 g; Cholesterol: 0 mg;
Sodium: 125 mg; Potassium: 70 mg; Total Carbohydrate: 12 g;
Dietary Fiber: 2 g; Sugar: 1 g; Protein: 3 g; Phosphorus: 60 mg

SIDE DISHES

Baked Asparagus

SERVES: 4 • **SERVING SIZE:** 4 MEDIUM SPEARS

1 1/2 pounds asparagus, trimmed

1 tablespoon extra-virgin olive oil

1/4 teaspoon kosher salt

1/8 teaspoon black pepper

1/4 lemon, juice only (1–2 tablespoons) (optional)

1/4–1/2 teaspoon salt-free lemon-pepper seasoning (optional)

1. Toss the asparagus spears with the oil, salt, pepper, and a squeeze of fresh lemon juice, or lemon-pepper seasoning, if desired. Roast flat in a baking dish in a single layer in the oven at 400°F until asparagus are slightly browned, about 15–20 minutes.

Whole-Grain Bread

SERVES: 4 • **SERVING SIZE:** 1 SLICE

4 slices whole-grain bread

1. Cover and warm the bread in a 300°F oven for 5–8 minutes, if desired.

> **TIP**
>
> Salmon fillets will occasionally have small, hard-to-see bones that should be removed before cooking. The easiest way to remove them is to lay the salmon on a flat surface and run your fingers down the length of the fillet. When you feel a bone, slide your hand under the fillet, letting it bend slightly so the bone sticks out a bit more. Grasp the tip of the bone with a clean pair of pliers or tweezers and pull gently until the bone comes free.

This salad is a crunchy alternative to taco night. You can get creative with the ingredients; consider adding cilantro, pistachios, diced sweet onion, or red bell peppers. For picky eaters, serve the ingredients separately. Little ones (ages 3 and up) might enjoy using a toothpick to pick up the beans, olives, and other morsels. Serve with Corn or Whole-Wheat Tortillas.

California Taco Salad

PREP + COOK: 25 MINUTES • **SERVES:** 6 • **SERVING SIZE:** 2 1/2 CUPS

1 small head iceberg or romaine lettuce, chopped (about 6 cups)

15 ounces canned black or red beans, drained and rinsed

1/2 cup shredded reduced-fat Monterey Jack cheese, or use cheddar or pepper jack, or more to taste

1 avocado, peeled and diced

1 mango, peeled and diced, or use 1–2 tomatoes

1/2 cup sliced black olives

1/2 pound cooked and shredded chicken breast, or use cooked ground beef, turkey, or vegetarian ground meat (optional)

1/2 lime, juice only, about 1 tablespoon

6 tablespoons vinaigrette dressing

1 cup multi-grain tortilla chips, crushed, or use corn kernels

1 cup nonfat sour cream, for serving (optional)

1 cup salsa, for serving (optional)

DO AHEAD OR DELEGATE: Chop and refrigerate the lettuce, shred the cheese, peel and dice the mango, cook the chicken, beef or turkey, juice the lime, and crush the tortilla chips, if using.

1. In a large serving bowl, combine the lettuce, beans, cheese, avocado, mango, olives, and cooked chicken (or other meat) (optional). Sprinkle with the lime juice and dressing and toss thoroughly.

2. Top the salad with the chips or corn kernels (and warm the tortillas). Serve immediately, topped with a dollop of sour cream and salsa, if desired.

FLAVOR BOOSTER
Add 1 diced and seeded fresh jalapeño pepper and use pepper jack cheese.

Corn or Whole-Wheat Tortillas

SERVES: 6 • **SERVING SIZE:** 1 TORTILLA

6 (6-inch) corn or whole-wheat tortillas

1. The tortillas can be warmed in the microwave for 30 seconds to 1 minute or over an open flame on a gas stove for a few seconds per side (use tongs).

TIP

If you are adding ground beef or turkey to the salad, brown it in a nonstick skillet over medium heat, and season it with a little salt and/or chili powder. Allow it to cool for several minutes before adding to the salad. If using meatless ground "meat," prepare it according to the package directions.

NUTRITIONAL INFORMATION | CALIFORNIA TACO SALAD:

EXCHANGES / CHOICES:
1 Starch; 1/2 Fruit; 1 Nonstarchy Vegetable; 1 Protein, lean; 2 Fat

Calories: 265; Calories from Fat: 125; Total Fat: 14 g;
Saturated Fat: 2.8 g; Trans Fat: 0 g; Cholesterol: 5 mg;
Sodium: 420 mg; Potassium: 445 mg; Total Carbohydrate: 30 g;
Dietary Fiber: 8 g; Sugar: 9 g; Protein: 8 g; Phosphorus: 150 mg

NUTRITIONAL INFORMATION | CORN OR WHOLE-WHEAT TORTILLAS:

EXCHANGES / CHOICES:
1 Starch

Calories: 60; Calories from Fat: 5; Total Fat: 0.5 g;
Saturated Fat: 0.1 g; Trans Fat: 0 g; Cholesterol: 0 mg;
Sodium: 0 mg; Potassium: 40 mg; Total Carbohydrate: 12 g;
Dietary Fiber: 1 g; Sugar: 0 g; Protein: 1 g; Phosphorus: 80 mg

This fun recipe is great for a time-pressed weeknight, and can easily be doubled for bigger families. Serve with Green Salad with Apples, Gorgonzola Cheese, and Pecans.

Tortellini Soup with Spinach and Tomatoes

PREP + COOK: 20 MINUTES • **SERVES:** 5 • **SERVING SIZE:** 2 CUPS

1 tablespoon extra-virgin olive oil

1 teaspoon minced garlic (about 2 cloves)

32 ounces low-sodium chicken or vegetable broth

9 ounces whole-wheat or regular cheese tortellini (sold refrigerated)

15 ounces no-salt-added diced tomatoes, with their liquid

1/4 teaspoon black pepper

1/2 teaspoon dried basil

1/2 teaspoon dried oregano

3 cups baby spinach (or use chopped Swiss chard)

1/4 cup shredded Parmesan cheese, or to taste

DO AHEAD OR DELEGATE: Peel the garlic and combine the dry seasonings.

1. (Make the salad first, if you are serving it.) In a stockpot, heat the oil over medium-high heat. Sauté the garlic for 30 seconds to 1 minute until fragrant, then stir in the broth. Bring to a boil, then add the tortellini, tomatoes, pepper, basil, and oregano.

2. Reduce the heat to a simmer for 7 minutes. Add the spinach. Simmer for 2 more minutes, then remove from the heat and serve immediately, topped with the cheese.

SLOW COOKER DIRECTIONS: Add all ingredients except tortellini and the cheese to the slow cooker. Cook on low 6–10 hours (this can simmer all day). Add the tortellini 30 minutes before serving. Serve topped with the cheese.

FLAVOR BOOSTER
Use an extra clove of garlic and double the black pepper. Use freshly grated Parmesan cheese.

Green Salad with Apples, Gorgonzola Cheese, and Pecans

SERVES: 5 • **SERVING SIZE:** 1 CUP

1 head Boston or butter lettuce, chopped or torn

1 red apple, such as Gala or Fuji, diced

2 tablespoons crumbled Gorgonzola or blue cheese

2 tablespoons pecans, lightly toasted

1/4 cup vinaigrette dressing

1. Toss the lettuce with the apples, cheese, pecans, and dressing.

NUTRITIONAL INFORMATION | TORTELLINI SOUP WITH SPINACH AND TOMATOES:

EXCHANGES / CHOICES:
1 1/2 Starch; 1 Nonstarchy Vegetable; 1 Protein, lean; 1 Fat

Calories: 225; Calories from Fat: 70; Total Fat: 8 g;
Saturated Fat: 2.3 g; Trans Fat: 0 g; Cholesterol: 35 mg;
Sodium: 375 mg; Potassium: 550 mg; Total Carbohydrate: 27 g;
Dietary Fiber: 5 g; Sugar: 4 g; Protein: 12 g; Phosphorus: 180 mg

NUTRITIONAL INFORMATION | GREEN SALAD WITH APPLES, GORGONZOLA CHEESE, AND PECANS:

EXCHANGES / CHOICES:
1/2 Carbohydrate; 1 1/2 Fat

Calories: 100; Calories from Fat: 70; Total Fat: 8 g;
Saturated Fat: 1.5 g; Trans Fat: 0 g; Cholesterol: 5 mg;
Sodium: 80 mg; Potassium: 140 mg; Total Carbohydrate: 6 g;
Dietary Fiber: 1 g; Sugar: 4 g; Protein: 2 g; Phosphorus: 35 mg

TIP
Buitoni sells a whole-wheat three cheese tortellini that is tender and delicious and much higher in dietary fiber than their traditional tortellini.

I know some people have an irrational fear of it, but tofu is a fantastic meat substitute and has a wonderful texture and flavor when cooked properly. However, if you really don't enjoy it, you can make this dish, inspired by a recipe from Jenna Weber on the Fresh Tastes blog on PBS.org, with chicken or fish. If you are in a hurry, just marinate and eat the tofu without baking it. It's delicious that way. Serve with Steamed Rice and Peas.

Savory Sesame Tofu

MARINATE: 10 MINUTES • **PREP:** 20 MINUTES • **COOK:** 30 MINUTES • **SERVES:** 4 • **SERVING SIZE:** 2 SLICES

16 ounces extra-firm tofu packed in water

2 tablespoons reduced-sodium soy sauce (use wheat/gluten-free if needed)

1 tablespoon sesame oil

1 tablespoon rice vinegar

1 tablespoon pure maple syrup

1 teaspoon chili-garlic sauce or sriracha (optional)

1 teaspoon minced garlic, about 2 cloves

1/4 teaspoon ground ginger

1 teaspoon toasted sesame seeds

DO AHEAD OR DELEGATE: Drain, wrap, and slice the tofu, make the marinade and marinate the tofu, and toast the sesame seeds, if necessary.

1. Drain the tofu and wrap it in a clean dishcloth for a few minutes (the longer the better) to absorb extra water. Preheat the oven to 400°F (unless you plan to marinate the tofu in advance).

2. In a large flat dish with sides, combine the remaining ingredients, except the sesame seeds. Cut the tofu from top to bottom the long way into 8 long thin slices, and lay them in the marinade, flipping and pressing several times to coat them. Let them sit for at least 10 minutes, and up to 24 hours.

3. Transfer the tofu in a single layer to a baking sheet lined with a silicone mat or aluminum foil. Bake for 30 minutes, or longer if you want darker and chewier, flipping once. (Meanwhile, make the rice and peas, if you are serving them.)

4. Remove the tofu from the oven, sprinkle on the sesame seeds, and serve immediately, or refrigerate and use in sandwiches or salads.

FLAVOR BOOSTER
Use the optional chili-garlic sauce and double the garlic.

Steamed Rice and Peas

SERVES: 4 • **SERVING SIZE:** 2/3 CUP

1 cup quick-cooking brown or regular white rice

2/3 cup frozen peas

2 teaspoons reduced-sodium soy sauce (use wheat/gluten-free if needed) (optional)

1. Cook the rice according to the package directions. Mix the frozen peas and a few shakes of salt or soy sauce into the rice while it is still hot, stir and cover for 1–2 minutes so the peas thaw.

TIP

Need more convincing to work tofu into your diet more often? Cup for cup, firm tofu has up to 60% more calcium than milk.

NUTRITIONAL INFORMATION | SAVORY SESAME TOFU:

EXCHANGES / CHOICES:
1/2 Carbohydrate; 2 Protein, lean; 1 Fat

Calories: 160; Calories from Fat: 90; Total Fat: 10 g;
Saturated Fat: 1.2 g; Trans Fat: 0 g; Cholesterol: 0 mg;
Sodium: 285 mg; Potassium: 185 mg; Total Carbohydrate: 7 g;
Dietary Fiber: 1 g; Sugar: 4 g; Protein: 12 g; Phosphorus: 170 mg

NUTRITIONAL INFORMATION | STEAMED RICE AND PEAS:

EXCHANGES / CHOICES:
1 1/2 Starch

Calories: 95; Calories from Fat: 5; Total Fat: 0.5 g;
Saturated Fat: 0.1 g; Trans Fat: 0 g; Cholesterol: 0 mg;
Sodium: 110 mg; Potassium: 55 mg; Total Carbohydrate: 19 g;
Dietary Fiber: 2 g; Sugar: 1 g; Protein: 3 g; Phosphorus: 75 mg

SPRING

WEEK 8

Thai Beef and Mango Salad (1)
SIDE DISH: Dinner Rolls (1a)

Baked Panko Shrimp with Oregano and Garlic (2)
SIDE DISH: Corn and Tomato Salad (2a)

Risotto with Sausage, Mushrooms, and Peas (3)
SIDE DISH: Crinkle-Cut or Baby Carrots (3a)

Chicken Parmesan with Garden Herbs (4)
SIDE DISH: Baby Greens with Blueberries and Feta Cheese (4a)

Texas Tornado Bake (5)
SIDE DISH: Watermelon (5a)

SHOPPING LIST

🥕 PRODUCE

1 pound **crinkle-cut or baby carrots** (3a)

2 cups **shredded (matchstick cut) carrots** (you can buy them pre-cut in bags) (1)

2 **scallions** (1)

2 **yellow onions** (3)(5)

1 **yellow bell pepper** (5)

1 pint **cherry or grape tomatoes** (2a)

1 small head **Boston lettuce** (1)

6 ounces **fresh spinach** (5)

6–8 cups **baby salad greens** (4a)

1 tablespoon **fresh basil or mint** (2a)

2 tablespoons **fresh basil and sage leaves** (4)

1/2 cup **fresh cilantro or basil** (1)*

4 ears **fresh corn** (2a)

8 ounces **sliced mushrooms** (3)

1 **lemon** (2)

2 1/4–2 1/2 **limes** (1)(2a)

1/2 cup **blueberries** (4a)

1 **mango** (1)

1 **watermelon** (5a)

🫓 MEAT AND FISH

1 1/2 pounds **chicken cutlets or chicken breasts** (4)

1 pound **shrimp, peeled and deveined** (2)

1 pound **lean top sirloin steak, or use boneless, skinless chicken breasts, or meatless chicken or steak strips** (1)

15 ounces **Italian sausage or meatless sausage** (use wheat/gluten-free if needed) (3)

🗄 SHELVED ITEMS

1 package **whole-wheat or white dinner rolls** (1a)

2 cups **arborio rice** (3)

1/2 cup **panko breadcrumbs** (use wheat/gluten-free if needed) (2)

1 cup **white wine** (3)

1/2–3/4 cup **red pasta sauce** (4)

28–30 ounces **low-sodium chicken or vegetable broth** (3)

1 3/4 cups **fire-roasted low-sodium salsa** (5)

🧂 SPICES

1/4 teaspoon **salt** (4)

1 tablespoon **salt-free Italian seasoning** (2)

1 teaspoon **dried oregano** (2)

1/2 teaspoon **black pepper** (3)

🧴 STAPLES

2 tablespoons **trans fat-free margarine or butter** (2)

7 tablespoons **extra-virgin olive oil** (2)(3)(5)

2 tablespoons **peanut or vegetable oil** (1)

2–4 tablespoons **light vinaigrette dressing** (4a)

3 tablespoons **reduced-sodium soy sauce** (use wheat/gluten-free if needed) (1)

1 teaspoon **sugar** (2a)*

2 tablespoons **brown sugar** (1)

1–2 **eggs** (4)

1 tablespoon + 2 teaspoons **minced garlic** (2)(3)

3/4 cup **flour** (use wheat/gluten-free if needed) (4)

3/4 cup **breadcrumbs or panko** (use wheat/gluten-free if needed) (4)

🧊 REFRIGERATED/FROZEN

1/4 cup **crumbled feta cheese** (4a)

1 1/4 cups **shredded reduced-fat cheddar or Monterey Jack cheese** (5)

3 tablespoons + 3/4 cup **grated Parmesan cheese** (2)(3)(4)

1/3 cup **shredded part-skim mozzarella cheese** (4)

1 cup **reduced-fat sour cream** (5)*

2 tablespoons refrigerated **pesto sauce** (4)*

4 cups **cooked brown rice** (5)

4 **veggie burgers**, such as Amy's Texas Veggie Burger or Morningstar Farms Spicy Black Bean Veggie Burgers (5)

1 cup **frozen peas** (3)

Get free, printable versions of the shopping lists from this book at TheScramble.com/diabetes.

*optional ingredients

SPRING WEEK 8 • 87

This is a sweet and tangy meal to liven up your evening! If your kids don't eat salad, serve them the steak, mango, and carrots separately. Serve with Whole-Wheat Dinner Rolls.

Thai Beef and Mango Salad

PREP + COOK: 30 MINUTES • **SERVES:** 4 • **SERVING SIZE:** 2 1/2 CUPS

2 limes, juice only (1/3–1/2 cup)

2 tablespoons brown sugar

3 tablespoons reduced-sodium soy sauce (use wheat/gluten-free if needed)

2 tablespoons peanut or vegetable oil

1 pound lean top sirloin steak (or use boneless, skinless chicken breasts or meatless chicken or steak strips)

2 scallions, thinly sliced

2 cups shredded (matchstick cut) carrots

1/2 cup fresh cilantro or basil, chopped (optional)

1 mango, peeled and diced

1 small head Boston lettuce, torn into bite-sized pieces

DO AHEAD OR DELEGATE: Make the marinade and marinate the meat in the refrigerator, slice the scallions, shred the carrots, if necessary, peel and dice the mango, and tear the lettuce.

1. In a medium bowl, whisk together the lime juice, sugar, soy sauce, and oil. Lay the steak in a flat dish with sides. Pour half the marinade over it and flip the meat to coat it thoroughly. Set it aside and reserve the remaining marinade to use as a dressing for the salad.

2. In a salad bowl, combine the scallions, carrots, cilantro or basil (optional), mango, and lettuce.

3. (Warm the rolls now, if you are serving them.) Heat a heavy skillet over medium-high heat. Remove the steak from the marinade, discard the marinade, and cook for about 5 minutes per side until it is just cooked to desired doneness. If the outside of the steak is cooking too quickly, reduce the heat and partially cover the pan. Transfer the steak to a cutting board, allow it to cool slightly, and slice it across the grain into 1/2-inch wide strips. Dress the salad with the reserved marinade (not the marinade you used for the steak) and serve the salad topped with slices of steak.

FLAVOR BOOSTER
Add 1/2 teaspoon Asian chili garlic sauce to the marinade and/or serve the salad with Thai sweet chili sauce. Sprinkle the salad with fresh lime juice and chopped peanuts.

Whole-Wheat Dinner Rolls

SERVES: 4 • **SERVING SIZE:** 1 ROLL

4 whole-wheat dinner rolls

1. Warm the dinner rolls in a 300°F oven for 5–10 minutes.

TIP

The reason you discard this marinade after marinating the steak is because it has come in contact with raw meat, which can have dangerous bacteria. If you'd like you use a marinade as a sauce, just boil the marinade for at least a minute and it will be safe to use.

NUTRITIONAL INFORMATION | THAI BEEF AND MANGO SALAD:

EXCHANGES / CHOICES:
1/2 Fruit; 1/2 Carbohydrate; 1 Nonstarchy Vegetable; 3 Protein, lean; 1 Fat

Calories: 275; Calories from Fat: 90; Total Fat: 10 g; Saturated Fat: 2.6 g; Trans Fat: 0.1 g; Cholesterol: 40 mg; Sodium: 450 mg; Potassium: 700 mg; Total Carbohydrate: 22 g; Dietary Fiber: 3 g; Sugar: 16 g; Protein: 25 g; Phosphorus: 235 mg

NUTRITIONAL INFORMATION | WHOLE-WHEAT DINNER ROLLS:

EXCHANGES / CHOICES:
1 Starch

Calories: 95; Calories from Fat: 15; Total Fat: 1.5 g; Saturated Fat: 0.3 g; Trans Fat: 0 g; Cholesterol: 0 mg; Sodium: 145 mg; Potassium: 100 mg; Total Carbohydrate: 18 g; Dietary Fiber: 3 g; Sugar: 3 g; Protein: 3 g; Phosphorus: 80 mg

This dish, a staple in the home of my colleague Betsy Goldstein, has all the rustic Italian flavors that I love, and makes the house smell fantastic while it's cooking. To make it look more elegant, scatter some freshly chopped parsley over the finished dish. Serve with Corn and Tomato Salad.

Baked Panko Shrimp with Oregano and Garlic

PREP + COOK: 30 MINUTES • **SERVES:** 4 • **SERVING SIZE:** 1 CUP

1 pound large, peeled, and deveined shrimp (preferably U.S. or Canadian)

1 lemon, juice only (2–3 tablespoons)

2 tablespoons trans fat-free margarine

2 tablespoons extra-virgin olive oil

1 teaspoon dried oregano

1 tablespoon salt-free Italian seasoning (or use dried parsley)

3 tablespoons grated Parmesan cheese

1 tablespoon minced garlic (5–6 cloves)

1/2 cup panko breadcrumbs

DO AHEAD OR DELEGATE: Peel and devein the shrimp, juice the lemon, grate the cheese and combine it with the oregano and Italian seasoning, and peel the garlic.

1. Preheat the oven to 350°F (and preheat the broiler if it is separate from the oven).

2. In an 8 × 8-inch baking dish, toss the shrimp with the lemon juice and arrange the shrimp evenly over the bottom of the dish.

3. In a medium microwave-safe bowl, melt the margarine. Add the remaining ingredients to the bowl with the margarine and stir gently to combine. Spread the mixture evenly over the shrimp.

4. Bake for 15–20 minutes until the shrimp are cooked through. (Meanwhile, prepare the salad, if you are serving it.) Transfer the dish to the broiler for 1–2 minutes until the topping turns golden brown (be careful not to let it scorch!). Serve immediately.

SLOW COOKER DIRECTIONS: In the slow cooker, toss the shrimp with the lemon juice and arrange the shrimp evenly over the bottom of the dish. Prepare the topping as directed, and spread evenly over the shrimp. Cook on low for 2 1/2–3 hours, until shrimp are pink. (Slow cooker cooking times may vary—get to know your slow cooker and, if necessary, adjust cooking times accordingly.)

FLAVOR BOOSTER

Season it with freshly ground black pepper and top it with fresh parsley before serving.

Corn and Tomato Salad

SERVES: 4 • **SERVING SIZE:** 1 1/4 CUPS

4 ears corn, kernels cut off cobs

1 pint cherry or grape tomatoes, halved or quartered

1 tablespoon fresh basil or mint, chopped

1/4–1/2 lime, juice only (about 1 tablespoon)

1 teaspoon sugar (optional)

1. Combine the corn kernels with the tomatoes, herbs, and lime juice (and the sugar if the corn isn't very sweet). Mix and chill until ready to serve. (If you prefer, you can steam the corn for 2–4 minutes before making the salad, especially if not super sweet and juicy.)

TIP

As fresh shrimp can be a bit costly, I often buy it frozen or purchase it when it's on sale at my store and then freeze it until I need it. Raw shrimp can be frozen for 4–6 months.

NUTRITIONAL INFORMATION | BAKED PANKO SHRIMP WITH OREGANO AND GARLIC:

EXCHANGES / CHOICES:
1/2 Starch; 3 Protein, lean; 1 1/2 Fat

Calories: 245; Calories from Fat: 110; Total Fat: 12 g; Saturated Fat: 2.5 g; Trans Fat: 0 g; Cholesterol: 190 mg; Sodium: 220 mg; Potassium: 295 mg; Total Carbohydrate: 8 g; Dietary Fiber: 1 g; Sugar: 1 g; Protein: 26 g; Phosphorus: 275 mg

NUTRITIONAL INFORMATION | CORN AND TOMATO SALAD:

EXCHANGES / CHOICES:
1 1/2 Starch

Calories: 115; Calories from Fat: 15; Total Fat: 1.5 g; Saturated Fat: 0.2 g; Trans Fat: 0 g; Cholesterol: 0 mg; Sodium: 5 mg; Potassium: 405 mg; Total Carbohydrate: 25 g; Dietary Fiber: 3 g; Sugar: 7 g; Protein: 4 g; Phosphorus: 100 mg

Our friend and Six O'Clock Scramble devotee Karen Murray gave me this terrific and easy recipe. The risotto smells as heavenly as it tastes. Serve with Crinkle-Cut or Baby Carrots.

Risotto with Sausage, Mushrooms, and Peas

PREP + COOK: 30 MINUTES • **SERVES:** 8 • **SERVING SIZE:** 2 CUPS

5 (3-ounce) links of sweet Italian style chicken sausage, fully cooked (such as Al Fresco)

2 tablespoons extra-virgin olive oil

1 yellow onion, diced

2 teaspoons minced garlic (about 4 cloves)

8 ounces sliced mushrooms

2 cups arborio rice, uncooked

28–30 ounces low-sodium chicken or vegetable broth

1 cup white wine (or use additional broth)

1/2 teaspoon black pepper

1 cup frozen peas

1/2 cup grated or shredded Parmesan cheese

DO AHEAD OR DELEGATE: Crumble or dice the sausage and refrigerate, dice the onion, peel the garlic, slice the mushrooms, and grate or shred the cheese, if necessary.

1. Dice the sausage into 1/4-inch pieces.

2. In a large saucepan or stockpot with a tight-fitting lid, heat the oil over medium heat. Add the onions, sausage, and garlic and sauté until the onions are tender and the sausage is browned, about 5 minutes.

3. Add the mushrooms and rice, and stir until the rice is coated and lightly browned, about 2 minutes.

4. Add the broth, wine, and pepper and bring to a boil. Cover and simmer the mixture for 15–20 minutes until the rice is tender. Stir in the peas and cheese and serve immediately.

FLAVOR BOOSTER
Use spicy Italian sausage and season the risotto with lots of freshly ground black pepper or salt-free lemon-pepper seasoning and use freshly grated cheese.

Crinkle-Cut or Baby Carrots

SERVES: 8 • **SERVING SIZE:** 5 BABY CARROTS

1 pound crinkle-cut or baby carrots

1. Serve crinkle-cut or baby carrots with the risotto.

TIP
If you don't like mushrooms, you can leave them out of this dish and it will still taste divine.

NUTRITIONAL INFORMATION | RISOTTO WITH SAUSAGE, MUSHROOMS, AND PEAS:

EXCHANGES / CHOICES:
2 1/2 Starch; 2 Protein, lean; 1 Fat

Calories: 320; Calories from Fat: 80; Total Fat: 9 g;
Saturated Fat: 2.6 g; Trans Fat: 0 g; Cholesterol: 45 mg;
Sodium: 420 mg; Potassium: 395 mg; Total Carbohydrate: 40 g;
Dietary Fiber: 3 g; Sugar: 2 g; Protein: 17 g; Phosphorus: 235 mg

NUTRITIONAL INFORMATION | CRINKLE-CUT OR BABY CARROTS:

EXCHANGES / CHOICES:
1 Nonstarchy Vegetable

Calories: 25; Calories from Fat: 0; Total Fat: 0 g;
Saturated Fat: 0 g; Trans Fat: 0 g; Cholesterol: 0 mg;
Sodium: 40 mg; Potassium: 180 mg; Total Carbohydrate: 5 g;
Dietary Fiber: 2 g; Sugar: 3 g; Protein: 1 g; Phosphorus: 20 mg

My friend Deb Ford says that this is one of her kids' favorite dinners, and her 15-year-old daughter often prepares it for the family. Serve with Baby Greens with Blueberries and Feta Cheese.

Chicken Parmesan with Garden Herbs

PREP + COOK: 30 MINUTES • **SERVES:** 6 • **SERVING SIZE:** 4 OUNCES

3/4 cup flour

1/4 teaspoon salt

1–2 eggs

3/4 cup breadcrumbs or panko

1 1/2 pounds chicken cutlets, or halved chicken breasts pounded to an even thickness

1/3 cup shredded part-skim mozzarella cheese

1/4 cup grated Parmesan cheese

2 tablespoons pesto sauce (optional)

1/2–3/4 cup red pasta sauce (marinara)

2 tablespoons fresh basil and sage leaves, minced, or use only basil

DO AHEAD OR DELEGATE: Combine the flour and the salt, beat and refrigerate the eggs, shred the mozzarella cheese, and grate the Parmesan cheese, if necessary.

1. Preheat the oven to 425°F. Spray a baking sheet with nonstick cooking spray.

2. Combine the flour and salt in a shallow dish and put the eggs and the breadcrumbs or panko in two separate shallow dishes. Coat each chicken cutlet lightly with the flour, then the egg, then the breadcrumbs, and lay them on the baking sheet. Bake for 6–8 minutes. Meanwhile, in a small bowl, combine the cheeses.

3. Remove the chicken from the oven, flip each cutlet over, and top each with 1 teaspoon of pesto (optional), 1 tablespoon of the marinara, spreading it to the edges, and a sprinkling of the fresh herbs and the cheese (make sure to use up all of the herbs and cheese).

4. Return the chicken to the oven for 6–8 more minutes until it is cooked through and the cheese is melted. Serve immediately.

FLAVOR BOOSTER
Use aged Parmesan such as Parmigiano-Reggiano and add a little black or red pepper to the breadcrumb mixture.

Baby Greens with Blueberries and Feta Cheese

SERVES: 6 • **SERVING SIZE:** 1 CUP

6–8 cups baby greens

1/2 cup blueberries

1/4 cup crumbled feta cheese

1/4 cup light vinaigrette dressing

1. In a large bowl, combine the greens with the blueberries, cheese, and dressing.

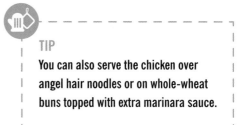

TIP
You can also serve the chicken over angel hair noodles or on whole-wheat buns topped with extra marinara sauce.

NUTRITIONAL INFORMATION | CHICKEN PARMESAN WITH GARDEN HERBS:

EXCHANGES / CHOICES:
1 1/2 Starch; 4 Protein, lean

Calories: 270; Calories from Fat: 65; Total Fat: 7 g;
Saturated Fat: 2.4 g; Trans Fat: 0 g; Cholesterol: 105 mg;
Sodium: 305 mg; Potassium: 320 mg; Total Carbohydrate: 20 g;
Dietary Fiber: 1 g; Sugar: 2 g; Protein: 31 g; Phosphorus: 285 mg

NUTRITIONAL INFORMATION | BABY GREENS WITH BLUEBERRIES AND FETA CHEESE:

EXCHANGES / CHOICES:
1/2 Carbohydrate; 1/2 Fat

Calories: 55; Calories from Fat: 20; Total Fat: 2.5 g;
Saturated Fat: 1.1 g; Trans Fat: 0.1 g; Cholesterol: 5 mg;
Sodium: 170 mg; Potassium: 215 mg; Total Carbohydrate: 6 g;
Dietary Fiber: 1 g; Sugar: 4 g; Protein: 2 g; Phosphorus: 45 mg

This casserole is so easy to make (especially if you use frozen precooked rice) and it's stick-to-your-ribs satisfying and very tasty! Serve with Watermelon.

Texas Tornado Bake

PREP: 30 MINUTES • **COOK:** 30 MINUTES • **SERVES:** 8 • **SERVING SIZE:** 1 3/4 CUPS

4 cups cooked brown rice, precooked, or made from 1 1/2 cups dry rice

1 tablespoon extra-virgin olive oil

1 yellow bell pepper, chopped

1 yellow onion, chopped

6 ounces fresh spinach, coarsely chopped (unless using baby spinach)

1 3/4 cups fire-roasted low-sodium salsa

4 veggie burgers, such as Amy's Texas Veggie Burger or Morningstar Farms Spicy Black Bean Veggie Burgers, defrosted and crumbled or chopped

1 1/4 cups shredded reduced-fat cheddar or Monterey Jack cheese, or a combination of the two

1 cup reduced-fat sour cream, for serving (optional)

DO AHEAD OR DELEGATE: Chop the bell pepper, onion, and spinach, cook the rice if necessary, defrost and crumble or chop the burgers, or fully prepare and refrigerate the recipe.

1. (Cook the rice, if necessary.) Heat a large heavy skillet, over medium-high heat and add the oil. When it's hot, add the bell peppers and onions. Sauté, stirring occasionally, for 6–8 minutes until tender and starting to brown. Stir in the spinach, cover, and steam for about 2 minutes until wilted. Remove from heat.

2. Meanwhile, spray a 9 × 13-inch baking dish with nonstick cooking spray and preheat the oven to 400°F. Spread the rice evenly in the bottom of the dish. Top it evenly with the sautéed vegetables, 1 cup of salsa, the crumbled veggie burgers, the remaining salsa, and the cheese. Cover with foil and bake for 30 minutes, uncovering after 20 minutes, and continuing cooking until the cheese is bubbly. (Meanwhile, cut the watermelon, if you are serving it.) Allow to cool for 10 minutes, if time allows, and cut into squares. Top with sour cream, if desired. You can also cover it tightly and refrigerate it for up to 3 days or freeze for up to 3 months.

SLOW COOKER DIRECTIONS: Place 1 cup dry rice, 2 cups water or broth, and all other ingredients except the sour cream in the slow cooker. (If you wish, you may reserve 1/2 cup of cheese to use as a topping.) Cook on low for 6–8 hours or on high for 3–4 hours, adding the reserved cheese 15–30 minutes before serving. (Slow cooker cooking times may vary—get to know your slow cooker and, if necessary, adjust cooking times accordingly.)

FLAVOR BOOSTER

Serve with hot pepper sauce, such as Tabasco.

Watermelon

SERVES: 8 • **SERVING SIZE:** 1 1/4 CUPS

1 medium watermelon

1. Slice or peel and chop the watermelon before serving.

NUTRITIONAL INFORMATION | TEXAS TORNADO BAKE:

EXCHANGES / CHOICES:
1 1/2 Starch; 1/2 Carbohydrate; 1 Nonstarchy Vegetable;
1 Protein, lean; 1 Fat

Calories: 260; Calories from Fat: 70; Total Fat: 8 g;
Saturated Fat: 2.8 g; Trans Fat: 0 g; Cholesterol: 10 mg;
Sodium: 455 mg; Potassium: 515 mg; Total Carbohydrate: 34 g;
Dietary Fiber: 5 g; Sugar: 4 g; Protein: 14 g; Phosphorus: 280 mg

NUTRITIONAL INFORMATION | WATERMELON:

EXCHANGES / CHOICES:
1 Fruit

Calories: 55; Calories from Fat: 0; Total Fat: 0 g;
Saturated Fat: 0 g; Trans Fat: 0 g; Cholesterol: 0 mg;
Sodium: 0 mg; Potassium: 215 mg; Total Carbohydrate: 14 g;
Dietary Fiber: 1 g; Sugar: 12 g; Protein: 1 g; Phosphorus: 20 mg

TIP
If you plan to freeze a
casserole, completely cool it
first to avoid condensation.

HOMEMADE DRESSINGS AND DIPS

Have you ever looked at the ingredients on a bottle of store-bought dressing? Not only are they often high in sodium, fat, and sugar, but they often include unnatural ingredients that you might not want to put into your body!

If you ever make your own dressing, you know how simple it is to make something healthy and delicious! Just whisk together the ingredients below or shake them up in a jar, and store any leftovers in the refrigerator for anywhere from 3 days to 2 weeks, depending on the ingredients (the creamier dressings generally don't last as long).

CAESAR DRESSING

2 tablespoons mayonnaise, 2 tablespoons extra-virgin olive oil, 1/2 teaspoon minced garlic (about 1 clove), 1/2 lemon, juice only (about 2 tablespoons), 1 teaspoon Worcestershire sauce, and 1/2 teaspoon anchovy paste (or use mashed capers or seasoned soybean paste for vegetarians)

RANCH DRESSING

2 tablespoons nonfat or low-fat sour cream or Greek yogurt, 2 tablespoons mayonnaise, 2 tablespoons reduced-fat buttermilk, 1 teaspoon white wine vinegar, 1 tablespoon fresh chives, minced, 1/4 teaspoon garlic powder, 1/4 teaspoon dried dill, 1/8 teaspoon salt, and 1/8 teaspoon black pepper

BLUE CHEESE DRESSING

1/4–1/2 cup crumbled blue cheese, (depending on how chunky you like the dressing), 1/4 cup mayonnaise (or use sour cream or plain yogurt), 1 teaspoon Worcestershire sauce, and 1 teaspoon white wine vinegar

TAHINI-LEMON DRESSING

2 tablespoons tahini (sesame paste) well stirred (or use hummus if you can't find tahini), 1 lemon, juice only (about 1/4 cup), 2 teaspoons Dijon mustard, 1 teaspoon minced garlic (about 2 cloves), 2 tablespoons water, 2 teaspoons honey, 1/4 teaspoon salt

RASPBERRY VINAIGRETTE

1/4 cup extra-virgin olive oil, 1/8 cup raspberry vinegar, 1 shallot, minced, and 1/4 teaspoon ground cinnamon

MAPLE-DIJON DRESSING

1/4 cup extra-virgin olive oil, 1/8 cup balsamic vinegar (or use red wine vinegar), 1 tablespoon pure maple syrup, 1 teaspoon Dijon mustard, 1/4 teaspoon herbes de Provence or thyme

LIGHT HONEY VINAIGRETTE

1/4 cup red wine vinegar, 1/8 yellow or white onion, minced (about 2 tablespoons), 1/2 teaspoon minced garlic (about 1 clove), 2 tablespoons extra-virgin olive oil, 2 tablespoons honey, 1/4 lemon, juice only (about 1 tablespoon), 1/4 teaspoon salt, 1/4 teaspoon black pepper

HONEY-LIME DRESSING

2 tablespoons extra-virgin olive oil, 2 tablespoons white wine vinegar, 1/2 lime, juice only (about 1 tablespoon), 1 tablespoon honey, 1/2 teaspoon curry powder, 1/2 teaspoon ground ginger, 1/4 teaspoon salt

ORANGE-BALSAMIC VINAIGRETTE

1/4 cup extra-virgin olive oil, 1/8 cup orange juice, 1/8 cup balsamic vinegar, 1 tablespoon Dijon mustard, and 1 tablespoon chopped fresh herbs, if desired

HONEY-LEMON DILL DRESSING

1/2–1 lemon, juice only (about 1/4 cup), 1 tablespoon honey, 2 tablespoons extra-virgin olive oil, 2 teaspoons fresh dill, finely chopped, or use 1/2 teaspoon dried dill

page 88 Thai Beef and Mango Salad

Fresh Corn, Tomato, and Avocado Salad with Shrimp
SIDE DISH: Whole-Wheat Dinner Rolls

page
142

SUMMER

Grilled Sesame Chicken (1)
SIDE DISH: Sesame Stir-Fried Broccoli (1a)

Baked Red Snapper with Golden Onions (2)
SIDE DISH: Wild Rice with Dried Cranberries and Pecans (2a); Snow or Sugar Snap Peas with Shallots (2b)

Crunchy Veggie Wraps (3)
SIDE DISH: Hard-Boiled Eggs (3a); Blended Iced Mocha (3b)

Ruffled Noodles with Spinach, Feta Cheese, and Tomatoes (4)
SIDE DISH: Green Salad with Grapes, Pistachio Nuts, and Maple-Dijon Dressing (4a)

Smoky Beans and Greens over Quick Grits (5)
SIDE DISH: Fresh Blackberries or Blueberries (5a)

SHOPPING LIST

PRODUCE

- 2 cups **shredded (matchstick cut) carrots** (you can buy them pre-cut in bags) (3)
- 1 small **shallot** (2b)
- 2 **scallions** (1)*
- 1 **yellow onion** (5)
- 1 **sweet yellow onion** such as Vidalia or Walla Walla (2)
- 3 **tomatoes** (4)(5)
- 1 head **lettuce, any variety** (4a)
- 12 ounces **baby spinach** (4)
- 8 ounces **kale** (5)
- 1 tablespoon **fresh ginger** (1)
- 1/4 cup **fresh flat-leaf parsley** (4)
- 2 teaspoons **fresh oregano** (4)
- 2 pounds **broccoli** (1a)
- 1–2 **cucumbers** (3)
- 12 ounces **snow or sugar snap peas** (2b)
- 1 **avocado** (3)
- 2 **lemons** (2)(3)(4)
- 1–2 pints **fresh blackberries or blueberries** (5a)
- 1/2 cup **seedless grapes** (4a)

MEAT AND FISH

- 3 pounds **skinless bone-in dark meat chicken**, such as drumsticks, thighs, and/or wings (1)
- 1 pound **red snapper fillets** (or use salmon, catfish, or other fillets) (2)
- 1/2 cup **smoked ham or cooked sausage** (5)*

🫙 SHELVED ITEMS

3/4 cup **quick-cooking or regular wild rice** (2a)

16 ounces **whole-wheat ruffles or radiatori or cavatelli shaped pasta** (4)

8 **whole-wheat tortillas** (use wheat/gluten-free if needed) (3)

1 cup **quick-cooking (not instant) grits** (5)

1/2 cup **reduced-sodium chicken or vegetable broth** (5)

1 1/2 cups water, **chicken, or vegetable broth** (2a)

1/3 cup **hoisin sauce** (sold with Asian foods) (1)

3 tablespoons **rice vinegar** (1)

15 ounces **canned black eyed peas or great northern beans** (5)

1 tablespoon **capers** (4)*

1/2 tablespoon **dried cranberries** (2a)

12 teaspoons **instant coffee** (3b)

8 tablespoons **chocolate syrup** (3b)

4 packets **Splenda** (3b)

4 teaspoons **unsweetened cocoa powder** (3b)

1/4 cup **shelled pistachio nuts** (4a)

1/2 tablespoon **pecans** (2a)

1/2 teaspoon **anchovy paste** (3)

1 cup **black beans** (3)

🧂 SPICES

5/8 teaspoon **salt** (2b)(5)

1/4 teaspoon **herbes de Provence or thyme** (4a)

1/2 teaspoon **Chinese five-spice powder or ground cloves** (1)

1/2 teaspoon **curry powder** (3a)*

1/2 teaspon **paprika** (3a)*

1 1/2 teaspoons **smoked paprika** (5)

1 tablespoon **toasted sesame seeds** (1)

🧴 STAPLES

1 tablespoon **butter** (5)*

4 tablespoons **reduced-sodium soy sauce** (use wheat/gluten-free if needed) (1)(1a)

7 tablespoons + 1–2 teaspoons + 1/4 cup **extra-virgin olive oil** (2)(2b)(3)(4)(4a)(5)

4 tablespoons **sesame oil** (1)(1a)

2 teaspoons + 1/8 cup **balsamic vinegar** (2)(4a)

1/2 tablespoon **vinaigrette dressing** (2a)

1 teaspoon **Dijon mustard** (use wheat/gluten-free if needed) (4a)

1 1/2 teaspoons **hot pepper sauce**, such as Tabasco (1)

1 tablespoon **pure maple syrup** (4a)

4 cups **nonfat milk** (3b)

6 **eggs** (3a)

3–4 teaspoons **minced garlic** (1)(1a)(3)

1 teaspoon **Worcestershire sauce** (3)

2 tablespoons **reduced-fat mayonnaise** (3)

🍦 REFRIGERATED/FROZEN

4 ounces **crumbled feta cheese** (4)

4 ounces **light chive or vegetable cream cheese or light Laughing Cow garlic and herb spreadable cheese** (3)

Get free, printable versions of the shopping lists from this book at TheScramble.com/diabetes.

*optional ingredients

SUMMER WEEK 1 • 103

My friend Esther Schrader often serves this delectable chicken, adapted from a recipe in Fine Cooking *magazine, to her family of five during the summer. This is a fabulous dish to grill in advance and reheat just before dinner or enjoy cold. Serve with Sesame Stir-Fried Broccoli.*

Grilled Sesame Chicken

MARINATE: 60 MINUTES • **PREP:** 10 MINUTES • **COOK:** 25 MINUTES • **SERVES:** 6
SERVING SIZE: 2 SMALL DRUMSTICKS, OR 2 SMALL THIGHS, OR 1 SMALL DRUMSTICK + 1 SMALL THIGH

1/3 cup hoisin sauce

2 tablespoons sesame oil

3 tablespoons rice vinegar

2 tablespoons reduced-sodium soy sauce (use wheat/gluten-free if needed)

1 tablespoon fresh ginger, peeled and grated or minced

1 1/2 teaspoons hot pepper sauce (such as Tabasco), or more to taste

1 teaspoon minced garlic (about 2 cloves)

1/2 teaspoon Chinese five-spice powder or ground cloves

3 pounds skinless bone-in dark meat chicken, such as drumsticks, thighs and/or wings

1 tablespoon toasted sesame seeds

2 scallions, thinly sliced, for garnish (optional)

DO AHEAD OR DELEGATE: Make the marinade and marinate the chicken in the refrigerator, toast the sesame seeds, slice the scallions, or fully prepare and refrigerate the dish.

1. In a large bowl, combine all the ingredients except the chicken, sesame seeds, and scallions (optional). Remove 2 tablespoons of the sauce and reserve it for later. Add the chicken to the bowl and coat it with the marinade. Refrigerate for at least one hour and up to 24 hours.

2. Preheat the grill to medium-high heat and oil the grates (or you can bake the chicken on a baking sheet at 400°F for 30 minutes). When the grill is hot, grill the chicken for 7–8 minutes (reserve the marinade), until it no longer sticks to the grates, flip it, and brush with the marinade. (Meanwhile, prepare the broccoli, if you are serving it.)

3. Grill the chicken for 7–8 more minutes, flip it, and brush with the sauce again, and let it cook for about 5 minutes. Flip the chicken once more, and let it cook for about 5 more minutes until it is nicely browned and cooked through (the chicken should have cooked for about 25–30 minutes total by now).

4. Transfer the chicken to a platter, brush with the reserved marinade, and sprinkle it with the sesame seeds and scallions (optional) before serving it. Alternatively, refrigerate it for up to 3 days.

SLOW COOKER DIRECTIONS: There is no need to marinate the chicken in advance. Combine all the ingredients except the chicken in the slow cooker and stir to combine. Then add the chicken, turning it over several times to coat it with the sauce. Cook on low for 8–10 hours or on high for 4–6 hours. Drizzle some of the sauce over the chicken when serving. (Slow cooker cooking times may vary—get to know your slow cooker and, if necessary, adjust cooking times accordingly.)

Sesame Stir-Fried Broccoli

SERVES: 6 • **SERVING SIZE:** 1 CUP

2 pounds broccoli, cut into florets
2 teaspoons minced garlic (about 4 cloves)
2 tablespoons sesame oil
2 tablespoons reduced-sodium soy sauce (use wheat/gluten-free if needed)

1. Heat the sesame oil in a wok or frying pan over medium-high heat. Lightly brown the garlic for about 30 seconds. Add the broccoli and 2 tablespoons water. Cover and cook for about 5 minutes, reducing the heat if necessary to keep it steaming, but prevent it from burning. Add the soy sauce, and stir-fry the broccoli for 1 more minute before serving.

FLAVOR BOOSTER
Double the hot pepper sauce and use 3/4 teaspoon five-spice powder in the marinade.

TIP
Chinese five-spice powder is a combination of spices that are intended to encompass sweet, sour, bitter, pungent, and salty flavors. There are many variants, but the spice mixture often contains cloves, star anise, cinnamon, Szechuan pepper, and ground fennel seeds. While it is generally available at local grocery stores, if you have an Asian market near you, you're likely to pay less for it there.

NUTRITIONAL INFORMATION | GRILLED SESAME CHICKEN:

EXCHANGES / CHOICES:
1/2 Carbohydrate; 4 Protein, lean; 1 Fat

Calories: 260; Calories from Fat: 115; Total Fat: 13 g;
Saturated Fat: 2.8 g; Trans Fat: 0 g; Cholesterol: 125 mg;
Sodium: 410 mg; Potassium: 320 mg; Total Carbohydrate: 5 g;
Dietary Fiber: 0 g; Sugar: 2 g; Protein: 29 g; Phosphorus: 235 mg

NUTRITIONAL INFORMATION | SESAME STIR-FRIED BROCCOLI:

EXCHANGES / CHOICES:
1 Nonstarchy Vegetable; 1 Fat

Calories: 80; Calories from Fat: 45; Total Fat: 5 g;
Saturated Fat: 0.7 g; Trans Fat: 0 g; Cholesterol: 0 mg;
Sodium: 220 mg; Potassium: 285 mg; Total Carbohydrate: 7 g;
Dietary Fiber: 3 g; Sugar: 1 g; Protein: 3 g; Phosphorus: 70 mg

A simple baked fish is a delightful dinner, especially with flavorful side dishes. Serve with Wild Rice with Dried Cranberries and Pecans, and Snow or Sugar Snap Peas with Shallots.

Baked Red Snapper with Golden Onions

PREP: 10 MINUTES • **COOK:** 25 MINUTES • **SERVES:** 4 • **SERVING SIZE:** 3 OUNCES

2 tablespoons extra-virgin olive oil, divided use

1 sweet yellow onion, such as Vidalia or Walla Walla, halved and thinly sliced

1 pound red snapper fillets (or use salmon, catfish, or other fillets)

1 lemon, juice only (about 1/4 cup)

2 teaspoons balsamic vinegar

1. (If you are making the rice, start that first.) Preheat the oven to 400°F. Heat a heavy skillet over medium-high heat and add half the oil and all of the onions. Sauté, stirring occasionally, until they are golden brown, about 5–7 minutes.

2. Meanwhile, lay the fish in a flat baking dish just large enough to hold it in one layer. In a small bowl, combine the lemon juice, remaining oil, and vinegar and pour it evenly over the fish.

3. When the onions are golden, spoon them over the fish. Bake the fish for 20–25 minutes until it is opaque and flakes easily. (Meanwhile, make the snow or sugar snap peas if you are serving them.) Season with salt and pepper to taste and serve it immediately.

TIP

To peel an onion easily, slice off both ends with a sharp knife. Score the skin and outside layer of the onion from the top to the bottom of the onion with the knife before peeling the skin and outer layer off with your fingers.

SIDE DISHES

Wild Rice with Dried Cranberries and Pecans

SERVES: 4 • **SERVING SIZE:** 2/3 CUP

3/4 cup wild rice
1 1/2 cups water, chicken or vegetable broth
1/2 tablespoon dried cranberries (optional)
1/2 tablespoon pecans (optional)
1/2 tablespoon balsamic vinaigrette

1. Prepare the rice, using water or broth, according to the package directions. To make it even more flavorful and colorful, stir the dried cranberries and chopped pecans into the just-cooked rice, and add the vinaigrette dressing.

Snow or Sugar Snap Peas with Shallots

SERVES: 4 • **SERVING SIZE:** 3/4 CUP

2 teaspoons extra-virgin olive oil
1 small shallot, peeled and minced
12 ounces snow or sugar snap peas
1/8 teaspoon salt, or to taste

1. Heat the oil over medium heat in a medium to large skillet. Add the shallots, and cook, stirring frequently, for 1–2 minutes until they just start to brown. Add the snow or sugar snap peas and continue sautéing, stirring frequently, for 1–2 minutes until they are tender crisp. Season with salt and serve.

Having a dinner that each family member can customize, usually means everybody's happy with the meal. These festive wraps are easy to adapt to your own tastes or refrigerator's contents. Consider adding sliced beets, chickpeas or white beans, romaine lettuce or baby greens, sliced red onion, sprouts, bell peppers, or whatever strikes your fancy. Serve with Hard-Boiled Eggs and with Blended Iced Mochas for dessert.

Crunchy Veggie Wraps

PREP + COOK: 10 MINUTES • **SERVES:** 8 • **SERVING SIZE:** 1 WRAP

4 ounces light chive or vegetable cream cheese or light Laughing Cow garlic and herb spreadable cheese

8 whole-wheat tortillas

2 cups shredded (matchstick cut) carrots (about 2 carrots)

1 avocado, peeled and sliced

1–2 cucumbers, peeled and cut into thin strips (2 cups)

1 cup black beans, rinsed and drained

LIGHT CAESAR DRESSING

2 tablespoons reduced-fat mayonnaise

2 tablespoons extra-virgin olive oil

1/2 teaspoon minced garlic (about 1 clove)

2 tablespoons fresh lemon juice (about 1/2 lemon)

1 teaspoon Worcestershire sauce

1/2 teaspoon anchovy paste (or use mashed capers, soy sauce, or seasoned soybean paste for a vegetarian alternative)

DO AHEAD OR DELEGATE: Shred the carrots if necessary, peel and cut the cucumbers, and make the dressing.

1. (Start the eggs first, if you are serving them.) Spread a thin layer of cream cheese or cheese spread on each tortilla. Fill each tortilla with about 1/4 cup shredded carrots, a couple of avocado slices, about 1/4 cup of cucumbers, and 1/4 cup black beans.

2. Combine and whisk together the Caesar dressing ingredients and drizzle the vegetables with about 1 teaspoon of the dressing. Fold up the bottom of the tortilla and roll them up as tightly as possible, letting the colorful vegetables peek out of the top. Cut in half, if desired, and enjoy immediately.

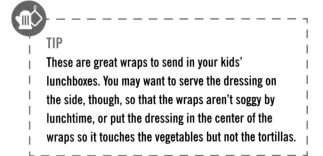

TIP

These are great wraps to send in your kids' lunchboxes. You may want to serve the dressing on the side, though, so that the wraps aren't soggy by lunchtime, or put the dressing in the center of the wraps so it touches the vegetables but not the tortillas.

SIDE DISHES

- -

Hard-Boiled Eggs

SERVES: 6 • **SERVING SIZE:** 1 EGG

6 eggs

1. In a medium saucepan, cover the eggs in cold water and bring the water to a boil. When the water boils, turn off the heat, cover the pot, and let the eggs sit in the hot water for 15 minutes (no peeking). Transfer the eggs to a bowl of ice water, then peel them, starting by cracking the skinny pointed end and peeling down from there.

Blended Iced Mocha

SERVES: 8 • **SERVING SIZE:** 1 1/8 CUPS

12 teaspoons instant coffee, regular or decaf
4 cups nonfat milk
8 tablespoons chocolate syrup, or more to taste
4 teaspoons unsweetened cocoa powder
4 packets Splenda, or use Equal or 4 teaspoons sugar

1. Blend all the ingredients with 8 cups of ice cubes in a standing blender until smooth. Enjoy immediately! Chococcino (great for kids): Follow directions above but omit the coffee and sweetener and double the chocolate syrup.

FLAVOR BOOSTER
Add some fresh ground pepper, lemon-pepper seasoning, or hot pepper sauce to the wraps before rolling them up.

NUTRITIONAL INFORMATION | CRUNCHY VEGGIE WRAPS:

EXCHANGES / CHOICES:
2 Starch; 1 Protein, lean; 1 1/2 Fat

Calories: 250; Calories from Fat: 100; Total Fat: 11 g;
Saturated Fat: 2.6 g; Trans Fat: 0 g; Cholesterol: 5 mg;
Sodium: 425 mg; Potassium: 420 mg; Total Carbohydrate: 32 g;
Dietary Fiber: 7 g; Sugar: 4 g; Protein: 7 g; Phosphorus: 225 mg

NUTRITIONAL INFORMATION | HARD-BOILED EGGS:

EXCHANGES / CHOICES:
1 Protein, medium fat

Calories: 70; Calories from Fat: 45; Total Fat: 5 g;
Saturated Fat: 1.6 g; Trans Fat: 0 g; Cholesterol: 185 mg;
Sodium: 70 mg; Potassium: 70 mg; Total Carbohydrate: 0 g;
Dietary Fiber: 0 g; Sugar: 0 g; Protein: 6 g; Phosphorus: 100 mg

NUTRITIONAL INFORMATION | BLENDED ICED MOCHA:

EXCHANGES / CHOICES:
1/2 Milk, fat-free; 1/2 Carbohydrate

Calories: 60; Calories from Fat: 0; Total Fat: 0 g;
Saturated Fat: 0.1 g; Trans Fat: 0 g; Cholesterol: 0 mg;
Sodium: 110 mg; Potassium: 275 mg; Total Carbohydrate: 11 g;
Dietary Fiber: 1 g; Sugar: 7 g; Protein: 5 g; Phosphorus: 140 mg

These fresh Greek flavors complement a textured pasta like ruffles or cavatelli. You can also enjoy this cold as a pasta salad. If you think your kids are unlikely to enjoy feta cheese and lemony noodles, remove some of the pasta before adding the stronger-flavored ingredients. Serve with Green Salad with Grapes, Pistachio Nuts, and Maple-Dijon Dressing.

Ruffled Noodles with Spinach, Feta Cheese, and Tomatoes

PREP + COOK: 30 MINUTES • **SERVES:** 8 • **SERVING SIZE:** 1 1/2 CUPS

16 ounces whole-wheat ruffles or radiator; or cavatelli-shaped pasta

12 ounces baby spinach

2 tablespoons extra-virgin olive oil

1 tablespoon capers, or use 1/4 cup pitted kalamata olives

2 tomatoes, diced

1/2 lemon, juice only (about 2 tablespoons), or use 1 tablespoon white wine vinegar

4 ounces crumbled feta cheese

2 teaspoons fresh oregano, or use 1/2 teaspoon dried

1/4 cup fresh flat-leaf parsley, chopped, or more to taste

DO AHEAD OR DELEGATE: Cook the pasta and store tossed with a little oil to prevent sticking, dice the tomatoes, chop the parsley, juice the lemon, or fully prepare and refrigerate the dish.

1. Cook the pasta according to the package directions, in salted water. (Meanwhile, prepare the salad, if you are serving it.) A minute before the pasta is done cooking, add the spinach to the water.

2. Remove about 1/2 cup of the cooking water, then drain both the pasta and the spinach and return to the pot. Gently stir in the remaining ingredients and serve immediately, or refrigerate for up to 2 days. (If noodles are too dry, stir in some or all of the reserved cooking water.)

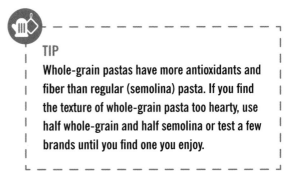

TIP

Whole-grain pastas have more antioxidants and fiber than regular (semolina) pasta. If you find the texture of whole-grain pasta too hearty, use half whole-grain and half semolina or test a few brands until you find one you enjoy.

- -

Green Salad with Grapes, Pistachio Nuts, and Maple-Dijon Dressing

SERVES: 8 • **SERVING SIZE:** 1 CUP

1 head lettuce, chopped
1/2 cup seedless grapes, halved
1/4 cup shelled pistachio nuts, toasted, if desired
1/4 cup extra-virgin olive oil
1/8 cup balsamic vinegar, or use red wine vinegar
1 tablespoon pure maple syrup
1 teaspoon Dijon mustard
1/4 teaspoon herbes de Provence or thyme

1. In a large bowl, combine the lettuce, grapes, and pistachio nuts. To make the dressing, whisk together the oil, vinegar, maple syrup, mustard, and herbes de Provence or thyme. Refrigerate any remaining dressing for future use.

FLAVOR BOOSTER
Use the optional capers or olives, add extra lemon juice, season with plenty of freshly ground black pepper.

NUTRITIONAL INFORMATION | RUFFLED NOODLES WITH SPINACH, FETA CHEESE, AND TOMATOES:

EXCHANGES / CHOICES:
2 1/2 Starch; 1 Nonstarchy Vegetable; 1 1/2 Fat

Calories: 295; Calories from Fat: 70; Total Fat: 8 g;
Saturated Fat: 2.8 g; Trans Fat: 0.1 g; Cholesterol: 15 mg;
Sodium: 250 mg; Potassium: 405 mg; Total Carbohydrate: 45 g;
Dietary Fiber: 7 g; Sugar: 3 g; Protein: 13 g; Phosphorus: 190 mg

NUTRITIONAL INFORMATION | GREEN SALAD WITH GRAPES, PISTACHIO NUTS, AND MAPLE-DIJON DRESSING:

EXCHANGES / CHOICES:
1/2 Carbohydrate; 1 1/2 Fat

Calories: 110; Calories from Fat: 80; Total Fat: 9 g;
Saturated Fat: 1.2 g; Trans Fat: 0 g; Cholesterol: 0 mg;
Sodium: 25 mg; Potassium: 160 mg; Total Carbohydrate: 7 g;
Dietary Fiber: 1 g; Sugar: 5 g; Protein: 2 g; Phosphorus: 35 mg

This is a modern healthy take on a Southern staple, inspired by a recipe from More Quick-Fix Vegan by Robin Robertson that was featured in The Washington Post. To make it more traditional, you can use collard greens and add some smoked ham, but I think your family will love this healthier version. Serve with Fresh Blueberries.

Smoky Beans and Greens over Quick Grits

PREP + COOK: 25 MINUTES • **SERVES:** 5 • **SERVING SIZE:** 1 1/4 CUPS

1 tablespoon extra-virgin olive oil

1 yellow onion, chopped

1 tomato, chopped

4 cups water

1 cup quick-cooking (not instant) grits

1 1/2 teaspoons smoked paprika, divided use

1/2 teaspoon salt

1 tablespoon butter (optional)

8 ounces kale, stemmed and chopped, or use collard greens

1/2 cup reduced-sodium chicken or vegetable broth, or use water and add 1/4 teaspoon salt

15 ounces canned black-eyed peas or great northern beans, drained and rinsed

1/2 cup smoked ham or cooked sausage, chopped (optional)

DO AHEAD OR DELEGATE: Chop the onion, tomato, and the ham or sausage and refrigerate, and stem and chop the kale.

1. Heat a large heavy skillet over medium heat and add the oil. When it is hot, add the onions and sauté for about 3 minutes until they are translucent, then add the tomatoes and continue to sauté for 2 more minutes.

2. Meanwhile, in a large saucepan, bring the water to a boil, and stir in the grits, 1/2–1 teaspoon paprika, to taste (use 1/2 teaspoon if you have picky eaters), and the salt. Stir, reduce the heat, and simmer, stirring occasionally, until the grits are thick and creamy, about 5–7 minutes (check the package directions). Remove from the heat and stir in the butter (optional).

3. To the onions and tomatoes: add the kale, 1/2 teaspoon paprika, and the broth. Cover and cook for about 3 minutes until the kale is wilted. Add the beans and ham or sausage (optional) and continue to sauté for 5 more minutes, stirring occasionally. Add salt and black pepper to taste. Serve the beans and greens over the grits.

SLOW COOKER DIRECTIONS: Combine the onions, tomatoes, kale, broth, peas or beans, and ham or sausage (optional) in the slow cooker. Cook on low for 3–4 hours. Serve over prepared grits. (Slow cooker cooking times may vary—get to know your slow cooker and, if necessary, adjust cooking times accordingly.)

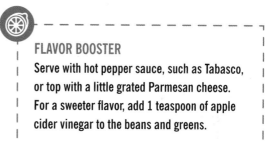

Fresh Blueberries

SERVES: 4 • **SERVING SIZE:** 3/4 CUP

1 1/2 pints fresh blueberries

1. Serve alongside Smoky Beans and Greens over Quick Grits.

FLAVOR BOOSTER

Serve with hot pepper sauce, such as Tabasco, or top with a little grated Parmesan cheese. For a sweeter flavor, add 1 teaspoon of apple cider vinegar to the beans and greens.

TIP

Grits, a breakfast favorite particularly in the South, come from dried corn kernels. There are both quick-cooking varieties (like those suggested here), and types that need to simmer for longer. On their own, grits taste fairly bland, but will absorb the flavors of whatever liquid they're cooked in.

NUTRITIONAL INFORMATION | SMOKY BEANS AND GREENS OVER QUICK GRITS:

EXCHANGES / CHOICES:
2 1/2 Starch; 1 Nonstarchy Vegetable; 1/2 Fat

Calories: 240; Calories from Fat: 35; Total Fat: 4 g;
Saturated Fat: 0.6 g; Trans Fat: 0 g; Cholesterol: 0 mg;
Sodium: 395 mg; Potassium: 460 mg; Total Carbohydrate: 44 g;
Dietary Fiber: 6 g; Sugar: 5 g; Protein: 9 g; Phosphorus: 145 mg

NUTRITIONAL INFORMATION | FRESH BLUEBERRIES:

EXCHANGES / CHOICES:
1 Fruit

Calories: 60; Calories from Fat: 5; Total Fat: 0.5 g;
Saturated Fat: 0 g; Trans Fat: 0 g; Cholesterol: 0 mg;
Sodium: 0 mg; Potassium: 160 mg; Total Carbohydrate: 15 g;
Dietary Fiber: 5 g; Sugar: 9 g; Protein: 1 g; Phosphorus: 20 mg

SUMMER

Chicken and Nectarine Salad with Honey-Lime Dressing (1)
SIDE DISH: Whole-Wheat Crackers (1a)

Grilled Trout Stuffed with Fresh Herbs and Lemon Slices (2)
SIDE DISH: Brown Rice (2a); Grilled Broccoli (2b)

New Mexican Rice Salad (3)
SIDE DISH: Strawberry Banana Smoothie (3a)

We Got the Beet Soup (4)
SIDE DISH: French Bread (4a); Green Salad with Shredded Carrots, Feta Cheese, and Pine Nuts (4b)

Creamy Ricotta Pasta with Cherry Tomatoes (5)
SIDE DISH: Swiss Chard with Garlic (5a)

SHOPPING LIST

🥕 PRODUCE

1 **carrot** (4b)

7–8 **scallions** (1)(3)

1 **yellow onion** (4)

1 **parsnip** (4)

1/2 **red bell pepper** (3)

1 medium **tomato** (3)

16 ounces **cherry or grape tomatoes** (5)

1 small head **lettuce** (4b)

1 head **Swiss chard** (5a)

1/2 cup **fresh basil** (5)

2 tablespoons **fresh rosemary** (2)

3–4 tablespoons **fresh mint leaves** (1)(2)

1 pound **beets** (4)

1–2 heads **broccoli** (2b)

1 **cucumber** (1)(4b)

1 pound **white potatoes** (4)

2 1/2–3 **lemons** (2)(4)

1/2 **lime** (1)

2 cups **strawberries**, fresh or frozen (3a)

2 **bananas** (3a)

3 **nectarines** (1)

🐟 MEAT AND FISH

1 pound **boneless, skinless chicken breasts** (1)

1/2 pound **cooked and diced chicken, sausage, or cooked shrimp** (3)*

4 **whole trout**, cleaned, gutted, heads removed (the fishmonger can do this for you) (2)

🫙 SHELVED ITEMS

1 loaf **French bread** (4a)

1 1/2 cups **quick-cooking brown rice** (2a)

1–1 1/4 cups **quick-cooking brown or wild rice or regular white rice** (3)

16 ounces **whole-wheat spaghetti** (5)

1 package **whole-wheat crackers,** such as Ak-Mak (1a)

4 cups **reduced-sodium chicken or vegetable broth** (4)

3 tablespoons **salsa** (3)

15 ounces **reduced-sodium canned black beans** (3)

15 ounces **corn kernels,** naturally sweetened (3)

3/4 cup **sliced almonds** (1)

1 tablespoon **pine nuts** (4b)

🧂 SPICES

1/2 teaspoon **salt** (1)(5a)

1–1 1/4 teaspoons **kosher salt** (2)(5)

5/8 teaspoon **black pepper** (2)(4)(5)

1/2 teaspoon **ground cumin** (3)

1/2 teaspoon **curry powder** (1)

1 teaspoon **dried dill,** or 1 tablespoon fresh (4)

1/2 teaspoon **ground ginger** (1)

🍾 STAPLES

11–12 tablespoons **extra-virgin olive oil** (1)(2)(2b)(4)(5)(5a)

1/4 cup **vinaigrette dressing** (4b)

2 tablespoons **Italian salad dressing** (3)

2 1/2 teaspoons **minced garlic** (5)(5a)

2 tablespoons **white wine vinegar** (1)

1 tablespoon **honey** (1)

🍦 REFRIGERATED/FROZEN

2 tablespoons **crumbled feta cheese** (4b)

2 tablespoons **shredded Parmesan cheese** (5a)

1 tablespoon **grated Parmesan cheese** (2b)*

1/4 cup **grated Asiago or Parmesan cheese** (5)

1 cup **part-skim ricotta cheese** (5)

1 cup **nonfat plain yogurt or kefir** (3a)

12 tablespoons **plain, fat-free Greek yogurt** (4)

1 cup **orange juice** (3a)

This combination of flavors and textures is delectable, and it's power food for your brain, according to neurosurgeon Larry McCleary, M.D., from whose book, Feed Your Brain, Lose Your Belly, I adapted the recipe. Serve with Whole-Wheat Crackers.

Chicken and Nectarine Salad with Honey-Lime Dressing

PREP + COOK: 30 MINUTES • **SERVES:** 4 • **SERVING SIZE:** 1 1/2 CUPS

1 pound boneless, skinless chicken breasts

1 tablespoon extra-virgin olive oil

3 nectarines, pitted and sliced

1/2 cucumber, peeled, seeded and sliced (1 cup)

3/4 cup sliced almonds

3–4 scallions, thinly sliced, green parts only (1/4 cup)

1–2 tablespoon fresh mint leaves, chopped (optional)

6 tablespoons Honey-Lime Dressing (page 98)

DO AHEAD OR DELEGATE: Slice, cook, and refrigerate the chicken, slice the nectarines, the cucumber, and the scallions, make the salad dressing, chop the mint if using, or fully prepare and refrigerate the salad.

1. Cut each chicken breast crosswise into thin strips. Heat a large skillet over medium to medium-high heat. Add the oil, and when it is hot, sauté the chicken, turning occasionally, until it is browned and cooked through, 5–7 minutes.

2. In a large serving bowl, combine the Honey-Lime Dressing ingredients (page 98). (Alternatively, you can shake them all up in a jar to emulsify them.) Pour the dressing over the salad and toss well to coat. Gently toss in the mint (optional). Refrigerate for at least 15 minutes and up to 2 days. Season the salad with salt and pepper to taste at the table.

FLAVOR BOOSTER
Add a little lime zest to the dressing and/or use the optional mint.

Whole-Wheat Crackers

SERVES: 6 • **SERVING SIZE:** 2 CRACKERS

12 whole-wheat crackers, such as Ak-Mak or Finn Crisp

1. Serve crackers alongside Chicken and Nectarine Salad with Honey-Lime Dressing.

TIP

Mint has been found to have a myriad of health benefits. Its healing properties are good for the digestive tract and for nasal symptoms associated with allergies. Peppermint can relieve some headache symptoms. Fresh mint is not only delicious in salads and smoothies, but is great in hot and iced teas.

NUTRITIONAL INFORMATION | CHICKEN AND NECTARINE SALAD (NUTRITION FOR SALAD ONLY):

EXCHANGES / CHOICES:
1 Fruit; 1/2 Carbohydrate; 4 Protein, lean; 2 Fat

Calories: 305; Calories from Fat: 135; Total Fat: 15 g; Saturated Fat: 1.9 g; Trans Fat: 0 g; Cholesterol: 65 mg; Sodium: 60 mg; Potassium: 585 mg; Total Carbohydrate: 16 g; Dietary Fiber: 4 g; Sugar: 10 g; Protein: 29 g; Phosphorus: 290 mg

NUTRITIONAL INFORMATION | WHOLE-WHEAT CRACKERS:

EXCHANGES / CHOICES:
1/2 Starch

Calories: 45; Calories from Fat: 10; Total Fat: 1 g; Saturated Fat: 0.1 g; Trans Fat: 0 g; Cholesterol: 0 mg; Sodium: 90 mg; Potassium: 40 mg; Total Carbohydrate: 8 g; Dietary Fiber: 2 g; Sugar: 0 g; Protein: 2 g; Phosphorus: 40 mg

This terrific recipe was suggested by my friend and food writer April Fulton. I love making trout on the grill or in the oven—it always tastes wonderful, never too fishy, and adapts to a variety of flavors and preparation techniques. What makes it even better is that trout is on the 'eco-best' list of the Environmental Defense Fund's Oceans Alive project. Serve with Brown Rice and Grilled Broccoli.

Grilled Trout with Fresh Herbs and Lemon Slices

PREP + COOK: 20 MINUTES • **SERVES:** 4 • **SERVING SIZE:** 1 TROUT

2 tablespoons fresh mint,
    finely chopped

2 tablespoons fresh rosemary,
    finely chopped

2 lemons

4 whole trout (about 7 ounces),
    cleaned, gutted, and heads removed
    (the fishmonger can do this for you)

1 tablespoon extra-virgin olive oil

1/2 teaspoon kosher salt

1/4 teaspoon black pepper

DO AHEAD OR DELEGATE: Zest and juice the lemons.

1. Preheat the grill to medium heat and oil the grates to prevent the fish from sticking. (Alternatively, bake the trout at 400°F for about 25 minutes.) In a small bowl, combine the chopped herbs, the zest of 1 1/2 lemons, and the juice of 1 lemon. Cut the other lemon into thin slices.

2. (Start the rice and broccoli now, if you are serving them.) Lay the trout on a cutting board, skin side up, and brush the skin with olive oil to coat. Flip the fish and rub the lemon-herb mixture over the flesh of the trout, season with the salt and pepper, and lay the lemon slices on top of one half of each trout. Close the trout around the herbs and lemon slices, and transfer the fish to the grill.

3. Grill the fish with the lid closed, without flipping, for 8 minutes or until the flesh is opaque and flaky. Using a spatula, carefully transfer the trout to a plate to serve. Garnish the plate with a few fresh mint leaves and sprigs of rosemary, if desired.

FLAVOR BOOSTER
Season the fish with freshly ground black pepper or lemon-pepper seasoning at the table.

SLOW COOKER DIRECTIONS: Place each piece of fish on an individual piece of foil, stuff each with the spices and lemon. Close the trout around the herbs and lemon slices, and fold the foil into a packet to completely surround the fish. Place the packets in the slow cooker and cook on low for 8–10 hours or on high for 4–5 hours. (Slow cooker cooking times may vary—get to know your slow cooker and, if necessary, adjust cooking times accordingly.)

NUTRITIONAL INFORMATION | GRILLED TROUT WITH FRESH HERBS AND LEMON SLICES:

EXCHANGES / CHOICES:
1/2 Carbohydrate; 4 Protein, lean; 1 Fat

Calories: 240; Calories from Fat: 110; Total Fat: 12 g;
Saturated Fat: 2 g; Trans Fat: 0 g; Cholesterol: 80 mg;
Sodium: 305 mg; Potassium: 570 mg; Total Carbohydrate: 5 g;
Dietary Fiber: 2 g; Sugar: 1 g; Protein: 29 g; Phosphorus: 340 mg

NUTRITIONAL INFORMATION | BROWN RICE:

EXCHANGES / CHOICES:
1 1/2 Starch

Calories: 115; Calories from Fat: 10; Total Fat: 1 g;
Saturated Fat: 0.2 g; Trans Fat: 0 g; Cholesterol: 0 mg;
Sodium: 5 mg; Potassium: 45 mg; Total Carbohydrate: 24 g;
Dietary Fiber: 2 g; Sugar: 0 g; Protein: 3 g; Phosphorus: 85 mg

NUTRITIONAL INFORMATION | GRILLED BROCCOLI:

EXCHANGES / CHOICES:
1 Nonstarchy Vegetable; 1 Fat

Calories: 65; Calories from Fat: 35; Total Fat: 4 g;
Saturated Fat: 0.7 g; Trans Fat: 0 g; Cholesterol: 0 mg;
Sodium: 50 mg; Potassium: 290 mg; Total Carbohydrate: 6 g;
Dietary Fiber: 2 g; Sugar: 2 g; Protein: 3 g; Phosphorus: 70 mg

SIDE DISHES

Brown Rice

SERVES: 4 • **SERVING SIZE:** 1/2 CUP

1 1/2 cups quick-cooking brown rice

1. Prepare the rice according to the package directions.

Grilled Broccoli

SERVES: 4 • **SERVING SIZE:** 4 SPEARS

1 pound broccoli, cut into 16 long spears
1 tablespoon extra-virgin olive oil
1 tablespoon grated Parmesan cheese

1. Toss or brush the broccoli with the oil. Grill the spears on medium to medium-high heat, directly on the grill or on a vegetable tray or aluminum foil, flipping once (use tongs), until they are lightly browned, about 10 minutes. Toss the grilled broccoli with the Parmesan cheese.

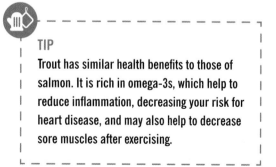

TIP
Trout has similar health benefits to those of salmon. It is rich in omega-3s, which help to reduce inflammation, decreasing your risk for heart disease, and may also help to decrease sore muscles after exercising.

This colorful salad is a good one to make ahead of time for a busy night or to bring to a picnic. You can also serve it warm, wrapped in tortillas. Serve with Strawberry Banana Smoothies.

New Mexican Rice Salad

MARINATE: 30 MINUTES • **PREP + COOK:** 30 MINUTES • **SERVES:** 6 • **SERVING SIZE:** 2 CUPS

1–1 1/4 cups quick-cooking brown or wild rice or regular white rice (2 cups cooked rice)

15 ounces canned black beans, drained and rinsed

15 ounces canned corn kernels, or 1 1/2 cups fresh or frozen corn kernels, thawed if frozen

4 scallions, thinly sliced (green and most of the white parts)

1 medium tomato, seeded and diced (about 1 cup)

1/2 red bell pepper, chopped (about 1/2 cup)

2 tablespoons vinaigrette dressing, or use 1 1/2 tablespoon olive oil and 1 1/2 teaspoon red wine vinegar

3 tablespoons salsa

1/2 teaspoon ground cumin

1/2 pound cooked and diced chicken, sausage, or cooked shrimp

DO AHEAD OR DELEGATE: Cook the rice, defrost the corn if necessary, slice the scallions, seed and dice the tomato, chop the bell pepper, combine the salad dressing, salsa, and cumin, cook the chicken, sausage, or shrimp, or fully prepare and refrigerate the dish.

1. Cook the rice according to package directions.

2. While the rice is cooking, in a large bowl, combine the beans, corn, scallions, tomatoes, and peppers. In a small bowl, combine the salad dressing, salsa, and cumin.

3. When the rice is cooked, add it to the ingredients in the large bowl, and toss everything with the dressing. Mix in the chicken, sausage, or shrimp. Chill for at least 30 minutes, if time allows, or up to 3 days, until you are ready to serve. (Meanwhile, prepare and refrigerate the smoothies, if you are serving them.)

FLAVOR BOOSTER
Stir in a little extra salsa or some fresh lime juice.

Strawberry Banana Smoothies

SERVES: 6 • **SERVING SIZE:** 1 CUP

4 cups strawberries, fresh or frozen
2 bananas
1 cup orange juice
1 cup nonfat plain yogurt or kefir
1 cup ice

1. In a blender, puree the strawberries, bananas, orange juice, yogurt, and ice, and serve immediately. For an extra nutritional boost, add a handful of spinach or kale.

TIP

To cook dried beans in a slow cooker: Put the beans in the slow cooker and cover with water. Add seasonings as desired. For 1 pound of beans, I recommend 1–2 teaspoons of salt and 1–2 teaspoons of other spices like chili powder, cumin, garlic powder (make sure it doesn't have added salt), paprika, or black pepper, if desired. Cook on low for 7–10 hours until the beans are tender. Drain and freeze or refrigerate in 1 1/2–cup increments, which is about the amount of beans in one 15 ounce can (measure the beans before freezing because they are very hard to separate when frozen.)

NUTRITIONAL INFORMATION | NEW MEXICAN RICE SALAD:

EXCHANGES / CHOICES:
2 Starch; 2 Protein, lean

Calories: 235; Calories from Fat: 45; Total Fat: 5 g;
Saturated Fat: 1.1 g; Trans Fat: 0 g; Cholesterol: 35 mg;
Sodium: 185 mg; Potassium: 475 mg; Total Carbohydrate: 31 g;
Dietary Fiber: 6 g; Sugar: 4 g; Protein: 17 g; Phosphorus: 210 mg

NUTRITIONAL INFORMATION | STRAWBERRY BANANA SMOOTHIES:

EXCHANGES / CHOICES:
1 1/2 Fruit

Calories: 105; Calories from Fat: 5; Total Fat: 0.5 g;
Saturated Fat: 0.1 g; Trans Fat: 0 g; Cholesterol: 0 mg;
Sodium: 25 mg; Potassium: 475 mg; Total Carbohydrate: 24 g;
Dietary Fiber: 3 g; Sugar: 16 g; Protein: 3 g; Phosphorus: 100 mg

My dear friend Jessica Honigberg, whose daughter is a vegetarian like my daughter, told me about a beet and potato soup she had made that her daughter loved. When my CSA delivered beets and potatoes that same week, I had to try making my own version. Serve with French Bread and Green Salad with Shredded Carrots, Feta Cheese, and Pine Nuts.

We Got the Beet Soup

PREP: 20 MINUTES • **COOK:** 25 MINUTES • **SERVES:** 6 • **SERVING SIZE:** 2 CUPS

1 tablespoon extra-virgin olive oil

1 yellow onion, chopped

1 pound beets, peeled and chopped (about 4 beets)

1 pound white potatoes, peeled and chopped (about 2 potatoes)

1 parsnip, peeled and chopped

1 teaspoon dried dill, or 1 tablespoon fresh

1/4 teaspoon black pepper

4 cups reduced-sodium chicken or vegetable broth

1/2–1 lemon, juice only, to taste

12 tablespoons plain, fat-free Greek yogurt

DO AHEAD OR DELEGATE: Chop the onion, peel and chop the beets, potatoes, and parsnip, and juice the lemon.

1. Heat a medium stockpot over medium-high heat. When it is hot, add the oil, and when the oil is hot, add the onions. Sauté for about 3 minutes until onions are tender. Add the beets, potatoes, parsnips, dill, pepper, and broth, cover and bring it to a boil. Reduce the heat to a simmer, covered, and cook for 25 minutes until the vegetables are very tender. (Meanwhile, warm the bread and make the salad, if you are serving them.)

2. Puree the soup with an immersion blender or a standing blender until it is smooth. Return it to the pot, if necessary, and stir in the lemon juice. (At this point you can serve it immediately or refrigerate the soup for up to 3 days.) Top the bowls of soup with the Greek yogurt and additional pepper, and garnish with additional dill, if desired.

SLOW COOKER DIRECTIONS: Combine all items except the lemon and yogurt in the slow cooker and cook on low for 8–12 hours or on high for 4–5 hours. Puree, stir in the lemon juice, and serve as directed. (Slow cooker cooking times may vary—get to know your slow cooker and, if necessary, adjust cooking times accordingly.)

FLAVOR BOOSTER
Top the soup with additional dill.

NUTRITIONAL INFORMATION | WE GOT THE BEET SOUP:

EXCHANGES / CHOICES:
1 Starch; 2 Nonstarchy Vegetable; 1/2 Fat

Calories: 145; Calories from Fat: 20; Total Fat: 2.5 g;
Saturated Fat: 0.4 g; Trans Fat: 0 g; Cholesterol: 0 mg;
Sodium: 400 mg; Potassium: 620 mg; Total Carbohydrate: 24 g;
Dietary Fiber: 4 g; Sugar: 8 g; Protein: 7 g; Phosphorus: 125 mg

NUTRITIONAL INFORMATION | FRENCH BREAD:

EXCHANGES / CHOICES:
1 Starch

Calories: 80; Calories from Fat: 5; Total Fat: 0.5 g;
Saturated Fat: 0.1 g; Trans Fat: 0 g; Cholesterol: 0 mg;
Sodium: 145 mg; Potassium: 35 mg; Total Carbohydrate: 16 g;
Dietary Fiber: 1 g; Sugar: 1 g; Protein: 3 g; Phosphorus: 30 mg

NUTRITIONAL INFORMATION | GREEN SALAD WITH SHREDDED
CARROTS, FETA CHEESE, AND PINE NUTS:

EXCHANGES / CHOICES:
1 Nonstarchy Vegetable; 1 Fat

Calories: 75; Calories from Fat: 55; Total Fat: 6 g;
Saturated Fat: 1.1 g; Trans Fat: 0 g; Cholesterol: 5 mg;
Sodium: 75 mg; Potassium: 190 mg; Total Carbohydrate: 5 g;
Dietary Fiber: 1 g; Sugar: 3 g; Protein: 2 g; Phosphorus: 45 mg

SIDE DISHES

French Bread

SERVES: 6 • **SERVING SIZE:** 1 OUNCES SLICE

1 loaf French bread, sliced

1. Warm the bread in a 300°F oven for 5–8 minutes, if desired.

Green Salad with Shredded Carrots, Feta Cheese, and Pine Nuts

SERVES: 6 • **SERVING SIZE:** 1 1/3 CUPS

1 medium head lettuce, torn or chopped
1 carrot, shredded (about 1/2 cup)
2 tablespoons crumbled feta cheese
1 tablespoon pine nuts, toasted, if desired
1/2 medium cucumber, diced
1/4 cup Orange Balsamic Vinaigrette (page 16)

1. In a large bowl, combine the lettuce, carrots, cheese, pine nuts, and cucumber. Toss the salad with dressing to taste.

TIP

If you've got extra lemons or limes sitting around and don't want that flavorful juice to go to waste before they go bad, freeze them. (Yes, you can freeze them!) Just cut them into quarters and put them in a single layer on a baking sheet. Place them in the freezer until frozen. Once frozen, you can place them in a freezer-safe bag and remove and use as needed.

I made this dish for the first time with our neighbor Gillian Ford when she was 10. She and her sister Charlotte, who was 11 at the time, thought this was one of the best pasta dishes they had ever had! Serve with Swiss Chard with Garlic.

Creamy Ricotta Pasta with Cherry Tomatoes

PREP + COOK: 30 MINUTES • **SERVES:** 8 • **SERVING SIZE:** 1 1/2 CUPS

16 ounces whole-wheat spaghetti, broken in half

16 ounces cherry or grape tomatoes, halved

1 1/2 teaspoons minced garlic (2–3 cloves)

4 tablespoons extra-virgin olive oil, divided use

1/2 teaspoon kosher salt

1 cup part-skim ricotta cheese

1/4 cup grated Asiago or Parmesan cheese

1/2 cup fresh basil, sliced (or use mostly basil and a little fresh oregano, if you have it)

1/8 teaspoon black pepper, or to taste (optional)

DO AHEAD OR DELEGATE: Cook the spaghetti and store tossed with a little oil to prevent sticking, halve the tomatoes, peel the garlic, combine the ingredients for the tomato mixture, and grate the cheese if necessary.

1. Cook the spaghetti according to the package directions until it is al dente, and drain, reserving 1/2 cup of the pasta's cooking water. (Start the Swiss chard now, if you are serving it.)

2. Meanwhile, in a large serving bowl, combine the tomatoes, garlic, 3 tablespoons oil, and the salt, and set aside.

3. When you drain the noodles, immediately transfer the tomato mixture to the pasta pot and cook over medium heat for 1–2 minutes until the tomatoes are hot and slightly softened. Meanwhile, put the pasta in the serving bowl and toss with 1 tablespoon olive oil, the ricotta cheese, the Asiago or Parmesan cheese, and the basil. (If the pasta is a little dry at this point, add a splash of the reserved cooking water.)

4. Top the spaghetti with the tomato mixture and serve immediately, topped with freshly ground black pepper, if desired.

FLAVOR BOOSTER
Double the garlic and serve the pasta sprinkled with crushed red pepper flakes, and/or add 1–2 teaspoons balsamic vinegar with the oil.

Swiss Chard with Garlic

SERVES: 8 • **SERVING SIZE:** 2/3 CUP

1 tablespoon extra-virgin olive oil
1 teaspoon minced garlic (about 2 cloves)
1 head Swiss chard, coarsely chopped
1/4 teaspoon salt
2 tablespoons shredded Parmesan cheese

1. Heat the oil over medium heat in a large nonstick skillet and add the garlic. After 30 seconds to 1 minute, when the garlic starts to brown, add the Swiss chard and 1/4 cup water. Cover and reduce the heat, if necessary, to steam the chard for about 10 minutes. Remove the cover, raise the heat to medium, and let the chard cook, stirring occasionally, until it is very tender, about 10 more minutes. Top with the salt and cheese before serving.

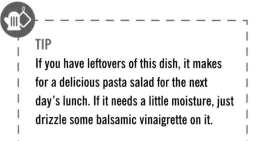

TIP
If you have leftovers of this dish, it makes for a delicious pasta salad for the next day's lunch. If it needs a little moisture, just drizzle some balsamic vinaigrette on it.

NUTRITIONAL INFORMATION | CREAMY RICOTTA PASTA WITH CHERRY TOMATOES:

EXCHANGES / CHOICES:
3 Starch; 1 Protein, lean; 1 Fat

Calories: 330; Calories from Fat: 100; Total Fat: 11 g;
Saturated Fat: 3 g; Trans Fat: 0 g; Cholesterol: 10 mg;
Sodium: 185 mg; Potassium: 245 mg; Total Carbohydrate: 45 g;
Dietary Fiber: 7 g; Sugar: 3 g; Protein: 14 g; Phosphorus: 195 mg

NUTRITIONAL INFORMATION | SWISS CHARD WITH GARLIC:

EXCHANGES / CHOICES:
1 Nonstarchy Vegetable; 1/2 Fat

Calories: 40; Calories from Fat: 20; Total Fat: 2 g;
Saturated Fat: 0.4 g; Trans Fat: 0 g; Cholesterol: 0 mg;
Sodium: 145 mg; Potassium: 380 mg; Total Carbohydrate: 4 g;
Dietary Fiber: 2 g; Sugar: 1 g; Protein: 2 g; Phosphorus: 55 mg

SUMMER

Cashew Garlic Chicken or Tofu with Sugar Snap Peas (1)
SIDE DISH: Brown Rice (1a)

Salmon Salad Melts with Havarti (2)
SIDE DISH: Cantaloupe (2a)

Indian Chickpeas with Spinach and Potatoes (3)
SIDE DISH: Curried Carrots with Dill (3a)

Cobb Salad with Bacon, Avocado, and Blue Cheese (4)
SIDE DISH: Whole-Grain Bread (4a)

Zucchini Noodles (Zoodles) with White Beans, Pesto, and Olives (5)
SIDE DISH: Corn on the Cob (5a)

SHOPPING LIST

🥕 PRODUCE

7–9 **carrots** (1)(3a)

1 **shallot** (2)

1 1/2 **yellow onions** (1)(3)

1 **red bell pepper** (3)

2 stalks **celery** (2)

2 **tomatoes** (4)

1 cup **cherry tomatoes** (5)

1 small head **romaine lettuce** (4)

5 cloves **garlic** (1)

1 tablespoon **fresh dill** (2)

2–3 **zucchini** (5)

1 **Yukon Gold or white potato** (3)

6 ears **fresh corn** (5a)

8 ounces **sugar snap peas** (1)

1 **avocado** (4)

1 1/2 **lemons** (2)(3)

1/2 **lime** (5a)*

1 **cantaloupe** (2a)

2 cups **fresh or frozen corn kernels** (4)

🐟 MEAT AND FISH

1 pound **boneless, skinless chicken breast or extra-firm tofu** (1)

4 slices **turkey bacon, or use pork or vegetarian bacon** (4)

SHELVED ITEMS

6 slices **whole-wheat bread** (2)

1 loaf **whole-grain bread** (4a)

1 1/2 cups **quick-cooking brown rice** (1a)

2 tablespoons **hoisin sauce** (sold with Asian foods) (1)

1 tablespoon **rice vinegar** (1)

1 tablespoon **mango chutney** (1)

15 ounces **canned white beans** (5)

15 ounces **canned chickpeas** (garbanzo beans) (3)

15 ounces **canned wild salmon** (2)

1/2 cup **pitted kalamata olives** (5)

1–3 teaspoons **capers** (2)

2 tablespoons **raisins** (3)

2 tablespoons **toasted pine nuts** (5)

1/2 cup **unsalted cashews** (1)

1 1/2 cups **no-salt-added black beans** (4)

1 tablespoon **Dijon mustard** (4)

SPICES

1/2 teaspoon **salt** (3)(3a)(5a)

1/8 teaspoon **black pepper** (3)

1 teaspoon **ground cumin** (3)

1 tablespoon + 1/2 teaspoon **curry powder** (3)(3a)

1/2 teaspoon **chili powder** (5a)*

1/2 teaspoon **dried or fresh dill** (3a)

STAPLES

2 teaspoons **butter** (5a)

1/4 cup + 2 teaspoons **extra-virgin olive oil** (3a)(4)

1 tablespoon **vegetable oil** (3)

1 tablespoon **canola or vegetable oil** (1)

1/4 cup **reduced-fat mayonnaise** (2)

1/8 cup **balsamic vinegar** (4)

1 1/2 tablespoons **reduced-sodium soy sauce** (use wheat/gluten-free if needed) (1)

2 hard-boiled **eggs** (4)

1 tablespoon **cornstarch** (1)

REFRIGERATED/FROZEN

3 tablespoons **crumbled blue cheese** (4)

1/2 cup + 1 tablespoon **shredded reduced-fat Havarti cheese** (2)

1 cup **plain nonfat yogurt** (3)*

1/2 cup **pesto sauce** (5)

10 ounces **frozen chopped spinach** (3)

1/8 cup **orange juice** (4)

Get free, printable versions of the shopping lists from this book at TheScramble.com/diabetes.

*optional ingredients

SUMMER WEEK 3 • 127

I never seem to make a stir-fry sauce the same way twice. That flexibility is one of the fun things about making a stir-fry. You can switch out the ingredients based on what you have in your 'fridge or what you like most. If you don't like your sauce a little sweet, replace one of the tablespoons of hoisin sauce with soy sauce. Serve with Brown Rice.

Cashew Garlic Chicken or Tofu with Sugar Snap Peas

PREP + COOK: 30 MINUTES • **SERVES:** 4 • **SERVING SIZE:** 1 1/2 CUPS

1 pound boneless, skinless chicken breast or use extra-firm tofu, drained and cut into 1-inch pieces

1 tablespoon cornstarch

1 tablespoon canola or vegetable oil

1 1/2 tablespoons reduced-sodium soy sauce (use wheat/gluten-free if needed)

1/2 cup unsalted cashews, toasted

5 cloves garlic, thinly sliced

1/2 yellow onion, chopped

3 carrots, halved lengthwise and sliced

8 ounces sugar snap peas

2 tablespoons hoisin sauce

1 tablespoon rice vinegar

1 tablespoon mango chutney (sold with Indian foods), or use apricot jam or orange marmalade

DO AHEAD OR DELEGATE: Cut the chicken and refrigerate, toast the cashews, slice the garlic, chop the onion, halve and slice the carrots, combine the soy sauce, hoisin sauce, vinegar, and chutney.

1. (Start the rice first, if you are serving it.) In a medium bowl, toss the chicken with the cornstarch to coat.

2. In a large nonstick skillet or wok, heat the oil over medium-high heat. When it is hot, add the chicken and cook for 3–4 minutes until just cooked through, drizzling with 1 tablespoon soy sauce about 1 minute before it is fully cooked. Meanwhile, toast the cashews. Using a slotted spoon or spatula, transfer the chicken to a clean bowl and set it aside, leaving any remaining oil in the pan.

3. Add the garlic, onions, and carrots to the pan and sauté for about 2 minutes, then add the sugar snap peas and cook for 3 more minutes until tender-crisp.

4. In a small bowl, combine the remaining soy sauce, hoisin sauce, vinegar, and chutney.

5. Add the chicken and cashews to the skillet, then add the soy sauce mixture, and stir-fry until it is heated through. Serve immediately over steamed rice, if desired, refrigerate for up to 3 days, or freeze for up to 3 months.

Brown Rice

SERVES: 4 • **SERVING SIZE:** 1/2 CUP

1 1/2 cups quick-cooking brown rice

1. Prepare the rice according to the package directions.

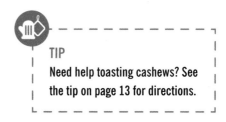

TIP
Need help toasting cashews? See the tip on page 13 for directions.

FLAVOR BOOSTER
Serve with extra soy sauce or some Asian chili garlic sauce.

NUTRITIONAL INFORMATION | CASHEW GARLIC CHICKEN OR TOFU
WITH SUGAR SNAP PEAS:

EXCHANGES / CHOICES:
1 Carbohydrate; 2 Nonstarchy Vegetable; 4 Protein, lean; 1 1/2 Fat

Calories: 360; Calories from Fat: 135; Total Fat: 15 g;
Saturated Fat: 2.7 g; Trans Fat: 0 g; Cholesterol: 65 mg;
Sodium: 450 mg; Potassium: 590 mg; Total Carbohydrate: 27 g;
Dietary Fiber: 4 g; Sugar: 11 g; Protein: 30 g; Phosphorus: 330 mg

NUTRITIONAL INFORMATION | BROWN RICE:

EXCHANGES / CHOICES:
1 1/2 Starch

Calories: 115; Calories from Fat: 10; Total Fat: 1 g;
Saturated Fat: 0.2 g; Trans Fat: 0 g; Cholesterol: 0 mg;
Sodium: 5 mg; Potassium: 45 mg; Total Carbohydrate: 24 g;
Dietary Fiber: 2 g; Sugar: 0 g; Protein: 3 g; Phosphorus: 85 mg

I've always been a sucker for tuna melts, ever since my mom used to make them for me, and now my son feels the same way about them. I decided to mix it up with canned salmon, which is even healthier in many ways. The results were just as satisfying as the classic tuna melt. Serve with Cantaloupe.

Salmon Salad Melts with Havarti

PREP + COOK: 20 MINUTES • **SERVES:** 6 • **SERVING SIZE:** 1 MELT

15 ounces canned wild salmon, drained

1/4 cup reduced-fat mayonnaise

2 stalks celery

1 shallot, finely diced

1 tablespoon fresh dill, finely chopped, or use 1 teaspoon dried

1 lemon, juice only (about 2 tablespoons)

1–3 teaspoons capers, to taste

6 slices whole-wheat bread

1/2 cup plus 1 tablespoon shredded light or reduced-fat Havarti cheese

DO AHEAD OR DELEGATE: Slice the celery, dice the shallot, chop the dill, juice the lemon, or fully prepare and refrigerate the salmon salad.

1. Preheat the broiler and line a baking sheet with aluminum foil or spray it with nonstick cooking spray.

2. In a mixing bowl, combine the salmon, mayonnaise, celery, shallots, dill, and lemon juice and mix thoroughly. Gently fold in the capers.

3. Lightly toast the bread. Spread a large spoonful of the salmon salad on each piece of toast and top with about 1 1/2 tablespoons of cheese. Transfer the sandwiches to the baking sheet and broil them in the oven for 3–5 minutes, or until the cheese is melted and bubbly. (Meanwhile, slice the cantaloupe, if you are serving it.) Slice the sandwiches in half diagonally to serve.

FLAVOR BOOSTER
Use extra capers and mix in 1/2 teaspoon lemon zest and 1/4 teaspoon black pepper.

Cantaloupe

SERVES: 6 • **SERVING SIZE:** 1 CUP

1 large cantaloupe, diced

1. Peel, remove seeds, and cut the cantaloupe into bite-sized pieces. If it needs more flavor, toss it with a little fresh lemon or lime juice.

TIP

Don't be alarmed if you find some salmon skin and bones in your canned salmon. They are cooked along with the meat so they are soft and edible. In fact, the skin and bones are packed with calcium and contain much of the nutritional value of the fish. Just mash it all together well so your family won't notice them.

NUTRITIONAL INFORMATION | SALMON SALAD MELTS WITH HAVARTI:

EXCHANGES / CHOICES:
1 Carbohydrate; 2 Protein, lean; 1/2 Fat

Calories: 180; Calories from Fat: 65; Total Fat: 7 g;
Saturated Fat: 1.9 g; Trans Fat: 0.1 g; Cholesterol: 50 mg;
Sodium: 440 mg; Potassium: 280 mg; Total Carbohydrate: 12 g;
Dietary Fiber: 3 g; Sugar: 2 g; Protein: 19 g; Phosphorus: 230 mg

NUTRITIONAL INFORMATION | CANTALOUPE:

EXCHANGES / CHOICES:
1 Fruit

Calories: 55; Calories from Fat: 0; Total Fat: 0 g;
Saturated Fat: 0.1 g; Trans Fat: 0 g; Cholesterol: 0 mg;
Sodium: 25 mg; Potassium: 415 mg; Total Carbohydrate: 13 g;
Dietary Fiber: 1 g; Sugar: 12 g; Protein: 1 g; Phosphorus: 25 mg

This colorful and flavorful Indian curry is simple to make. If you prefer, use 1 pound of boneless, skinless chicken breast instead of the chickpeas. Serve with Curried Carrots with Dill.

Indian Chickpeas with Spinach and Potatoes

PREP + COOK: 30 MINUTES • **SERVES:** 4 • **SERVING SIZE:** 2 CUPS

1 tablespoon vegetable oil

1 yellow onion, diced

1 Yukon Gold or white potato, peeled and diced into 1/2-inch pieces

10 ounces frozen chopped spinach, or use 6–9 ounces fresh baby spinach

1 red bell pepper, diced

1 teaspoon ground cumin

1 tablespoon curry powder, or to taste

15 ounces canned chickpeas (garbanzo beans), with their liquid

2 tablespoons raisins

1/2 lemon, juice only (about 2 tablespoons)

1/8 teaspoon salt, or to taste

1/8 teaspoon black pepper, or to taste

1 cup plain nonfat yogurt, for serving (optional)

DO AHEAD OR DELEGATE: Dice the onion and the bell pepper, peel and dice the potato and store it covered with water to prevent browning, defrost the spinach, juice the lemon, or fully prepare and refrigerate the dish.

1. In a large heavy skillet, heat the oil over medium heat. Sauté the onions and potatoes, stirring occasionally, until the onions are softened, about 5 minutes.

2. Meanwhile, defrost the spinach, drain thoroughly (press it with a bowl or your hands to squeeze out the extra liquid), and set it aside.

3. To the onions and potatoes in the skillet, add the bell peppers, cumin, and curry powder. Cover and continue to cook for about 5 more minutes. (Meanwhile, start the carrots, if you are serving them.) Stir in the chickpeas and the raisins, and cook for about 5 more minutes, until the potatoes are fork tender. Add the spinach and the lemon juice and heat it through for a couple more minutes (if using fresh spinach, until it is wilted). Season with salt and pepper to taste.

4. Serve immediately, topped with a spoonful of yogurt, if desired, or refrigerate for up to 3 days.

SLOW COOKER DIRECTIONS: Omit the oil. Combine all ingredients except the yogurt in the slow cooker and cook on low for 7–8 hours (or longer if necessary) or on high for 3–4 hours. (Slow cooker cooking times may vary—get to know your slow cooker and, if necessary, adjust cooking times accordingly.)

FLAVOR BOOSTER
Use spicy curry powder and serve with chutney on the side.

Curried Carrots with Dill

SERVES: 4 • **SERVING SIZE:** 3/4 CUP

2 teaspoons extra-virgin olive oil

4–6 carrots, sliced

1/2 teaspoon curry powder

1/2 teaspoon dried or fresh dill, to taste

1/8 teaspoon salt

1. Heat the oil in a small saucepan over medium heat. Add the carrots, curry powder, dill, and salt. Sauté for 2 minutes, stirring occasionally. Cover the pan, reduce the heat, and steam the carrots for about 8 minutes, until just tender when pierced with a fork.

TIP

Raisins, a food that often appeals to both kids and adults, are great for you! The *Journal of Food Science* found that raisins pack a nutritional punch. They can reduce the risk of cardiovascular disease and improve blood sugar control. Sprinkle some raisins into trail mix, cereal, yogurt, or more savory foods like this dish.

NUTRITIONAL INFORMATION | INDIAN CHICKPEAS WITH SPINACH AND POTATOES:

EXCHANGES / CHOICES:
2 Starch; 2 Nonstarchy Vegetable; 1 Fat

Calories: 255; Calories from Fat: 55; Total Fat: 6 g;
Saturated Fat: 0.6 g; Trans Fat: 0 g; Cholesterol: 0 mg;
Sodium: 455 mg; Potassium: 665 mg; Total Carbohydrate: 44 g;
Dietary Fiber: 10 g; Sugar: 11 g; Protein: 9 g; Phosphorus: 170 mg

NUTRITIONAL INFORMATION | CURRIED CARROTS WITH DILL:

EXCHANGES / CHOICES:
1 Nonstarchy Vegetable; 1/2 Fat

Calories: 45; Calories from Fat: 20; Total Fat: 2.5 g;
Saturated Fat: 0.3 g; Trans Fat: 0 g; Cholesterol: 0 mg;
Sodium: 115 mg; Potassium: 205 mg; Total Carbohydrate: 6 g;
Dietary Fiber: 2 g; Sugar: 3 g; Protein: 1 g; Phosphorus: 25 mg

Andrew and I enjoy this hearty and flavorful salad, especially on a warm night. If your kids aren't eating salad yet, you can serve it with extra hard-boiled eggs, and make a little plate for them with elements of the salad for them to taste. Serve with Whole-Grain Bread.

Cobb Salad with Bacon, Avocado, and Blue Cheese

PREP + COOK: 25 MINUTES • **SERVES:** 6 • **SERVING SIZE:** 2 1/2 CUPS

2 hard-boiled eggs, sliced

4 slices turkey bacon, or use pork or vegetarian bacon

1 small head romaine lettuce, chopped (about 8 cups total)

2 tomatoes, chopped

1 avocado, peeled and chopped

3 tablespoons crumbled blue cheese

6 tablespoons Orange Balsamic Vinaigrette (page 16)

2 cups fresh or frozen corn kernels, from 3–4 ears of corn if using fresh

1 1/2 cups no-salt-added black beans, drained and rinsed

DO AHEAD OR DELEGATE: Cook and chop the bacon, hard-boil the eggs, slice and refrigerate the eggs, chop the romaine and the tomatoes, and make the dressing.

1. Hard-boil the eggs, if necessary.

2. Cook the bacon over medium heat in a skillet, turning occasionally, until crisp, about 8 minutes. Remove to a paper towel to drain. Chop or crumble it into small pieces (and warm the bread, if you are serving it).

3. Combine all the ingredients in a large bowl and toss thoroughly.

FLAVOR BOOSTER
Top the salad with plenty of freshly ground black pepper.

Whole-Grain Bread

SERVES: 6 • **SERVING SIZE:** 1 SLICE

6 slices whole-grain bread

1. Warm the bread in a 300°F oven for 5–8 minutes, if desired.

TIP

Eggs are not just for breakfast. Many hearty and healthy meals can be built around eggs, which can easily cost 1/2 the price of meat. You can put fried eggs on sandwiches with cheese and greens, and on top of noodles to make a pasta dish richer and more filling. Scramble eggs with some cooked vegetables, or top with salsa and a spoonful of cheese and wrap in a whole-wheat tortilla. Hard-boiled eggs make a healthy and satisfying snack, just be sure to cook them yourself to save money.

NUTRITIONAL INFORMATION | COBB SALAD WITH BACON, AVOCADO, AND BLUE CHEESE:

EXCHANGES / CHOICES:
1 1/2 Starch; 1 Nonstarchy Vegetable; 1 Protein, lean; 1 Fat

Calories: 215; Calories from Fat: 80; Total Fat: 9 g;
Saturated Fat: 2.4 g; Trans Fat: 0 g; Cholesterol: 70 mg;
Sodium: 215 mg; Potassium: 730 mg; Total Carbohydrate: 26 g;
Dietary Fiber: 7 g; Sugar: 4 g; Protein: 11 g; Phosphorus: 215 mg

NUTRITIONAL INFORMATION | WHOLE-GRAIN BREAD:

EXCHANGES / CHOICES:
1 Starch

Calories: 70; Calories from Fat: 10; Total Fat: 1 g;
Saturated Fat: 0.2 g; Trans Fat: 0 g; Cholesterol: 0 mg;
Sodium: 125 mg; Potassium: 70 mg; Total Carbohydrate: 12 g;
Dietary Fiber: 2 g; Sugar: 1 g; Protein: 3 g; Phosphorus: 60 mg

We have so much fun making zucchini noodles with an awesome little gadget called a Veggetti. I make these at almost all of my cooking demos because people are always amazed how easy they are to make and how great they taste. If you prefer the noodles warm, you can sauté them for 1–2 minutes in a nonstick skillet. Serve with Corn on the Cob.

Zucchini Noodles (Zoodles) with White Beans, Pesto, and Olives

PREP (NO COOK): 10 MINUTES • **SERVES:** 6 • **SERVING SIZE:** 1 1/2 CUPS

2 –3 zucchini (6 cups total)

1/4–1/2 teaspoon salt (optional)

1 (15-ounce) can cannellini beans, drained and rinsed

1/2 cup pesto sauce

1/2 cup pitted kalamata olives, chopped

1 cup cherry tomatoes, quartered

2 tablespoons toasted pine nuts

1. Using a spiral vegetable slicer such as a Veggetti, a food processor, a mandolin, or a box grater turned on its largest side, shred the zucchini lengthwise into long thin strips. If using a spiral vegetable slicer, run a knife a couple of times across the long strips of zucchini so they are shorter and easier to eat. (If you did not use a spiral vegetable slicer and the zucchini seems a little moist, transfer it to a colander, sprinkle it with the salt, and let the zucchini drain for 15–20 minutes, gently pressing the liquid out occasionally.)

2. Transfer the zucchini to a serving bowl, add the beans and pesto, and toss thoroughly. Sprinkle the olives, tomatoes, and pine nuts on top. Serve immediately.

FLAVOR BOOSTER
Top the noodles with freshly grated Parmesan cheese and freshly ground black pepper.

Corn on the Cob

SERVES: 6 • **SERVING SIZE:** 1 EAR

6 ears corn

2 teaspoons butter or margarine

1/4 teaspoon salt

1/2 teaspoon chili powder (optional)

1/2 lime (optional)

1. Steam the corn in the microwave for 3–5 minutes (steam them right in the husks, or remove the husks and sprinkle them with water, partially cover the bowl, and cook on high power) and then toss them in the still-warm bowl with the butter or margarine and the salt before serving. (Note: some people like to cook corn longer, but we prefer it crisp and juicy.) Alternatively, boil or steam it for 2–3 minutes on the stovetop. For a flavor boost, add a few shakes of chili powder and/or a squeeze of lime juice just before serving.

NUTRITIONAL INFORMATION | ZUCCHINI NOODLES (ZOODLES) WITH WHITE BEANS, PESTO, AND OLIVES:

EXCHANGES / CHOICES:
1/2 Starch; 1 Nonstarchy Vegetable; 1 Protein, lean; 2 1/2 Fat

Calories: 220; Calories from Fat: 135; Total Fat: 15 g;
Saturated Fat: 2 g; Trans Fat: 0 g; Cholesterol: 0 mg;
Sodium: 380 mg; Potassium: 575 mg; Total Carbohydrate: 16 g;
Dietary Fiber: 5 g; Sugar: 3 g; Protein: 7 g; Phosphorus: 150 mg

NUTRITIONAL INFORMATION | CORN ON THE COB:

EXCHANGES / CHOICES:
1 1/2 Starch; 1/2 Fat

Calories: 110; Calories from Fat: 25; Total Fat: 3 g;
Saturated Fat: 1 g; Trans Fat: 0.1 g; Cholesterol: 5 mg;
Sodium: 110 mg; Potassium: 225 mg; Total Carbohydrate: 22 g;
Dietary Fiber: 2 g; Sugar: 5 g; Protein: 4 g; Phosphorus: 80 mg

SUMMER

WEEK 4

Grilled Pork and Pineapple Kabobs (1)
SIDE DISH: Whole-Wheat Couscous (1a)

Fresh Corn, Tomato, and Avocado Salad with Shrimp (2)
SIDE DISH: Whole-Wheat Dinner Rolls (2a)

Classic Crunchy Tacos (3)
SIDE DISH: Homemade Ranch Dressing with Carrots and Broccoli (3a)

Eggplant Caponata Stew (4)
SIDE DISH: Farro (4a)

Pasta with White Beans, Tomatoes, and Basil (5)
SIDE DISH: Spinach Salad with Mushrooms, Onions, and Parmesan Cheese (5a)

SHOPPING LIST

🥕 PRODUCE
1/2 pound **carrots** (3a)
1 **shallot** (4)
1 tablespoon **fresh chives** (3a)
1/2 **yellow or red onion** (5a)
1 **red bell pepper** (1)
1 **green bell pepper** (4)
2 **tomatoes** (4)
2 cups **cherry tomatoes** (2)
1/2 head **iceberg lettuce** (3)
12 ounces **baby spinach** (5a)
1 tablespoon **fresh ginger** (1)
3/4 cup **fresh basil** (2)(4)
10 fresh **basil leaves** (5)
1 tablespoon **fresh flat-leaf parsley** (4a)*
1 pound **Japanese eggplants or regular eggplant** (4)
1 **zucchini or yellow squash** (4)
2 ears **fresh corn** (2)
2 cups **sliced mushrooms** (5a)
2 **avocados** (2)

🍞 MEAT AND FISH
1 pound **lean ground turkey or vegetarian ground meat** (3)
1 pound **medium or large shrimp**, peeled and deveined (2)
1 pound **boneless pork center cut loin or tenderloin** (1)

🗄 SHELVED ITEMS

1 package **whole-wheat dinner rolls** (2a)

1–2 cups **whole-wheat couscous** (1a)

3/4 cups **farro perlato** (or use pearled barley) (4a)

16 ounces **whole-wheat large pasta shells** (5)

12 (6-inch) **corn tortillas** (3)

28 ounce **no-salt-added whole peeled tomatoes with basil** (5)

1 1/2 cups **reduced-sodium chicken or vegetable broth** (4a)

1 cup **salsa** (3)

2 tablespoons **rice vinegar** (1)

2 (15-ounce) cans **cannellini beans** (5)

1 tablespoon **capers** (4)

20 ounces **pineapple chunks in 100% juice** (1)

🧂 SPICES

7/8 teaspoon **salt** (2)(3)(3a)(4)(4a)

1/4 teaspoon **crushed red pepper flakes** (5)

3/8 teaspoon **black pepper** (2)(3a)

1/4 teaspoon **garlic powder** (3a)

1 tablespoon **chili powder** (3)

1/4 teaspoon **dried dill** (3a)

🍶 STAPLES

6 tablespoons + 1/2 teaspoon **extra-virgin olive oil** (1)
(2)(4)(4a)(5)

1 teaspoon **white wine vinegar** (3a)

2–3 tablespoons **balsamic vinegar** (2)(4)

2 tablespoons **reduced-fat mayonnaise** (3a)

1/4 cup **vinaigrette dressing** (5a)

2 3/4 tablespoons **reduced-sodium soy sauce** (use
wheat/gluten-free if needed) (1)

2 tablespoons **pure maple syrup** (1)

3 teaspoons **minced garlic** (1)(5)

🍴 REFRIGERATED/FROZEN

1/4 cup **crumbled feta cheese** (4)

1/2 cup **reduced-fat shredded cheddar cheese** (3)

3 ounces **reduced-fat feta cheese** (2)

3 tablespoons **grated Parmesan cheese** (5)

1/4 cup **grated or shredded Parmesan cheese** (5a)

2 tablespoons **nonfat sour cream or Greek yogurt** (3a)

2 tablespoons **reduced-fat buttermilk** (3a)

Get free, printable versions of the shopping lists from this book at **TheScramble.com/diabetes**.

*optional ingredients

SUMMER WEEK 4 • 139

These flavors are a magical combination, and the pattern of the pork, red peppers, and pineapple on the skewer looks so appetizing that it would be ideal to serve to company. Serve with Whole-Wheat Couscous.

Grilled Pork and Pineapple Kabobs

MARINATE: 1 HOUR • **PREP:** 10 MINUTES • **COOK:** 20 MINUTES • **SERVES:** 4 • **SERVING SIZE:** 2 KABOBS

20 ounces pineapple chunks in 100% juice, drained (save the juice—see Tip)

1 pound boneless pork center-cut loin or tenderloin, cut into 1-inch cubes

1 red bell pepper, cut into 1-inch chunks

2 3/4 tablespoons reduced-sodium soy sauce or tamari (use wheat/gluten-free if needed)

1 tablespoon extra-virgin olive oil

2 tablespoons rice vinegar

2 tablespoons pure maple syrup, or use honey

1 teaspoon minced garlic (about 2 cloves)

1 tablespoon fresh ginger, peeled and minced

DO AHEAD OR DELEGATE: Cube the pork, cut the bell pepper, or fully prepare the skewers and marinate in the refrigerator ahead of time.

1. Thread pieces of pineapple, pork, and bell pepper onto about 8 metal skewers, creating a repeating pattern. Lay the skewers in a large pan or dish with sides, just large enough to hold them in one layer.

2. In a large measuring cup, combine the remaining ingredients and pour it over the kebabs, turning them to coat. Marinate, refrigerated, for at least 1 hour, and up to 24 hours, turning occasionally.

3. Preheat the grill to medium-high heat (about 400°F), and oil the grates. (Start the couscous now, if serving it.) Remove the kabobs from the marinade, reserving the marinade, and grill for about 5 minutes per side until the meat is browned and just cooked through.

4. In a small saucepan, bring the reserved marinade to a boil and simmer for 2 minutes. Transfer to a small pitcher or bowl to serve with the kabobs.

SLOW COOKER DIRECTIONS: Use bamboo skewers, cutting to fit the slow cooker if necessary. Combine marinade ingredients as directed. Thread pineapple, pork, and bell pepper onto skewers, stack in slow cooker, and then drizzle or brush with marinade, turning to coat. Reserve remaining marinade for serving. Cook on low for 6–8 hours or on high for 3–5 hours. (Slow cooker cooking times may vary—get to know your slow cooker and, if necessary, adjust cooking times accordingly.)

FLAVOR BOOSTER
Add 1/2 teaspoon black pepper to the marinade.

Whole-Wheat Couscous

SERVES: 8 • **SERVING SIZE:** 2/3 CUP

1 1/2 cups whole-wheat couscous

1. Prepare the couscous according to package directions, using water or broth for the liquid. For even more flavor, stir fresh herbs, toasted pine nuts, slivered almonds, and/or dried cranberries or currants into the hot couscous.

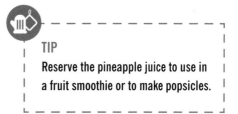

TIP
Reserve the pineapple juice to use in a fruit smoothie or to make popsicles.

NUTRITIONAL INFORMATION | GRILLED PORK AND PINEAPPLE KABOBS:

EXCHANGES / CHOICES:
1 1/2 Fruit; 1/2 Carbohydrate; 3 Protein, lean; 1/2 Fat

Calories: 285; Calories from Fat: 65; Total Fat: 7 g;
Saturated Fat: 1.5 g; Trans Fat: 0 g; Cholesterol: 60 mg;
Sodium: 425 mg; Potassium: 655 mg; Total Carbohydrate: 33 g;
Dietary Fiber: 2 g; Sugar: 28 g; Protein: 24 g; Phosphorus: 230 mg

NUTRITIONAL INFORMATION | WHOLE-WHEAT COUSCOUS:

EXCHANGES / CHOICES:
1 1/2 Starch

Calories: 105; Calories from Fat: 5; Total Fat: 0.5 g;
Saturated Fat: 0 g; Trans Fat: 0 g; Cholesterol: 0 mg;
Sodium: 0 mg; Potassium: 60 mg; Total Carbohydrate: 24 g;
Dietary Fiber: 4 g; Sugar: 0 g; Protein: 4 g; Phosphorus: 20 mg

I could eat this salad every day during the summer! I got the delectable recipe from Shawn Askew, who works at Bella Bethesda hair salon (one of my favorite places to spend time). Serve with Whole-Wheat Dinner Rolls.

Fresh Corn, Tomato, and Avocado Salad with Shrimp

PREP (NO COOK): 20 MINUTES • **SERVES:** 8 • **SERVING SIZE:** 1 1/2 CUP

1 pound medium or large shrimp, peeled and deveined

2 cups cherry tomatoes, halved

2 avocados, peeled and cubed

2 ears corn, kernels sliced off (no need to cook if it's fresh sweet corn. If not, steam it for 3 minutes)

3 ounces reduced-fat feta cheese, cubed, or use Mexican queso fresco or cotija

1/4 cup fresh basil, slivered

1–2 tablespoons balsamic vinegar, to taste

1 tablespoon extra-virgin olive oil

1/8 teaspoon salt

1/4 teaspoon black pepper, freshly ground, or to taste

DO AHEAD OR DELEGATE: Cook and refrigerate the shrimp, halve the tomatoes, remove the corn kernels from the cobs, or fully prepare and refrigerate the salad (wait to chop and add the avocado until just before serving).

1. Pan-fry, steam, or grill the shrimp until they are pink, 3–4 minutes total. (Meanwhile, warm the rolls, if you are serving them.) Combine all the ingredients except the shrimp in a large serving bowl. Serve the shrimp on top of the salad.

FLAVOR BOOSTER
Add 1/4 teaspoon celery seeds or cumin and 1 tablespoon fresh lemon or lime juice to the salad.

Whole-Wheat Dinner Rolls

SERVES: 6 • **SERVING SIZE:** 1 SMALL DINNER ROLL

6 whole-wheat or white dinner rolls

1. Warm the dinner rolls in a 300°F oven for 5 minutes, if desired.

TIP

Corn can be considered nature's sunglasses. It contains zeaxanthin and lutein, important antioxidants that help break down the sun's harmful rays that can damage eyes over time.

NUTRITIONAL INFORMATION | FRESH CORN, TOMATO, AND AVOCADO SALAD WITH SHRIMP:

EXCHANGES / CHOICES:
1 Carbohydrate; 2 Protein, lean; 1 Fat

Calories: 195; Calories from Fat: 90; Total Fat: 10 g;
Saturated Fat: 2.2 g; Trans Fat: 0 g; Cholesterol: 125 mg;
Sodium: 435 mg; Potassium: 460 mg; Total Carbohydrate: 12 g;
Dietary Fiber: 4 g; Sugar: 3 g; Protein: 17 g; Phosphorus: 260 mg

NUTRITIONAL INFORMATION | WHOLE-WHEAT DINNER ROLLS:

EXCHANGES / CHOICES:
1 Starch

Calories: 95; Calories from Fat: 15; Total Fat: 1.5 g;
Saturated Fat: 0.3 g; Trans Fat: 0 g; Cholesterol: 0 mg;
Sodium: 145 mg; Potassium: 100 mg; Total Carbohydrate: 18 g;
Dietary Fiber: 3 g; Sugar: 3 g; Protein: 3 g; Phosphorus: 80 mg

Who doesn't love crispy tacos, even though they are practically designed to fall apart at first bite? If the crumbling factor bothers you; make soft tacos, or crumble up the shells, or use tortilla chips, and make taco salad instead. I use lower fat (and less greasy) turkey instead of ground beef, and my own seasonings to flavor the meat. Serve with Homemade Ranch Dressing with Carrots and Broccoli.

Classic Crunchy Tacos

PREP + COOK: 20 MINUTES • **SERVES:** 6 • **SERVING SIZE:** 2 TACOS

1 pound lean ground turkey or vegetarian ground meat

1 tablespoon chili powder

1/8 teaspoon salt, or more to taste

1 cup salsa, or to taste

1/2 head iceberg lettuce, thinly shredded (3 cups)

1/2 cup 50% reduced-fat shredded cheddar cheese

12 (6-inch) corn tortillas or 12 taco shells

DO AHEAD OR DELEGATE: Shred the lettuce and the cheese, if necessary, and refrigerate.

1. Preheat the oven to 425°F. In a nonstick skillet, brown the turkey over medium heat, mixing in the chili powder, salt, and 2 tablespoons salsa, and breaking the turkey into small pieces with a spatula as it browns, about 8–10 minutes. (Meanwhile, make the ranch dressing and cut the vegetables, if you are serving them.)

2. Put the lettuce, cheese, and extra salsa in serving bowls.

3. When the meat is nearly done, put the taco shells on a baking sheet, overlapping them a little bit, and heat for about 2 minutes until they are warm (this makes them extra crispy—watch them carefully so they don't burn).

4. Serve the tacos immediately, letting family members layer the fillings to their own tastes. (We like to add the meat, then cheese, then lettuce, and finally drizzle salsa over everything.)

FLAVOR BOOSTER
Use hot Mexican or chipotle chili powder and spicy salsa.

Homemade Ranch Dressing with Carrots and Broccoli

SERVES: 6
SERVING SIZE: 1 TABLESPOON DRESSING AND 1 CUP RAW VEGETABLES

2 tablespoons nonfat sour cream or Greek yogurt

2 tablespoons reduced-fat mayonnaise

2 tablespoons reduced-fat buttermilk

1 teaspoon white wine vinegar

1 tablespoon fresh chives, minced

1/4 teaspoon garlic powder

1/4 teaspoon dried dill

1/8 teaspoon salt

1/8 teaspoon black pepper

1/2 pound carrots, cut into sticks

1 medium head broccoli, cut into florets (steamed for 1–2 minutes until bright green)

1. Whisk all ingredients, except the carrots and broccoli, with a fork and serve with the vegetables. Refrigerate any leftovers in an airtight container for up to a week.

TIP

If you shred the lettuce ahead of time, wrap it in a wet paper towel, seal in a baggy, and store in the refrigerator. This will keep it nice and crisp until you're ready to use it.

NUTRITIONAL INFORMATION | CLASSIC CRUNCHY TACOS:

EXCHANGES / CHOICES:
1 1/2 Starch; 1 Nonstarchy Vegetable; 2 Protein, lean; 1 Fat

Calories: 275; Calories from Fat: 80; Total Fat: 9 g;
Saturated Fat: 2.8 g; Trans Fat: 0.1 g; Cholesterol: 60 mg;
Sodium: 430 mg; Potassium: 445 mg; Total Carbohydrate: 29 g;
Dietary Fiber: 4 g; Sugar: 2 g; Protein: 21 g; Phosphorus: 375 mg

NUTRITIONAL INFORMATION | HOMEMADE RANCH DRESSING WITH CARROTS AND BROCCOLI:

EXCHANGES / CHOICES:
1 Nonstarchy Vegetable; 1 Fat

Calories: 60; Calories from Fat: 30; Total Fat: 3.5 g;
Saturated Fat: 0.6 g; Trans Fat: 0 g; Cholesterol: 0 mg;
Sodium: 120 mg; Potassium: 245 mg; Total Carbohydrate: 6 g;
Dietary Fiber: 2 g; Sugar: 3 g; Protein: 2 g; Phosphorus: 45 mg

In the summer, I often get a basket of fresh fruits and vegetables delivered from local farms through a service in the D.C. area called "From the Farmer." A recent basket included darling mini-eggplants called fairytale eggplants. They are mild and have thin skins just like Japanese eggplants, so the two are interchangeable in recipes. You can substitute whatever fresh summer produce you have lying around for any of the other vegetables. Serve over Farro, a hearty grain.

Eggplant Caponata Stew

PREP: 20 MINUTES • **COOK:** 25 MINUTES • **SERVES:** 4 • **SERVING SIZE:** 2 CUPS

2 tablespoons extra-virgin olive oil

1 shallot, finely chopped, or use 2 cloves garlic or 1/2 onion

1 green bell pepper, seeded and chopped

1 zucchini or yellow squash, halved lengthwise and sliced

1 pound Japanese or fairytale eggplants or regular eggplant, chopped

2 tomatoes, chopped, or use 15 ounces canned diced tomatoes

1 tablespoon capers, or use chopped green olives

1/4 teaspoon salt

1 tablespoon balsamic vinegar

15 ounces canned cannellini beans, drained and rinsed

1/2 cup fresh basil, chopped, or use some basil and some oregano or parsley

1/4 cup crumbled feta cheese

DO AHEAD OR DELEGATE: Chop the shallot, the eggplant, and the tomatoes, seed and chop the bell pepper, halve and slice the zucchini, drain and rinse the beans, or fully prepare and refrigerate or freeze the stew.

1. (Start the farro, if you are serving it.) Heat a large heavy skillet over medium heat. Add the oil, and when it is hot, add the shallots. Stir them for about 30 seconds until they are fragrant, then add the peppers, zucchini, eggplant, and tomatoes (you can add them as you chop, they don't all need to go in at precisely the same time), and sauté for about 5 minutes until they start to get tender. Stir in the capers, salt, and vinegar, cover the pan, reduce the heat if necessary to keep any liquid simmering, and steam everything for about 5 minutes.

2. Remove the lid, add the beans, and continue sautéing the vegetable mixture for about 20 more minutes or until any liquid has thickened and the vegetables are very tender. Stir in the fresh herbs and let them soften for 1–2 minutes. Serve the stew immediately, topped with 1 tablespoon of cheese per serving, or refrigerate for up to 4 days, or freeze for up to 3 months.

SLOW COOKER DIRECTIONS: Omit the oil. Combine all ingredients except the cheese in the slow cooker. Cook on low for 8–10 hours or on high for 4–5 hours. Serve topped with feta cheese as directed. (Slow cooker cooking times may vary—get to know your slow cooker and, if necessary, adjust cooking times accordingly.)

Farro

SERVES: 4 • **SERVING SIZE:** 1/2 CUP

3/4 cup farro perlato (or use pearled barley), or use quinoa for a gluten-free option

1 1/2 cups reduced-sodium chicken or vegetable broth, or use water or combination or water and broth

1/2 teaspoon extra-virgin olive oil

1 tablespoon fresh flat-leaf parsley, chopped (optional)

1. In a medium stockpot, cook the farro in broth or water according to package directions, adding the salt to the water (no need to add the salt if you are using broth). Cook for 20–30 minutes until tender but still chewy. Drain if necessary, toss with the oil, and top with the parsley, if desired.

FLAVOR BOOSTER
Add 1/4 teaspoon crushed red pepper flakes with the shallots, use garlic salt instead of regular salt, and season the dish at the table with freshly ground black pepper.

TIP
When you halve oblong vegetables like zucchini or carrots, halve them lengthwise and put the flat sides down on the cutting board for quick, easy, and safe slicing.

NUTRITIONAL INFORMATION | EGGPLANT CAPONATA STEW:

EXCHANGES / CHOICES:
1 Starch; 3 Nonstarchy Vegetable; 2 Fat

Calories: 235; Calories from Fat: 90; Total Fat: 10 g; Saturated Fat: 2.5 g; Trans Fat: 0.1 g; Cholesterol: 10 mg; Sodium: 385 mg; Potassium: 795 mg; Total Carbohydrate: 31 g; Dietary Fiber: 9 g; Sugar: 8 g; Protein: 9 g; Phosphorus: 180 mg

NUTRITIONAL INFORMATION | FARRO:

EXCHANGES / CHOICES:
2 Starch

Calories: 140; Calories from Fat: 15; Total Fat: 1.5 g; Saturated Fat: 0.2 g; Trans Fat: 0 g; Cholesterol: 0 mg; Sodium: 195 mg; Potassium: 185 mg; Total Carbohydrate: 27 g; Dietary Fiber: 3 g; Sugar: 0 g; Protein: 6 g; Phosphorus: 140 mg

Six O'Clock Scramble member Hillary Bratton of Portola Valley, California, sent me her family's favorite weeknight pasta recipe. I love how the white beans break down into the sauce while it's cooking, making it thicker, richer, and healthier! Serve with Spinach Salad with Mushrooms, Onions, and Parmesan Cheese.

Pasta with White Beans, Tomatoes, and Basil

PREP + COOK: 30 MINUTES • **SERVES:** 9 • **SERVING SIZE:** 1 1/3 CUPS

16 ounces whole-wheat large pasta shells

2 tablespoons extra-virgin olive oil

2 teaspoons minced garlic (3–4 cloves)

15 ounces cannellini beans, drained and rinsed

28 ounces no-salt-added whole peeled tomatoes with basil, with their liquid, or use 2 pounds fresh tomatoes, coarsely chopped

10 fresh basil leaves, chopped

1/4 teaspoon crushed red pepper flakes

1/4 teaspoon salt

1/8 teaspoon black pepper

3 tablespoons grated Parmesan cheese

DO AHEAD OR DELEGATE: Cook the pasta and store it tossed with a little oil to prevent sticking, peel the garlic, drain and rinse the beans, chop the tomatoes if using fresh, grate the cheese if necessary, or fully prepare and refrigerate the dish.

1. Cook the pasta according to the package directions until it is al dente.

2. Meanwhile, in a large heavy skillet, heat 1 tablespoon oil over medium heat. When the oil is hot, add the garlic and stir it for about 30 seconds until it is very fragrant. Stir in the beans for about 1 minute. Add the tomatoes, basil, and crushed red pepper flakes. Bring to a boil, and simmer for about 20 minutes, or until the pasta is done, breaking up the tomatoes and beans a bit with the back of a wooden spoon while it cooks. (Meanwhile, make the salad, if you are serving it.)

3. Drain the shells and combine them with the sauce. Season with the salt and pepper. Serve immediately topped with the Parmesan cheese and drizzled with olive oil, or refrigerate for up to 3 days.

SLOW COOKER DIRECTIONS: Combine the garlic, beans, tomatoes, basil, and red pepper flakes in the slow cooker and cook on low for 5–6 hours or on high for 2–3 hours. Combine with cooked, drained pasta shells and top with the cheese and oil as directed. (Slow cooker cooking times may vary—get to know your slow cooker and, if necessary, adjust cooking times accordingly.)

Spinach Salad with Mushrooms, Onions, and Parmesan Cheese

SERVES: 9 • **SERVING SIZE:** 1 1/2 CUPS

12 ounces baby spinach

2 cups sliced mushrooms

1/2 yellow or red onion, sliced

1/4 cup grated or shredded Parmesan cheese

6 tablespoons Orange Balsamic Vinaigrette (page 16)

1. To make the salad, combine the spinach, mushrooms, sliced onions, and Parmesan cheese, and toss thoroughly with balsamic vinaigrette or dressing of your choice.

FLAVOR BOOSTER
Double the crushed red pepper flakes and use freshly grated aged Parmesan cheese.

TIP
When adding dry spices to a recipe, never measure or shake them over a boiling pot, as the moisture and humidity from the pot may affect the color and flavor of the remainder of the bottle.

NUTRITIONAL INFORMATION | PASTA WITH WHITE BEANS, TOMATOES, AND BASIL:

EXCHANGES / CHOICES:
3 Starch; 1/2 Fat

Calories: 255; Calories from Fat: 40; Total Fat: 4.5 g; Saturated Fat: 0.8 g; Trans Fat: 0 g; Cholesterol: 0 mg; Sodium: 130 mg; Potassium: 345 mg; Total Carbohydrate: 47 g; Dietary Fiber: 7 g; Sugar: 3 g; Protein: 11 g; Phosphorus: 190 mg

NUTRITIONAL INFORMATION | SPINACH SALAD WITH MUSHROOMS, ONIONS, AND PARMESAN CHEESE:

EXCHANGES / CHOICES:
1 Nonstarchy Vegetable; 1 Fat

Calories: 65; Calories from Fat: 45; Total Fat: 5 g; Saturated Fat: 0.9 g; Trans Fat: 0 g; Cholesterol: 0 mg; Sodium: 90 mg; Potassium: 285 mg; Total Carbohydrate: 4 g; Dietary Fiber: 1 g; Sugar: 1 g; Protein: 2 g; Phosphorus: 50 mg

SUMMER WEEK 5

Cuban-Spiced Chicken (1)
SIDE DISH: Roasted Beets (1a)

Foil Packet Salmon with Cherry Tomatoes, Basil, and Capers (2)
SIDE DISH: Boiled New or Red Potatoes (2a)

Spicy Szechuan Green Beans and Ground Turkey or Pork (3)
SIDE DISH: Brown Rice (3a)

Orecchiette with Baby Spinach, Mint, and Feta Cheese (4)
SIDE DISH: Russian Radish and Cucumber Salad (4a)

Classic Gazpacho with Diced Avocado (Cold Vegetable Soup) (5)
SIDE DISH: Tortilla Chips (5a); Watermelon (5b)

SHOPPING LIST

🥕 PRODUCE

1/4 cup **scallions or chives** (3)
1/4 **red or yellow onion** (5)
1 **green bell pepper** (5)
1/2–1 **jalapeño pepper** (5)
2 cups **radishes** (4a)
2 1/2 pounds **tomatoes** (5)
1 1/2 cups **cherry tomatoes** (2)
16–18 ounces **baby spinach** (4)
1 clove **garlic** (5)
1 tablespoon **fresh ginger** (3)
2 tablespoons **fresh basil** (2)
2 tablespoons **fresh dill** (4a)
1/4–1/2 cup **fresh flat-leaf parsley** (5)
1/4 cup **fresh mint** (4)
1/2 pound **beets** (1a)
1 pound **green beans** (3)
2 **cucumbers** (4a)(5)
1 pound **new or red potatoes** (2a)
1 **avocado** (5)
1/2 **lemon** (4)
1/2 **lime** (1)
1 **watermelon** (5b)

🌀 MEAT AND FISH

2 pounds **boneless, skinless chicken thighs** (1)

1 pound **ground turkey, pork, or meatless crumble** (3)

1 1/2 pounds **salmon fillet** (preferably wild Alaskan salmon) (2)

🗄 SHELVED ITEMS

1 1/2 cups **quick-cooking brown rice or regular white rice** (3a)

16 ounces **whole-wheat orecchiette noodles** (4)

4 cups **tortilla chips** (5a)

2 tablespoons **sherry or apple cider vinegar** (5)

1 tablespoon **rice wine, mirin, or dry sherry** (3)

1 1/2 tablespoons **capers** (2)

15 ounces canned **black beans** (1)

🧂 SPICES

2 3/4 teaspoons **salt** (1)(1a)(2)(2a)(4)(4a)(5)

1/4 teaspoon **salt-free lemon pepper seasoning** (2a)*

1/2 teaspoon **dried oregano** (1)

1/2 teaspoon **dried thyme** (1)

1/4–1/2 teaspoon **crushed red pepper flakes** (3)*

7/8 teaspoon **black pepper** (1)(1a)(2)(4)

1/4 teaspoon **ground ginger** (1a)

1 teaspoon **ground cumin** (1)

5/8 teaspoon **garlic powder** (1)(2a)

2 teaspoons **paprika** (1)

🧴 STAPLES

1 tablespoon **butter** (1a)

1 1/2 tablespoons **extra-virgin olive oil or butter** (2a)

1/2 cup **extra-virgin olive oil** (1)(2)(4)(5)

1 tablespoon **vegetable or coconut oil** (3)

2 teaspoons **white wine vinegar** (4a)

2 1/2 tablespoons **reduced-sodium soy sauce or tamari** (use wheat/gluten- free if needed) (3)

1 teaspoon **brown sugar** (3)

2 tablespoon **pure maple syrup** (1a)

2 1/2 teaspoons **minced garlic** (3)(4)

1 teaspoon **cornstarch** (3)

🍦 REFRIGERATED/FROZEN

3/4 cup **crumbled feta cheese** (4)

1 cup **nonfat sour cream** (4a)

1/4 cup **orange juice** (1a)

1 1/2 cups **plain nonfat Greek yogurt** (5)

Get free, printable versions of the shopping lists from this book at **TheScramble.com/diabetes**.

*optional ingredients

SUMMER WEEK 5 • 151

You can vary the spices in this quickie chicken to make it more or less pungent. The lime and oil help bring out the flavor of the spice mix, in addition to helping the spices adhere to the chicken. The chicken would also be excellent shredded and served over a salad or in a sandwich. Serve with Roasted Beets.

Cuban-Spiced Chicken

PREP: 5 MINUTES • **COOK:** 40 MINUTES • **SERVES:** 6 • **SERVING SIZE:** 1 THIGH

2 teaspoons paprika

1 teaspoon ground cumin

1/2 teaspoon garlic powder

1/2 teaspoon black pepper

1/2 teaspoon dried thyme

1/2 teaspoon dried oregano

1/2 teaspoon salt

2 pounds boneless, skinless chicken thighs

1/2 lime, juice only (1–2 tablespoons)

1 tablespoon extra-virgin olive oil

15 ounces canned black beans, drained and rinsed

DO AHEAD OR DELEGATE: Combine the dry spices, marinate the chicken in the refrigerator, or fully prepare and refrigerate the chicken.

1. (Start the beets first, if you are serving them.) Preheat the oven to 400°F (unless you plan to marinate the chicken). Line a baking sheet with a silicone mat, parchment paper, or spray it with nonstick cooking spray.

2. In a small bowl, combine all the dry spices (the paprika through the salt).

3. In a medium bowl, toss the chicken with the lime juice and oil, then add the spice mixture and coat the chicken thoroughly. (At this point you can proceed with the recipe or refrigerate the chicken for up to 24 hours.)

4. Transfer the chicken to the baking sheet and bake, uncovered, for 30–40 minutes until the chicken is cooked through in the center of the largest piece. When the chicken is about 3 minutes from being done, warm the beans in a microwave-safe dish for 1–2 minutes. Serve immediately over a scoop of beans (about 1/4 cup) or refrigerate for up to 3 days.

SLOW COOKER DIRECTIONS: Prepare and coat the chicken with the spice mixture as directed. Place the chicken in the slow cooker and cook on low for 6–8 hours or on high for 3–4 hours. Serve it over the beans as directed above. (Slow cooker cooking times may vary—get to know your slow cooker and, if necessary, adjust cooking times accordingly.)

FLAVOR BOOSTER
Replace 1/4 teaspoon of the paprika with cayenne pepper.

Roasted Beets

PREP + COOK: 40 MINUTES • **SERVES:** 6 • **SERVING SIZE:** 3/4 CUP

1 1/2 pounds beets, peeled and cubed (4–5 beets)

1 1/2 tablespoons extra-virgin olive oil

1/2 teaspoon kosher salt, to taste

1. Preheat the oven to 425°F. In a bowl, toss the beets with the oil, and lay them on a rimmed baking sheet (you can toss them with the oil on the sheet, but I find doing it in a bowl coats them more evenly). Sprinkle them with the salt. Roast them for 25–30 minutes, flipping them after 20 minutes (use tongs!), until they are browned in spots and tender. Serve immediately.

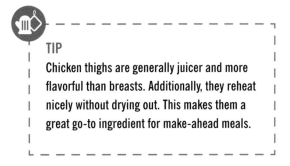

TIP

Chicken thighs are generally juicer and more flavorful than breasts. Additionally, they reheat nicely without drying out. This makes them a great go-to ingredient for make-ahead meals.

NUTRITIONAL INFORMATION | CUBAN-SPICED CHICKEN:

EXCHANGES / CHOICES:
1/2 Starch; 4 Protein, lean; 1 Fat

Calories: 260; Calories from Fat: 100; Total Fat: 11 g;
Saturated Fat: 2.7 g; Trans Fat: 0 g; Cholesterol: 135 mg;
Sodium: 340 mg; Potassium: 465 mg; Total Carbohydrate: 11 g;
Dietary Fiber: 4 g; Sugar: 1 g; Protein: 28 g; Phosphorus: 285 mg

NUTRITIONAL INFORMATION | ROASTED BEETS:

EXCHANGES / CHOICES:
1 Nonstarchy Vegetable; 1 Fat

Calories: 60; Calories from Fat: 30; Total Fat: 3.5 g;
Saturated Fat: 0.5 g; Trans Fat: 0 g; Cholesterol: 0 mg;
Sodium: 210 mg; Potassium: 215 mg; Total Carbohydrate: 7 g;
Dietary Fiber: 1 g; Sugar: 6 g; Protein: 1 g; Phosphorus: 25 mg

Wrapping fish in a foil packet is a way to ensure a juicy and flavorful meal. Serve with Boiled New or Red Potatoes.

Foil Packet Salmon with Cherry Tomatoes, Basil, and Capers

PREP: 10 MINUTES • **COOK:** 25 MINUTES • **SERVES:** 4 • **SERVING SIZE:** 1 PACKET

1 1/2 cups cherry tomatoes, halved

1 1/2 tablespoons capers, with a little of their liquid

2 tablespoons fresh basil, chopped

1 tablespoon extra-virgin olive oil

1 1/2 pounds salmon fillet (preferably wild Alaskan salmon)

1/4 teaspoon salt

1/8 teaspoon black pepper

DO AHEAD OR DELEGATE: Halve the tomatoes and combine the ingredients for the salmon's topping.

1. Preheat the oven to 450°F. In a medium bowl, combine the tomatoes, capers, basil, and oil. Set them aside.

2. Lay a big sheet of heavy-duty aluminum foil on a baking sheet, and put the salmon in the middle. Fold up the sides of the foil, and pour the tomato mixture evenly over the salmon. Season it with salt and freshly ground pepper to taste. Wrap the foil into an airtight packet around the fish and sauce, folding and sealing the edges, and put the packet on the baking sheet.

3. Bake the fish for 25 minutes. (Meanwhile, prepare the potatoes, if you are serving them.) Remove from the oven and open the packet immediately (and carefully) so the fish stops cooking. Serve immediately.

SLOW COOKER DIRECTIONS: Cut the salmon into pieces that will fit into the slow cooker, if needed. Prepare one packet as directed for each piece of salmon, then place the packets in the slow cooker, layering as needed. Cook on low for 6–8 hours or on high for 3–4 hours. (Slow cooker cooking times may vary—get to know your slow cooker and, if necessary, adjust cooking times accordingly.)

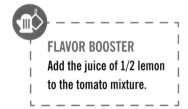

FLAVOR BOOSTER
Add the juice of 1/2 lemon to the tomato mixture.

Boiled New or Red Potatoes

SERVES: 4 • **SERVING SIZE:** 3/4 CUP

1 pound new or red potatoes

1 tablespoon extra-virgin olive oil or butter

1/8 teaspoon garlic powder

1/4 teaspoon salt-free lemon-pepper seasoning (optional)

1. Cover the potatoes with water in a medium pot. Bring the water to a boil. Simmer the potatoes until they are fork tender, about 10–15 minutes, and drain them. Toss them immediately (cut them in half first, if desired) with the oil or butter, garlic powder, and lemon-pepper seasoning (optional).

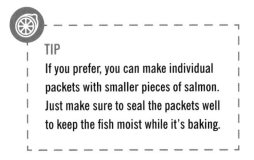

TIP

If you prefer, you can make individual packets with smaller pieces of salmon. Just make sure to seal the packets well to keep the fish moist while it's baking.

NUTRITIONAL INFORMATION | FOIL PACKET SALMON WITH CHERRY TOMATOES, BASIL, AND CAPERS:

EXCHANGES / CHOICES:
5 Protein, lean; 1 1/2 Fat

Calories: 290; Calories from Fat: 125; Total Fat: 14 g;
Saturated Fat: 2.6 g; Trans Fat: 0 g; Cholesterol: 75 mg;
Sodium: 315 mg; Potassium: 890 mg; Total Carbohydrate: 3 g;
Dietary Fiber: 1 g; Sugar: 2 g; Protein: 37 g; Phosphorus: 465 mg

NUTRITIONAL INFORMATION | BOILED NEW OR RED POTATOES:

EXCHANGES / CHOICES:
1 1/2 Starch; 1/2 Fat

Calories: 125; Calories from Fat: 30; Total Fat: 3.5 g;
Saturated Fat: 0.5 g; Trans Fat: 0 g; Cholesterol: 0 mg;
Sodium: 150 mg; Potassium: 420 mg; Total Carbohydrate: 22 g;
Dietary Fiber: 2 g; Sugar: 1 g; Protein: 2 g; Phosphorus: 50 mg

I used a technique I learned from Cooks Illustrated *to make these tasty Szechuan green beans, and combined it with enough ground meat to make it a meal. My son, Solomon, and my husband, Andrew, polished it off before I could contemplate seconds! Serve with Brown Rice.*

Spicy Szechuan Green Beans and Ground Turkey or Pork

PREP + COOK: 25 MINUTES • **SERVES:** 4 • **SERVING SIZE:** 1 1/2 CUPS

2 1/2 tablespoons reduced-sodium soy sauce or tamari (use wheat/gluten-free if needed)

1 tablespoon rice wine, mirin, or dry sherry

1 teaspoon brown sugar

1 teaspoon cornstarch

1/4–1/2 teaspoon crushed red pepper flakes, to taste (optional)

1 tablespoon vegetable oil

1 pound green beans, ends trimmed and cut in half, or use frozen

1 pound lean ground turkey, pork, or meatless crumble

2 teaspoons minced garlic (3–4 cloves)

1 tablespoon fresh ginger, peeled and minced

1/4 cup scallions or chives, thinly sliced

DO AHEAD OR DELEGATE: Prepare the sauce, trim and cut the green beans, brown the turkey, pork, or meatless crumbles and refrigerate, peel the garlic, peel and mince the ginger, slice the scallions or chives, or fully prepare and refrigerate or freeze the dish.

1. (Start the rice first, if you are serving it.) In a small bowl or measuring cup, whisk together the soy sauce, rice wine, brown sugar, cornstarch, and red pepper flakes (optional). Set it aside.

2. Heat a large nonstick skillet over high heat and add the oil. When it is smoking, add the beans (if using frozen beans, defrost them first) and cook, stirring frequently, until beans are shriveled and black in spots, about 5–8 minutes. (Reduce the heat if necessary to keep them from burning.) Transfer the beans to a plate.

3. Reduce the heat to medium and add the turkey, pork, or meatless crumbles. Cook until no pink remains, about 5 minutes, then add the garlic and ginger, stirring until fragrant, about 1 minute. Return the beans to the pan, stir the sauce again, and add it to the pan. Cook until heated through and the sauce is thickened, about 1 minute. Stir in the scallions or chives and serve immediately, refrigerate for up to 3 days, or freeze for up to 3 months.

SLOW COOKER DIRECTIONS: Whisk together the sauce ingredients as directed, adding the garlic and ginger as well. Place the turkey, pork, or meatless crumbles into the slow cooker, lay the beans and scallions on top, and pour the sauce on top. Cook on low for 6–8 hours or on high for 3–4 hours, until the meat is cooked through with no pink remaining. (Slow cooker cooking times may vary—get to know your slow cooker and, if necessary, adjust cooking times accordingly.)

Brown Rice

SERVES: 4 • **SERVING SIZE:** 1/2 CUP

1 1/2 cups quick-cooking brown rice

1. Prepare the rice according to package directions.

FLAVOR BOOSTER
Use the optional red pepper flakes and sprinkle sesame seeds on the finished dish.

TIP
For a really quick way to trim green beans, line up the stems (the tough end) of the beans on a cutting board, making sure that the stem ends all face the same direction. Push the ends up against the palm of your hand so they're even, and cut off the stem with a chef's knife. Then repeat the process with the other ends.

NUTRITIONAL INFORMATION | SPICY SZECHUAN GREEN BEANS AND GROUND TURKEY OR PORK:

EXCHANGES / CHOICES:
2 Nonstarchy Vegetable; 3 Protein, lean; 1 1/2 Fat

Calories: 265; Calories from Fat: 110; Total Fat: 12 g;
Saturated Fat: 2.8 g; Trans Fat: 0.1 g; Cholesterol: 85 mg;
Sodium: 430 mg; Potassium: 440 mg; Total Carbohydrate: 12 g;
Dietary Fiber: 3 g; Sugar: 3 g; Protein: 25 g; Phosphorus: 260 mg

NUTRITIONAL INFORMATION | BROWN RICE:

EXCHANGES / CHOICES:
1 1/2 Starch

Calories: 115; Calories from Fat: 10; Total Fat: 1 g;
Saturated Fat: 0.2 g; Trans Fat: 0 g; Cholesterol: 0 mg;
Sodium: 5 mg; Potassium: 45 mg; Total Carbohydrate: 24 g;
Dietary Fiber: 2 g; Sugar: 0 g; Protein: 3 g; Phosphorus: 85 mg

I am crazy about the flavor combination in this Greek-inspired pasta recipe, and it is so simple to prepare. Serve with Russian Radish and Cucumber Salad.

Orecchiette with Baby Spinach, Mint, and Feta Cheese

PREP + COOK: 30 MINUTES • **SERVES:** 8 • **SERVING SIZE:** 1 1/2 CUPS

16 ounces whole-wheat orecchiette noodles

16–18 ounces baby spinach

2 tablespoons extra-virgin olive oil

1/2 teaspoon minced garlic (about 1 clove)

1/4 cup fresh mint, coarsely chopped

1/2 lemon, juice only (about 2 tablespoons)

3/4 cup crumbled feta cheese

1/4 teaspoon salt, or to taste

1/8 teaspoon black pepper, or to taste

DO AHEAD OR DELEGATE: Peel the garlic, juice the lemon, or fully prepare and refrigerate the dish.

1. Cook the noodles in a large pot of salted boiling water, leaving some room at the top of the pot for the spinach, until it is al dente. (Meanwhile, make the salad, if you are serving it.)

2. One minute before the pasta is done, stir in the spinach until it is just wilted, then drain the noodles and spinach. Return them to the pot or to a large metal serving bowl and toss with the oil, garlic, mint, and lemon juice. Top with the cheese and season with salt and pepper to taste. Serve immediately or refrigerate for up to 2 days.

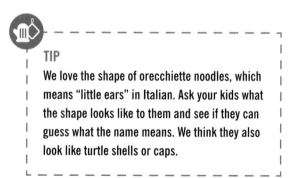

TIP

We love the shape of orecchiette noodles, which means "little ears" in Italian. Ask your kids what the shape looks like to them and see if they can guess what the name means. We think they also look like turtle shells or caps.

Russian Radish and Cucumber Salad

SERVES: 8 • **SERVING SIZE:** 1/2 CUP

1 cup nonfat sour cream

2 tablespoons fresh dill, or use 2 teaspoons dried

2 teaspoons white wine vinegar

1/4 teaspoon salt

2 cups radishes, chopped

1 cucumber, chopped (about 2 cups)

1. In a medium-sized serving bowl, combine the sour cream, dill, vinegar, and salt. Add the radishes and cucumbers and toss gently. Serve immediately or refrigerate for up to 3 days. (Thanks to Olga Berman of MangoTomato.com for the inspiration!)

NUTRITIONAL INFORMATION | ORECCHIETTE WITH BABY SPINACH, MINT, AND FETA CHEESE:

EXCHANGES / CHOICES:
3 Starch; 1 Fat

Calories: 275; Calories from Fat: 65; Total Fat: 7 g;
Saturated Fat: 2.8 g; Trans Fat: 0.1 g; Cholesterol: 10 mg;
Sodium: 300 mg; Potassium: 410 mg; Total Carbohydrate: 45 g;
Dietary Fiber: 6 g; Sugar: 2 g; Protein: 12 g; Phosphorus: 215 mg

NUTRITIONAL INFORMATION | RUSSIAN RADISH AND CUCUMBER SALAD:

EXCHANGES / CHOICES:
1/2 Carbohydrate

Calories: 35; Calories from Fat: 0; Total Fat: 0 g;
Saturated Fat: 0.1 g; Trans Fat: 0 g; Cholesterol: 5 mg;
Sodium: 120 mg; Potassium: 150 mg; Total Carbohydrate: 7 g;
Dietary Fiber: 1 g; Sugar: 2 g; Protein: 2 g; Phosphorus: 45 mg

I must admit that it's taken me a very long time to come around to enjoying gazpacho. Maybe my taste buds have matured, or maybe it's because my 18-year-old neighbor, Will Witkop, brought me some of his homemade gazpacho and shared his recipe with me, but I am really starting to enjoy eating gazpacho. This recipe produces a pretty classic gazpacho flavor, but I have also seen delicious variations adding melon, cumin, or fresh lime juice, or blending in stale bread to thicken the soup. Serve with Tortilla Chips and Watermelon.

Classic Gazpacho with Diced Avocado (Cold Vegetable Soup)

PREP (NO COOK): 20 MINUTES • **SERVES:** 6 • **SERVING SIZE:** 1 1/4 CUPS

1 clove garlic, halved

2 1/2 pounds tomatoes (5–6 tomatoes), quartered

1 cucumber, halved across

1 green bell pepper, seeds and ribs removed, quartered

1/2–1 jalapeño pepper, seeded, to taste

1/4 red or yellow onion, quartered

1/4–1/2 cup fresh flat-leaf parsley, to taste

1 teaspoon salt

1/4 cup extra-virgin olive oil

2 tablespoons sherry or apple cider vinegar

1 avocado, peeled and diced

1 1/2 cups plain nonfat Greek yogurt

DO AHEAD OR DELEGATE: Peel the garlic, quarter the tomatoes and the onion, remove seeds and ribs from the green pepper and quarter, halve the cucumber, or fully prepare and refrigerate the soup.

1. Put the garlic, half of the tomatoes, half of the cucumber, half of the bell pepper, and the jalapeño into a food processor or powerful blender and puree. Transfer to a large bowl.

2. Add all the remaining ingredients, except the avocado and yogurt, into the food processor or blender and pulse to desired consistency, either chunky or more finely chopped. Transfer to the bowl. Chill for at least an hour and up to 3 days.

3. (Meanwhile, slice the watermelon, if you are serving it.) Serve with the diced avocado, and add 1/4 cup yogurt to each serving of gazpacho at the table, if desired.

FLAVOR BOOSTER
Add some fresh mint along with the parsley and serve with hot sauce.

SIDE DISHES

- - - - - - - - - - - - - - - - - - - -

Tortilla Chips

SERVES: 6 • **SERVING SIZE:** 1 OUNCE

4 cups multi-grain tortilla chips

1. Serve alongside Gazpacho or crumble or dip them in the soup.

Watermelon

SERVES: 8 • **SERVING SIZE:** 1 1/4 CUPS

1 6-pound watermelon

1. Slice and chop the watermelon before serving.

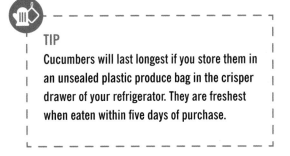

TIP
Cucumbers will last longest if you store them in an unsealed plastic produce bag in the crisper drawer of your refrigerator. They are freshest when eaten within five days of purchase.

NUTRITIONAL INFORMATION | CLASSIC GAZPACHO WITH DICED AVOCADO:

EXCHANGES / CHOICES:
2 Nonstarchy Vegetable; 1 Protein, lean; 2 Fat

Calories: 200; Calories from Fat: 115; Total Fat: 13 g;
Saturated Fat: 1.8 g; Trans Fat: 0 g; Cholesterol: 0 mg;
Sodium: 425 mg; Potassium: 685 mg; Total Carbohydrate: 13 g;
Dietary Fiber: 4 g; Sugar: 8 g; Protein: 8 g; Phosphorus: 140 mg

NUTRITIONAL INFORMATION | TORTILLA CHIPS:

EXCHANGES / CHOICES:
1 Starch; 1 1/2 Fat

Calories: 150; Calories from Fat: 70; Total Fat: 8 g;
Saturated Fat: 1 g; Trans Fat: 0 g; Cholesterol: 0 mg;
Sodium: 135 mg; Potassium: 60 mg; Total Carbohydrate: 18 g;
Dietary Fiber: 2 g; Sugar: 1 g; Protein: 2 g; Phosphorus: 55 mg

NUTRITIONAL INFORMATION | WATERMELON:

EXCHANGES / CHOICES:
1 Fruit

Calories: 55; Calories from Fat: 0; Total Fat: 0 g;
Saturated Fat: 0 g; Trans Fat: 0 g; Cholesterol: 0 mg;
Sodium: 0 mg; Potassium: 215 mg; Total Carbohydrate: 14 g;
Dietary Fiber: 1 g; Sugar: 12 g; Protein: 1 g; Phosphorus: 20 mg

SUMMER

WEEK 6

Thai Herb Grilled Chicken (1)
SIDE DISH: Grilled Zucchini (1a)

Pan-Fried Tilapia with Mango Lime Salsa (2)
SIDE DISH: Roasted Green or Wax Beans (2a)

Farmer's Market Pasta with Sweet Corn and Tomatoes (3)
SIDE DISH: Spinach Salad with Strawberries and Almonds (3a)

Indian Spiced Lentils with Rice (4)
SIDE DISH: Fresh Cherries (4a)

Israeli Chopped Salad with Tahini Lemon Dressing (5)
SIDE DISH: Hummus or Baba Ghanoush with Pita Chips and Baby Carrots (5a)

SHOPPING LIST

PRODUCE
16 ounces **baby carrots** (5a)

1 large **yellow onion** (4)

1/2 **sweet yellow onion** such as Vidalia or Walla Walla (2)

1/2 **red onion** (5)

1 **jalapeño or other hot chili pepper** (1)*

2 pounds **cherry tomatoes** (3)(5)

12 ounces **baby spinach** (3a)

4 cloves **garlic** (1)

1/2 cup **fresh basil** (1)(3)

1/3 cup **fresh cilantro** (1)

1/2 cup **fresh flat-leaf parsley** (5)

1/2 cup **fresh mint** (1)(2)

1 pound **green or wax beans** (2a)

2–3 **zucchini or yellow squash** (1a)

2 **cucumbers** (5)

4 ears **fresh corn** (3)

1 **lemon** (5)

3 **limes** (1)(2)

2 cups **strawberries** (3a)

1 **mango** (2)

1 pound **cherries** (4a)

🍖 MEAT AND FISH

3 pounds **boneless chicken thighs** (1)

4 (1 1/4–1 1/2 pounds) **tilapia fillets or other thin white fish** (2)

1/4–1/2 pound **spicy sausage such as chorizo** (use wheat/gluten-free if needed) (4)*

4 ounces **prosciutto or precooked sausage** (3)*

📦 SHELVED ITEMS

1 cup **conventional brown rice** (not quick-cooking) (4)

3/4 pound **whole-wheat conchiglie** (medium pasta shells) (3)

2 1/2 cups **pita chips** (5)(5a)

2 tablespoons **tahini (sesame paste)**, or use hummus if you can't find tahini (5)

1 cup **dried green/brown lentils** (4)

1/2 cup **raisins** (4)

1/4 cup **slivered almonds** (3a)

🧂 SPICES

2 teaspoons **salt** (1a)(3)(4)(5)

1/4 teaspoon **kosher salt** (2a)

2 bay **leaves** (4)

1/4 teaspoon **black pepper** (1a)(2a)

2 teaspoons **curry powder** (4)

🍶 STAPLES

3/4 cup **extra-virgin olive oil** (1a)(2)(2a)(3)(4)

1 1/2 tablespoons **vegetable or canola oil** (1)

1/4 cup **vinaigrette dressing** (3a)

2 teaspoons **Dijon mustard** (use wheat/gluten-free if needed) (5)

3 1/3 tablespoons **reduced-sodium soy sauce** (use wheat/gluten-free if needed) (1)

2 teaspoons **honey** (5)

4 hard-boiled **eggs** (5)

1 teaspoon **minced garlic** (5)

🍦 REFRIGERATED/FROZEN

1/4 cup **grated Parmesan cheese** (3)

1 cup **low-fat plain yogurt** (4)

6 ounces **hummus or baba ghanoush** (5a)

2 tablespoons **basil pesto** (3)

Get free, printable versions of the shopping lists from this book at **TheScramble.com/diabetes**.

*optional ingredients

SUMMER WEEK 6 • 163

As soon as the warm weather arrives, I fill the pots on our deck with all kinds of herbs. I use fresh herbs to boost the flavor (and nutrition) of salads, pasta, marinades, smoothies, iced tea, cocktails, and just about anything else I can think of. Pulverizing them in a food processor or blender makes their flavors really burst, as in this marinade. Serve with Grilled Zucchini or Yellow Squash.

Thai Herb Grilled Chicken

MARINATE: 30 MINUTES • **PREP:** 15 MINUTES • **COOK:** 15 MINUTES • **SERVES:** 6 • **SERVING SIZE:** 2 THIGHS

1/3 cup fresh basil

1/3 cup fresh mint

1/3 cup fresh cilantro

4 cloves garlic, coarsely chopped

3 1/3 tablespoons reduced-sodium soy sauce or tamari (use wheat/gluten-free if needed)

1 1/2 tablespoons vegetable or canola oil

1–2 limes, juice only (2–4 tablespoons), to taste

1 jalapeño or other hot chili pepper, seeded and coarsely chopped (optional)

3 pounds boneless, skinless chicken thighs, or use chicken breasts

DO AHEAD OR DELEGATE: Peel and chop the garlic, juice the limes, seed and chop the jalapeño pepper, if using, make the marinade and marinate the chicken in the refrigerator, or fully prepare and refrigerate the chicken.

1. In a food processor (a mini one works well for this) or blender, combine the fresh herbs, garlic, soy sauce, oil, lime juice, and jalapeño pepper (optional). Put the chicken in a large flat dish with sides, and poke holes in the flesh with the tines of a fork. Spoon the mixture over the chicken, cover, and marinate in the refrigerator for at least 30 minutes and up to 24 hours, turning it once or twice.

2. Heat the grill to medium-high heat, remove the chicken from the marinade, reserving the marinade, and grill the chicken with the cover on the grill for 7–10 minutes until it is nicely browned on the bottom. (Meanwhile, start the zucchini, if you are serving it.) Flip the chicken, spoon the remaining marinade over it, and cook for about 7 more minutes until cooked through and browned on both sides. Transfer the chicken to a clean dish and serve immediately, refrigerate for up to 3 days, or freeze for up to 3 months.

FLAVOR BOOSTER
Use the jalapeño pepper and leave its seeds in for extra spice or add 1/2 teaspoon lime zest to the marinade.

Grilled Zucchini or Yellow Squash

SERVES: 6 • **SERVING SIZE:** 1 CUP

3 zucchini or yellow squash
1 tablespoon extra-virgin olive oil
1/4 teaspoon salt
1/8 teaspoon black pepper

1. Cut the zucchini or yellow squash lengthwise into quarters, and then cut the strips crosswise into several shorter pieces. Toss with the oil, salt, and pepper.

2. Spread the squash slices on a vegetable tray or sturdy piece of aluminum foil, and grill over medium or medium-high heat for 10–20 minutes, flipping once, until they reach desired tenderness. (Alternatively, sauté the zucchini or squash in the oil over medium heat for about 10 minutes until lightly browned and tender.)

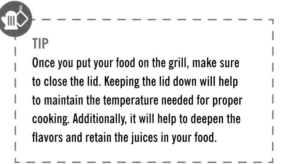

TIP

Once you put your food on the grill, make sure to close the lid. Keeping the lid down will help to maintain the temperature needed for proper cooking. Additionally, it will help to deepen the flavors and retain the juices in your food.

NUTRITIONAL INFORMATION | THAI HERB GRILLED CHICKEN:

EXCHANGES / CHOICES:
5 Protein, lean; 1 1/2 Fat

Calories: 315; Calories from Fat: 145; Total Fat: 16 g;
Saturated Fat: 3.7 g; Trans Fat: 0.1 g; Cholesterol: 205 mg;
Sodium: 440 mg; Potassium: 480 mg; Total Carbohydrate: 2 g;
Dietary Fiber: 0 g; Sugar: 0 g; Protein: 38 g; Phosphorus: 345 mg

NUTRITIONAL INFORMATION | GRILLED ZUCCHINI OR YELLOW SQUASH:

EXCHANGES / CHOICES:
1 Nonstarchy Vegetable; 1/2 Fat

Calories: 35; Calories from Fat: 20; Total Fat: 2.5 g;
Saturated Fat: 0.3 g; Trans Fat: 0 g; Cholesterol: 0 mg;
Sodium: 105 mg; Potassium: 255 mg; Total Carbohydrate: 3 g;
Dietary Fiber: 1 g; Sugar: 2 g; Protein: 1 g; Phosphorus: 35 mg

You can use this sweet and tangy salsa in so many ways—serve it with fish, chicken, beans, or scoop it up with tortilla chips. You'll love how it livens up the mild flavor of a white fish like tilapia. Serve with Roasted Green or Wax Beans.

Pan-Fried Tilapia with Mango Lime Salsa

PREP + COOK: 20 MINUTES • **SERVES:** 4 • **SERVING SIZE:** 1 FILLET

1 mango, peeled and diced

1/2 sweet yellow onion such as Vidalia or Walla Walla, diced

1 tablespoon fresh mint leaves, finely chopped, or more to taste

1 lime, juice only (about 2 tablespoons)

1 tablespoon extra-virgin olive oil

4 tilapia fillets, or other thin white fish fillets (1 1/4–1 1/2 pounds)

DO AHEAD OR DELEGATE: Make and refrigerate the salsa.

1. (Start the beans first, if you are serving them.) In a medium serving bowl, combine the mango, onions, mint, and half the lime juice. Set it aside. (The salsa can be made up to 24 hours in advance and stored in the refrigerator.)

2. In a large nonstick skillet, heat the oil over medium-high heat. When the pan is hot, add the fillets and press down with a spatula to ensure each fillet is completely touching the pan. Cook the fillets 2–3 minutes per side until they are lightly browned. After flipping the fish, sprinkle the fillets with the remaining lime juice.

3. Serve the fish immediately, topped with the mango salsa.

SLOW COOKER DIRECTIONS: Add all ingredients to the slow cooker and cook on low for 4–5 hours, or on high for 2–2 1/2 hours. (Slow cooker cooking times may vary—get to know your slow cooker and, if necessary, adjust cooking times accordingly.)

FLAVOR BOOSTER
Add more mint and/or hot sauce or a finely diced hot chili pepper to the mango salsa.

TIP
If you're lured in by the strong, sweet fragrance of the mangos at the market, go ahead and buy an extra one. You can peel and dice a mango and keep it in the freezer for up to 6 months for use in smoothies or salsas. Mangos are not only delicious, but great for you as well—one cup is just 100 calories and provides 100% of your vitamin C. It's also a good source of vitamin A and fiber.

Roasted Green or Wax Beans

SERVES: 4 • **SERVING SIZE:** 3/4 CUP

1 pound green or wax beans, ends trimmed

1 tablespoon extra-virgin olive oil

1/4 teaspoon kosher salt

1/8 teaspoon black pepper

1. Preheat the oven to 400°F. Toss the beans in a large bowl with the oil. Spread the beans on a baking sheet and season them with the salt and pepper.

2. Bake them for 25–30 minutes until they are nicely browned, tossing them once after 15–20 minutes.

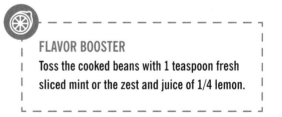

FLAVOR BOOSTER
Toss the cooked beans with 1 teaspoon fresh sliced mint or the zest and juice of 1/4 lemon.

NUTRITIONAL INFORMATION | PAN-FRIED TILAPIA WITH MANGO LIME SALSA:

EXCHANGES / CHOICES:
1 Fruit; 4 Protein, lean

Calories: 215; Calories from Fat: 55; Total Fat: 6 g; Saturated Fat: 1.5 g; Trans Fat: 0 g; Cholesterol: 60 mg; Sodium: 65 mg; Potassium: 550 mg; Total Carbohydrate: 12 g; Dietary Fiber: 1 g; Sugar: 10 g; Protein: 29 g; Phosphorus: 235 mg

NUTRITIONAL INFORMATION | SERVE WITH ROASTED GREEN OR WAX BEANS:

EXCHANGES / CHOICES:
1 Nonstarchy Vegetable; 1 Fat

Calories: 65; Calories from Fat: 30; Total Fat: 3.5 g; Saturated Fat: 0.5 g; Trans Fat: 0 g; Cholesterol: 0 mg; Sodium: 115 mg; Potassium: 140 mg; Total Carbohydrate: 7 g; Dietary Fiber: 3 g; Sugar: 1 g; Protein: 2 g; Phosphorus: 25 mg

Fresh and just-picked-flavor are the best words to describe this pasta dish. It's so sweet that our kids gobbled it up. Serve with Spinach Salad with Strawberries and Slivered Almonds.

Farmer's Market Pasta with Sweet Corn and Tomatoes

PREP + COOK: 25 MINUTES • **SERVES:** 8 • **SERVING SIZE:** 1 3/4 CUPS

3/4 pound whole-wheat conchiglie (medium pasta shells)

4 ears corn

1 pound cherry tomatoes, halved or quartered

1/4 cup extra-virgin olive oil

2 tablespoons basil pesto

1/2 teaspoon salt

10 fresh basil leaves, slivered

4 ounces prosciutto or precooked sausage, diced (optional)

1/4 cup grated Parmesan cheese, for serving

DO AHEAD OR DELEGATE: Cook the pasta and store it tossed with a little oil to prevent sticking, cook the corn and remove the kernels from the cob, chop the tomatoes, dice the prosciutto or sausage and refrigerate, grate the Parmesan cheese, or fully prepare and refrigerate the dish.

1. (Prepare the salad first, if you are serving it.) Cook the pasta according to the package directions and drain.

2. Meanwhile, boil the ears of corn for 2 minutes (or steam them in the microwave for about 4 minutes). Run the corn under cold water to cool and cut the kernels off the cob with a sharp knife (hold the cob upright on the base of a large serving bowl). Add the tomatoes, oil, pesto, salt, basil, prosciutto or sausage (optional), and pasta to the bowl. Toss it thoroughly and serve immediately, topped with the cheese, or refrigerate for up to 2 days. It's also good chilled!

FLAVOR BOOSTER
Add the juice of 1/2 fresh lime or lemon, 1 tablespoon balsamic vinegar, or 1/2 teaspoon salt-free lemon-pepper seasoning.

Spinach Salad with Strawberries and Slivered Almonds

SERVES: 8 • **SERVING SIZE:** 1 3/4 CUP

2 cup strawberries, sliced

12 ounces baby spinach

1/4 cup slivered almonds

1/4 cup vinaigrette dressing, to taste

1. In a large bowl, combine the spinach, strawberries, and almonds. Toss with the dressing and serve immediately.

TIP

You can freeze your remaining pesto sauce for use in future recipes. This can be done in one container or you can divide the pesto into smaller portions by using an ice cube tray. Once the small portions are frozen, you can store them in a freezer-safe resealable bag and pull them out when you want to add a burst of flavor to pasta, chicken, soup, or sandwiches.

NUTRITIONAL INFORMATION | FARMER'S MARKET PASTA WITH SWEET CORN AND TOMATOES:

EXCHANGES / CHOICES:
2 1/2 Starch; 1 Nonstarchy Vegetable; 1 1/2 Fat

Calories: 285; Calories from Fat: 90; Total Fat: 10 g; Saturated Fat: 1.7 g; Trans Fat: 0 g; Cholesterol: 0 mg; Sodium: 255 mg; Potassium: 305 mg; Total Carbohydrate: 44 g; Dietary Fiber: 5 g; Sugar: 5 g; Protein: 10 g; Phosphorus: 175 mg

NUTRITIONAL INFORMATION | SPINACH SALAD WITH STRAWBERRIES AND SLIVERED ALMONDS:

EXCHANGES / CHOICES:
1/2 Carbohydrate; 1 Fat

Calories: 65; Calories from Fat: 30; Total Fat: 3.5 g; Saturated Fat: 0.4 g; Trans Fat: 0 g; Cholesterol: 0 mg; Sodium: 105 mg; Potassium: 325 mg; Total Carbohydrate: 6 g; Dietary Fiber: 2 g; Sugar: 3 g; Protein: 2 g; Phosphorus: 45 mg

When I first saw this recipe, I wondered how lentils and rice could be as good as Six O'Clock Scramble member Sena Murphy suggested. But it was a big hit in our family, too! My more carnivorous friends report that this dish is great with a little cooked spicy sausage thrown in at the end. Serve with Fresh Cherries.

Indian Spiced Lentils with Rice

PREP: 15 MINUTES • **COOK:** 55 MINUTES • **SERVES:** 8 • **SERVING SIZE:** 1 1/2 CUPS

1/4 cup extra-virgin olive oil

1 large yellow onion, chopped

1 cup conventional brown rice (not quick-cooking)

2 teaspoons curry powder

2 bay leaves

1 cup dried green/brown lentils, rinsed

4 1/2 cups water

1 teaspoon salt, or to taste

1/2 cup raisins

1/4–1/2 pound spicy sausage (optional)

1 cup low-fat plain yogurt

DO AHEAD OR DELEGATE: Chop the onion, dice and refrigerate the sausage, or fully prepare and refrigerate the dish.

1. In a stockpot with a tight-fitting lid, heat the oil over medium-high heat and sauté the onions for about 5 minutes, until they start to turn golden.

2. Add the rice, curry powder, and bay leaves and stir for a minute to coat the grains of rice. Add the remaining ingredients, except the sausage (optional) and the yogurt, and bring to a boil. Cover and simmer until the water is absorbed and the rice is tender, 50–55 minutes. Meanwhile, crumble or dice and brown the sausage in a nonstick skillet.

3. Remove the bay leaves, stir in the cooked sausage (optional), and serve immediately, topped with a dollop of yogurt, or refrigerate for up to 3 days.

SLOW COOKER DIRECTIONS: Use cooked rice for the slow cooker version of this recipe. Combine the oil, onion, curry powder, bay leaves, lentils, sausage, raisins, and 3 cups water in the slow cooker. Cook on low for 8–10 hours or on high for 4–5 hours. Add the cooked rice 15–30 minutes before serving time. (Slow cooker cooking times may vary—get to know your slow cooker and, if necessary, adjust cooking times accordingly.)

Fresh Cherries

SERVES: 8 • **SERVING SIZE:** 6 CHERRIES

1 pound cherries

1. Serve alongside Indian Spiced Lentils with Rice.

FLAVOR BOOSTER

Add 1/2 teaspoon ground cumin with the other spices, and/or stir in a couple of tablespoons of chopped fresh cilantro before serving.

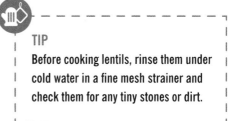

TIP

Before cooking lentils, rinse them under cold water in a fine mesh strainer and check them for any tiny stones or dirt.

NUTRITIONAL INFORMATION | INDIAN SPICED LENTILS WITH RICE:

EXCHANGES / CHOICES:
2 Starch; 1/2 Fruit; 1 Nonstarchy Vegetable; 1 1/2 Fat

Calories: 280; Calories from Fat: 70; Total Fat: 8 g;
Saturated Fat: 1.4 g; Trans Fat: 0 g; Cholesterol: 0 mg;
Sodium: 320 mg; Potassium: 445 mg; Total Carbohydrate: 43 g;
Dietary Fiber: 8 g; Sugar: 10 g; Protein: 10 g; Phosphorus: 235 mg

NUTRITIONAL INFORMATION | FRESH CHERRIES:

EXCHANGES / CHOICES:
1/2 Fruit

Calories: 30; Calories from Fat: 0; Total Fat: 0 g;
Saturated Fat: 0 g; Trans Fat: 0 g; Cholesterol: 0 mg;
Sodium: 0 mg; Potassium: 115 mg; Total Carbohydrate: 8 g;
Dietary Fiber: 1 g; Sugar: 7 g; Protein: 1 g; Phosphorus: 10 mg

When my family traveled in Israel, we were astounded by the endless array of beautiful, healthy, and creative salads, even at breakfast. Here I've recreated one of our favorites that we enjoyed at Israel's homegrown version of Starbucks, called Aroma. (This salad was a finalist in the Eggland's Best Recipe contest!) Serve with Hummus or Baba Ghanoush with Pita Chips and Carrots.

Israeli Chopped Salad with Tahini Lemon Dressing

PREP (NO COOK): 20 MINUTES • **SERVES:** 6 • **SERVING SIZE:** 2 CUPS

4 hard-boiled eggs, chopped

2 cucumbers, peeled and diced into small pieces

1 pound cherry tomatoes, diced into small pieces, or use 2 large tomatoes

1/2 red onion, finely diced

1/2 cup fresh parsley, chopped

2 tablespoons tahini (sesame paste), or hummus if you can't find tahini, well stirred

1 lemon, juice only (about 1/4 cup)

2 teaspoons Dijon mustard (use wheat/gluten-free if needed)

1 teaspoon minced garlic (about 2 cloves)

2 tablespoon water

2 teaspoons honey

1/4 teaspoon salt

1 cup pita chips, broken into small pieces

DO AHEAD OR DELEGATE: Hard boil, chop, and refrigerate the eggs, peel and chop the cucumbers, dice the tomatoes and the onion, chop the parsley, juice the lemon, make the salad dressing, or fully assemble the salad and the dressing and refrigerate (separately).

1. Hard boil the eggs, if necessary. In a medium serving bowl, combine the chopped eggs, cucumbers, tomatoes, onions, and parsley.

2. In a small bowl or large measuring cup, combine the tahini, lemon juice, mustard, garlic, water, honey, and salt. Toss the salad with the dressing (you might not need all of the dressing) and pita chips, and serve immediately. (You can make the salad and dressing up to 4 hours in advance but don't combine them until you are ready to serve.)

FLAVOR BOOSTER
Add olives, capers, or tuna to the salad.

Hummus or Baba Ghanoush with Pita Chips and Baby Carrots

SERVES: 6
SERVING SIZE: 4 CHIPS, 7–8 MEDIUM BABY CARROTS, AND 2 1/3 TABLESPOONS HUMMUS

6 ounces hummus or baba ghanoush (roasted eggplant dip)

1 1/2 cups (about 24) pita chips, or pita bread

16 ounces baby carrots

1. Serve the hummus or baba ghanoush with pita chips or pita bread and baby carrots.

TIP

Have you ever noticed that the yolks of some hard-boiled eggs have a greenish tint? It's harmless and is due to a chemical reaction between sulfur in the egg white and the iron in the yolk. You can minimize its occurrence by keeping the cooking time of the eggs to the bare minimum and quickly submerging them in an ice bath after cooking.

NUTRITIONAL INFORMATION | ISRAELI CHOPPED SALAD WITH TAHINI LEMON DRESSING:

EXCHANGES / CHOICES:
1/2 Starch; 1 Nonstarchy Vegetable; 1 Protein, medium fat; 1/2 Fat

Calories: 150; Calories from Fat: 65; Total Fat: 7 g;
Saturated Fat: 1.6 g; Trans Fat: 0 g; Cholesterol: 125 mg;
Sodium: 260 mg; Potassium: 410 mg; Total Carbohydrate: 15 g;
Dietary Fiber: 3 g; Sugar: 6 g; Protein: 7 g; Phosphorus: 155 mg

NUTRITIONAL INFORMATION | HUMMUS OR BABA GHANOUSH WITH PITA CHIPS AND BABY CARROTS:

EXCHANGES / CHOICES:
1 Carbohydrate; 1 Fat

Calories: 120; Calories from Fat: 40; Total Fat: 4.5 g;
Saturated Fat: 0.6 g; Trans Fat: 0 g; Cholesterol: 0 mg;
Sodium: 255 mg; Potassium: 255 mg; Total Carbohydrate: 17 g;
Dietary Fiber: 4 g; Sugar: 6 g; Protein: 4 g; Phosphorus: 85 mg

SUMMER (WEEK 7)

Spiced Chicken Soft Tacos (1)
SIDE DISH: Black Bean Dip with Red Pepper Strips (1a)

Grilled Halibut with Lemon-Basil Vinaigrette (2)
SIDE DISH: Grilled Broccoli (2a)

Light and Fluffy Spinach and Cheese Strata (3)
SIDE DISH: Blueberries (3a)

Farro Salad with Grilled Italian Vegetables (4)
SIDE DISH: Chickpea Salad (4a)

Sicilian Pasta with Eggplant and Fresh Tomatoes (5)
SIDE DISH: Vegetable Platter with Carrots, Red Peppers, and Snow Peas (5a)

SHOPPING LIST

🥕 PRODUCE
1/2 pound **baby carrots** (5a)
1/2 **shallot** (2)
3/4 **yellow onion** (1a)(5)
1 **red onion** (4)
3 **red bell peppers** (1)(1a)(5a)
5 **tomatoes** (4)(5)
1/4 cup + 1–2 tablespoons **fresh basil** (2)(5)
2 tablespoons **fresh cilantro** (1a)*
1/4 cup **fresh flat-leaf parsley** (4)
1 tablespoon **fresh oregano** or 1 teaspoon dried (5)
1–2 heads **broccoli** (2a)
1 medium **eggplant** (5)
1 **zucchini** (4)
1/2 pound **snow peas** (5a)
8 ounces **portobello mushroom caps** (4)
1 ripe **avocado** (1)*
1 **lemon** (2)
1/2 **lime** (1a)
1/2–1 pints **blueberries or blackberries** (3a)

🍖 MEAT AND FISH
1 1/2 pounds **boneless, skinless chicken breasts** (1)
1 1/2 pounds **halibut fillet** (2)
12 ounces **precooked Italian turkey, chicken, or meatless sausage** (4)*
3 slices **bacon** (turkey, pork, or meatless) (3)*

SHELVED ITEMS

6 slices **ciabatta bread** (3)

1 1/2 cups **farro perlato** (sold with grains) (4)

16 ounces **whole-wheat rigatoni noodles** (5)

4 cups **tortilla chips** (1a)*

12 **corn or wheat tortillas** (1)

2 tablespoons **tomato paste** (5)

1 cup **reduced-sodium vegetable broth** (4)

1/2 cup **reduced-sodium chicken broth or water** (1)

12 ounces **salsa or picante sauce** (1)

15 ounces **canned chickpeas** (garbanzo beans) (4a)

15 ounces **reduced-sodium canned black beans** (1a)

1–2 tablespoons **capers** (5)

1 tablespoon **toasted pine nuts** (4)

7 ounces **roasted red peppers** (4a)

1/2 cup **pitted black olives** (4a)

SPICES

1 1/2–1 3/4 teaspoons **salt** (1a)(2)(3)(4)(5)

1 teaspoon **herbes de Provence or thyme** (3)

1/8 teaspoon **black pepper** (4)

1/2 teaspoon **cinnamon** (1)

1 teaspoon **ground cumin** (1)(1a)

3/4 teaspoon **garlic powder** (1a)(3)

1/2 teaspoon **chili powder** (1a)

STAPLES

8 tablespoons + 1/4 cup + 1 teaspoon **extra-virgin olive oil** (1)(1a)(2)(2a)(4)(5)

2–3 teaspoons **balsamic vinegar** (4)

2 teaspoons **Dijon mustard** (use wheat/gluten-free if needed) (2)

1 tablespoon + 2 teaspoons **honey** (1)(2)

1 1/2 cups **nonfat or low-fat milk** (3)

6 **eggs** (3)

1 teaspoon **minced garlic** (4)

REFRIGERATED/FROZEN

1 cup **shredded reduced-fat cheddar cheese** (3)

1 tablespoon + 1/4 cup **grated Parmesan cheese** (2a)(5)

1/2 cup **shredded Swiss cheese** (3)

1 tablespoon **orange juice** (1a)

10 ounces **frozen chopped spinach** (3)

1/4 cup **crumbled Feta cheese** (4a)

Get free, printable versions of the shopping lists from this book at **TheScramble.com/diabetes**.

*optional ingredients

SUMMER WEEK 7 • 175

These tacos are melt-in-your-mouth delicious. The filling can be served over rice instead of inside tortillas, if you prefer a neater feast. Serve with Black Bean Dip with Red Bell Pepper Strips.

Spiced Chicken Soft Tacos

PREP + COOK: 30 MINUTES • **SERVES:** 6 • **SERVING SIZE:** 2 TACOS

1 tablespoon extra-virgin olive oil

1 red bell pepper, chopped

1 1/2 pounds boneless, skinless chicken breasts, cut in half crosswise (the short way)

12 ounces salsa or picante sauce

1/2 cup reduced-sodium chicken broth or water

1/2 teaspoon ground cumin

1/2 teaspoon cinnamon

1 tablespoon honey

12 corn or wheat tortillas

1 ripe avocado, peeled and diced (optional)

DO AHEAD OR DELEGATE: Core and chop the bell pepper and cut and refrigerate the chicken.

1. In a large heavy skillet, heat the oil over medium heat. Add the bell peppers and cook for 4–5 minutes until they start to get tender. Push the peppers to one side of the pan and add the chicken, cooking for about 2 minutes per side until the outsides start to brown. Pour the salsa, broth or water, spices, and honey over the chicken, stir to combine, and simmer for 8–10 minutes, flipping the chicken once or twice. (Meanwhile, make the dip, if you are serving it.)

2. When the chicken is just cooked through, remove it from the sauce. Using two forks, pull it apart to shred it into bite-sized strips. Return the chicken to the sauce to warm.

3. Heat the tortillas by wrapping them in a clean damp dishtowel and warming them in the microwave for about 1 minute until they are warm and soft. Serve the chicken inside the tortillas (use a slotted spoon to avoid getting too much of the liquid in the tacos), and top with the avocado (optional), if desired.

SLOW COOKER DIRECTIONS: Omit the chicken broth or water. Cut the chicken into bite-size strips. Place all ingredients except the tortillas and avocado into the slow cooker, and give it a stir to evenly distribute the spices. Cook on low for 6–8 hours or on high for 3–4 hours, or until the chicken is tender and cooked through. Warm the tortillas just before serving.

NUTRITIONAL INFORMATION | SPICED CHICKEN SOFT TACOS:

EXCHANGES / CHOICES:
2 Starch; 1 Nonstarchy Vegetable; 3 Protein, lean

Calories: 300; Calories from Fat: 65; Total Fat: 7 g;
Saturated Fat: 1.3 g; Trans Fat: 0 g; Cholesterol: 65 mg;
Sodium: 435 mg; Potassium: 515 mg; Total Carbohydrate: 32 g;
Dietary Fiber: 4 g; Sugar: 6 g; Protein: 28 g; Phosphorus: 365 mg

NUTRITIONAL INFORMATION | BLACK BEAN DIP WITH
RED PEPPER STRIPS:

EXCHANGES / CHOICES:
1/2 Starch; 1 Nonstarchy Vegetable; 1/2 Fat

Calories: 95; Calories from Fat: 20; Total Fat: 2.5 g;
Saturated Fat: 0.4 g; Trans Fat: 0 g; Cholesterol: 0 mg;
Sodium: 175 mg; Potassium: 265 mg; Total Carbohydrate: 14 g;
Dietary Fiber: 5 g; Sugar: 3 g; Protein: 4 g; Phosphorus: 75 mg

SIDE DISH

Black Bean Dip with Red Pepper Strips

SERVES: 6 • **SERVING SIZE:** 2 1/2 TABLESPOONS

15 ounces reduced-sodium canned black beans, drained and rinsed, or use 1 1/2 cups cooked black beans

1 tablespoon extra-virgin olive oil

1 tablespoon orange juice

1/2 lime, juice only (about 2 tablespoons)

1/4 teaspoon garlic powder, or use 1 clove fresh garlic, minced

1/4 teaspoon salt

1/2 teaspoon chili powder

1/2 teaspoon ground cumin

2 tablespoons fresh cilantro, chopped (optional)

1/4 yellow onion, finely diced (optional)

2 medium red bell peppers, sliced into 36 strips

1. In a food processor or blender, puree all the ingredients together except the cilantro, onion, and bell peppers. If too thick, add 1/8–1/4 cup water. For spicier flavor, add 1 chipotle pepper or 1/8 teaspoon cayenne pepper. Serve topped with cilantro and onions, and with red bell pepper strips for dipping.

FLAVOR BOOSTER
Use spicy salsa/picante sauce and/or double the cumin.

This gourmet dinner is so easy to prepare and the flavors are fresh and summery. Serve with Grilled Broccoli.

Grilled Halibut with Lemon-Basil Sauce

PREP + COOK: 25 MINUTES • **SERVES:** 4 • **SERVING SIZE:** 5 OUNCES FISH + 2 1/2 TABLESPOONS SAUCE

3 tablespoons extra-virgin olive oil, divided use

1 1/2 pounds halibut fillet, or use cod, mahi mahi, or other thick white fish

3/8 teaspoon salt, plus additional for seasoning the fish

1 lemon, juice only (about 1/4 cup), plus 1/2 teaspoon zest, if desired

2 teaspoons Dijon mustard (use wheat/gluten-free if needed)

2 teaspoons honey

1/2 shallot, minced (about 2 tablespoons)

1/4 cup fresh basil, finely chopped

DO AHEAD OR DELEGATE: Juice the lemon, mince the shallot, prepare the sauce for the fish, and refrigerate.

1. Preheat the grill to medium-high heat. Pour 1 tablespoon oil in a small bowl, and using a pastry brush, lightly brush the tops and bottoms of the fillets with oil. Season the top of the halibut with about 1/8 teaspoon salt.

2. In a small to medium serving bowl, whisk together the remaining oil with the rest of the ingredients, including 1/4 teaspoon salt.

3. (Put the broccoli on the grill a few minutes before the fish, if serving it.) Grill the fish directly on the grates or on a fish/vegetable grilling tray for 5 minutes with the skin side down, then flip it and grill for 1–2 minutes until it is just cooked through and flakes easily. Serve with the lemon-basil sauce spooned over it.

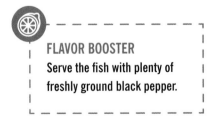

FLAVOR BOOSTER
Serve the fish with plenty of freshly ground black pepper.

Grilled Broccoli

SERVES: 4 • **SERVING SIZE:** 4 SPEARS

1 pound broccoli, tough bottoms cut off, cut into 16 spears

1 tablespoon extra-virgin olive oil

1 tablespoon grated Parmesan cheese (optional)

1. Toss or brush the broccoli with the oil. Grill the spears on medium or medium-high heat, directly on the grill or on a vegetable tray or aluminum foil, flipping once (use tongs), until they are lightly browned, about 10 minutes. Toss the grilled broccoli with the Parmesan cheese, if desired.

TIP

Halibut, a member of the flounder family, has a mild flavor, a dense texture, and is low in fat. It's a great choice for grilling because it holds together well and grilling helps to bring out its sweet flavor.

NUTRITIONAL INFORMATION | GRILLED HALIBUT WITH LEMON-BASIL SAUCE:

EXCHANGES / CHOICES:
1/2 Carbohydrate; 5 Protein, lean; 1 Fat

Calories: 295; Calories from Fat: 125; Total Fat: 14 g;
Saturated Fat: 2 g; Trans Fat: 0 g; Cholesterol: 55 mg;
Sodium: 375 mg; Potassium: 815 mg; Total Carbohydrate: 5 g;
Dietary Fiber: 0 g; Sugar: 4 g; Protein: 36 g; Phosphorus: 385 mg

NUTRITIONAL INFORMATION | GRILLED BROCCOLI:

EXCHANGES / CHOICES:
1 Nonstarchy Vegetable; 1 Fat

Calories: 65; Calories from Fat: 35; Total Fat: 4 g;
Saturated Fat: 0.7 g; Trans Fat: 0 g; Cholesterol: 0 mg;
Sodium: 50 mg; Potassium: 290 mg; Total Carbohydrate: 6 g;
Dietary Fiber: 2 g; Sugar: 2 g; Protein: 3 g; Phosphorus: 70 mg

It took me a few attempts, but I finally made the strata of my dreams. In case you aren't familiar with it, strata is an Italian baked egg and bread dish. This is a great dish to serve at a brunch, especially because you can make it in advance, but it also makes a nice change for a family dinner. Serve with Blueberries or Blackberries.

Light and Fluffy Spinach and Cheese Strata

MARINATE: 4 HOURS • **PREP:** 15 MINUTES • **COOK:** 50 MINUTES • **SERVES:** 8 • **SERVING SIZE:** 2 1/4 × 3 1/4-INCH PIECE

10 ounces frozen chopped spinach

6 eggs

1 1/2 cups nonfat or low-fat milk

1 cup shredded reduced-fat cheddar cheese

1/2 cup shredded Swiss cheese

1 teaspoon herbes de Provence or thyme, or other Italian herbs

1/2 teaspoon garlic powder

1/4 teaspoon salt

3 slices bacon (turkey, pork, or meatless), cooked and diced (optional)

6 slices ciabatta bread, about 1/2 inch thick, cubed, or use any day-old bread (about 4 cups)

DO AHEAD OR DELEGATE: Defrost the spinach, combine and refrigerate the eggs and the milk, shred the cheese, if necessary, and refrigerate, combine the dry seasonings, cube the bread, or fully assemble and refrigerate the strata.

1. Defrost the spinach in the microwave or on the stovetop. Spray a 9 × 13-inch glass or ceramic baking dish with nonstick cooking spray. Cook the bacon, if necessary.

2. In a large bowl, whisk together the eggs and the milk. Whisk in the cheeses, herbs, garlic powder, and salt. Stir in the spinach, bacon (optional), and bread cubes until the bread is completely moistened. Pour the egg mixture into the baking dish, smoothing it with the back of a spoon, if necessary. Refrigerate, covered, for at least 4 hours and up to 24 hours.

2. When you are ready to bake it, remove the strata from the refrigerator and preheat the oven to 350°F. Bake it in the center of the oven, uncovered, for 45–50 minutes until it is browned on the edges and cooked through in the center. Cut into squares to serve.

SLOW COOKER DIRECTIONS: In the slow cooker, whisk together the eggs and the milk, then whisk in the cheeses, herbs, garlic powder, and salt. Stir in the spinach, bacon, and bread cubes until the bread is completely moistened. Cook on low for 4–5 hours or on high for 2–3 hours. (Slow cooker cooking times may vary—get to know your slow cooker and, if necessary, adjust cooking times accordingly.)

SIDE DISH

- -

Blueberries or Blackberries

SERVES: 4
SERVING SIZE: 3/4 CUP BLUEBERRIES OR 1 CUP BLACKBERRIES

1 1/2 pints fresh blueberries or 2 pints blackberries

1. Serve alongside Light and Fluffy Spinach and Cheese Strata.

FLAVOR BOOSTER
Double the salt and add
1/8 teaspoon black pepper.

NUTRITIONAL INFORMATION | LIGHT AND FLUFFY SPINACH AND CHEESE STRATA:

EXCHANGES / CHOICES:
1 Carbohydrate; 2 Protein, medium fat

Calories: 200; Calories from Fat: 90; Total Fat: 10 g;
Saturated Fat: 4.3 g; Trans Fat: 0.1 g; Cholesterol: 155 mg;
Sodium: 420 mg; Potassium: 250 mg; Total Carbohydrate: 12 g;
Dietary Fiber: 1 g; Sugar: 3 g; Protein: 15 g; Phosphorus: 285 mg

NUTRITIONAL INFORMATION | BLUEBERRIES OR BLACKBERRIES:

EXCHANGES / CHOICES:
1 Fruit

Calories: 60; Calories from Fat: 5; Total Fat: 0.5 g;
Saturated Fat: 0 g; Trans Fat: 0 g; Cholesterol: 0 mg;
Sodium: 0 mg; Potassium: 160 mg; Total Carbohydrate: 15 g;
Dietary Fiber: 5 g; Sugar: 9 g; Protein: 1 g; Phosphorus: 20 mg

I am madly in love with the farro blends from Tuscan Fields, sold at many Whole Foods and some other specialty markets. If you can't find Tuscan Fields, this will still be delicious with any type of farro. Serve with Chickpea Salad.

Farro with Grilled Italian Vegetables

PREP + COOK: 30 MINUTES • **SERVES:** 6 • **SERVING SIZE:** 1 1/2 CUPS

1 1/2 cups farro perlato

1 cup reduced-sodium vegetable broth plus 2 cups water

1/4 cup extra-virgin olive oil

1 teaspoon minced garlic (about 2 cloves)

8 ounces portobello mushroom caps

1 zucchini (about 10 ounces), halved the short way and thinly sliced lengthwise

1 red onion, halved and sliced

1/4–1/2 teaspoon salt, to taste

1/8 teaspoon black pepper

1 tomato, diced

1/4 cup fresh flat-leaf parsley, chopped, or use a combination of parsley, basil, and oregano

1 tablespoon pine nuts, toasted

2–3 teaspoons balsamic vinegar, to taste

DO AHEAD OR DELEGATE: Cook the farro, peel and mince the garlic, combine the oil and garlic, halve and slice the zucchini, slice the onion, chop the parsley, dice the tomato, toast the pine nuts if using, or fully prepare and refrigerate the dish.

1. Cook the farro according to the package directions with the vegetable broth and water. Preheat the grill to medium-high heat.

2. Meanwhile, in a small bowl, whisk together the oil and garlic. Put the mushrooms, zucchini, and onions in a large flat dish. Using a pastry brush, brush both sides with the oil-garlic mixture. Season both sides with salt and pepper to taste. Grill the vegetables directly on the grill or on a vegetable grilling tray for about 5 minutes per side until they are tender and browned. (Meanwhile, make the salad if serving it.) Transfer the vegetables to a cutting board and coarsely chop them.

3. Put the tomatoes and herbs in a medium serving bowl, add the hot cooked farro, grilled vegetables, pine nuts, and vinegar, and toss to combine. Serve immediately or refrigerate for up to 2 days.

FLAVOR BOOSTER
Stir 2–4 tablespoons feta cheese into the dish once it cools.

Chickpea Salad

SERVES: 6 • **SERVING SIZE:** 1/2 CUP

15 ounces canned chickpeas (garbanzo beans), drained and rinsed

7 ounces roasted red peppers (sold in jars), drained and diced, or use 1 pint grape tomatoes, halved

1/2 cup pitted black olives, chopped

1/4 cup crumbled feta cheese

1/2 cup pita chips (optional)

1. In a medium bowl, combine the chickpeas with the roasted red peppers. Stir in the olives, feta, and pita chips (optional).

TIP

In 2013, the Institute of Medicine determined that, on average, Americans consume about 3,400 milligrams of sodium daily. For people with diabetes, a healthier goal is to aim for no more than 1,500 milligrams daily. The most effective way to lower your sodium intake is to cut back on processed foods like deli meat, pizza, and packaged snacks. Also noteworthy is that adding a little salt when cooking or serving food is less of a culprit than the processed items many Americans have as staples in their diet.

NUTRITIONAL INFORMATION | FARRO WITH GRILLED ITALIAN VEGETABLES:

EXCHANGES / CHOICES:
2 1/2 Starch; 1 Nonstarchy Vegetable; 2 Fat

Calories: 300; Calories from Fat: 100; Total Fat: 11 g; Saturated Fat: 1.5 g; Trans Fat: 0 g; Cholesterol: 0 mg; Sodium: 150 mg; Potassium: 600 mg; Total Carbohydrate: 44 g; Dietary Fiber: 6 g; Sugar: 4 g; Protein: 9 g; Phosphorus: 265 mg

NUTRITIONAL INFORMATION | CHICKPEA SALAD:

EXCHANGES / CHOICES:
1 Starch; 1/2 Fat

Calories: 105; Calories from Fat: 30; Total Fat: 3.5 g; Saturated Fat: 1.2 g; Trans Fat: 0.1 g; Cholesterol: 5 mg; Sodium: 260 mg; Potassium: 170 mg; Total Carbohydrate: 14 g; Dietary Fiber: 4 g; Sugar: 4 g; Protein: 5 g; Phosphorus: 95 mg

This is a great dish for late summer or early fall when the last of the eggplants and tomatoes are harvested. The capers are essential for a nice salty and tangy finish. Serve with Vegetable Platter with Carrots, Red Peppers, and Snow Peas.

Sicilian Pasta with Eggplant and Fresh Tomatoes

PREP: 20 MINUTES • **COOK:** 20 MINUTES • **SERVES:** 8 • **SERVING SIZE:** 1 3/4 CUPS

2 tablespoons extra-virgin olive oil, divided use

1/2 yellow onion, quartered and thinly sliced

12 ounces whole-wheat rigatoni noodles

1 medium eggplant, diced

1/2 teaspoon salt

4 tomatoes, diced (or use 28 ounces canned whole or diced tomatoes)

1 tablespoon fresh oregano, or use 1 teaspoon dried

1–2 tablespoons fresh basil, or use 1 teaspoon dried

2 tablespoons tomato paste (you can freeze the remaining tomato paste by the tablespoon for future use)

1–2 tablespoons capers, to taste

1/4 cup grated Parmesan cheese, for serving

DO AHEAD OR DELEGATE: Quarter and slice the onion, dice the eggplant and the tomatoes, if using fresh, or fully prepare and refrigerate or freeze the dish.

1. In a large heavy skillet, heat 1 tablespoon of the oil over medium heat. Sauté the onions until they are fragrant and tender, about 3–5 minutes.

2. Meanwhile, cook the rigatoni according to the package directions.

3. Add the eggplant to the skillet and drizzle with the remaining oil and the salt, then add the tomatoes and bring it to a low boil (there will be enough liquid as the tomatoes begin to break down from the heat.) Cover the pan, reduce the heat, and steam the vegetables for about 5 minutes until the eggplant begins to darken. Remove the lid and add the herbs and tomato paste.

4. Simmer the sauce, stirring occasionally, for 15–20 minutes until the eggplant is very tender. Stir in the capers. Combine the sauce and pasta and serve immediately, topped with the cheese, or refrigerate for up to 3 days, or freeze for up to 3 months.

Vegetable Platter with Carrots, Red Peppers, and Snow Peas

SERVES: 8 • **SERVING SIZE:** 3/4 CUP

1/2 pound baby carrots

1 red bell pepper, sliced

1/2 pound snow peas

1. Serve with a colorful platter of baby carrots, red bell pepper slices, and snow peas.

TIP

When selecting onions, the freshest ones will be firm and dry and have a mild scent. Avoid those that are sprouting or soft.

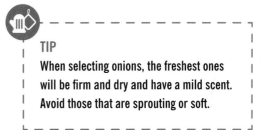

FLAVOR BOOSTER

Sauté 1 teaspoon minced garlic with the onions, stir about 1 tablespoon fresh lemon juice into the sauce with the capers, and top the dish with feta cheese instead of Parmesan.

NUTRITIONAL INFORMATION | SICILIAN PASTA WITH EGGPLANT AND FRESH TOMATOES:

EXCHANGES / CHOICES:
2 Starch; 2 Nonstarchy Vegetable; 1/2 Fat

Calories: 230; Calories from Fat: 45; Total Fat: 5 g;
Saturated Fat: 1 g; Trans Fat: 0 g; Cholesterol: 0 mg;
Sodium: 250 mg; Potassium: 410 mg; Total Carbohydrate: 43 g;
Dietary Fiber: 7 g; Sugar: 7 g; Protein: 9 g; Phosphorus: 160 mg

NUTRITIONAL INFORMATION | VEGETABLE PLATTER WITH CARROTS, RED PEPPERS, AND SNOW PEAS:

EXCHANGES / CHOICES:
1 Nonstarchy Vegetable

Calories: 25; Calories from Fat: 0; Total Fat: 0 g;
Saturated Fat: 0 g; Trans Fat: 0 g; Cholesterol: 0 mg;
Sodium: 25 mg; Potassium: 160 mg; Total Carbohydrate: 5 g;
Dietary Fiber: 2 g; Sugar: 3 g; Protein: 1 g; Phosphorus: 25 mg

SUMMER

Grilled Mexican Flank Steak Fajitas (1)

SIDE DISH: Easiest Grilled Corn (1a)

Shrimp, Mango, and Avocado Salad with Lime (2)

SIDE DISH: Whole-Grain Baguette (2a)

Caramelized Tofu and Broccoli Stir-Fry (3)

SIDE DISH: Brown Rice (3a)

Healthy Fettuccine Alfredo with Cherry Tomatoes (4)

SIDE DISH: Baby Greens with Sliced Peaches and Pecans (4a)

Indian Summer Vegetable Stew (5)

SIDE DISH: Bulgur Wheat (5a)

SHOPPING LIST

🥕 PRODUCE

2 **carrots** (5)

1 3/4 **red onions** (2)(3)(5)

1 1/2 **red bell peppers** (3)(5)

1 **jalapeño pepper** (2)*

5 **tomatoes** (5)

8 ounces **cherry tomatoes** (4)

10 ounces **baby salad greens** (4a)

1/4 cup **fresh basil leaves** (4)

2 tablespoons **fresh cilantro** (2)

1 head **broccoli** (3)

6 ears **corn** (1a)

1 head **cauliflower** (5)

1 **avocado** (2)

3 **limes** (1)(2)

2 **peaches** (4a)

1 **mango** (2)

1 1/2 cups **iceberg lettuce** (1)

🍖 MEAT AND FISH

1 pound **cooked shrimp** (preferably U.S. or Canadian farmed or wild shrimp) (2)

1 1/2 pounds **flank steak** (1)

🫙 SHELVED ITEMS

1 **whole-grain baguette** (2a)

1 1/2 cups **quick-cooking brown rice** (3a)

1 cup **bulgur wheat or quinoa** (5a)

16 ounces **whole-wheat fettuccine** (4)

2 cups **reduced-sodium chicken or vegetable broth** (5a)

2 tablespoons **barbecue sauce** (5)

15 ounces **canned chickpeas** (garbanzo beans) (5)

1/2 cup + 8 teaspoons **pecans** (3)(4a)

1/2 cup **raw unsalted cashews** (4)

6 (6-inch) **corn tortillas** (1)

3/4 cup **salsa** (1)

🧂 SPICES

2 1/4 teaspoons **salt** (1)(2)(4)(5)

1 teaspoon **dried oregano** (1)

1/4 teaspoon **crushed red pepper flakes** (3)*

1/4 teaspoon **black pepper** (5)

1 teaspoon **ground cumin** (1)

1 tablespoon **garam masala** (an Indian spice blend) (5)

1 tablespoon **chili powder** (1)

1 teaspoon **smoked paprika** (1)

🫙 STAPLES

1 tablespoon **no-trans-fat margarine** (4)

5 tablespoons **extra-virgin olive oil** (1)(2)(5)

2 tablespoons **coconut or peanut oil** (3)

1/4 cup **vinaigrette dressing** (4a)

3 tablespoons **reduced-sodium soy sauce** (use wheat/ gluten-free if needed) (3)

2 tablespoons **brown sugar** (3)

4 teaspoons **minced garlic** (3)(4)(5)

1 1/2 teaspoons **butter-flavored nonstick cooking spray** (1a)

🍦 REFRIGERATED/FROZEN

1/4 cup **grated Parmesan cheese** (4)

1 cup **part-skim ricotta cheese** (4)

3/4 cup **plain nonfat Greek yogurt** (5)*

15 ounces **extra-firm tofu** (3)

6 tablespoons **fat-free sour cream** (1)

Get free, printable versions of the shopping lists from this book at **TheScramble.com/diabetes**.

*optional ingredients

SUMMER WEEK 8 • 187

Flank steak is an inexpensive cut of meat that takes well to the high heat of the grill or broiler. I think it's best with an acidic marinade to help tenderize the meat, and if you can let it marinate for a few hours, or even up to 2 days, all the better. Serve with Easiest Grilled Corn.

Grilled Mexican Flank Steak Fajitas

MARINATE: 30 MINUTES • **PREP + COOK:** 20 MINUTES • **SERVES:** 6 • **SERVING SIZE:** 3 OUNCES MEAT

1 1/2 pounds flank steak (also called skirt steak)

2 limes, juice only (about 1/4 cup)

2 tablespoons extra-virgin olive oil

1 teaspoon salt

1 tablespoon chili powder

1 teaspoon ground cumin

1 teaspoon dried oregano

1 teaspoon smoked paprika

6 (6-inch) corn tortillas

3/4 cup salsa

6 tablespoons fat-free sour cream

1 1/2 cups finely chopped iceberg lettuce

DO AHEAD OR DELEGATE: Combine the dry seasonings, make the marinade and marinate the meat in the refrigerator, or fully prepare and refrigerate the steak, finely chop the lettuce.

1. Put the steak in a large flat dish with sides and poke some holes in the meat with the tines of a fork. In a measuring cup or bowl whisk together lime juice, oil, salt, chili powder, cumin, oregano, and paprika and pour them over the meat, flipping it several times to coat. Marinate, refrigerated, for at least 30 minutes and up to 2 days, flipping occasionally. Discard extra marinade.

2. When you are ready to cook, preheat the grill (or broiler) to medium-high heat. (Put the corn on the grill about 5 minutes before the meat, if you are serving it.) Grill the meat for 4 minutes per side for medium-rare or 6 minutes for medium. Transfer the steak to a cutting board and let it rest for 10 minutes if time allows, then slice it thinly across the grain.

3. Serve the sliced steak wrapped in warm tortillas and topped with 1–2 tablespoons salsa, 1 tablespoon sour cream, and 1/4 cup of lettuce.

SLOW COOKER DIRECTIONS: There's no need to marinate in advance. Combine the lime juice, oil, and spices in the slow cooker and stir to combine well. Add the steak, turning several times to be sure it's well coated. Cook on low for 4–5 hours or on high for 2–3 hours. Serve as directed above. (Slow cooker cooking times may vary—get to know your slow cooker and, if necessary, adjust cooking times accordingly.)

FLAVOR BOOSTER
Add 1/4–1/2 teaspoon of cayenne pepper to the dry spices.

Easiest Grilled Corn

SERVES: 6 • **SERVING SIZE:** 1 EAR

6 medium ears corn

1 1/2 teaspoons butter-flavored nonstick cooking spray
(2 sprays per ear), or use melted butter or margarine

1. Preheat the grill to medium-high heat.
   Peel the husk and silk off the corn.
   Spray the corn evenly with the butter-
   flavored spray. Grill the corn for 10–15
   minutes directly on the grates, turning
   occasionally, until it is browned or
   blackened in spots. Serve immediately
   seasoned with a little salt or fresh lime
   juice, if desired.

TIP
Use any leftover flank steak for breakfast:
Dice leftover steak and scramble with eggs,
onions, and cheese. Wrap in tortillas and
serve with salsa and sour cream.

NUTRITIONAL INFORMATION | GRILLED MEXICAN FLANK STEAK FAJITAS:

EXCHANGES / CHOICES:
1 Carbohydrate; 3 Protein, lean; 1 Fat

Calories: 255; Calories from Fat: 80; Total Fat: 9 g;
Saturated Fat: 3 g; Trans Fat: 0 g; Cholesterol: 65 mg;
Sodium: 455 mg; Potassium: 480 mg; Total Carbohydrate: 18 g;
Dietary Fiber: 2 g; Sugar: 2 g; Protein: 25 g; Phosphorus: 285 mg

NUTRITIONAL INFORMATION | EASIEST GRILLED CORN:

EXCHANGES / CHOICES:
1 1/2 Starch

Calories: 105; Calories from Fat: 20; Total Fat: 2 g;
Saturated Fat: 0.3 g; Trans Fat: 0 g; Cholesterol: 0 mg;
Sodium: 0 mg; Potassium: 225 mg; Total Carbohydrate: 22 g;
Dietary Fiber: 2 g; Sugar: 5 g; Protein: 4 g; Phosphorus: 80 mg

My husband, Andrew, couldn't get enough of this tangy and colorful salad, inspired by a recipe by Stephanie Witt Sedgwick in The Washington Post. *It would be great for a potluck as long as you keep it cool. This is also good with about a cup of peeled and diced cucumber tossed in. Serve with Whole-Grain Baguette.*

Shrimp, Mango, and Avocado Salad with Lime

PREP + COOK: 30 MINUTES • **SERVES:** 4 • **SERVING SIZE:** 1 1/2 CUPS

1 tablespoon extra-virgin olive oil

1/4 teaspoon salt

1 lime, juice only (about 1/4 cup)

2 tablespoons fresh cilantro, chopped

1 mango, peeled and diced

1/4 red onion, finely diced

1 avocado, peeled and diced

1 jalapeño pepper, seeded, halved and thinly sliced (optional)

1 pound peeled and deveined cooked shrimp, or use lobster or crab

DO AHEAD OR DELEGATE: Cook the shrimp if necessary, peel and dice the mango, dice the onion, seed, halve, and slice the jalapeño pepper, chop the cilantro, juice the lime, or fully prepare and refrigerate the salad.

1. (Warm the baguette if you are serving it.) Combine all the ingredients in a medium salad bowl. If time allows, let the salad sit for 10 minutes to meld the flavors. Serve immediately or refrigerate for up to 24 hours.

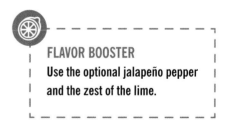

FLAVOR BOOSTER
Use the optional jalapeño pepper and the zest of the lime.

- -

Whole-Grain Baguette

SERVES: 6 • **SERVING SIZE:** 1 SLICE

1 whole-grain baguette

1. Warm the baguette in a 300°F oven for about 5 minutes. Slice into 6 pieces. Alternatively, brush thin slices of the baguette with olive oil and toast or broil them for a few minutes until they are lightly browned and crispy.

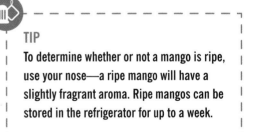

TIP

To determine whether or not a mango is ripe, use your nose—a ripe mango will have a slightly fragrant aroma. Ripe mangos can be stored in the refrigerator for up to a week.

NUTRITIONAL INFORMATION | SHRIMP, MANGO, AND AVOCADO SALAD WITH LIME:

EXCHANGES / CHOICES:
1 Carbohydrate; 4 Protein, lean

Calories: 245; Calories from Fat: 80; Total Fat: 9 g; Saturated Fat: 1.4 g; Trans Fat: 0 g; Cholesterol: 215 mg; Sodium: 275 mg; Potassium: 600 mg; Total Carbohydrate: 14 g; Dietary Fiber: 4 g; Sugar: 9 g; Protein: 29 g; Phosphorus: 300 mg

NUTRITIONAL INFORMATION | WHOLE-GRAIN BAGUETTE:

EXCHANGES / CHOICES:
1 Starch

Calories: 70; Calories from Fat: 10; Total Fat: 1 g; Saturated Fat: 0.2 g; Trans Fat: 0 g; Cholesterol: 0 mg; Sodium: 125 mg; Potassium: 70 mg; Total Carbohydrate: 12 g; Dietary Fiber: 2 g; Sugar: 1 g; Protein: 3 g; Phosphorus: 60 mg

My friend and food writer April Fulton shared her wonderful recipe for this savory and healthy meatless dish. If you don't like tofu, you can use chicken or beef instead. Serve with Brown Rice.

Caramelized Tofu and Broccoli Stir-Fry

PREP + COOK: 20 MINUTES • **SERVES:** 4 • **SERVING SIZE:** 1 3/4 CUPS

15 ounces extra-firm tofu, or use boneless chicken or beef

2 tablespoons peanut oil or coconut oil

1 teaspoon minced garlic (1–2 cloves)

1/2 cup pecans, coarsely chopped

2 tablespoons brown sugar

3 tablespoons reduced-sodium soy sauce (use wheat/gluten-free if needed), divided use

1/4 teaspoon crushed red pepper flakes (optional)

1 head broccoli, cut into florets (about 3 cups)

1/2 red bell pepper, cut into thin 1-inch long strips

1/2 red onion, thinly sliced

DO AHEAD OR DELEGATE: Drain, wrap, and slice the tofu or slice the chicken or beef into strips if you are using it, and refrigerate. Peel the garlic, chop the pecans, chop the broccoli, and slice the bell pepper and the onion.

1. (Start the rice first, if you are serving it.) Drain the tofu and wrap it in a clean dishcloth to draw out the extra water. Cut the tofu into 3 crosswise slices, and cut those slices into 3 or 4 long strips.

2. In a large skillet, heat the oil over medium-high heat. Add the tofu strips and cook them without stirring for about 3 minutes until they have browned on the bottom. Flip the tofu (tongs work well for this) and add the garlic and pecans, stirring for a minute until the garlic becomes fragrant. Add the sugar, 1 1/2 tablespoons soy sauce, and the red pepper flakes (optional), and stir until the sugar blends with the rest of the ingredients. Remove the tofu and nuts to a plate, allowing some of the sauce to remain in the pan.

3. Add the broccoli, red peppers, onions, and the remaining soy sauce and cook for 3–4 minutes until they are tender. Add the tofu and other ingredients back into the skillet to heat them through, and serve immediately.

FLAVOR BOOSTER
Serve with extra soy sauce and/or Asian chili garlic sauce.

Brown Rice

SERVES: 4 • **SERVING SIZE:** 1/2 CUP

1 1/2 cups quick-cooking brown rice

1. Prepare the rice according to package directions.

TIP

Beware of the sodium content (and of course calories and fat) in restaurant foods! According to a Cambridge University study, restaurant-industry supported logos used to point out healthier choices on menus use guidelines that are more generous than recommendations by the USDA. The biggest discrepancy in this area is sodium. All the more reason to plan ahead and eat healthier meals at home.

NUTRITIONAL INFORMATION | CARAMELIZED TOFU AND BROCCOLI STIR-FRY:

EXCHANGES / CHOICES:
1 Carbohydrate; 1 Nonstarchy Vegetable; 2 Protein, medium fat; 2 Fat

Calories: 325; Calories from Fat: 215; Total Fat: 24 g;
Saturated Fat: 2.6 g; Trans Fat: 0 g; Cholesterol: 0 mg;
Sodium: 440 mg; Potassium: 470 mg; Total Carbohydrate: 18 g;
Dietary Fiber: 4 g; Sugar: 11 g; Protein: 15 g; Phosphorus: 245 mg

NUTRITIONAL INFORMATION | BROWN RICE:

EXCHANGES / CHOICES:
1 1/2 Starch

Calories: 115; Calories from Fat: 10; Total Fat: 1 g;
Saturated Fat: 0.2 g; Trans Fat: 0 g; Cholesterol: 0 mg;
Sodium: 5 mg; Potassium: 45 mg; Total Carbohydrate: 24 g;
Dietary Fiber: 2 g; Sugar: 0 g; Protein: 3 g; Phosphorus: 85 mg

We love this Alfredo sauce because it tastes rich but is low in saturated fat and high in protein and calcium. Serve with Baby Greens with Sliced Peach and Pecans.

Healthy Fettuccine Alfredo with Cherry Tomatoes

PREP + COOK: 30 MINUTES • **SERVES:** 8 • **SERVING SIZE:** 1 3/4 CUPS

1/2 cup raw, unsalted cashews

16 ounces whole-wheat fettuccine

1 tablespoon no-trans-fat margarine

2 teaspoons minced garlic (about 4 cloves)

1 cup part-skim ricotta cheese

1/4 cup grated Parmesan cheese

1/2 teaspoon salt

8 ounces cherry tomatoes, halved or quartered

1/4 cup fresh basil leaves, thinly sliced, or use fresh parsley

DO AHEAD OR DELEGATE: Cook the pasta and store tossed with a little oil to prevent sticking (don't forget to reserve 1/2 cup of the pasta's cooking water), peel the garlic, grate the Parmesan cheese if necessary, and refrigerate, and halve or quarter the tomatoes.

1. In a small bowl, cover the cashews with water (about 1/3 cup) and heat in the microwave for 30–60 seconds until the water is hot. Set aside.

2. Cook the pasta according to the package directions until it is al dente. Scoop out 1/2 cup of the boiling water before draining the pasta and set it aside. (Meanwhile, prepare the salad, if you are serving it.) When the pasta goes in the water, melt the butter in a small skillet over medium heat, and when it is melted, add the garlic. Sauté for 30 seconds to 1 minute until it is fragrant, and remove from the heat.

3. In a blender or food processor, combine the butter, garlic, ricotta, Parmesan cheese, salt, cashews and their soaking water, and 1/4 cup of the water reserved from the boiling pasta, and blend until smooth (if it is too thick, add the rest of the reserved water).

4. Return the drained pasta to the pot (or transfer it to a large metal bowl), letting some water cling to the noodles. Toss with the Alfredo sauce and stir in the tomatoes and basil. Serve immediately, seasoning with black pepper to taste at the table. (It will thicken if you don't serve it immediately.)

Baby Greens with Sliced Peaches and Pecans

SERVES: 8 • **SERVING SIZE:** 1 CUP

10 ounces baby greens

2 medium peaches, sliced

8 teaspoons pecans, coarsely chopped, or broken and lightly toasted

1/4 cup vinaigrette dressing

1. Toss the greens with the peaches, pecans, and vinaigrette.

FLAVOR BOOSTER

Serve the dish with freshly ground pepper or sprinkled with crushed red pepper flakes at the table.

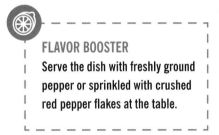

TIP

Cashews, which are rich in iron, phosphorus, and zinc, are an excellent source of protein. While nuts have a high fat content, the great majority of this fat is heart-healthy monounsaturated fat, similar to the fats found in olive oil.

NUTRITIONAL INFORMATION | HEALTHY FETTUCCINE ALFREDO WITH CHERRY TOMATOES:

EXCHANGES / CHOICES:
2 1/2 Starch; 1/2 Carbohydrate; 1 Protein, lean; 1 Fat

Calories: 325; Calories from Fat: 80; Total Fat: 9 g;
Saturated Fat: 3 g; Trans Fat: 0 g; Cholesterol: 10 mg;
Sodium: 260 mg; Potassium: 230 mg; Total Carbohydrate: 47 g;
Dietary Fiber: 7 g; Sugar: 2 g; Protein: 15 g; Phosphorus: 245 mg

NUTRITIONAL INFORMATION | BABY GREENS WITH SLICED PEACHES AND PECANS:

EXCHANGES / CHOICES:
1/2 Carbohydrate; 1/2 Fat

Calories: 50; Calories from Fat: 25; Total Fat: 3 g;
Saturated Fat: 0.3 g; Trans Fat: 0 g; Cholesterol: 0 mg;
Sodium: 145 mg; Potassium: 155 mg; Total Carbohydrate: 6 g;
Dietary Fiber: 2 g; Sugar: 4 g; Protein: 1 g; Phosphorus: 25 mg

I was thrilled by how much my family loved this stew, especially because I served it as a cleansing meal after a vacation weekend of overindulgence. You can vary the vegetables—zucchini, potatoes, or eggplant would all work well, and you could even stir in some shrimp for the last few minutes until they turn pink. Serve over Bulgur Wheat.

Indian Summer Vegetable Stew

PREP: 25 MINUTES • **COOK:** 20 MINUTES • **SERVES:** 6 • **SERVING SIZE:** 2 CUPS

2 tablespoons extra-virgin olive oil

1 red onion, finely diced

1 teaspoon minced garlic (about 2 cloves)

1 tablespoon garam masala (an Indian spice blend), or use 1 tablespoon curry powder and 1/4 teaspoon cinnamon and/or cardamom

1 head cauliflower, cut into florets (7 cups)

2 carrots, halved and sliced

1 red bell pepper, finely diced

2 cups water

5 tomatoes, chopped

15 ounces canned chickpeas, drained and rinsed, or use 1 1/2 cups cooked chickpeas

1/2 teaspoon salt

1/4 teaspoon black pepper

2 tablespoons barbecue sauce, or use red pasta sauce

3/4 cup plain nonfat Greek yogurt, or use nonfat sour cream

DO AHEAD OR DELEGATE: Dice the onion and the bell pepper, peel the garlic, cut the cauliflower, halve and slice the carrots, and chop the tomatoes.

1. Heat a large Dutch oven or deep skillet over medium heat. Add the oil, and when it is hot, add the onions and garlic, and sauté for 2–3 minutes until the onions are tender. Add the garam masala and cook for 1 more minute.

2. Stir in the cauliflower, carrots, bell peppers, and water. Increase the heat to medium-high and bring it to a boil. (Meanwhile, start the bulgur, if you are serving it.) Cover, reduce the heat, and simmer for 5 minutes. Add the tomatoes, chickpeas, salt, and pepper and cover and simmer for 10–15 more minutes until the vegetables are tender, stirring occasionally.

3. Remove the cover and stir in the barbecue sauce. Heat through for another minute. Serve immediately, topped with a little Greek yogurt, or refrigerate for up to 3 days, or freeze for up to 3 months.

SLOW COOKER DIRECTIONS: Omit the oil. Place all ingredients except the yogurt into the slow cooker and cook on low for 8–10 hours or on high for 4–5 hours. Serve with yogurt as directed. (Slow cooker cooking times may vary—get to know your slow cooker and, if necessary, adjust cooking times accordingly.)

FLAVOR BOOSTER
Use extra garlic and garam masala or curry powder.

Bulgur Wheat

SERVES: 6 • **SERVING SIZE:** 1/2 CUP

1 cup bulgur wheat

2 cups reduced-sodium chicken or vegetable broth, or use a combination of water and broth

1. In a medium saucepan, combine the bulgur wheat and the broth or combination of broth and water. Bring to a boil, cover, and simmer for 15 minutes until the bulgur is tender.

TIP

To make chickpeas in the slow cooker, soak 1 pound dried beans in cold water for a few hours or overnight and drain them. (This is not necessary but it may reduce the beans' gassy effect when you eat them.) Put the drained (or dry) beans in the slow cooker and cover them with water until they are immersed. Add seasonings as desired. I recommend 1–2 teaspoons of salt and then 1–2 teaspoons of cumin if desired. Cook them on low for 7–10 hours until the beans are tender. Drain and freeze or refrigerate them in 1 1/2 cup increments. (Measure and divide the beans before freezing them because they are very hard to separate when frozen.)

NUTRITIONAL INFORMATION | INDIAN SUMMER VEGETABLE STEW:

EXCHANGES / CHOICES:
1 Starch; 3 Nonstarchy Vegetable; 1 Fat

Calories: 210; Calories from Fat: 55; Total Fat: 6 g;
Saturated Fat: 0.9 g; Trans Fat: 0 g; Cholesterol: 0 mg;
Sodium: 395 mg; Potassium: 930 mg; Total Carbohydrate: 31 g;
Dietary Fiber: 8 g; Sugar: 13 g; Protein: 10 g; Phosphorus: 205 mg

NUTRITIONAL INFORMATION | BULGUR WHEAT:

EXCHANGES / CHOICES:
1 1/2 Starch

Calories: 95; Calories from Fat: 0; Total Fat: 0 g;
Saturated Fat: 0.1 g; Trans Fat: 0 g; Cholesterol: 0 mg;
Sodium: 175 mg; Potassium: 165 mg; Total Carbohydrate: 21 g;
Dietary Fiber: 5 g; Sugar: 0 g; Protein: 4 g; Phosphorus: 90 mg

SNACK ATTACK:
25 Healthy Snacks to Keep You Going Between Meals

Afternoon hunger strikes like a cobra! Before it attacks and rattles your brain, it's best to be armed with a list of nourishing and delicious snacks.

1. Plain or flavored nonfat yogurt or cottage cheese with sliced fruit and granola

2. Whole-grain cereals or oatmeal, dry or with milk, yogurt, or raisins

3. Reduced-fat cheese sticks, cubes, or shredded cheese

4. Nut and raisin mix or homemade trail mix

5. Peanut butter sandwich on whole-wheat bread with sliced apples or bananas

6. Sliced banana topped with 1 tablespoon almond butter and sprinkled with ground cinnamon and unsweetened cocoa powder

7. Cinnamon toast (toasted whole-grain bread spread lightly with butter and sprinkled with cinnamon)

8. Cinnamon graham crackers with nonfat cottage cheese

9. Chocolate graham crackers with peanut butter

10. Brown rice cakes, plain or topped with peanut butter or cheese

11. Whole-grain crackers with spreadable cheese, such as Laughing Cow Creamy Light Swiss

12. Mini whole-grain bagels with cream cheese and sliced cucumbers

13. Pizza bagels (whole-grain bagel topped with sauce, cheese, herbs, and other toppings)

14. Whole-grain bagel chips with cream cheese or hummus

15. Hummus dip with fresh vegetables

16. Sliced avocados with whole-grain crackers

17. Hard-boiled eggs

18. Reduced-sodium turkey slices served plain or rolled in a whole-wheat tortilla

19. Celery filled with cream cheese, Boursin cheese, or peanut butter

20. Sliced bell peppers, celery, baby carrots, or sugar snap peas with light ranch dip or other dressing (see page 98 for homemade dressings and dips)

21. Edamame in the shell, sprinkled lightly with sea salt

22. Reduced-sodium black beans topped with reduced-fat cheddar cheese and salsa

23. Apple slices with peanut or almond butter

24. Smoothies: blend fresh and/or frozen fruit, spinach or other greens, chia seeds, low-fat yogurt, kefir or soy milk

25. Dried fruit such as mango, apricots, raisins, or plums

page 180   Light and Fluffy Spinach and Cheese Strata

Corn and Scallion Pancakes
SIDE DISH: French Beet Salad

page
212

FALL

FALL  WEEK 1

Thai Garlic and Basil Chicken (1)
SIDE DISH: Steamed Rice and Peas (1a)

Stuffed Zucchini Gondolas (2)
SIDE DISH: Whole-Grain Bread (2a)

Penne Pesto with Baby Spinach (3)
SIDE DISH: Green Salad with Apples, Gorgonzola Cheese, and Pecans (3a)

Greek Chopped Salad (4)
SIDE DISH: Seedless Grapes (4a)

Corn and Scallion Pancakes (5)
SIDE DISH: French Beet Salad (5a)

SHOPPING LIST

- -

🥕 PRODUCE

4 **scallions** (5)

1/2 **yellow onion** (2)

1 large **red onion** (1)

1 **red onion or red bell pepper** (4)

1/2 **bell pepper**, any variety (2)

1 **red bell pepper** (1)

1 **tomato** (4)

1 head **romaine lettuce** (4)

1 head **lettuce**, any variety (3a)

12 ounces **baby spinach** (3)

1 1/2–2 cups **fresh basil leaves** (1)

2 tablespoons **fresh dill** (4)

1/2 cup **fresh parsley** (2)

3 medium to large **beets** (or use precooked beets) (5a)

3 medium **zucchini** (2)

1 **cucumber** (4)

1 cup **corn kernels, fresh, frozen, or canned** (5)

1–2 **lemons** (4)

1 **red apple**, such as Gala or Fuji (3a)

1 bunch **seedless grapes** (4a)

🍖 MEAT AND FISH

1 1/2 pounds **boneless, skinless chicken breasts** (1)

8 ounces **meatless crumbles, or lean ground beef or turkey** (2)

SHELVED ITEMS

1 loaf **whole-grain bread** (2a)

1 1/2 cups **quick-cooking brown rice** (1a)

16 ounces **whole-wheat penne noodles** (3)

1/2 cup **stone-ground cornmeal** (5)

1 cup **tomato and basil–flavored pasta sauce** (2)

1/2 cup **salsa** (5)*

6 1/2 ounces **light tuna in water or olive oil** (4)*

15 ounces **cannellini beans** (4)

1/2 cup **pitted kalamata olives** (4)

2 tablespoons **capers** (3)

2 tablespoons **pecans** (3a)

SPICES

1 teaspoon **salt** (1a)(3)(5)

1 teaspoon **dried oregano** (4)

3/8 teaspoon **black pepper** (3)(4)

STAPLES

2 teaspoons **butter** (5)

1/2 cup **extra-virgin olive oil** (2)(3)(4)

1/3 cup **canola or vegetable oil** (1)(5)

2 teaspoons **white wine vinegar** (5a)

1/4 cup **vinaigrette dressing** (3a)

2 teaspoons **grainy Dijon mustard** (use wheat/gluten-free if needed) (5a)

5 tablespoons **reduced-sodium soy sauce** (use wheat/gluten-free if needed) (1)(1a)

1 tablespoon **brown sugar** (1)

1/4 cup pure **maple syrup** (5)*

1 tablespoon **honey** (5)

1/2 cup **nonfat or low-fat milk** (5)

2 **eggs** (5)

2 tablespoons + 2 1/2 teaspoons **minced garlic** (1)(2)(3)(4)

1/2 cup **flour** (use wheat/gluten-free if needed) (5)

1 teaspoon **baking powder** (5)

REFRIGERATED/FROZEN

2 tablespoons **crumbled Gorgonzola or blue cheese** (3a)

1/2 cup **reduced-fat feta cheese** (4)

1/4 cup **shredded Parmesan cheese** (3)

2 tablespoons **grated Parmesan cheese** (2)

1/3 cup **shredded part-skim mozzarella cheese** (2)

1/2 cup **nonfat sour cream** (5)*

1/2 cup **refrigerated pesto sauce** (3)

2/3 cup **frozen peas** (1a)

Get free, printable versions of the shopping lists from this book at **TheScramble.com/diabetes**.

*optional ingredients

When I made this Thai-style chicken for our guests, the kids all wanted seconds. Serve with Steamed Rice and Peas.

Thai Garlic and Basil Chicken

PREP + COOK: 20 MINUTES • **SERVES:** 6 • **SERVING SIZE:** 1 1/4 CUPS

1 1/2 tablespoons canola or vegetable oil

2 tablespoons minced garlic (10–12 cloves)

1 large red onion, quartered top-to-bottom and cut into thin strips

1 red bell pepper, cut into thin strips, about 1 inch long

1 1/2 pounds boneless, skinless chicken breasts, cut into 1-inch pieces

3 1/3 tablespoons reduced-sodium soy sauce or tamari (use wheat/gluten-free if needed)

1 tablespoon brown sugar

1 1/2–2 cups fresh basil leaves, coarsely chopped

DO AHEAD OR DELEGATE: Peel the garlic, cut the onion and the bell pepper, cut and refrigerate the chicken, or fully prepare and refrigerate or freeze the meal.

1. (Start the steamed rice and peas, if you are making it.) In a large nonstick skillet over medium-high heat, heat the oil. Add the garlic, onions, and peppers, and sauté for 2 minutes. Add the chicken and stir-fry until it starts to brown on all sides, but is not cooked through, 3–5 minutes.

2. Meanwhile, in a small bowl, combine the soy sauce and sugar, and add that to the pan. Continue to cook the chicken, uncovered, tossing it occasionally, until the chicken is just cooked through, 2–3 more minutes. (At this point you can cool and refrigerate the chicken for up to 3 days, or freeze it for up to 3 months. Add the basil just before serving.) Add the basil, toss it well, and serve immediately.

SLOW COOKER DIRECTIONS: Combine all ingredients except the basil in the slow cooker, and cook on low for 6–7 hours or on high for 3–3 1/2 hours. Add the basil just before serving. (Slow cooker cooking times may vary—get to know your slow cooker and, if necessary, adjust cooking times accordingly.)

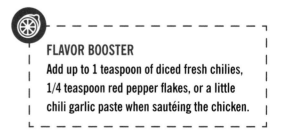

FLAVOR BOOSTER
Add up to 1 teaspoon of diced fresh chilies, 1/4 teaspoon red pepper flakes, or a little chili garlic paste when sautéing the chicken.

Steamed Rice and Peas

SERVES: 6 • **SERVING SIZE:** 3/4 CUP

1 cup quick-cooking brown rice

2/3 cup frozen peas

1/4 teaspoon salt (optional)

1 tablespoon reduced-sodium soy sauce (use wheat/gluten- free if needed) (optional)

1. Cook the rice according to the package directions. Mix the frozen peas and a few shakes of salt or soy sauce into the rice while it is still hot. Stir and cover for 1–2 minutes so the peas thaw.

TIP

Would you like your family to describe you as attentive, thoughtful, and capable? A study done by the Cornell University Food and Brand Lab determined that when the cook (usually mom or dad) included vegetables with the meal they prepared, they (and the meal) were perceived more positively. So, load some veggies onto your family's plates. Maybe someone will even kiss the cook!

NUTRITIONAL INFORMATION | THAI GARLIC AND BASIL CHICKEN:

EXCHANGES / CHOICES:

1/2 Carbohydrate; 1 Nonstarchy Vegetable; 3 Protein, lean; 1/2 Fat

Calories: 220; Calories from Fat: 70; Total Fat: 8 g;
Saturated Fat: 1.2 g; Trans Fat: 0 g; Cholesterol: 65 mg;
Sodium: 430 mg; Potassium: 390 mg; Total Carbohydrate: 10 g;
Dietary Fiber: 2 g; Sugar: 5 g; Protein: 26 g; Phosphorus: 215 mg

NUTRITIONAL INFORMATION | EDAMAME:

EXCHANGES / CHOICES:

1 1/2 Starch

Calories: 130; Calories from Fat: 10; Total Fat: 1 g;
Saturated Fat: 0.1 g; Trans Fat: 0 g; Cholesterol: 0 mg;
Sodium: 30 mg; Potassium: 95 mg; Total Carbohydrate: 26 g;
Dietary Fiber: 2 g; Sugar: 1 g; Protein: 4 g; Phosphorus: 120 mg

I don't find zucchini to be the most flavorful or exciting vegetable, but I love it as a crunchy crust stuffed with flavorful filling. I was going to call these zucchini boats but the imagery of gondolas better matches their Italian flavor. Serve with Whole-Grain Bread.

Stuffed Zucchini Gondolas

PREP: 30 MINUTES • **COOK:** 10 MINUTES • **SERVES:** 6 • **SERVING SIZE:** 1 BOAT

3 medium zucchini (8–10 ounces each)

2 tablespoons extra-virgin olive oil, divided use

1/2 bell pepper, any color, finely diced

1/2 yellow onion, finely diced

1 teaspoon minced garlic (about 2 cloves)

8 ounces meatless crumbles, or lean ground beef or turkey

1 cup tomato basil pasta sauce

1/2 cup fresh parsley, chopped

2 tablespoons grated Parmesan cheese

1/3 cup shredded part-skim mozzarella cheese, or a little more if needed

DO AHEAD OR DELEGATE: Cut and scoop out the zucchini, dice the bell pepper and the onion, peel the garlic, chop the parsley, grate the cheeses, if necessary, and refrigerate, or fully prepare and refrigerate the dish.

1. Preheat the oven to 450°F. Spray a baking sheet with nonstick cooking spray.

2. Cut the zucchini in half lengthwise and, using a grapefruit spoon, or a teaspoon if you don't have a grapefruit spoon, scoop out about half of the flesh of the zucchini to create a well in the center, reserving the zucchini flesh. Lay the zucchini on the baking sheet and put half the oil in a small bowl. Using a pastry brush, brush the flesh of the zucchini with oil and bake it for 10 minutes.

3. Meanwhile, heat a large heavy skillet over medium heat, and add the remaining oil. When it is hot, add the peppers and onions and sauté them for about 3 minutes until they start to get tender. Chop the reserved zucchini flesh and add it to the skillet. Stir in the garlic until it is fragrant, about 30 seconds, then add the meat and brown it for 3–4 minutes. Add the sauce and bring it to a low boil. Remove from the heat and stir in the parsley and the Parmesan cheese.

4. Remove the zucchini from the oven and scoop the vegetable mixture into the wells of the zucchini, mounding as necessary to use all the filling, and topping with the mozzarella cheese. Return it to the oven for 10 more minutes until the zucchini is fork tender. (Meanwhile, warm the bread, if you are serving it.) For a browner top, broil the zucchini for the final 2 minutes until it is browned in spots. Serve immediately or refrigerate for up to 3 days.

Whole-Grain Bread

SERVES: 6 • **SERVING SIZE:** 1 (1-OUNCE) SLICE

1 loaf whole-grain bread

1. Warm the bread in a 300°F oven for 5–8 minutes, if desired.

FLAVOR BOOSTER

Add 1/4–1/2 teaspoon crushed red pepper flakes when you add the sauce. Use Gorgonzola cheese instead of mozzarella.

TIP

Instead of using the meat or meatless crumbles, you can crumble frozen veggie burgers into the sauce.

NUTRITIONAL INFORMATION | STUFFED ZUCCHINI GONDOLAS:

EXCHANGES / CHOICES:
1/2 Carbohydrate; 1 Nonstarchy Vegetable; 1 Protein, lean; 1 Fat

Calories: 165; Calories from Fat: 70; Total Fat: 8 g;
Saturated Fat: 1.8 g; Trans Fat: 0 g; Cholesterol: 5 mg;
Sodium: 430 mg; Potassium: 720 mg; Total Carbohydrate: 15 g;
Dietary Fiber: 5 g; Sugar: 8 g; Protein: 11 g; Phosphorus: 155 mg

NUTRITIONAL INFORMATION | WHOLE-GRAIN BREAD:

EXCHANGES / CHOICES:
1 Starch

Calories: 70; Calories from Fat: 10; Total Fat: 1.0 g;
Saturated Fat: 0.2 g; Trans Fat: 0 g; Cholesterol: 0 mg;
Sodium: 125 mg; Potassium: 70 mg; Total Carbohydrate: 12 g;
Dietary Fiber: 2 g; Sugar: 1 g; Protein: 3 g; Phosphorus: 60 mg

My family loves this combination so much that we could eat it every week (and sometimes do!). But you can always remove some of the noodles before tossing them with the pesto, and toss them with butter and Parmesan cheese for picky eaters. Serve with Green Salad with Apples, Gorgonzola Cheese, and Pecans.

Penne Pesto with Baby Spinach

PREP + COOK: 25 MINUTES • **SERVES:** 8 • **SERVING SIZE:** 1 1/2 CUPS

1/2 teaspoon minced garlic (about 1 clove)

8 tablespoons homemade pesto (see below), or use store-bought

2 tablespoons extra-virgin olive oil

2 tablespoons capers, drained

16 ounces whole-wheat penne noodles

12 ounces baby spinach

1/4 teaspoon salt, or to taste

1/8 teaspoon black pepper, or to taste

1/4 cup shredded Parmesan cheese, or more to taste

PESTO

2 cups (tightly packed) fresh basil leaves

2 chopped garlic cloves

2 tablespoons pine nuts

1/2 cup extra-virgin olive oil

1/2 cup grated Parmesan cheese

1/2 teaspoon salt

1/4 teaspoon pepper

1/2 lemon (optional)

DO AHEAD OR DELEGATE: Peel the garlic, make the pesto if using homemade, and cook the pasta (and toss with a little oil to prevent sticking).

1. To make fresh pesto, combine all ingredients in a blender or food processor. Blend until coarsely chopped.

2. Boil the water for the pasta in a large stockpot (and start the salad, if you are serving it). Meanwhile, in a large serving bowl, combine the garlic, pesto, oil, and capers. Add the noodles to the boiling water and cook them until they are about 1 minute short of being done. Add the spinach to the boiling water with the pasta and cook for about 1 minute.

3. Drain the pasta and spinach briefly and toss it with the ingredients in the large bowl. Season with salt and pepper and top with the Parmesan cheese. Serve immediately, or refrigerate for up to 2 days.

FLAVOR BOOSTER
Use extra garlic and serve the pasta with crushed red pepper flakes.

Green Salad with Apples, Gorgonzola Cheese, and Pecans

SERVES: 8 • **SERVING SIZE:** 1 CUP

1 head lettuce, any variety, torn or chopped into bite-sized pieces

1 red apple, such as Gala or Fuji, diced

2 tablespoons crumbled Gorgonzola or blue cheese

2 tablespoons pecans, lightly toasted

1/4 cup vinaigrette dressing

1. Toss the lettuce with the apples, cheese, pecans, and dressing, to taste.

NUTRITIONAL INFORMATION | PENNE PESTO WITH BABY SPINACH:

EXCHANGES / CHOICES:
3 Starch; 2 Fat

Calories: 320; Calories from Fat: 100; Total Fat: 11 g;
Saturated Fat: 1.9 g; Trans Fat: 0 g; Cholesterol: 0 mg;
Sodium: 285 mg; Potassium: 330 mg; Total Carbohydrate: 47 g;
Dietary Fiber: 7 g; Sugar: 2 g; Protein: 10 g; Phosphorus: 155 mg

NUTRITIONAL INFORMATION | GREEN SALAD WITH APPLES, GORGONZOLA CHEESE, AND PECANS:

EXCHANGES / CHOICES:
1/2 Carbohydrate; 1 Fat

Calories: 65; Calories from Fat: 30; Total Fat: 3.5 g;
Saturated Fat: 0.7 g; Trans Fat: 0 g; Cholesterol: 0 mg;
Sodium: 110 mg; Potassium: 135 mg; Total Carbohydrate: 7 g;
Dietary Fiber: 1 g; Sugar: 5 g; Protein: 1 g; Phosphorus: 30 mg

TIP
You can use extra pesto sauce as a spread for crackers, toss it with steamed green beans, or freeze it for a future use. To freeze leftover pesto, spoon it into ice cube trays and, after it freezes, remove from the tray and store in resealable bags in the freezer. You can take them out as needed and add them to pasta recipes for a flavor boost.

This tantalizing salad came from longtime Six O'Clock Scramble member Michele Houghton, who sent it with this advice: "I like to make all of my salads in a pasta bowl that is very wide and shallow. This allows me to layer the salad ingredients without the need to toss, since I never toss my salads with the dressing. I make really large salads like this one and serve them for 2–3 days, which saves me tons of time having to make a new salad each day." Serve with Seedless Grapes.

Greek Chopped Salad

PREP (NO COOK): 25 MINUTES • **SERVES:** 6 • **SERVING SIZE:** 2 1/2 CUPS

1 head romaine lettuce, chopped

1 red onion or red bell pepper, diced

1 cucumber, peeled, halved, seeded, and chopped

1/2 cup pitted kalamata olives

15 ounces canned cannellini beans (also called white kidney beans), drained and rinsed

1/2 cup reduced-fat feta cheese, cubed

1 tomato, chopped

2 tablespoons fresh dill or 2 teaspoons dried

1–2 lemons, juice only (1/4 cup)

1/4 cup extra-virgin olive oil

1 teaspoon dried oregano

1/4 teaspoon black pepper

1 teaspoon minced garlic (about 2 cloves)

DO AHEAD OR DELEGATE: Wash and chop the lettuce, dice the onion or pepper, peel, seed, and chop the cucumber, drain and rinse the beans, chop the tomato, dice the cheese if necessary, juice the lemons, and make the dressing.

1. In a large, wide, and shallow bowl, layer the lettuce, onions or bell peppers, cucumbers, olives, beans, cheese, tomatoes, and dill.

2. In a large measuring cup or jar, combine the lemon juice, oil, oregano, black pepper, and garlic. Whisk or shake the dressing until it is emulsified (thickened).

3. When you are ready to serve, toss the salad with the dressing, or drizzle the dressing over individual servings at the table.

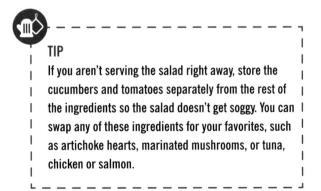

TIP

If you aren't serving the salad right away, store the cucumbers and tomatoes separately from the rest of the ingredients so the salad doesn't get soggy. You can swap any of these ingredients for your favorites, such as artichoke hearts, marinated mushrooms, or tuna, chicken or salmon.

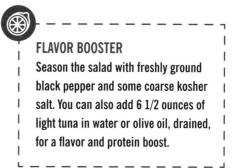

- -

Seedless Grapes

SERVES: 6 • **SERVING SIZE:** 3 OUNCES (17 SMALL GRAPES)

1 1/4 pounds seedless grapes

1. Serve either purple or green grapes (or you can serve frozen grapes for a sweet and crunchy treat). Safety note: Young children (3 and younger) should only eat halved or quartered grapes to prevent choking.

FLAVOR BOOSTER

Season the salad with freshly ground black pepper and some coarse kosher salt. You can also add 6 1/2 ounces of light tuna in water or olive oil, drained, for a flavor and protein boost.

NUTRITIONAL INFORMATION | GREEK CHOPPED SALAD:

EXCHANGES / CHOICES:
1/2 Starch; 1 Nonstarchy Vegetable; 1 Protein, lean; 1/2 Fat

Calories: 140; Calories from Fat: 55; Total Fat: 6 g;
Saturated Fat: 1.3 g; Trans Fat: 0 g; Cholesterol: 5 mg;
Sodium: 365 mg; Potassium: 460 mg; Total Carbohydrate: 16 g;
Dietary Fiber: 5 g; Sugar: 3 g; Protein: 7 g; Phosphorus: 130 mg

NUTRITIONAL INFORMATION | SEEDLESS GRAPES:

EXCHANGES / CHOICES:
1 Fruit

Calories: 60; Calories from Fat: 0; Total Fat: 0 g;
Saturated Fat: 0 g; Trans Fat: 0 g; Cholesterol: 0 mg;
Sodium: 0 mg; Potassium: 160 mg; Total Carbohydrate: 15 g;
Dietary Fiber: 1 g; Sugar: 13 g; Protein: 1 g; Phosphorus: 15 mg

These little cuties make a great main course, side dish, or a weekend brunch delight. Serve with French Beet Salad.

Corn and Scallion Pancakes

PREP + COOK: 20 MINUTES • **SERVES:** 4 • **SERVING SIZE:** 3 PANCAKES

1/2 cup flour

1/2 cup stone-ground cornmeal

1 teaspoon baking powder

1/2 teaspoon salt

2 eggs

1/2 cup nonfat or low-fat milk

1/4 cup canola or vegetable oil

1 tablespoon honey

1 cup corn kernels, fresh, frozen, or canned, thawed if frozen, steamed if fresh

4 scallions, thinly sliced (about 1/2 cup)

2 teaspoons butter, divided use

1/2 cup nonfat sour cream (optional)

1/2 cup salsa (optional)

1/4 cup pure maple syrup or butter (optional)

DO AHEAD OR DELEGATE: Combine the dry ingredients or prepare and refrigerate the batter.

1. (Start the beet salad first, if you are serving it.) In a large mixing bowl, whisk together the flour, cornmeal, baking powder, and salt. Add the eggs, milk, oil, and honey and mix gently until it is combined (do not over mix). Stir in the corn and scallions. (The batter can be made up to 12 hours in advance and stored in the refrigerator.)

2. Heat 1 teaspoon butter in a large nonstick skillet or electric frying pan over medium to medium-high heat. When the pan is hot and the butter is bubbly, ladle about half the batter into small pancakes in the pan (they should be about 3 inches wide, using about 1/4–1/2 cup of batter each). Cook them for about 2 minutes per side, until they are nicely browned on each side. Add a second teaspoon of butter to the pan and repeat with remaining batter. (Loosely cover the first batch with foil while the second batch is cooking.)

3. Serve immediately with sour cream, salsa, butter, maple syrup, or your favorite toppings.

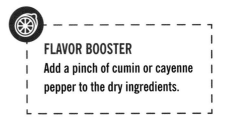

FLAVOR BOOSTER
Add a pinch of cumin or cayenne pepper to the dry ingredients.

French Beet Salad

SERVES: 4 • **SERVING SIZE:** 1/2 CUP

3 medium to large beets (or use precooked beets)

2 teaspoons grainy Dijon mustard (use wheat/gluten-free if needed)

2 teaspoons white wine vinegar

1. Scrub the beets. Cut off the greens, leaving about 1 inch of stems, and steam them in about 1 inch of gently boiling water, covered, for 45 minutes, until they are fork tender. Drain the beets, rinse them in cold water, and peel the skins, using your fingers or a vegetable peeler (or use precooked beets).

2. Dice the beets and place them in a medium serving bowl. Combine the mustard and vinegar and pour it over the beets, tossing thoroughly. Refrigerate the salad for at least 20 minutes. (Note: you can cook and peel the beets or make the whole salad up to 2 days in advance.)

TIP

If you try flipping the pancakes and they're sticking to the pan, that's an indication that they're not quite ready to be flipped. Let them continue to cook for another 30 seconds or so and try again. If the pancakes appear to be getting too brown for your liking, reduce the heat slightly and take the pan off the heat for a minute to let it cool.

NUTRITIONAL INFORMATION | CORN AND SCALLION PANCAKES:

EXCHANGES / CHOICES:
2 1/2 Starch; 1 Protein, lean; 2 1/2 Fat

Calories: 355; Calories from Fat: 170; Total Fat: 19 g;
Saturated Fat: 3.1 g; Trans Fat: 0.1 g; Cholesterol: 100 mg;
Sodium: 450 mg; Potassium: 240 mg; Total Carbohydrate: 40 g;
Dietary Fiber: 2 g; Sugar: 7 g; Protein: 8 g; Phosphorus: 260 mg

NUTRITIONAL INFORMATION | FRENCH BEET SALAD:

EXCHANGES / CHOICES:
1 Nonstarchy Vegetable

Calories: 25; Calories from Fat: 0; Total Fat: 0 g;
Saturated Fat: 0 g; Trans Fat: 0 g; Cholesterol: 0 mg;
Sodium: 105 mg; Potassium: 190 mg; Total Carbohydrate: 6 g;
Dietary Fiber: 2 g; Sugar: 4 g; Protein: 1 g; Phosphorus: 25 mg

FALL ⬤ WEEK 2

Creamy Herbed Chicken with Spinach and Sundried Tomatoes (1)
SIDE DISH: Green Beans with Lemon and Garlic (1a)

Indian Spiced Salmon (2)
SIDE DISH: Indian Quinoa Pilaf (2a)

Corn, Tomato, and Bacon Salad with Creamy Basil Dressing (3)
SIDE DISH: Lavish Crackers (3a); Sliced Apples (3b)

Fettuccine with Shredded Zucchini, Carrots, and Garlic (4)
SIDE DISH: Green Salad with Dried Cranberries and Parmesan Cheese (4a)

Cauliflower and Sweet Potato Stir-Fry (5)
SIDE DISH: Brown Rice (5a)

SHOPPING LIST

- -

🥕 PRODUCE
3 **carrots** or use 2 cups preshredded carrots (4)

1/2 **yellow onion** (2a)

1 **red bell pepper** (5)

1/2 **green chili pepper** (2a)*

1 pint **cherry tomatoes** (3)

1 small head **lettuce** (4a)

6 ounces **baby spinach** (1)

1 teaspoon + 1 tablespoon **fresh ginger** (2a)(5)

1 cup **fresh basil** (3)

1 pound **green beans, fresh or frozen** (1a)

2 **zucchini** (4)

1 **yellow squash** (4)

1 **sweet potato** (5)

4 ears **fresh corn** (3)

1 small to medium head **cauliflower** (5)

8 ounces **sliced mushrooms** (1)

1/8 **lemon** (1a)

2–4 **apples** (3b)

1 medium **avocado** (3)

🍖 MEAT AND FISH
1 pound **boneless, skinless chicken breasts** (1)

1 1/2 pounds **salmon fillet**, preferably wild Alaskan salmon (2)

6 ounces **cooked turkey sausage** (4)*

6 strips **bacon** (turkey, pork, or meatless) (3)

🗄 SHELVED ITEMS

1–2 cups **quick-cooking brown rice** (5a)

1 bag **Success Rice Whole-Grain Brown Rice or 1 cup quick-cooking brown rice** (1)

2/3 cup **quinoa** (2a)

16 ounces **whole-wheat fettuccine** (4)

12 **lavash crackers** (Armenian cracker bread) or use gluten/wheat-free crackers (3a)

1/2 cup sliced **sundried tomatoes in oil** (1)

1/2 cup **reduced-sodium chicken broth** (1)

1/4 cup **white wine** (1)

2 tablespoons **dried cranberries** (4a)

🧂 SPICES

3/8 teaspoons **salt** (1a)(2a)(3)(4)

1/2 teaspoon **kosher salt** (2)

1/2 teaspoon **Italian seasoning blend** (1)

3/8 teaspoon **black pepper** (1)(1a)

1/4 teaspoon **ground cinnamon** (2a)

1/2 teaspoon **ground cumin** (2a)

1 teaspoon **turmeric** (2a)

1/2 teaspoon **curry powder** (2)

🫙 STAPLES

2 tablespoons **trans fat-free margarine** (1)

1 tablespoon + 1 teaspoon + 1/4 cup **extra-virgin olive oil** (1a)(2)(4)

3 tablespoons **canola or vegetable oil** (2a)(5)

1/4 cup **vinaigrette dressing** (4a)

2 2/3 tablespoons **reduced-sodium soy sauce** (use wheat/gluten-free if needed) (5)

2 teaspoons **brown sugar** (2)

1/4 cup **honey** (3b)*

5 1/2 teaspoons **minced garlic** (1a)(3)(4)(5)

🍦 REFRIGERATED/FROZEN

1 1/4 cup **grated Parmesan cheese** (4)(4a)

6-ounce package **light Laughing Cow garlic and herb spreadable cheese wedges** (1)

1/2 cup **nonfat sour cream** (3)

15 ounces **extra-firm tofu** (5)

1 cup **frozen peas** (2a)

Get free, printable versions of the shopping lists from this book at TheScramble.com/diabetes.

*optional ingredients

FALL WEEK 2 • 215

This mouth-watering, all-in-one-dish recipe is adapted from the Success Rice kitchens. It has a classic rich Italian flavor but I've lightened it up with reduced-fat cheese and stirred in whole grains and lots of veggies. Serve with Green Beans with Lemon and Garlic.

Creamy Herbed Chicken with Spinach and Sundried Tomatoes

PREP + COOK: 30 MINUTES • **SERVES:** 6 • **SERVING SIZE:** 1 1/2 CUPS

1 bag Success Rice Whole-Grain Brown Rice or 1 cup quick-cooking brown rice (2 cups cooked rice), or use frozen brown rice

1 pound boneless, skinless chicken breasts

1/4 teaspoon black pepper

1/2 teaspoon Italian seasoning blend, or use 1/4 teaspoon each of dried oregano and basil

2 tablespoons trans fat-free margarine type spread, divided use, or use butter

1/4 cup white wine, or use 1/4 cup chicken broth plus 1 teaspoon white vinegar

8 ounces sliced mushrooms

1/2 cup reduced-sodium chicken broth

6-ounce package light Laughing Cow Creamy Swiss Garlic and Herb spreadable cheese wedges

1/2 cup sliced sundried tomatoes in oil, drained

6 ounces baby spinach

DO AHEAD OR DELEGATE: Cook the rice, cut and refrigerate the chicken, combine the dry seasonings, slice the mushrooms, if necessary, or fully prepare and refrigerate the dish.

1. Prepare the rice according to the package directions, taking it out about 1 minute before the package says it is done.

2. Cut the chicken into 1-inch pieces and season with the pepper and Italian seasoning. Meanwhile, melt 1 tablespoon margarine in a large heavy skillet over medium-high heat until it is bubbling. Add the chicken to the skillet in a single layer, and sauté for about 5 minutes total, flipping occasionally, until it is cooked on the outside, and nearly cooked through. Transfer the chicken to a plate and set aside.

3. Add the remaining margarine or butter to the skillet, along with the wine and mushrooms, and sauté for about 5 minutes until tender. (Meanwhile, start the green beans, if you are serving them.) Stir the rice, broth, and cheese into the skillet until the cheese mostly melts and begins to turn creamy. Stir in the chicken to coat, and then stir in the sundried tomatoes and the spinach. Cover, reduce the heat, and simmer the mixture for 5 minutes, stirring once, until the spinach is wilted. Remove from the heat and serve immediately or refrigerate for up to 24 hours.

SLOW COOKER DIRECTIONS: This is best in a slow cooker that is at least 3.3L in size. Add all ingredients to the slow cooker except the chicken (rice should be uncooked). Stir all the ingredients, then lay the chicken on top. Your slow cooker will be very full, but the spinach will cook down. Cook on high for 4–5 hours or on low for 6–10 hours. (Slow cooker cooking times may vary—get to know your slow cooker and, if necessary, adjust cooking times accordingly.)

NUTRITIONAL INFORMATION | CREAMY HERBED CHICKEN WITH SPINACH AND SUNDRIED TOMATOES:

EXCHANGES / CHOICES:
1 Starch; 1 Nonstarchy Vegetable; 3 Protein, lean; 1/2 Fat

Calories: 270; Calories from Fat: 80; Total Fat: 9 g; Saturated Fat: 2.8 g; Trans Fat: 0 g; Cholesterol: 50 mg; Sodium: 440 mg; Potassium: 635 mg; Total Carbohydrate: 21 g; Dietary Fiber: 3 g; Sugar: 3 g; Protein: 23 g; Phosphorus: 405 mg

NUTRITIONAL INFORMATION | GREEN BEANS WITH LEMON AND GARLIC:

EXCHANGES / CHOICES:
1 Nonstarchy Vegetable; 1/2 Fat

Calories: 45; Calories from Fat: 20; Total Fat: 2.5 g; Saturated Fat: 0.4 g; Trans Fat: 0 g; Cholesterol: 0 mg; Sodium: 0 mg; Potassium: 95 mg; Total Carbohydrate: 5 g; Dietary Fiber: 2 g; Sugar: 1 g; Protein: 1 g; Phosphorus: 20 mg

SIDE DISH

Green Beans with Lemon and Garlic

SERVES: 6 • **SERVING SIZE:** 2/3 CUP

1 tablespoon extra-virgin olive oil
1 teaspoon minced garlic (about 2 cloves)
1 pound green beans, fresh or frozen
1/8 lemon, juice only (about 1 teaspoon)
1/8 teaspoon salt (optional)
1/8 teaspoon black pepper (optional)

1. Heat the oil in a large skillet over medium heat. Add the garlic and stir for 30 seconds until it is fragrant. Stir in the green beans. Cover the pan and steam the beans until they are tender, 5–8 minutes. Add the lemon juice for the last minute of cooking, and season with salt and black pepper, if desired. To make them in the slow cooker: Put all ingredients in the slow cooker and add 1 cup of water or broth. Cook on low for 8–10 hours or on high for 4–5 hours. Use a slotted spoon to serve.

FLAVOR BOOSTER
Add 1 teaspoon minced garlic to the skillet with the wine and mushrooms.

TIP
Italian seasoning, a common herb blend used to add flavor to many dishes including tomato sauces, soups, vegetables and pasta dishes, is typically comprised of basil, oregano, rosemary, parsley, and garlic.

Our friend (and Six O'Clock Scramble member since the very beginning) Jolynn Dellinger sent me this delightfully easy, yet sophisticated recipe for salmon that people go crazy for. Serve with Indian Quinoa Pilaf.

Indian Spiced Salmon

PREP + COOK: 20 MINUTES • **SERVES:** 4 • **SERVING SIZE:** 1 FILLET

1 1/2 pounds salmon fillet, preferably wild Alaskan salmon

1 teaspoon extra-virgin olive oil

2 teaspoons brown sugar

1/2 teaspoon curry powder

1/2 teaspoon kosher salt

DO AHEAD OR DELEGATE: Combine the dry seasonings.

1. Preheat the broiler. (If you are making the quinoa, start that first.) Line a baking pan with aluminum foil, and set the rack about 4 inches from the heating element.

2. Cut the salmon into 4 serving-size pieces. Pour the olive oil in a small bowl or dish and brush it over the fish with a pastry brush. In a small bowl, combine the brown sugar, curry powder, and salt and rub it evenly over the fillets.

3. Broil the fish for 12–14 minutes, without flipping it, until it is browned on top and cooked through, and flakes easily in the thickest part of the fillet. Watch it carefully so it doesn't burn, and lower the rack if it is browning too quickly before the inside is cooked through.

SLOW COOKER DIRECTIONS: Cut the salmon into pieces that will fit easily into the slow cooker. Place each piece of salmon on a piece of aluminum foil large enough to fold into a packet. Pour the oil in a small bowl or dish and brush it over the fish with a pastry brush. In another small bowl, combine the brown sugar, curry powder, and salt and rub it evenly over the fillets. Fold the aluminum foil around the fillets to form a packet, then stack the packets in the slow cooker. Cook on low for 4 hours or on high for 2–3 hours. (Slow cooker cooking times may vary—get to know your slow cooker and, if necessary, adjust cooking times accordingly.)

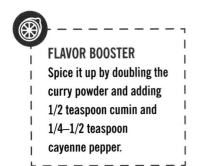

FLAVOR BOOSTER
Spice it up by doubling the curry powder and adding 1/2 teaspoon cumin and 1/4–1/2 teaspoon cayenne pepper.

Indian Quinoa Pilaf

SERVES: 4 • **SERVING SIZE:** 4/5 CUP

2/3 cup quinoa
2 teaspoons canola or vegetable oil
1/2 yellow onion, finely chopped
1 teaspoon fresh ginger, peeled and finely chopped
1/2 green chili pepper, minced (optional)
1 teaspoon turmeric
1/2 teaspoon ground cumin
1/4 teaspoon ground cinnamon
1/4 teaspoon salt
1 1/3 cups water
1 cup frozen peas

1. Rinse the quinoa in a fine strainer. In a medium saucepan, heat the oil over medium heat and sauté the onions until they are translucent, about 3 minutes. Add the ginger, quinoa, chili pepper (optional), turmeric, cumin, and cinnamon and stir for about 1 minute. Add the salt and water and bring it to a boil. Cover, reduce the heat, and simmer for 15 minutes. Remove the cover, stir in the frozen peas, cover for a minute to let the peas thaw, and serve immediately or refrigerate for up to 3 days.

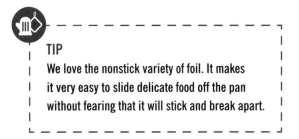

TIP
We love the nonstick variety of foil. It makes it very easy to slide delicate food off the pan without fearing that it will stick and break apart.

NUTRITIONAL INFORMATION | INDIAN SPICED SALMON:

EXCHANGES / CHOICES:
5 Protein, lean; 1 Fat

Calories: 270; Calories from Fat: 110; Total Fat: 12 g;
Saturated Fat: 2.8 g; Trans Fat: 0 g; Cholesterol: 95 mg;
Sodium: 350 mg; Potassium: 625 mg; Total Carbohydrate: 2 g;
Dietary Fiber: 0 g; Sugar: 2 g; Protein: 34 g; Phosphorus: 465 mg

NUTRITIONAL INFORMATION | INDIAN QUINOA PILAF:

EXCHANGES / CHOICES:
2 Starch; 1/2 Fat

Calories: 170; Calories from Fat: 40; Total Fat: 4.5 g;
Saturated Fat: 0.5 g; Trans Fat: 0 g; Cholesterol: 0 mg;
Sodium: 190 mg; Potassium: 260 mg; Total Carbohydrate: 27 g;
Dietary Fiber: 5 g; Sugar: 4 g; Protein: 6 g; Phosphorus: 180 mg

I think corn and tomatoes are a perfect pair. They ripen at the same time of year and the tangy sweet flavor of tomatoes complements the crisp juiciness of the corn kernels. Here, with a creamy basil dressing and a smattering of bacon, it's downright irresistible. Serve with Lavash Crackers and Sliced Apples.

Corn, Tomato, and Bacon Salad with Creamy Basil Dressing

PREP + COOK: 25 MINUTES • **SERVES:** 4 • **SERVING SIZE:** ABOUT 2 CUPS + 2 1/2 TABLESPOONS DRESSING

4 ears corn

6 strips bacon (turkey, pork, or meatless)

1/2 cup nonfat sour cream

1 cup fresh basil, coarsely chopped

1/2 teaspoon salt

1/2 teaspoon minced garlic (about 1 clove)

1 pint cherry tomatoes, halved

1 medium avocado, sliced

DO AHEAD OR DELEGATE: Steam the corn and cut the kernels off, cook, chop, and refrigerate the bacon, halve the cherry tomatoes, peel the garlic, make and refrigerate the salad dressing, or fully prepare and refrigerate the dish.

1. Steam the corn (right in its husk if you bought it with the husk on) in the microwave for 4–6 minutes until the ears are very hot. Meanwhile, cook the bacon according to the package directions. (I like to put it on a lined baking sheet in a cold oven, heat the oven to 400°F and let it cook for about 10 minutes until it is well browned.) (While the corn and bacon are cooking, slice the apples if you are serving them.) Transfer the bacon to a cutting board.

2. In a small food processor or a blender, puree the sour cream, basil, salt, and garlic until creamy and light green.

3. Shuck the corn and cut the kernels off the cobs into a serving bowl. Add the tomatoes and the basil dressing and stir to combine evenly. Chop the bacon and stir in gently just before serving. Serve immediately with the avocado slices, or refrigerate for up to 24 hours.

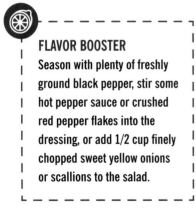

FLAVOR BOOSTER
Season with plenty of freshly ground black pepper, stir some hot pepper sauce or crushed red pepper flakes into the dressing, or add 1/2 cup finely chopped sweet yellow onions or scallions to the salad.

NUTRITIONAL INFORMATION | CORN, TOMATO, AND BACON SALAD (ANALYSIS FOR SALAD ONLY):

EXCHANGES / CHOICES:
1 1/2 Starch; 1 Nonstarchy Vegetable; 2 Fat

Calories: 220; Calories from Fat: 100; Total Fat: 11 g;
Saturated Fat: 2.0 g; Trans Fat: 0 g; Cholesterol: 10 mg;
Sodium: 280 mg; Potassium: 630 mg; Total Carbohydrate: 28 g;
Dietary Fiber: 6 g; Sugar: 7 g; Protein: 8 g; Phosphorus: 170 mg

(ANALYSIS FOR CREAMY BASIL DRESSING ONLY):

EXCHANGES / CHOICES:
Free food

Calories: 10; Calories from Fat: 0; Total Fat: 0 g;
Saturated Fat: 0.1 g; Trans Fat: 0.0 g; Cholesterol: 0 mg;
Sodium: 45 mg; Potassium: 40 mg; Total Carbohydrate: 2 g;
Dietary Fiber: 0 g; Sugar: 1 g; Protein: 1 g; Phosphorus: 15 mg

NUTRITIONAL INFORMATION | LAVASH CRACKERS:

EXCHANGES / CHOICES:
1 Starch

Calories: 80; Calories from Fat: 10; Total Fat: 1 g;
Saturated Fat: 0.4 g; Trans Fat: 0 g; Cholesterol: 0 mg;
Sodium: 110 mg; Potassium: 25 mg; Total Carbohydrate: 16 g;
Dietary Fiber: 1 g; Sugar: 1 g; Protein: 3 g; Phosphorus: 25 mg

NUTRITIONAL INFORMATION | SLICED APPLES:

EXCHANGES / CHOICES:
1 Fruit

Calories: 55; Calories from Fat: 0; Total Fat: 0 g;
Saturated Fat: 0 g; Trans Fat: 0 g; Cholesterol: 0 mg;
Sodium: 0 mg; Potassium: 110 mg; Total Carbohydrate: 14 g;
Dietary Fiber: 2 g; Sugar: 11 g; Protein: 0 g; Phosphorus: 10 mg

SIDE DISHES

Lavash Crackers (Armenian Cracker Bread)

SERVES: 4 • **SERVING SIZE:** 5 CRACKERS

20 lavash crackers (Armenian cracker bread) (or use wheat/ gluten-free crackers if needed)

1. Enjoy the dish with lavash crackers (also known as Armenian cracker bread).

Sliced Apples

SERVES: 4 • **SERVING SIZE:** 1 SMALL APPLE

4 small apples, cored and sliced
1/4 cup honey (optional)

1. Slice the apples. For a simple dessert, serve them with the honey for dipping.

TIP
Cut a bunch of cherry tomatoes at once by putting them on a rimmed plate, topping with another rimmed plate to stabilize, and cutting through them at once with a long serrated knife inserted between the plates.

I love this recipe because you basically double the volume of the pasta by adding all the shredded vegetables, which makes it a much healthier dish. The zucchini and carrots give it a sweetness, which is counterbalanced with Parmesan cheese. For a sharper contrast, use feta cheese instead, and if the kids balk, you can always top their veggies with tomato sauce. Serve with Green Salad with Dried Cranberries and Parmesan Cheese.

Fettuccine with Shredded Zucchini, Carrots, and Garlic

PREP + COOK: 30 MINUTES • **SERVES:** 8 • **SERVING SIZE:** 2 CUPS

16 ounces whole-wheat fettuccine

1/4 cup extra-virgin olive oil, divided use

2 zucchini

1 yellow squash, or use extra zucchini

3 carrots, or use 2 cups pre-shredded carrots

2 teaspoons minced garlic (about 4 cloves)

6 ounces cooked turkey sausage, diced (optional)

1/2 teaspoon salt

1 cup grated Parmesan cheese, for serving

DO AHEAD OR DELEGATE: Cook the pasta and store it tossed with a little oil to prevent sticking, shred the zucchini, yellow squash, and carrots, peel the garlic, and grate the Parmesan cheese if necessary.

1. Cook the noodles according to the package directions, drain, and toss with 1 tablespoon oil to prevent sticking.

2. Meanwhile, using a food processor (this task is worth pulling it out for) or a grater, shred the zucchini, yellow squash, and carrots to yield 7–9 cups of vegetables.

3. Heat a large heavy skillet over medium heat, and add the remaining 3 tablespoons oil. When it is hot, add the garlic. Stir the garlic for about 30 seconds until it is fragrant but don't let it brown. If using the sausage, add it to the skillet now. Add the shredded vegetables including any liquid, and the salt. Cook the vegetables for about 10 minutes or until the pasta is done, stirring occasionally, until they are tender. (Meanwhile, prepare the salad, if you are serving it.)

4. Top the noodles with the vegetables and serve with plenty of cheese and lots of freshly ground black pepper at the table.

Green Salad with Dried Cranberries and Parmesan Cheese

SERVES: 8 • **SERVING SIZE:** 1 CUP

8 cups chopped or torn lettuce
2 tablespoons dried cranberries
1/4 cup grated Parmesan cheese
1/4 cup vinaigrette dressing

1. In a large salad bowl, toss the lettuce, cranberries, cheese, and dressing.

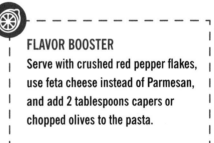

FLAVOR BOOSTER
Serve with crushed red pepper flakes, use feta cheese instead of Parmesan, and add 2 tablespoons capers or chopped olives to the pasta.

TIP
Because the skin of zucchini and yellow squash is particularly rich in antioxidants including beta-carotene and lutein, it's a vegetable where it definitely makes sense to keep the skin intact. If you'd like to avoid any potential pesticides that may be on the skin, purchase organic squash.

NUTRITIONAL INFORMATION | FETTUCCINE WITH SHREDDED ZUCCHINI, CARROTS, AND GARLIC:

EXCHANGES / CHOICES:
2 1/2 Starch; 1 Nonstarchy Vegetable; 1 Protein, lean; 1 1/2 Fat

Calories: 325; Calories from Fat: 90; Total Fat: 10 g;
Saturated Fat: 2.6 g; Trans Fat: 0 g; Cholesterol: 5 mg;
Sodium: 315 mg; Potassium: 330 mg; Total Carbohydrate: 46 g;
Dietary Fiber: 7 g; Sugar: 4 g; Protein: 13 g; Phosphorus: 210 mg

NUTRITIONAL INFORMATION | GREEN SALAD WITH DRIED CRANBERRIES AND PARMESAN CHEESE:

EXCHANGES / CHOICES:
1/2 Carbohydrate; 1/2 Fat

Calories: 40; Calories from Fat: 20; Total Fat: 2.0 g;
Saturated Fat: 0.4 g; Trans Fat: 0 g; Cholesterol: 0 mg;
Sodium: 100 mg; Potassium: 80 mg; Total Carbohydrate: 4 g;
Dietary Fiber: 1 g; Sugar: 3 g; Protein: 1 g; Phosphorus: 20 mg

I wouldn't normally think about putting sweet potato in a stir-fry but when Six O'Clock Scramble member Ailea Sneller sent me her recipe, I was willing to take a leap of faith. It not only tasted fantastic but the colors popped out of the pan and the flavors blended beautifully. Serve with Brown Rice.

Cauliflower and Sweet Potato Stir-Fry

PREP + COOK: 30 MINUTES • **SERVES:** 4 • **SERVING SIZE:** 2 CUPS

2 tablespoons vegetable oil

15 ounces extra-firm tofu, drained and wrapped in a clean dishtowel to remove excess water, and diced, or use 1 pound boneless, skinless chicken breast, diced, or 12 ounces sliced mushrooms

1 medium sweet potato, peeled and diced

1 medium head cauliflower, cut into small florets (about 7 cups)

1 red bell pepper, seeded and diced

1 tablespoon fresh ginger, peeled and minced

2 teaspoons minced garlic (about 4 cloves)

2 2/3 tablespoons reduced-sodium soy sauce (use wheat/gluten-free if needed)

DO AHEAD OR DELEGATE: Drain and dice the tofu or dice the chicken if using and refrigerate, peel and dice the sweet potato, cut the cauliflower, seed and dice the red pepper, peel and mince the ginger, peel the garlic, or fully prepare and refrigerate the dish.

1. Heat the oil in a large nonstick skillet (use the largest skillet you have) or wok over medium-high heat. Add the tofu and sweet potatoes and stir-fry for 6–8 minutes until they are golden brown and the potatoes are becoming tender.

2. Add the cauliflower and bell peppers and stir-fry for another 5 minutes until they are tender (cover the pan for a few minutes if the cauliflower isn't getting tender enough). (Meanwhile, make the rice, if you are serving it.)

3. Add the ginger and garlic and cook for another minute until they are fragrant. Drizzle the soy sauce over everything and toss to coat evenly. Season with black pepper to taste and with a little extra soy sauce, if desired. Serve immediately over steamed rice, or refrigerate for up to 3 days.

SLOW COOKER DIRECTIONS: Omit the oil. Combine all other ingredients in the slow cooker, stirring well. Cook on low for 7–8 hours or on high for 3–4 hours until the cauliflower and sweet potatoes are tender. (Slow cooker cooking times may vary—get to know your slow cooker and, if necessary, adjust cooking times accordingly.)

Brown Rice

SERVES: 4 • **SERVING SIZE:** 1/2 CUP

1 1/2 cups quick-cooking brown rice

1. Prepare the rice according to package directions.

FLAVOR BOOSTER
Add 1 tablespoon of chopped cilantro or scallions with the garlic and ginger and serve with sweet Asian chili sauce or sriracha.

TIP
Cauliflower, which is an excellent source of vitamin C, is a vegetable you can use to add more volume to many dishes without a ton of additional calories. It can also be a great substitute for starchy ingredients like pasta, potatoes, and rice.

NUTRITIONAL INFORMATION | CAULIFLOWER AND SWEET POTATO STIR-FRY:

EXCHANGES / CHOICES:
1/2 Starch; 2 Nonstarchy Vegetable; 1 Protein, medium fat; 1 1/2 Fat

Calories: 245; Calories from Fat: 125; Total Fat: 14 g;
Saturated Fat: 1.2 g; Trans Fat: 0 g; Cholesterol: 0 mg;
Sodium: 440 mg; Potassium: 795 mg; Total Carbohydrate: 20 g;
Dietary Fiber: 5 g; Sugar: 7 g; Protein: 15 g; Phosphorus: 245 mg

NUTRITIONAL INFORMATION | BROWN RICE:

EXCHANGES / CHOICES:
1 1/2 Starch

Calories: 115; Calories from Fat: 10; Total Fat: 1 g;
Saturated Fat: 0.2 g; Trans Fat: 0 g; Cholesterol: 0 mg;
Sodium: 5 mg; Potassium: 45 mg; Total Carbohydrate: 24 g;
Dietary Fiber: 2 g; Sugar: 0 g; Protein: 3 g; Phosphorus: 85 mg

FALL  WEEK 3

Honey-Glazed Chicken with Mango Salsa (1)
SIDE DISH: Steamed Edamame (Japanese Soybeans) (1a)

Tilapia Packets with Fresh Herbs and Baby Spinach (2)
SIDE DISH: Roasted Brussels Sprouts (2a)

Meatball and Orzo Soup (3)
SIDE DISH: Sliced Pears (3a)

Mexican Poached Eggs (4)
SIDE DISH: Applesauce with Cinnamon and Granola (4a)

Luscious Chickpea, Avocado, and Cucumber Salad (5)
SIDE DISH: Indian Naan, Middle Eastern Flatbread, or Pita (5a)

SHOPPING LIST

🥕 PRODUCE
2 **carrots** (3)

1/4 cup **scallions or chives** (5)

1/2 **yellow onion** (3)

1 small **yellow onion** (4)

1/2 **red bell pepper** (4)

1 **yellow bell pepper** (2)

1/2–1 **jalapeño pepper** (4)

2 **tomatoes** (5)

2 cups **baby spinach** (2)

3 cups **fresh spinach** (3)

1 tablespoon **fresh ginger** (1)

1/4 cup **fresh cilantro** (1)

2 tablespoons **fresh cilantro or fresh flat-leaf parsley** (4)*

1/2 cup **fresh flat-leaf parsley** (5)

1 tablespoon **fresh sage, thyme, parsley, basil, or any combination** (2)

1 pound **brussels sprouts** (2a)

1 small **cucumber** (5)

1 **avocado** (5)

1 **lemon** (2)(5)

1/2 **lime** (1)

3–4 **pears** (3a)

1 large **mango** (1)

MEAT AND FISH

1 1/2 pounds **boneless, skinless chicken breasts** (1)

1 pound **tilapia**, or use flounder, cod, or other thin fish fillets (2)

SHELVED ITEMS

1 package **Indian naan, Middle Eastern flatbread, or pita** (5a)

1/2 cup **whole-wheat orzo or ditalini noodles** (3)

6 **corn or whole-wheat tortillas** (4)

2 tablespoons **low-fat granola or muesli** (4a)

1 cup **no-salt-added tomato sauce** (4)

15 ounces **no-salt-added petite-diced tomatoes** (3)

32 ounces **low-sodium chicken or vegetable broth** (3)

1 cup **chunky salsa** (4)

2 tablespoons **white wine** (2)

1/4 cup **vegetarian refried beans** (Amy's is our favorite) (4)*

15 ounces **canned chickpeas** (garbanzo beans) (5)

3 cups **unsweetened applesauce** (4a)

SPICES

1/2–3/4 teaspoon **salt** (2)(5)

3/8–3/4 teaspoon **kosher salt** (1a)(2a)

1/4 teaspoon **crushed red pepper flakes** (1)*

1/4–3/8 teaspoon **black pepper** (2)(5)

1/3 teaspoon **ground cinnamon** (4a)

1/2 teaspoon **ground cumin** (5)

STAPLES

6–7 tablespoons **extra-virgin olive oil** (2)(2a)(3)(4)(5)

2 1/2 tablespoons **reduced-sodium soy sauce** (use wheat/gluten-free if needed) (1)

1 2/3 tablespoons **honey** (1)

6 **eggs** (4)

2 teaspoons **minced garlic** (1)(3)

REFRIGERATED/FROZEN

1/2 cup **shredded cheddar or Monterey Jack cheese** (4)

3/4 cup **reduced-fat sour cream** (4)*

1 **dill pickle** (such as Claussen) (5)

16 ounces **edamame** (Japanese soybeans, sold frozen) or frozen peas (1a)

12 ounces **meatless mini meatballs** (3)

Get free, printable versions of the shopping lists from this book at **TheScramble.com/diabetes**.

*optional ingredients

FALL WEEK 3 • 227

My whole family gobbled up this chicken, inspired by a recipe from The National Mango Board's website, www.mango.org. Serve with Steamed Edamame (Japanese Soybeans).

Honey-Glazed Chicken with Mango Salsa

PREP + COOK: 25 MINUTES • **SERVES:** 4 • **SERVING SIZE:** 5 OUNCES AND 1/3 CUP SALSA

2 1/2 tablespoons reduced-sodium soy sauce (use wheat/gluten-free if needed)

1 2/3 tablespoons honey, divided use

1/2 teaspoon minced garlic (about 1 clove)

1 tablespoon fresh ginger, peeled and minced

1 1/2 pounds boneless, skinless chicken breasts, cut in half crosswise (the short way)

1 large mango, or use 2 peaches, peeled and cubed, or use 1 1/2 cups frozen mango

1/4 cup fresh cilantro, chopped

1/2 lime, juice only (about 1 tablespoon)

1/4 teaspoon crushed red pepper flakes (optional)

DO AHEAD OR DELEGATE: Peel the garlic, peel and mince the ginger, make the marinade and marinate the chicken in the refrigerator for up to 24 hours, peel and cube the mango, chop the cilantro, juice the lime, make the salsa.

1. Preheat the broiler and put the oven rack 3–4 inches from the heating element. Spray a broiler pan with nonstick cooking spray.

2. In a medium bowl, combine the soy sauce, 1 tablespoon honey, the garlic, and ginger. Add the chicken to the bowl with the sauce and turn until it is coated.

3. Place the chicken on the broiling pan, reserving the marinade, and cook for 5 minutes until it turns golden. Flip the chicken and drizzle the reserved marinade evenly over the top. Broil it for about 5 more minutes until it is cooked through (the chicken should no longer be pink in the middle or its internal temperature should be 165°F.) (Meanwhile, prepare the edamame, if you are serving it.) Remove from the oven.

4. Meanwhile, in a medium serving bowl, toss together the mango, cilantro, lime juice, 2/3 tablespoon honey, and crushed red pepper flakes (optional). Serve the chicken topped with the mango salsa.

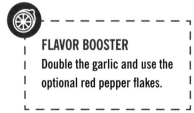

FLAVOR BOOSTER
Double the garlic and use the optional red pepper flakes.

Steamed Edamame (Japanese Soybeans)

SERVES: 6 • **SERVING SIZE:** 1 CUP

1 1/2 pounds edamame (Japanese soybeans, sold frozen) or frozen peas

1/8–1/4 teaspoon kosher salt (optional)

1. Prepare the edamame according to the package directions. Sprinkle the cooked edamame with kosher salt, if desired.

TIP

Fruits and vegetables high in vitamin C are not only great for your immune system, but they may also protect against stroke. Vitamin C helps to build collagen, a substance vital for blood vessel health. Some good options to help you fill up on vitamin C are mangos, red peppers, and oranges.

NUTRITIONAL INFORMATION | HONEY-GLAZED CHICKEN WITH MANGO SALSA:

EXCHANGES / CHOICES:
1 Fruit; 5 Protein, lean

Calories: 270; Calories from Fat: 40; Total Fat: 4.5 g; Saturated Fat: 1.2 g; Trans Fat: 0 g; Cholesterol: 100 mg; Sodium: 430 mg; Potassium: 450 mg; Total Carbohydrate: 19 g; Dietary Fiber: 1 g; Sugar: 17 g; Protein: 38 g; Phosphorus: 290 mg

NUTRITIONAL INFORMATION | STEAMED EDAMAME:

EXCHANGES / CHOICES:
2 Nonstarchy Vegetable; 1 Protein, lean; 1 Fat

Calories: 140; Calories from Fat: 55; Total Fat: 6 g; Saturated Fat: 0.7 g; Trans Fat: 0 g; Cholesterol: 0 mg; Sodium: 5 mg; Potassium: 495 mg; Total Carbohydrate: 11 g; Dietary Fiber: 6 g; Sugar: 2 g; Protein: 12 g; Phosphorus: 190 mg

Six O'Clock Scramble member Lizzy Smith kindly shared her family's favorite fish recipe with me. You can use chicken tenderloins or thin chicken cutlets instead of the fish, and you can vary the vegetables, herbs, and seasonings to your tastes: Try slivered carrots or onions or use dill or oregano instead of the suggested herbs. Serve with Roasted Brussels Sprouts.

Tilapia Packets with Fresh Herbs and Baby Spinach

PREP + COOK: 30 MINUTES • **SERVES:** 4 • **SERVING SIZE:** 1 PACKET

1 pound tilapia, or use flounder, cod, or other thin fish fillets

1 tablespoon extra-virgin olive oil

1/2 lemon, juice only (about 2 tablespoons)

2 tablespoons white wine, or use chicken or vegetable broth or 1 additional tablespoon lemon juice

1 tablespoon fresh sage, thyme, parsley, basil, or any combination, chopped, or substitute 1 teaspoon dried herbs

1/4 teaspoon salt

1/8–1/4 teaspoon black pepper, to taste

1 yellow bell pepper, cut into thin strips, or use 1 cup slivered carrots or slivered onions

2 cups baby spinach

DO AHEAD OR DELEGATE: Juice the lemon, chop the fresh herbs, if you are using them, and cut the bell pepper.

1. (Start the brussels sprouts first, if you are serving them.) Preheat the oven to 400°F. Put each fillet in the center of its own large square of heavy-duty aluminum foil. Combine the oil, lemon juice, and wine and drizzle it evenly over the fish and season it with the herbs, salt, and pepper. Top the fillets with the bell peppers and spinach, divided evenly, and fold and seal the foil packets.

2. Place the packets directly on the rack and bake them for 15–20 minutes (check doneness after 15 minutes) until the fish flakes easily with a fork and is opaque throughout. Carefully unwrap the packets and serve immediately.

SLOW COOKER DIRECTIONS: Prepare the packets as directed. Stack them, one on top of the other, in the slow cooker, and cook on low for 6–8 hours or high for 3–4 hours. (Slow cooker cooking times may vary—get to know your slow cooker and, if necessary, adjust cooking times accordingly.)

FLAVOR BOOSTER
Add 1/4 teaspoon fresh lemon zest with the lemon juice and use fresh herbs.

Roasted Brussels Sprouts

SERVES: 4 • **SERVING SIZE:** 1 CUP

1 pound brussels sprouts

1 tablespoon extra-virgin olive oil

1/4 teaspoon kosher salt

1. Preheat the oven to 450°F. Trim the stems of the brussels sprouts a little and peel off any tough outer leaves. If the sprouts are large, cut them in half from top to bottom. Toss the sprouts with the oil and the salt and roast them for 20 minutes, tossing occasionally, until they are browned and tender. (Optional twist: Toss roasted sprouts with 1 tablespoon dried cranberries and 1 teaspoon grated Parmesan cheese.)

TIP
Cooking with foil packets is very friendly to your waistline. It's an easy way to prepare delicious, flavorful meals without a lot of added fat. You can also customize the packets and leave ingredients out of individual packets if you know someone in your family doesn't like a certain ingredient.

NUTRITIONAL INFORMATION | TILAPIA PACKETS WITH FRESH HERBS AND BABY SPINACH:

EXCHANGES / CHOICES:
1 Nonstarchy Vegetable; 3 Protein, lean

Calories: 165; Calories from Fat: 55; Total Fat: 6 g;
Saturated Fat: 1.2 g; Trans Fat: 0 g; Cholesterol: 55 mg;
Sodium: 230 mg; Potassium: 595 mg; Total Carbohydrate: 4 g;
Dietary Fiber: 1 g; Sugar: 1 g; Protein: 24 g; Phosphorus: 220 mg

NUTRITIONAL INFORMATION | ROASTED BRUSSELS SPROUTS:

EXCHANGES / CHOICES:
1 Nonstarchy Vegetable; 1 Fat

Calories: 65; Calories from Fat: 35; Total Fat: 4 g;
Saturated Fat: 0.6 g; Trans Fat: 0 g; Cholesterol: 0 mg;
Sodium: 140 mg; Potassium: 325 mg; Total Carbohydrate: 7 g;
Dietary Fiber: 3 g; Sugar: 2 g; Protein: 3 g; Phosphorus: 55 mg

This is a really fun recipe from my friend Jill Rabach. It's also great for a busy night because it's a one-pot meal to cook and a one-bowl meal to eat, so cleanup is a breeze. Serve with Sliced Pears.

Meatball and Orzo Soup

PREP + COOK: 30 MINUTES • **SERVES:** 6 • **SERVING SIZE:** 1 1/2 CUPS

1 tablespoon extra-virgin olive oil

1/2 yellow onion, finely diced (about 1 cup)

2 carrots, finely diced (about 2 cups)

1 1/2 teaspoons minced garlic (about 3 cloves)

32 ounces low-sodium chicken or vegetable broth

1 cup water

15 ounces no-salt-added petite-diced tomatoes, with their liquid

12 ounces precooked meatless mini meatballs (often sold frozen), or use beef or turkey meatballs

1/2 cup whole-wheat orzo or ditalini noodles

3 cups fresh spinach, coarsely chopped

DO AHEAD OR DELEGATE: Dice the onion and the carrots, peel the garlic, and chop the spinach.

1. In a large stockpot, heat the oil over medium heat. When it is hot, add the onions, carrots, and garlic, and sauté until the onions and carrots are tender, about 5 minutes.

2. Add the broth, water, and tomatoes, cover, and bring to a boil. Add the meatballs (if they are large, cut them in quarters) and orzo, and stir frequently for a minute or two so the pasta doesn't stick to the bottom of the pot. Simmer the soup for 15 minutes, partially covered, stirring occasionally. (Meanwhile, slice the pears, if you are serving them.) Stir in the spinach and let it wilt for 1 minute. Serve the soup immediately, seasoned with salt and pepper, if desired.

SLOW COOKER DIRECTIONS: Omit the oil. Combine all ingredients except the orzo and spinach in the slow cooker, and cook on low for 8–10 hours or on high for 4–5 hours. Add the orzo 30 minutes before serving. Stir in the spinach 5 minutes before serving. (Slow cooker cooking times may vary—get to know your slow cooker and, if necessary, adjust cooking times accordingly.)

FLAVOR BOOSTER
Use fire-roasted diced tomatoes rather than plain, and/or add a pinch of crushed red pepper flakes to the soup along with the orzo.

SIDE DISH

Sliced Pears

SERVES: 6 • **SERVING SIZE:** 1/2 LARGE PEAR

3 large pears

1. Slice the pears just before serving.

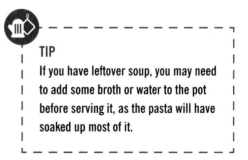

TIP

If you have leftover soup, you may need to add some broth or water to the pot before serving it, as the pasta will have soaked up most of it.

NUTRITIONAL INFORMATION | MEATBALL AND ORZO SOUP:

EXCHANGES / CHOICES:
1 Starch; 2 Nonstarchy Vegetable; 1 Protein, lean; 1 Fat

Calories: 225; Calories from Fat: 70; Total Fat: 8 g;
Saturated Fat: 1.3 g; Trans Fat: 0 g; Cholesterol: 5 mg;
Sodium: 440 mg; Potassium: 635 mg; Total Carbohydrate: 23 g;
Dietary Fiber: 6 g; Sugar: 6 g; Protein: 17 g; Phosphorus: 285 mg

NUTRITIONAL INFORMATION | SLICED PEARS:

EXCHANGES / CHOICES:
1 Fruit

Calories: 65; Calories from Fat: 0; Total Fat: 0 g;
Saturated Fat: 0 g; Trans Fat: 0 g; Cholesterol: 0 mg;
Sodium: 0 mg; Potassium: 135 mg; Total Carbohydrate: 18 g;
Dietary Fiber: 4 g; Sugar: 11 g; Protein: 0 g; Phosphorus: 15 mg

I was inspired by an enticing recipe for baked Italian eggs that I saw on my friend Domenica Marchetti's blog, www.domenicacooks.com. I wanted to try a similar idea with Mexican or Southwestern flavors to create a homey, healthy, and easy dinner. Serve with Applesauce with Cinnamon and Granola.

Mexican Poached Eggs

PREP + COOK: 25 MINUTES • **SERVES:** 6 • **SERVING SIZE:** 1 SANDWICH

1 tablespoon extra-virgin olive oil

1 small onion, diced

1/2 red bell pepper, seeded and diced

1/2–1 jalapeño pepper, to taste, seeded and finely diced

1 cup chunky salsa

1 cup no-added-salt tomato sauce

6 eggs

1/2 cup shredded cheddar or Monterey Jack cheese

3/4 cup reduced-fat sour cream (optional)

2 tablespoons fresh cilantro or flat-leaf parsley, finely chopped (optional)

1/4 cup vegetarian refried beans (Amy's is our favorite)

6 corn tortillas or whole-wheat tortillas

DO AHEAD OR DELEGATE: Dice the onion, bell pepper, and jalapeño.

1. Heat the oil in a large heavy skillet over medium heat. Add the onions, bell and jalapeño peppers, and sauté them until they are very tender and slightly browned, about 5–7 minutes.

2. Meanwhile, in a large measuring cup, combine the salsa and tomato sauce. Crack the eggs into a medium bowl, trying to keep their yolks intact.

3. When the vegetables are tender, add the salsa-tomato sauce mixture to the skillet, bring it to a low boil, and gently add the eggs, topping them evenly with the cheese. Cover, reduce the heat, and poach the eggs over the simmering sauce for 6–10 minutes, until they are just firm. (Meanwhile, assemble the bowls of applesauce, if you are serving them.) Top with the sour cream and fresh herbs, if desired, and serve immediately over or wrapped in the tortillas (coat the tortillas first with a couple of teaspoons of the beans, if desired).

SLOW COOKER DIRECTIONS: Add the oil, onion, peppers, salsa, and tomato sauce to the slow cooker and stir to combine. Cook on high for 3–4 hours or low for 6–10 hours. 30 minutes before serving, crack the eggs into a bowl, and gently pour over the simmering sauce. Replace the slow cooker lid and cook for 30 minutes more until the eggs are set. Serve as directed. Note: this will produce eggs with fully cooked yolks. If you prefer runny yolks, reduce the time to cook the eggs to approximately 15 minutes, and watch carefully for desired level of doneness. (Slow cooker cooking times may vary—get to know your slow cooker and, if necessary, adjust cooking times accordingly.)

FLAVOR BOOSTER
Use spicy salsa and/or spicy jack cheese.

- - - - - - - - - - - - - - - - - - -

Applesauce with Cinnamon and Granola

SERVES: 6 • **SERVING SIZE:** 1/2 CUP

3 cups unsweetened applesauce

1/3 teaspoon ground cinnamon

2 tablespoons low-fat granola or muesli

1. In each small bowl, top 1/2 cup applesauce with a sprinkle of cinnamon and 1 teaspoon of granola or muesli. Some people also like to mix their applesauce with cottage cheese or yogurt for a creamier taste.

TIP
Use a serrated spoon to seed the jalapeño pepper, and wear gloves or wash hands afterwards to avoid getting the hot pepper oil in your eyes. To turn this meal into huevos rancheros: Fry the corn tortillas over medium heat in a skillet with about 1 teaspoon butter or oil per tortilla until they are a little browned and puffy, coat the tortillas with refried beans, and top them with the poached egg mixture.

NUTRITIONAL INFORMATION | MEXICAN POACHED EGGS:

EXCHANGES / CHOICES:
1 Starch; 1 Nonstarchy Vegetable; 1 Protein, lean; 2 Fat

Calories: 230; Calories from Fat: 100; Total Fat: 11 g;
Saturated Fat: 4 g; Trans Fat: 0.1 g; Cholesterol: 195 mg;
Sodium: 435 mg; Potassium: 480 mg; Total Carbohydrate: 23 g;
Dietary Fiber: 4 g; Sugar: 5 g; Protein: 12 g; Phosphorus: 275 mg

NUTRITIONAL INFORMATION | APPLESAUCE WITH CINNAMON AND GRANOLA:

EXCHANGES / CHOICES:
1 Fruit

Calories: 60; Calories from Fat: 0; Total Fat: 0 g;
Saturated Fat: 0 g; Trans Fat: 0 g; Cholesterol: 0 mg;
Sodium: 5 mg; Potassium: 100 mg; Total Carbohydrate: 15 g;
Dietary Fiber: 2 g; Sugar: 12 g; Protein: 0 g; Phosphorus: 10 mg

This flavorful salad can be a meal if served with some warm pita bread or naan, or a hearty side dish with some chicken or fish. About the pickle: I've never used a pickle in a salad before but I had one less cucumber than I wanted for the dish, so I decided to try a pickle, and I loved the tangy element it added to the salad. Serve with Indian Naan, Middle Eastern Flatbread, or Pita Bread.

Luscious Chickpea, Avocado, and Cucumber Salad

PREP (NO COOK): 15 MINUTES • **SERVES:** 4 • **SERVING SIZE:** 2 CUPS

15 ounces canned chickpeas (garbanzo beans), or use 1 1/2 cups cooked chickpeas

2 tomatoes, diced (about 2 cups)

1 small cucumber, quartered lengthwise and diced (no need to peel if it has a thin skin)

1 dill pickle, quartered lengthwise and diced

1 avocado, peeled and diced

1/2 cup fresh flat-leaf parsley, chopped

1/4 cup scallions or chives, finely chopped

1/2 lemon, juice only (about 2 tablespoons)

2 tablespoons extra-virgin olive oil

1/2 teaspoon ground cumin

1/4 teaspoon salt, or to taste

1/8 teaspoon black pepper

DO AHEAD OR DELEGATE: Dice the tomatoes, quarter and dice the cucumber and the pickle, chop the parsley and the scallions or chives, juice the lemon, prepare the salad dressing, or fully prepare and refrigerate the salad.

1. In a medium serving bowl, combine the chickpeas, tomatoes, cucumbers, pickles, avocado, parsley, and scallions. (Warm the bread now, if you are serving it.)

2. In a small bowl or measuring cup, whisk together the lemon juice, oil, cumin, salt, and pepper. Drizzle it over the salad and toss gently. Serve immediately or refrigerate for up to 24 hours. (You can make it up to 2 days in advance if you wait until just before serving to add the avocado).

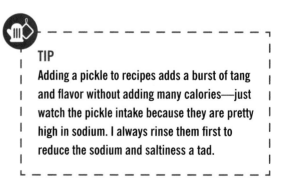

TIP

Adding a pickle to recipes adds a burst of tang and flavor without adding many calories—just watch the pickle intake because they are pretty high in sodium. I always rinse them first to reduce the sodium and saltiness a tad.

- -

Indian Naan, Middle Eastern Flatbread, or Pita Bread

SERVES: 4 • **SERVING SIZE:** 3 1/4-INCH SQUARE

4 pieces Indian naan, Middle Eastern flatbread, or pita

1. Warm the bread either in the microwave for about 1 minute or wrapped in foil in the oven at 300°F for 8–10 minutes.

NUTRITIONAL INFORMATION | LUSCIOUS CHICKPEA, AVOCADO, AND CUCUMBER SALAD:

EXCHANGES / CHOICES:
1 Starch; 2 Nonstarchy Vegetable; 1 1/2 Fat

Calories: 190; Calories from Fat: 65; Total Fat: 7 g;
Saturated Fat: 1 g; Trans Fat: 0 g; Cholesterol: 0 mg;
Sodium: 260 mg; Potassium: 685 mg; Total Carbohydrate: 26 g;
Dietary Fiber: 9 g; Sugar: 7 g; Protein: 8 g; Phosphorus: 160 mg

NUTRITIONAL INFORMATION | INDIAN NAAN, MIDDLE EASTERN FLATBREAD, OR PITA BREAD:

EXCHANGES / CHOICES:
1 Starch

Calories: 90; Calories from Fat: 20; Total Fat: 2.5 g;
Saturated Fat: 0.3 g; Trans Fat: 0 g; Cholesterol: 10 mg;
Sodium: 110 mg; Potassium: 45 mg; Total Carbohydrate: 15 g;
Dietary Fiber: 1 g; Sugar: 1 g; Protein: 3 g; Phosphorus: 35 mg

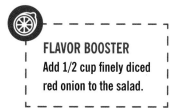

FLAVOR BOOSTER
Add 1/2 cup finely diced
red onion to the salad.

FALL

WEEK 4

Pork (or Chicken) Souvlaki (1)
SIDE DISH: Pomegranates (1a)

Grilled Yellowfin Tuna with Fresh Lemon and Garlic Marinade (2)
SIDE DISH: Whole-Wheat Couscous (2a); Grilled Zucchini (2b)

Lentil Stew with Bacon (3)
SIDE DISH: Carrot and Celery Sticks (3a)

Super Foods Salad with Cilantro-Avocado Dressing (4)
SIDE DISH: Multi-Grain Tortilla Chips (4a)

Rigatoni with Tomatoes and Tapenade (5)
SIDE DISH: Green Salad with Beets, Goat Cheese, and Pecans (5a)

SHOPPING LIST

🥕 PRODUCE

1/2 pound **baby carrots or large carrots** (3a)

3 **carrots** (3)

1 large **yellow or white onion** (1)

1 **yellow onion** (3)

1/2 **orange bell pepper** (4)

4–5 stalks **celery** (3)

1/2 pound **celery** (3a)

2 **tomatoes** (5)

1 head (6 ounces) **Boston, butter, or Bibb lettuce** (4)

1 head **lettuce, any variety** (5a)

1 clove **garlic** (4)

1/8 cup **fresh cilantro** (4)

2–3 tablespoons **fresh mint** (5)

1/2 cup **cooked beets** (5a)

2–3 **zucchini or yellow squash** (2b)

1 **avocado** (4)

2 **lemons** (1)(2)(4)

2 **pomegranates** (1a)

🐟 MEAT AND FISH

1 pound **yellowfin tuna** (use U.S. Atlantic, pole-caught, if possible) (2)

1 1/2 pounds **boneless pork loin roast or boneless, skinless chicken thighs** (1)

8 ounces **bacon** (turkey, pork, or meatless) (3)

SHELVED ITEMS

6 **whole-wheat or white pita breads** (1)

1/2 cup **quinoa** (4)

1–2 cups **whole-wheat couscous** (2a)

16 ounces **whole-wheat rigatoni noodles** (5)

4 ounces **multi-grain tortilla chips** (4a)

4 cups water, **chicken, or vegetable broth** (3)

3/4 cup **light ranch dressing or other dip** (3a)

2 tablespoons **red wine** (3)*

1 cup **brown or green lentils** (3)

2 tablespoons **capers** (5)

1/4 cup **tapenade or olive paste** (5)

2 tablespoons **pecans** (5a)

2 tablespoons **unsalted sunflower seeds** (4)

SPICES

1/2 teaspoon **salt** (2b)(4)

1/3 teaspoon **kosher salt** (1)

1 **bay leaf** (3)

1 teaspoon **dried oregano** (1)

1/2 teaspoon **crushed red pepper flakes** (2)(5)

1/2 teaspoon **black pepper** (1)(2b)(3)

STAPLES

6 tablespoons + 1/2 cup **extra-virgin olive oil** (1)(2) (2b)(3)(4)(5)

1/4 cup **vinaigrette dressing** (5a)

1 tablespoon **reduced-sodium soy sauce** (use wheat/ gluten-free if needed) (2)

2 1/2 teaspoons **minced garlic** (1)(2)(5)

REFRIGERATED/FROZEN

3/4 cup **crumbled feta cheese** (1)*

2 tablespoons **crumbled goat cheese** (5a)

1/2 cup **grated Parmesan cheese** (5)

2 tablespoons **orange juice** (4)

6 ounces **frozen shelled edamame** (4)

Get free, printable versions of the shopping lists from this book at **TheScramble.com/diabetes**.

optional ingredients

FALL WEEK 4 • 239

Souvlaki is a classic Greek meal, served in nearly every eatery in that sun-drenched country. Depending on the weather and your preference, you can grill or broil the meat. Serve with Pomegranates.

Pork (or Chicken) Souvlaki

MARINATE: 60 MINUTES • **PREP + COOK:** 20 MINUTES • **SERVES:** 6 • **SERVING SIZE:** 1 SANDWICH

1 1/2 pounds boneless pork loin roast or boneless, skinless chicken thighs, trimmed of fat and cut into 1-inch cubes

1 large yellow or white onion, cut into large chunks

1 lemon, juice only (about 4 tablespoons)

3 tablespoons extra-virgin olive oil

1 teaspoon minced garlic (about 2 cloves)

1 teaspoon dried oregano (or 1 tablespoon fresh)

1/3 teaspoon kosher salt

1/4 teaspoon black pepper

6 whole-wheat or white pita breads

3/4 cup crumbled feta cheese (optional)

DO AHEAD OR DELEGATE: Cut and refrigerate the pork or chicken and the onion, make the marinade and marinate the meat in the refrigerator, and thread the meat and the onion onto skewers and refrigerate.

1. Place the meat and onions in a large resealable bag or flat dish with sides. In a large measuring cup, whisk together the lemon juice, oil, garlic, oregano, salt, and pepper, and pour the mixture over the meat and onions. Flip the meat to coat it, and marinate it in the refrigerator for at least 1 hour and up to 24 hours.

2. Remove the meat from the marinade, reserving the marinade, and thread the meat onto metal skewers, alternating with the onion, or transfer it to a grilling or broiling tray without skewers. Grill or broil the meat and onions for 4–6 minutes per side, turning once, and brushing with the marinade (don't brush the marinade on the meat during the last 2 minutes of cooking), until it is lightly browned and just cooked through. (Meanwhile, prepare the pomegranates, if you are serving them.)

3. Meanwhile, warm the pita in the oven, microwave, or on the grill. To serve, wrap the meat and onions in the warm pita, and top with the feta cheese (optional).

SLOW COOKER DIRECTIONS: Choose wooden skewers that will fit into your slow cooker, cutting to fit if necessary. Mix the marinade as directed. Thread the meat, alternating with the onion, onto the skewers, then place in slow cooker. Brush or drizzle the marinade over the kebabs, turning to coat. Cook on low for 8–10 hours or on high for 4–6 hours. (Slow cooker cooking times may vary—get to know your slow cooker and, if necessary, adjust cooking times accordingly.)

SIDE DISH

-- -- -- -- -- -- -- -- -- -- -- -- -- -- -- --

Pomegranates

SERVES: 6 • **SERVING SIZE:** 1/2 CUP SEEDS

2 large pomegranates

1. To cut the pomegranates, slice off the top of the fruit and use a paring knife to score the rind from top to bottom in several places. Tear the fruit into sections and eat the beautiful red seeds (called arils).

2. Or, to remove the pomegranate seeds from the fruit, deeply score the pomegranate and place it in a bowl of water. Break it open underwater to free the seeds. Keep breaking and freeing seeds until they're released from the pomegranate's skin.

FLAVOR BOOSTER
Double the oregano and pepper and serve the souvlaki with chopped tomatoes and cucumbers.

TIP
Brush the pitas lightly with olive oil and grill or broil them briefly on both sides to heat them.

NUTRITIONAL INFORMATION | PORK (OR CHICKEN) SOUVLAKI:

EXCHANGES / CHOICES:
2 Starch; 1 Nonstarchy Vegetable; 3 Protein, lean; 1 1/2 Fat

Calories: 380; Calories from Fat: 135; Total Fat: 15 g;
Saturated Fat: 3.7 g; Trans Fat: 0 g; Cholesterol: 60 mg;
Sodium: 450 mg; Potassium: 465 mg; Total Carbohydrate: 35 g;
Dietary Fiber: 5 g; Sugar: 2 g; Protein: 27 g; Phosphorus: 290 mg

NUTRITIONAL INFORMATION | POMEGRANATES:

EXCHANGES / CHOICES:
1 Fruit

Calories: 70; Calories from Fat: 10; Total Fat: 1 g;
Saturated Fat: 0.1 g; Trans Fat: 0 g; Cholesterol: 0 mg;
Sodium: 0 mg; Potassium: 205 mg; Total Carbohydrate: 16 g;
Dietary Fiber: 3 g; Sugar: 12 g; Protein: 1 g; Phosphorus: 30 mg

When it comes to cooking fish, I'd rather splurge on the best quality, even if it's pricier, and stick with smaller portions. With fresh tuna, the key is to cook it for a very short time on high heat so the inside stays pink and tender. This light, lemony marinade enhances the flavor of the fish without overwhelming it. Serve with Whole-Wheat Couscous and Grilled Zucchini or Yellow Squash.

Grilled Yellowfin Tuna with Fresh Lemon and Garlic Marinade

PREP + COOK: 30 MINUTES • **SERVES:** 4 • **SERVING SIZE:** 3 OUNCES

1 lemon (use the juice of 1/2 lemon and slice the rest into wedges for serving)

1 tablespoon extra-virgin olive oil

1 tablespoon reduced-sodium soy sauce (use wheat/gluten-free if needed)

1 teaspoon minced garlic (about 2 cloves)

1/4 teaspoon crushed red pepper flakes

1 pound yellowfin tuna (use U.S. Atlantic, pole-caught, if possible), or use halibut or salmon

DO AHEAD OR DELEGATE: Juice the lemon, cut the other half lemon into wedges (cover them to prevent them from drying out), peel the garlic, make the marinade, and marinate the fish in the refrigerator.

1. In a small flat dish with sides, whisk together all the ingredients except the tuna, then add the tuna, flipping it a couple of times to coat. Set it aside for at least 10 minutes and up to 30 minutes, flipping occasionally.

2. (Start the zucchini now, if you are serving it.) Preheat the grill to medium-high heat (alternatively, cook in a cast iron or other heavy skillet). Put the tuna over direct heat and cook for 2–3 minutes. Flip it, spoon a little of the marinade on top, and cook for 2–3 more minutes. (Meanwhile, prepare the couscous, if you are serving it.)

3. Remove the tuna from the grill and let it sit for 3–5 minutes, then slice and serve immediately with extra lemon wedges, if desired.

TIP
To protect our fish supply, purchase pole-caught tuna if possible. Purchasing fish that was caught in this way benefits the environment in a number of ways including sparing sharks, turtles, and whales (that would otherwise get caught in large fishing nets), preventing overfishing and helping to employ people to catch the fish.

FLAVOR BOOSTER
Serve with lemon wedges and freshly ground black pepper.

SIDE DISHES

- - - - - - - - - - - - - - - - - - - -

Whole-Wheat Couscous

SERVES: 8 • SERVING SIZE: 2/3 CUP

1 1/2 cups whole-wheat couscous

1. Prepare the couscous according to package directions, using water or broth for the liquid. For even more flavor, stir 1–2 tablespoons fresh herbs, toasted pine nuts, slivered almonds, or dried cranberries or currants into the hot couscous.

Grilled Zucchini or Yellow Squash

SERVES: 4 • SERVING SIZE: 1 1/4 CUPS

3 zucchini or yellow squash

1 tablespoon extra-virgin olive oil

1/4 teaspoon salt

1/8 teaspoon black pepper

1. Cut the zucchini or yellow squash lengthwise into quarters, and then cut the strips crosswise into several shorter pieces. Toss them with the oil, salt, and pepper, to taste. Spread the squash slices on a vegetable tray or sturdy piece of aluminum foil, and grill over medium or medium-high heat for 10–20 minutes, flipping once, until they reach desired tenderness. (Alternatively, sauté the zucchini or squash in the oil over medium heat for about 10 minutes, until it is lightly browned and tender.)

This stew is nourishing and tastes wonderful, especially if you let the flavors meld overnight (but it's also delicious if you want to eat it right away). Serve with Carrot and Celery Sticks.

Lentil Stew with Bacon

PREP: 20 MINUTES • **COOK:** 1 HOUR AND 25 MINUTES • **SERVES:** 6 • **SERVING SIZE:** 1 3/4 CUPS

1 tablespoon extra-virgin olive oil

1 yellow onion, diced

3 carrots, thinly sliced

4–5 stalks celery, thinly sliced (1 cup total)

8 ounces bacon (turkey, pork, or meatless), cut into thin strips

1 bay leaf

1 cup brown or green lentils, rinsed and drained, soaked overnight for faster cooking

4 cups water, chicken or vegetable broth

1/8 teaspoon black pepper, or to taste

2 tablespoons red wine (optional)

DO AHEAD OR DELEGATE: Dice the onion, slice the carrots and the celery, cut the bacon, soak the lentils overnight to cut down on cooking time, or fully prepare and refrigerate the stew.

1. In a medium to large heavy stockpot, heat the oil over medium heat. Add the onions, carrots, celery, bacon, and bay leaf and sauté them, stirring occasionally, for about 10 minutes, until the onions are translucent.

2. Add the lentils and the water or broth and bring it to a low boil. Cover and simmer it, stirring occasionally, for about 1 hour and 20 minutes, until the lentils are tender (check it after an hour if you soaked the lentils overnight). (Meanwhile, slice the carrots and celery, if you are serving them.)

3. Add the pepper and wine (optional), and simmer it uncovered for about 5 more minutes. Take out the bay leaf and serve it immediately or, better yet, refrigerate it for a day or two to let the flavors meld.

SLOW COOKER DIRECTIONS: Reduce the liquid to 2–3 cups, depending on whether you like your stew thinner or thicker. Add all ingredients to the slow cooker, and cook on low for 6–8 hours or high for 4–5 hours. (Slow cooker cooking times may vary—get to know your slow cooker and, if necessary, adjust cooking times accordingly.)

Carrot and Celery Sticks

SERVES: 6
SERVING SIZE: 2/3 CUP VEGGIE STICKS + 1 1/3 TABLESPOONS DRESSING

1/2 pound baby carrots or large carrots

1/2 pound celery

1/2 cup light ranch dressing or other dip (see homemade ranch dressing recipe on page 345)

1. Serve carrot and celery sticks with light ranch dressing or your favorite dip.

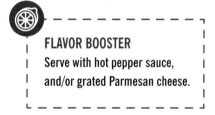

FLAVOR BOOSTER
Serve with hot pepper sauce, and/or grated Parmesan cheese.

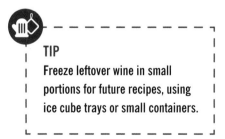

TIP
Freeze leftover wine in small portions for future recipes, using ice cube trays or small containers.

NUTRITIONAL INFORMATION | LENTIL STEW WITH BACON:

EXCHANGES / CHOICES:
1 1/2 Starch; 1 Protein, lean; 1 1/2 Fat

Calories: 220; Calories from Fat: 80; Total Fat: 9 g;
Saturated Fat: 2.1 g; Trans Fat: 0.1 g; Cholesterol: 35 mg;
Sodium: 440 mg; Potassium: 580 mg; Total Carbohydrate: 22 g;
Dietary Fiber: 8 g; Sugar: 3 g; Protein: 14 g; Phosphorus: 245 mg

NUTRITIONAL INFORMATION | CARROT AND CELERY STICKS:

EXCHANGES / CHOICES:
1 Nonstarchy Vegetable; 1 Fat

Calories: 70; Calories from Fat: 45; Total Fat: 5 g;
Saturated Fat: 0.7 g; Trans Fat: 0 g; Cholesterol: 5 mg;
Sodium: 250 mg; Potassium: 205 mg; Total Carbohydrate: 6 g;
Dietary Fiber: 2 g; Sugar: 4 g; Protein: 1 g; Phosphorus: 60 mg

Believe it or not, this recipe was inspired by a salad I purchased at LAX airport. I was looking for something healthy after a week of indulgence (not easy at an airport) and found a "super foods" salad that looked and tasted relatively appealing; however, I felt I could make it better in my own kitchen. The salad tastes not only super nourishing, but is also bursting with flavor—so much so that we scraped the salad bowl clean at the end of the meal. Serve with Multi-Grain Tortilla Chips.

Super Foods Salad with Cilantro-Avocado Dressing

PREP + COOK: 30 MINUTES • **SERVES:** 4 • **SERVING SIZE:** 1 3/4 CUPS SALAD + 1 TABLESPOON DRESSING

1/2 cup quinoa

6 ounces (1 cup) shelled edamame

CILANTRO-AVOCADO DRESSING

1/4 cup extra-virgin olive oil

1/2 lemon, juice only (about 2 tablespoons)

2 tablespoons orange juice, preferably fresh

1 avocado (use 1/4 in the dressing and dice the remaining 3/4 for salad)

1/8 cup coarsely chopped cilantro, or use parsley

1/4 teaspoon salt

1 clove garlic, peeled and halved

1 head (6 ounces) Boston, butter, or Bibb lettuce, or use kale, baby arugula, or spring mix, chopped or torn, if necessary

1/2 orange bell pepper, cored and diced

2 tablespoons unsalted sunflower seeds, or use pecans or pistachios

DO AHEAD OR DELEGATE: Cook the quinoa and the edamame, juice the orange, chop the cilantro, peel the garlic, prepare the dressing, and dice the bell pepper.

1. Rinse and cook the quinoa in 1 cup water for about 10 minutes or until the water is just absorbed. Fluff it and remove it from the heat.

2. Meanwhile, cook the edamame for 5 minutes in about 4 cups of boiling water.

3. In a small food processor or blender, puree the oil, lemon and orange juices, 1/4 avocado, cilantro, salt, and garlic.

4. In a large salad bowl, combine the lettuce, bell pepper, quinoa, edamame, remaining avocado, and sunflower seeds. Pour the dressing over everything and toss gently. Serve immediately.

SIDE DISH

- -

Multi-Grain Tortilla Chips

SERVES: 6 • **SERVING SIZE:** 1 OUNCE

6 ounces multi-grain tortilla chips

1. Serve alongside Super Foods Salad.

FLAVOR BOOSTER
Add 4 teaspoons dried cranberries, 1/4 cup pomegranate seeds, a diced orange, or use baby arugula for the greens.

NUTRITIONAL INFORMATION | SUPER FOODS SALAD WITH CILANTRO-AVOCADO DRESSING (ANALYSIS FOR SALAD ONLY):

EXCHANGES / CHOICES:
1 Starch; 1 Nonstarchy Vegetable; 1 Protein, lean; 1 1/2 Fat

Calories: 210; Calories from Fat: 90; Total Fat: 10 g;
Saturated Fat: 1.3 g; Trans Fat: 0 g; Cholesterol: 0 mg;
Sodium: 10 mg; Potassium: 575 mg; Total Carbohydrate: 24 g;
Dietary Fiber: 7 g; Sugar: 3 g; Protein: 9 g; Phosphorus: 250 mg

(ANALYSIS FOR CILANTRO-AVOCADO DRESSING ONLY):

EXCHANGES / CHOICES:
1 Fat

Calories: 55; Calories from Fat: 55; Total Fat: 6 g;
Saturated Fat: 0.8 g; Trans Fat: 0 g; Cholesterol: 0 mg;
Sodium: 60 mg; Potassium: 30 mg; Total Carbohydrate: 1 g;
Dietary Fiber: 0 g; Sugar: 0 g; Protein: 0 g; Phosphorus: 0 mg

NUTRITIONAL INFORMATION | MULTI-GRAIN TORTILLA CHIPS:

EXCHANGES / CHOICES:
1 Starch; 1 1/2 Fat

Calories: 150; Calories from Fat: 70; Total Fat: 8 g;
Saturated Fat: 1 g; Trans Fat: 0 g; Cholesterol: 0 mg;
Sodium: 135 mg; Potassium: 60 mg; Total Carbohydrate: 18 g;
Dietary Fiber: 2 g; Sugar: 1 g; Protein: 2 g; Phosphorus: 55 mg

This oh-so-flavorful pasta was inspired by a recipe from the Food Network's Melissa d'Arabian (who is a friend and a Six O'Clock Scramble member). If you fear it may be a little too flavorful for your picky eaters, you can either leave some of the pasta plain and just toss it with the tomatoes and olive oil, or you can rinse some of the noodles under cold water before serving them to wash off the sauce. Serve with Green Salad with Beets, Goat Cheese, and Pecans.

Rigatoni with Tomatoes and Tapenade

PREP + COOK: 30 MINUTES • **SERVES:** 8 • **SERVING SIZE:** 1 1/2 CUPS

16 ounces whole-wheat rigatoni noodles

1/4 cup extra-virgin olive oil

1/4 cup tapenade or olive paste, preferably made with kalamata olives (or use finely chopped or pureed flavorful pitted olives)

2 tomatoes, diced, or 2 cups cherry tomatoes, halved

2–3 tablespoons fresh mint, chopped, or use parsley or basil

2 tablespoons capers

1/2 teaspoon minced garlic (about 1 clove)

1/4 teaspoon crushed red pepper flakes, or more to taste

1/2 cup grated Parmesan cheese, for serving

DO AHEAD OR DELEGATE: Cook the pasta and store tossed with a little oil to prevent sticking, dice the tomatoes, chop the mint, peel the garlic, grate the Parmesan cheese and refrigerate, or fully prepare and refrigerate the dish.

1. Cook the rigatoni according to the package directions in a large pot of water.

2. Meanwhile, in a large serving bowl, combine the oil, tapenade, tomatoes, mint, capers, garlic, and red pepper flakes, and press them with the back of a large spoon or potato masher to combine the flavors. Let it sit until the pasta is cooked to let the flavors meld. (Meanwhile, prepare the salad, if you are serving it.)

3. Drain the pasta and toss with the tomato mixture. Serve immediately, topped with the cheese, if desired, or refrigerate for up to 2 days before serving.

FLAVOR BOOSTER
Double the garlic and top the pasta with freshly grated Parmesan cheese.

Green Salad with Beets, Goat Cheese, and Pecans

SERVES: 8 • **SERVING SIZE:** 1 CUP

8 cups lettuce, any variety, chopped

1/2 cup cooked beets, chopped

2 tablespoons crumbled goat cheese

2 tablespoons pecans, coarsely chopped

1/4 cup vinaigrette dressing

1. In a large bowl, combine the lettuce, beets, goat cheese, pecans, and vinaigrette or dressing of your choice.

TIP

Tapenade, often used as a spread on sandwiches or crackers, is generally made with a puree of olives, sometimes with additional flavorful ingredients, such as capers, garlic, lemon, and anchovies.

NUTRITIONAL INFORMATION | RIGATONI WITH TOMATOES AND TAPENADE:

EXCHANGES / CHOICES:
3 Starch; 1 1/2 Fat

Calories: 300; Calories from Fat: 90; Total Fat: 10 g;
Saturated Fat: 2.1 g; Trans Fat: 0 g; Cholesterol: 5 mg;
Sodium: 220 mg; Potassium: 220 mg; Total Carbohydrate: 45 g;
Dietary Fiber: 6 g; Sugar: 4 g; Protein: 10 g; Phosphorus: 190 mg

NUTRITIONAL INFORMATION | GREEN SALAD WITH BEETS, GOAT CHEESE, AND PECANS:

EXCHANGES / CHOICES:
1 Nonstarchy Vegetable; 1 Fat

Calories: 55; Calories from Fat: 30; Total Fat: 3.5 g;
Saturated Fat: 0.9 g; Trans Fat: 0 g; Cholesterol: 0 mg;
Sodium: 95 mg; Potassium: 120 mg; Total Carbohydrate: 4 g;
Dietary Fiber: 1 g; Sugar: 3 g; Protein: 1 g; Phosphorus: 35 mg

FALL  WEEK 5

Chicken with Dijon-Sage Crumbs (1)
SIDE DISH: Roasted Cauliflower Poppers (1a)

Cilantro Lime Shrimp (2)
SIDE DISH: Buckwheat (Kasha) (2a); Steamed Broccoli with Lemon-Pepper Seasoning (2b)

Fusilli with Prosciutto and Kale (3)
SIDE DISH: Clementines (3a)

Incan Quinoa Delight (4)
SIDE DISH: Avocados with Lime (4a)

Frittata with Red Potato and Greens (5)
SIDE DISH: Sourdough Bread (5a); Green Salad with Grapes, Pistachios, and Gorgonzola Cheese (5b)

SHOPPING LIST

- -

🥕 PRODUCE
1/2 **yellow or white onion** (4)
1 **red onion** (5)
1 **green bell pepper** (4)
1 **tomato** (4)
1 head **lettuce, any variety** (5b)
4 ounces **kale, spinach, or other greens** (5)
1 head **kale** (3)
1/4 cup **fresh cilantro** (2)
1/4 cup **fresh cilantro and/or chives** (4)
1 tablespoon **fresh sage leaves** (1)
2 pounds **broccoli** (2b)
1 1/2 pounds **red potatoes** (5)
2 ears **fresh corn** (4)
1 head **cauliflower** (1a)
2 **avocados** (4a)
1 **lemon** (4)
1 1/2 **limes** (2)(4a)
8 **clementines** (3a)
1/2 cup **seedless grapes** (5b)

🍖 MEAT AND FISH
4 **boneless, skinless chicken breast halves** (1)
1 pound **large shrimp**, peeled and deveined (2)
4 ounces **prosciutto, smoked ham, or soy chorizo** (3)

🧴 SHELVED ITEMS

3 slices **wheat or rye bread** (1)

1 loaf **sourdough bread** (use wheat/gluten-free bread if needed) (5a)

1 cup **quinoa** (Inca Red if you can find it) (4)

1 cup **buckwheat** (kasha) (2a)

16 ounces **whole-wheat fusilli noodles** (use wheat/gluten-free if needed) (3)

15 onces **reduced-sodium canned black beans** (4)

4 ounces **sliced black olives** (4)

1/4 cup **shelled pistachio nuts** (5b)

Sriracha or salsa for serving (5)

🧂 SPICES

1 5/8–2 1/4 teaspoons **salt** (1)(1a)(2)(4)(4a)(5)

1/2 teaspoon **salt-free lemon pepper seasoning** (2b)

1/2 teaspoon **dried oregano** (5)

1/4–1/2 teaspoon **crushed red pepper flakes** (3)

7/8 teaspoon **black pepper** (1)(2)(4)(5)

1/2 teaspoon **ground coriander** (4)

3/4 teaspoon **ground cumin** (1a)(4)

1/2 teaspoon **garlic powder** (4)(5)

1/2 teaspoon **chili powder** (1a)

🍯 STAPLES

1 cup **extra-virgin olive oil** (1)(1a)(2)(3)(4)(5)

1/4 cup **vinaigrette dressing** (5b)

4 teaspoons **Dijon mustard** (use wheat/gluten-free if needed) (1)

1 teaspoon **honey** (4)

8 **eggs** (5)

2 1/2 teaspoons **minced garlic** (1)(2)(3)

1/4 cup **breadcrumbs** (3)

❄️ REFRIGERATED/FROZEN

2 tablespoons **crumbled Gorgonzola cheese** (5b)

3/4 cup **crumbled reduced-fat feta cheese** (5)

1/4 cup **grated Parmesan cheese** (3)

Get free, printable versions of the shopping lists from this book at **TheScramble.com/diabetes**.

*optional ingredients

FALL WEEK 5 • 251

I was looking for a new way to jazz up chicken breasts, and decided that a crispy and tangy topping would make my family happy. I adapted this recipe from an old clipping I had for pork chops from Gourmet magazine (RIP). Serve with Roasted Cauliflower Poppers.

Chicken with Dijon-Sage Crumbs

PREP + COOK: 30 MINUTES • **SERVES:** 4 • **SERVING SIZE:** 1 BREAST HALF

3 slices wheat or rye bread, stale or toasted

3 tablespoons extra-virgin olive oil

1 teaspoon minced garlic (about 2 cloves)

1 tablespoon fresh sage leaves, minced, or 1 teaspoon dried

1/4 teaspoon salt

1/8 teaspoon black pepper

4 boneless, skinless chicken breast halves

4 teaspoons Dijon mustard

DO AHEAD OR DELEGATE: Make the breadcrumbs and peel the garlic.

1. Preheat the oven to 400°F. Put the bread in a food processor or blender to make coarse breadcrumbs.

2. (Start the cauliflower now, if you are serving it.) Heat a large oven-safe heavy skillet, such as a cast iron skillet, over medium-high heat. Add 2 tablespoons oil, and when it is hot, add the breadcrumbs, garlic, sage, salt, and pepper. Stir frequently until the crumbs are golden brown, 3–4 minutes. Remove them from the skillet and wipe the skillet clean.

3. Pat the chicken dry with paper towels. Heat the remaining oil and brown the chicken, without moving it, for about 5 minutes per side or until it is golden brown on each side. Spread about 1 teaspoon of mustard on top of each breast (you may want to leave one plain for picky eaters), then spoon 1/4 of the crumbs over each. Transfer it to the oven and cook for about 5 more minutes or until the thickest breast is just cooked through. Serve immediately.

SLOW COOKER DIRECTIONS: (Note: This won't result in chicken with a crispy topping but is still delicious.) On a plate or other flat surface, mix together the breadcrumbs, garlic, sage, salt, and pepper. Brush the chicken breasts with olive oil (you'll only need about 1 tablespoon) and mustard, then coat with the breadcrumb mixture. Place in the slow cooker and cook on low for 6–8 hours or on high for 4–6 hours. (Slow cooker cooking times may vary—get to know your slow cooker and, if necessary, adjust cooking times accordingly.)

FLAVOR BOOSTER
Use extra Dijon mustard on the chicken.

Roasted Cauliflower Poppers

SERVES: 4 • **SERVING SIZE:** 3/4 CUP

1 head cauliflower

1 tablespoon extra-virgin olive oil

1/2 teaspoon chili powder, or more to taste

1/4 teaspoon ground cumin, or more to taste

1/4 teaspoon salt

1. Preheat the oven to 400°F. Cut the cauliflower into florets. Toss them with the olive oil, chili powder, cumin, and salt. Roast them on a baking sheet for 20–30 minutes until the florets are browned and soft, tossing once.

TIP

I recommend using a cast iron skillet for browning meat. They can be purchased for about $25 and last forever as long as you follow the instructions to care for them. The only drawback is that they are extremely heavy so it can be hard to lift and pour ingredients out of the pan.

NUTRITIONAL INFORMATION | CHICKEN WITH DIJON-SAGE CRUMBS:

EXCHANGES / CHOICES:
1/2 Starch; 4 Protein, lean; 1 1/2 Fat

Calories: 275; Calories from Fat: 125; Total Fat: 14 g;
Saturated Fat: 2.3 g; Trans Fat: 0 g; Cholesterol: 65 mg;
Sodium: 415 mg; Potassium: 260 mg; Total Carbohydrate: 10 g;
Dietary Fiber: 2 g; Sugar: 1 g; Protein: 26 g; Phosphorus: 225 mg

NUTRITIONAL INFORMATION | ROASTED CAULIFLOWER POPPERS:

EXCHANGES / CHOICES:
1 Nonstarchy Vegetable; 1/2 Fat

Calories: 55; Calories from Fat: 30; Total Fat: 3.5 g;
Saturated Fat: 0.5 g; Trans Fat: 0 g; Cholesterol: 0 mg;
Sodium: 175 mg; Potassium: 270 mg; Total Carbohydrate: 5 g;
Dietary Fiber: 2 g; Sugar: 2 g; Protein: 2 g; Phosphorus: 40 mg

This refreshing dish is low in calories, high in flavor, and so versatile. It can be served hot or cold, and it's great for a picnic (if you can keep it cool or it won't be sitting out for too long), and could be wrapped in tortillas as easily as served over lettuce or rice. Serve with Buckwheat (Kasha) and Steamed Broccoli with Lemon-Pepper Seasoning.

Cilantro Lime Shrimp

PREP + COOK: 10 MINUTES • **SERVES:** 4 • **SERVING SIZE:** 1 1/2 CUPS

1 tablespoon extra-virgin olive oil

1/2 teaspoon minced garlic (about 1 clove)

1 pound large peeled and deveined shrimp, fresh (never frozen), if possible

1 lime, juice only (2 tablespoons), or more to taste

1/4 cup fresh cilantro, chopped, or more to taste

1/4 teaspoon salt

1/8 teaspoon black pepper

DO AHEAD OR DELEGATE: Peel the garlic, juice the lime, chop the cilantro, combine the lime juice, cilantro, salt, and pepper.

1. (Start the buckwheat and the broccoli first, if you are serving them.) In a large heavy skillet over medium-high heat, heat the oil. Add the garlic and cook it for 30 seconds or so until it is fragrant, then add the shrimp and cook, turning once, until the shrimp are pink and cooked through, about 2–3 minutes per side.

2. Transfer the shrimp to a bowl, and combine with the lime juice, cilantro, salt, and pepper. Serve immediately or refrigerate for up to 2 days and serve cold.

FLAVOR BOOSTER
Double the garlic and sprinkle the finished dish with 1/2 teaspoon lime zest or salt-free lemon-pepper seasoning.

TIP
Before juicing an orange, lime, or lemon, remove the zest. You can refrigerate it for 3 days or freeze it for up to a month. You can then use the zest as you need it to add flavor to dressings, marinades, and stir-fries.

NUTRITIONAL INFORMATION | CILANTRO LIME SHRIMP:

EXCHANGES / CHOICES:
3 Protein, lean

Calories: 130; Calories from Fat: 30; Total Fat: 3.5 g;
Saturated Fat: 0.5 g; Trans Fat: 0 g; Cholesterol: 190 mg;
Sodium: 260 mg; Potassium: 275 mg; Total Carbohydrate: 1 g;
Dietary Fiber: 0 g; Sugar: 0 g; Protein: 24 g; Phosphorus: 240 mg

NUTRITIONAL INFORMATION | BUCKWHEAT:

EXCHANGES / CHOICES:
1 1/2 Starch

Calories: 95; Calories from Fat: 5; Total Fat: 0.5 g;
Saturated Fat: 0.1 g; Trans Fat: 0 g; Cholesterol: 0 mg;
Sodium: 0 mg; Potassium: 90 mg; Total Carbohydrate: 21 g;
Dietary Fiber: 3 g; Sugar: 1 g; Protein: 4 g; Phosphorus: 75 mg

NUTRITIONAL INFORMATION | STEAMED BROCCOLI WITH LEMON-PEPPER SEASONING:

EXCHANGES / CHOICES:
2 Nonstarchy Vegetable

Calories: 40; Calories from Fat: 0; Total Fat: 0 g;
Saturated Fat: 0 g; Trans Fat: 0 g; Cholesterol: 0 mg;
Sodium: 40 mg; Potassium: 385 mg; Total Carbohydrate: 8 g;
Dietary Fiber: 3 g; Sugar: 2 g; Protein: 3 g; Phosphorus: 80 mg

SIDE DISHES

Buckwheat (Kasha)

SERVES: 4 • **SERVING SIZE:** 2/3 CUP

1 cup buckwheat (kasha)

1. Prepare the buckwheat (kasha) according to the package directions, using 2 cups of water or reduced-sodium vegetable or chicken broth.

Steamed Broccoli with Lemon-Pepper Seasoning

SERVES: 6 • **SERVING SIZE:** 5 SPEARS

2 pounds broccoli, trim the bottom 1/2 inch of stalk, remove leaves, and cut into about 30 spears

1/8 teaspoon salt (optional)

1/2 teaspoon salt-free lemon-pepper seasoning

1. Steam the broccoli in 1 inch of simmering water for 8–10 minutes, to desired tenderness. Drain and season to taste with salt and lemon-pepper seasoning.

Lately I've been obsessed with kale because of its powerful health properties, low cost, and because it is so easy to grow in my garden. So, when long-time Six O'Clock Scramble member Debbie Firestone sent me her recipe for pasta with kale, I had little doubt I would love it. The addition of prosciutto or ham gives it a smoky and savory flavor, but you can leave it out or use soy-chorizo for a vegetarian meal. Serve with Clementines.

Fusilli with Prosciutto and Kale

PREP + COOK: 25 MINUTES • **SERVES:** 8 • **SERVING SIZE:** 1 1/2 CUPS

16 ounces whole-wheat fusilli noodles

1 bunch kale, large stems removed, coarsely chopped (about 1 pound)

3 tablespoons extra-virgin olive oil, divided use

1 teaspoon minced garlic (about 2 cloves)

1/4–1/2 teaspoon crushed red pepper flakes, to taste

1/4 cup breadcrumbs (use wheat/gluten-free if needed), preferably fresh

4 ounces prosciutto, smoked ham, or soy chorizo, chopped

1/4 cup grated Parmesan cheese, for serving

DO AHEAD OR DELEGATE: Remove the stems from the kale, cook the pasta and kale (and toss with a little oil to prevent sticking), prepare the breadcrumbs, chop the prosciutto, ham, or soy chorizo.

1. Cook the pasta in salted water according to the package directions until it is al dente. Two minutes before the pasta is done, scoop out 1/4 cup of the pasta's water and set it aside. Add the kale to the pasta pot and cook for 2 more minutes.

2. Meanwhile, heat a large heavy skillet over medium heat and add 2 tablespoons oil. When the oil is hot, add the garlic and crushed red pepper flakes, stir for about 30 seconds but don't let the garlic brown, then add the breadcrumbs, toasting them until they are golden. Remove this mixture to a plate.

3. Wipe out the skillet and add the remaining tablespoon of oil. Add the prosciutto, ham, or soy chorizo and sauté until browned and crisp, 3–5 minutes. Transfer to the plate with the breadcrumbs.

4. Drain the pasta and kale, return to the pot or to a large serving bowl, and toss with the breadcrumbs (and meat, if using), adding the reserved water if it is too dry. Serve immediately, topped with Parmesan cheese, or refrigerate for up to 3 days.

FLAVOR BOOSTER
Double the garlic and serve the dish with freshly ground pepper.

Clementines

SERVES: 8 • **SERVING SIZE:** 1 CLEMENTINE

8 clementines

1. Peel and serve with Fusilli with Prosciutto and Kale.

TIP
Make sure to thoroughly rinse or soak the kale, as it may have sand or dirt clinging to it. You can easily separate the leaves from the stems by sliding your fingers up the stems from the bottom—the leaves should slide right off the stems. Any portions of the stem that are still attached to the leaves should be tender enough to eat.

NUTRITIONAL INFORMATION | FUSILLI WITH PROSCIUTTO AND KALE:

EXCHANGES / CHOICES:
3 Starch; 1 Protein, lean; 1/2 Fat

Calories: 290; Calories from Fat: 70; Total Fat: 8 g;
Saturated Fat: 1.6 g; Trans Fat: 0 g; Cholesterol: 10 mg;
Sodium: 315 mg; Potassium: 275 mg; Total Carbohydrate: 46 g;
Dietary Fiber: 6 g; Sugar: 3 g; Protein: 14 g; Phosphorus: 210 mg

NUTRITIONAL INFORMATION | CLEMENTINES:

EXCHANGES / CHOICES:
1/2 Fruit

Calories: 35; Calories from Fat: 0; Total Fat: 0 g;
Saturated Fat: 0 g; Trans Fat: 0 g; Cholesterol: 0 mg;
Sodium: 0 mg; Potassium: 130 mg; Total Carbohydrate: 9 g;
Dietary Fiber: 1 g; Sugar: 7 g; Protein: 1 g; Phosphorus: 15 mg

Six O'Clock Scramble member Michele Houghton sent me her healthy and flavorful quinoa salad recipe. This dish would be great for a picnic or potluck, especially if you can find the Inca Red quinoa, sold by Ancient Harvest, which makes the dish even prettier. Quinoa is an ancient Incan whole grain grown in South America. Serve with Avocados with Lime.

Incan Quinoa Delight

PREP + COOK: 30 MINUTES • **SERVES:** 6 • **SERVING SIZE:** 2 CUPS + 1 1/3 TABLESPOONS DRESSING

1 cup quinoa (Inca Red if you can find it)

2 ears corn, or use 1 1/2 cups frozen or canned corn kernels

1/2 yellow or white onion, finely diced

1 green bell pepper, finely diced

1 tomato, diced

15 ounces canned black beans, drained and rinsed

4 ounces sliced black olives, drained

1/4 cup fresh cilantro and/or chives, chopped

INCAN DRESSING

1/4 cup extra-virgin olive oil

1 lemon, juice only (about 1/4 cup)

1/2 teaspoon black pepper

1/4 teaspoon garlic powder

1/2 teaspoon ground coriander

1/2 teaspoon ground cumin

1 teaspoon honey

DO AHEAD OR DELEGATE: Cook and refrigerate the quinoa, steam the corn, if necessary, dice the onion, bell pepper, and tomato, chop the cilantro/chives, make and refrigerate the dressing, or fully prepare and refrigerate the dish.

1. Rinse the quinoa in a fine mesh strainer. Combine the quinoa and 2 cups of water in a medium-sized heavy saucepan with a lid. Bring to a boil, cover the pot, reduce the heat and simmer for 10 minutes. (Meanwhile, slice the avocados, if you are serving them.) Remove from the heat and let it sit for 5 more minutes. Lift the lid and fluff the quinoa.

2. Meanwhile, remove the kernels from the cobs, if necessary, and cover and steam them in the microwave or on the stovetop (no additional water is necessary) for 2–3 minutes (no need to steam the corn if using canned).

3. In a large serving bowl, combine the onions, peppers, tomatoes, beans, olives, corn, and cilantro and/or chives. In a large measuring cup or bowl, combine the oil, lemon juice, pepper, garlic powder, coriander, cumin, and honey. Add the quinoa to the serving bowl with the vegetables and toss it all with the dressing. Serve immediately, seasoned with salt, to taste, or refrigerate for up to 3 days.

SIDE DISHES

Avocados with Lime

SERVES: 6 • **SERVING SIZE:** 2 SLICES

2 medium avocados, cut in half, then each half sliced into 3 slices (12 slices total)

1/2 lime, juice only, 1–2 teaspoons

1/2 teaspoon salt

1. Peel and slice the avocados and sprinkle them with the lime juice and the salt (or mash the avocados, lime juice, and salt to make guacamole).

NUTRITIONAL INFORMATION | INCAN QUINOA DELIGHT (ANALYSIS FOR SALAD ONLY):

EXCHANGES / CHOICES:
2 1/2 Starch; 1 Nonstarchy Vegetable; 1/2 Fat

Calories: 240; Calories from Fat: 40; Total Fat: 4.5 g; Saturated Fat: 0.6 g; Trans Fat: 0 g; Cholesterol: 0 mg; Sodium: 195 mg; Potassium: 515 mg; Total Carbohydrate: 43 g; Dietary Fiber: 10 g; Sugar: 6 g; Protein: 9 g; Phosphorus: 250 mg

(ANALYSIS FOR INCAN DRESSING ONLY):

EXCHANGES / CHOICES:
2 Fat

Calories: 85; Calories from Fat: 80; Total Fat: 9 g; Saturated Fat: 1.3 g; Trans Fat: 0 g; Cholesterol: 0 mg; Sodium: 0 mg; Potassium: 20 mg; Total Carbohydrate: 2 g; Dietary Fiber: 0 g; Sugar: 1 g; Protein: 0 g; Phosphorus: 0 mg

NUTRITIONAL INFORMATION | AVOCADOS WITH LIME:

EXCHANGES / CHOICES:
1 1/2 Fat

Calories: 80; Calories from Fat: 65; Total Fat: 7 g; Saturated Fat: 1.1 g; Trans Fat: 0 g; Cholesterol: 0 mg; Sodium: 195 mg; Potassium: 245 mg; Total Carbohydrate: 4 g; Dietary Fiber: 3 g; Sugar: 0 g; Protein: 1 g; Phosphorus: 25 mg

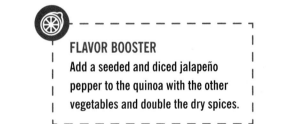

FLAVOR BOOSTER
Add a seeded and diced jalapeño pepper to the quinoa with the other vegetables and double the dry spices.

TIP
Cook at home if you're watching your waistline! According to the USDA, people consume an average of 135 more calories per meal when they eat at a restaurant.

Eggs are the perfect protein—affordable and healthy, they are low in calories and saturated fat and high in protein and minerals. Plus they can stay in the fridge for weeks so they're always there for you in a pinch. The potatoes and greens in this frittata give it a great texture and color and make the meal extra nutritious and filling. Serve with Sourdough Bread and Green Salad with Grapes, Pistachios, and Gorgonzola Cheese.

Frittata with Red Potato and Greens

PREP + COOK: 30 MINUTES • **SERVES:** 8 • **SERVING SIZE:** 1 SLICE

3 tablespoons extra-virgin olive oil

1 red onion, quartered and sliced

1 1/2 pounds red potatoes, halved and thinly sliced (about 1/4 inch)

1/2 teaspoon dried oregano

1/4 teaspoon salt, or up to 1/2 teaspoon to taste

1/4 teaspoon garlic powder

1/8 teaspoon black pepper

4 ounces kale, spinach, or other greens, coarsely chopped

8 eggs

3/4 cup reduced-fat crumbled feta cheese

sriracha or salsa for serving

1. Heat a large heavy oven-safe skillet, preferably cast iron, over medium to medium-high heat. When it is hot, add the oil, and when the oil is hot add the onions and potatoes, oregano, salt, garlic powder, and pepper. Cook, stirring occasionally, for 15–17 minutes until the potatoes and onions are lightly browned and potatoes are fork tender. Add the greens to the skillet and sauté for about 5 minutes until they are wilted and tender.

2. Meanwhile, in a medium bowl, whisk together the eggs and cheese and preheat the broiler.

3. Pour the eggs over the potato mixture and smooth them with the back of the spatula. Cook them for 3–5 more minutes until the edges of the eggs start to harden. Put the skillet under the broiler for 2–3 minutes until the top is browned. Remove it from the heat, allow it to cool for a couple of minutes, and using a pizza cutter, cut the frittata into 8 slices. Serve immediately topped with a little sriracha or salsa, if desired, or refrigerate for up to 3 days.

FLAVOR BOOSTER
Serve it with hot sauce.

TIP
While still very mild, red potatoes have a slightly more robust flavor than their lighter-skinned counterparts. Additionally, red skinned potatoes absorb flavors well so are a great addition to a wide variety of both hot and cold dishes—they're perfect for potato salads!

- - - - - - - - - - - - - - - - - -

Sourdough Bread

SERVES: 6 • **SERVING SIZE:** 1-OUNCE SLICE

1 loaf sourdough bread

1. Warm the bread in a 300-degree oven for
5 minutes before serving, if desired.

Green Salad with Grapes, Pistachios, and Gorgonzola Cheese

SERVES: 6 • **SERVING SIZE:** 1 CUPS

1 head (6 cups) lettuce, any variety, torn into bite-sized
pieces

1/2 cup seedless grapes, halved

1/4 cup shelled pistachio nuts

2 tablespoons crumbled Gorgonzola cheese

1/4 cup vinaigrette dressing

1. Combine the lettuce with the grapes,
pistachios, cheese, and the vinaigrette or
dressing of your choice.

**NUTRITIONAL INFORMATION | FRITTATA WITH RED POTATO
AND GREENS:**

EXCHANGES / CHOICES:
1 Starch; 1 Protein, medium fat; 1 Fat

Calories: 215; Calories from Fat: 110; Total Fat: 12 g;
Saturated Fat: 3.2 g; Trans Fat: 0 g; Cholesterol: 190 mg;
Sodium: 315 mg; Potassium: 525 mg; Total Carbohydrate: 17 g;
Dietary Fiber: 2 g; Sugar: 2 g; Protein: 11 g; Phosphorus: 200 mg

NUTRITIONAL INFORMATION | SOURDOUGH BREAD:

EXCHANGES / CHOICES:
1 Starch

Calories: 80; Calories from Fat: 5; Total Fat: 0.5 g;
Saturated Fat: 0.1 g; Trans Fat: 0 g; Cholesterol: 0 mg;
Sodium: 145 mg; Potassium: 35 mg; Total Carbohydrate: 16 g;
Dietary Fiber: 1 g; Sugar: 1 g; Protein: 3 g; Phosphorus: 30 mg

**NUTRITIONAL INFORMATION | GREEN SALAD WITH GRAPES,
PISTACHIOS, AND GORGONZOLA CHEESE:**

EXCHANGES / CHOICES:
1/2 Carbohydrate; 1 Fat

Calories: 80; Calories from Fat: 45; Total Fat: 5 g;
Saturated Fat: 1.1 g; Trans Fat: 0 g; Cholesterol: 0 mg;
Sodium: 145 mg; Potassium: 165 mg; Total Carbohydrate: 7 g;
Dietary Fiber: 1 g; Sugar: 4 g; Protein: 2 g; Phosphorus: 50 mg

FALL  WEEK 6

Spanish Picadillo (1)
SIDE DISH: Brown Rice (1a); Steamed Green Beans with Goat or Feta Cheese (1b)

Lump Crab Quesadillas (2)
SIDE DISH: Roasted Parsnips or Carrots (2a)

Lentil, Chickpea, and Carrot Salad with Feta Cheese (3)
SIDE DISH: Baked Kale Chips (3a)

Hot and Sour Soup (4)
SIDE DISH: Fruity Swirl Smoothies (4a)

Pasta with Roasted Tomato Sauce (5)
SIDE DISH: Green Salad with Diced Orange, Walnuts, and Parmesan Cheese (5a)

SHOPPING LIST

🥕 PRODUCE
6 **carrots** (3)(4)(5)
4 **scallions** (2)(4)
1 **yellow onion** (5)
1 1/2 pounds **parsnips or carrots** (2a)
1 **red onion** (1)
1 **red bell pepper** (5)
1/2 **yellow bell pepper** (2)
4 pounds **tomatoes** (5)(2)
9 cups **lettuce, any variety** (5a)
1 bunch **kale** (3a)
4 cloves **garlic** (5)
1 teaspoon **fresh ginger** (4)
1/4 cup **fresh cilantro** (1)*
1/2 cup **fresh flat-leaf parsley** (3)
1 pound **green beans** (1b)
2 ounces **shiitake or oyster mushrooms** (4)
3/4 **lemon** (1b)(3)
1 **lime** (2)
1 **orange** (5a)
1/3 cup **blueberries, fresh or frozen** (4a)
1 **extra-small banana** (4a)
1 1/3 cups **mango, fresh or frozen** (4a)

MEAT AND FISH

1 pound **lean ground turkey or beef**, preferably lean grass-fed beef (1)

1 pound **jumbo lump crab meat** (2)

2 **precooked sausage links, pork, chicken or meatless** (use wheat/gluten-free if needed) (3)*

SHELVED ITEMS

1–2 cups **quick-cooking brown rice or regular white rice** (1a)

16 ounces **whole-wheat radiatori pasta** (5)

8 medium **whole-wheat or flour tortillas** (soft taco size) (2)

15 ounces **fire-roasted diced tomatoes** (1)

4 cups **low-sodium chicken or vegetable broth** (4)

1 cup **salsa** (2)*

1/4 cup **rice vinegar** (4)

15 ounces **canned chickpeas** (garbanzo beans) (3)

2 1/2 cups **precooked lentils** (3)

2 tablespoons **capers** (1)

1/4 cup **raisins** (1)

2–4 tablespoons **walnuts** (5a)

SPICES

3/4 teaspoon **salt** (1b)(5)

1/2 teaspoon **kosher salt** (2a)(3a)

1/2 teaspoon **dried tarragon** (3)

1/8 teaspoon **crushed red pepper flakes** (4)*

1/4–3/8 teaspoon **black pepper** (1b)(2a)

1/4 teaspoon **ground cinnamon** (1)

1/2 teaspoon **ground cumin** (1)

3/4 teaspoon **chili powder** (1)

STAPLES

3/4 cup **extra-virgin olive oil** (1)(2a)(3)(3a)(5)

1 teaspoon **sesame oil** (4)

2 tablespoons **balsamic vinegar** (1)(3)

1/4 cup **vinaigrette dressing** (5a)

1 tablespoon **Dijon mustard** (use wheat/gluten-free if needed) (3)

2 tablespoons **reduced-sodium soy sauce** (use wheat/gluten-free if needed) (4)

1 **egg** (4)

2 1/2 teaspoons **minced garlic** (1)(4)

4 teaspoons **cornstarch** (4)

REFRIGERATED/FROZEN

1 cup **shredded reduced-fat Monterey Jack or pepper jack cheese** (2)

1–2 tablespoons + 3/4 cup **crumbled reduced-fat feta or goat cheese** (1b)(3)

1/2 cup + 2 tablespoons **grated Parmesan cheese** (5)(5a)

2/3 cup **nonfat plain or vanilla yogurt** (4a)

1 cup **orange juice** (4a)

8 ounces **extra-firm tofu** (4)

Get free, printable versions of the shopping lists from this book at TheScramble.com/diabetes.

*optional ingredients

FALL WEEK 6 • 263

Picadillo is a sweet, spiced, and tangy ground meat mixture popular in Spain and other Spanish-speaking countries. It may sound like an odd combination of ingredients but it bursts with flavor and is super-flexible. You can serve it over rice or potatoes or eat it in a tortilla or a lettuce leaf, scooped up with tortilla chips, stuffed inside empanada dough, or with a fried egg on top. Serve with Brown Rice and Steamed Green Beans with Goat or Feta Cheese.

Spanish Picadillo

PREP + COOK: 30 MINUTES • **SERVES:** 6 • **SERVING SIZE:** 3/4 CUP

1 tablespoon extra-virgin olive oil

1 red onion, finely diced

1 1/2 teaspoons minced garlic (about 3 cloves)

1 pound lean ground turkey or beef, preferably lean grass fed beef

3/4 teaspoon chili powder

1/2 teaspoon ground cumin

1/4 teaspoon ground cinnamon, or more to taste

15 ounces fire-roasted diced tomatoes, with their liquid

1/4 cup raisins

2 tablespoons capers, or use 1/4 cup sliced green olives

1 tablespoon balsamic vinegar

1/4 cup fresh cilantro, for serving (optional)

1. Heat a large heavy skillet over medium heat, and when it is hot add the oil. Let the oil heat for a minute, then add the onions and let them cook for about 5 minutes until they are tender and just starting to get golden. Stir in the garlic for about 30 seconds, then add the meat and spices. Cook, stirring occasionally, for 3–4 minutes until the meat is mostly cooked through.

2. Add the tomatoes, raisins, capers, and vinegar, bring it to a low boil, and simmer, stirring occasionally, for about 15 minutes until the liquid is reduced by about half and the flavors are melded. Season with salt and pepper to taste, and serve immediately, topped with cilantro, or refrigerate for up to 3 days, or freeze it for up to 3 months. This is one of those dishes that's even better the next day.

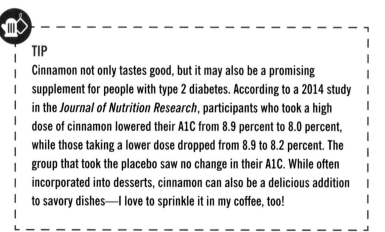

TIP

Cinnamon not only tastes good, but it may also be a promising supplement for people with type 2 diabetes. According to a 2014 study in the *Journal of Nutrition Research*, participants who took a high dose of cinnamon lowered their A1C from 8.9 percent to 8.0 percent, while those taking a lower dose dropped from 8.9 to 8.2 percent. The group that took the placebo saw no change in their A1C. While often incorporated into desserts, cinnamon can also be a delicious addition to savory dishes—I love to sprinkle it in my coffee, too!

SIDE DISHES

- - - - - - - - - - - - - - - - - - - -

Brown Rice

SERVES: 4 • **SERVING SIZE:** 1/2 CUP

1 1/2 cups quick-cooking brown rice

1. Prepare the rice according to package directions.

Steamed Green Beans with Goat or Feta Cheese

SERVES: 4 • **SERVING SIZE:** 1 CUP

1 pound green beans, trimmed and halved
1 tablespoon goat or feta cheese, crumbled
1/4 lemon, juice only (about 1 tablespoon)
1/4 teaspoon salt
1/8 teaspoon black pepper

1. Steam the green beans in 1–2 inches of boiling water for 5–8 minutes, to desired tenderness. Drain and toss immediately with the goat or feta cheese, lemon juice, salt, and pepper to taste.

FLAVOR BOOSTER
Serve with hot pepper sauce or sriracha.

NUTRITIONAL INFORMATION | SPANISH PICADILLO:

EXCHANGES / CHOICES:
1/2 Carbohydrate; 2 Protein, lean; 1 Fat

Calories: 180; Calories from Fat: 70; Total Fat: 8 g;
Saturated Fat: 2 g; Trans Fat: 0.1 g; Cholesterol: 55 mg;
Sodium: 315 mg; Potassium: 375 mg; Total Carbohydrate: 9 g;
Dietary Fiber: 1 g; Sugar: 6 g; Protein: 15 g; Phosphorus: 165 mg

NUTRITIONAL INFORMATION | BROWN RICE:

EXCHANGES / CHOICES:
1 1/2 Starch

Calories: 115; Calories from Fat: 10; Total Fat: 1 g;
Saturated Fat: 0.2 g; Trans Fat: 0 g; Cholesterol: 0 mg;
Sodium: 5 mg; Potassium: 45 mg; Total Carbohydrate: 24 g;
Dietary Fiber: 2 g; Sugar: 0 g; Protein: 3 g; Phosphorus: 85 mg

NUTRITIONAL INFORMATION | STEAMED GREEN BEANS WITH
GOAT OR FETA CHEESE:

EXCHANGES / CHOICES:
2 Nonstarchy Vegetable

Calories: 45; Calories from Fat: 10; Total Fat: 1 g;
Saturated Fat: 0.6 g; Trans Fat: 0 g; Cholesterol: 0 mg;
Sodium: 155 mg; Potassium: 145 mg; Total Carbohydrate: 8 g;
Dietary Fiber: 3 g; Sugar: 2 g; Protein: 3 g; Phosphorus: 45 mg

Longtime Six O'Clock Scramble member Nancy Bolen sent me her family's favorite recipe for these yummy quesadillas. The crab filling is so versatile—you can use it as a sandwich filling, or serve it as a salad over lettuce, or even as a dip with crackers or toast. Serve with Roasted Parsnips or Carrots.

Lump Crab Quesadillas

PREP + COOK: 25 MINUTES • **SERVES:** 8 • **SERVING SIZE:** 1 QUESADILLA

1 tomato, seeded and diced

1/2 yellow bell pepper, seeded and diced

2 scallions, thinly sliced

1 pound jumbo lump crab meat, or use 12–16 ounces canned crab meat

1 cup shredded reduced-fat pepper jack cheese

1 lime, juice only (about 2 tablespoons)

8 medium (8-inch) whole-wheat or flour tortillas (soft taco size)

1 cup salsa (optional)

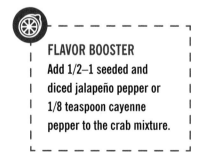

FLAVOR BOOSTER

Add 1/2–1 seeded and diced jalapeño pepper or 1/8 teaspoon cayenne pepper to the crab mixture.

DO AHEAD OR DELEGATE: Seed and dice the tomato and the bell pepper, slice the scallions, shred the cheese if necessary and refrigerate, juice the lime, or fully prepare and refrigerate the filling.

1. (Start the parsnips first, if you are serving them.) Preheat the oven to 300°F.

2. In a medium bowl, thoroughly combine all of the ingredients except the tortillas and salsa. Let it sit for about 5 minutes to meld the flavors. (The filling can be prepared and refrigerated up to 12 hours in advance, and then drained just before using.) Transfer the ingredients to a colander to drain any remaining liquid, pressing gently, if necessary. (Although most of the lime juice will drain out, much of the lime flavor will be retained, and draining will prevent the quesadillas from getting soggy.)

3. Spray 2 heavy skillets with nonstick cooking spray, or use nonstick skillets. Heat the skillets over medium heat. Add a tortilla to each pan, spreading a scoop of the mixture (about 1/8 of it) on half of each tortilla. Fold the tortillas and repeat with a second tortilla in each skillet, so that their curved edges point to the outside of the pan. (With two skillets, you can cook four quesadillas at once!) Once the bottoms of the tortillas are lightly browned, after 3–5 minutes, flip the quesadillas and lightly brown the second sides for another 3–5 minutes. When both sides are browned, transfer the tortillas to a baking sheet to keep warm in the oven until all the quesadillas are cooked. Repeat with the remaining tortillas and crab salad mixture. Slice the quesadillas in halves or quarters (a pizza cutter works well for this) and serve immediately, with salsa, if desired.

SIDE DISH

- - - - - - - - - - - - - - - - - -

Roasted Parsnips or Carrots

SERVES: 8 • **SERVING SIZE:** 1/2 CUP

1 1/2 pounds parsnips or carrots, or use a combination of both

1 tablespoon extra-virgin olive oil

1/4 teaspoon kosher salt

1/8 teaspoon black pepper

1. Preheat the oven to 450°F. Cut the parsnips and/or carrots lengthwise into halves or quarters (depending on their size) and cut those strips into 1-inch pieces.

2. In a roasting pan, toss the pieces with the oil, salt, and pepper (add 1/2–1 teaspoon fresh thyme, if desired). Roast them until they are lightly browned, 15–20 minutes, tossing once. The longer they cook, the sweeter they become.

TIP

Jumbo lump crab meat is prized for the size of the crab meat, but is more costly than the other grades of crab. Keep in mind if you decide to go with a lower-priced option, that all of the grades are white meat and taste the same, with the exception of claw meat, which is darker and has a more intense flavor.

NUTRITIONAL INFORMATION | LUMP CRAB QUESADILLAS:

EXCHANGES / CHOICES:
1 1/2 Starch; 2 Protein, lean; 1/2 Fat

Calories: 220; Calories from Fat: 65; Total Fat: 7 g;
Saturated Fat: 2.4 g; Trans Fat: 0 g; Cholesterol: 85 mg;
Sodium: 450 mg; Potassium: 365 mg; Total Carbohydrate: 24 g;
Dietary Fiber: 4 g; Sugar: 1 g; Protein: 18 g; Phosphorus: 280 mg

NUTRITIONAL INFORMATION | ROASTED PARSNIPS OR CARROTS:

EXCHANGES / CHOICES:
1 Nonstarchy Vegetable; 1/2 Fat

Calories: 40; Calories from Fat: 20; Total Fat: 2 g;
Saturated Fat: 0.3 g; Trans Fat: 0 g; Cholesterol: 0 mg;
Sodium: 80 mg; Potassium: 170 mg; Total Carbohydrate: 7 g;
Dietary Fiber: 2 g; Sugar: 2 g; Protein: 1 g; Phosphorus: 25 mg

Six O'Clock Scramble member Jen Grosman said she makes a version of this salad every week for her family and serves it with pita chips. It's so nourishing, and it fills you up with fiber and protein. If you can find precooked lentils, which are often sold in a vacuum-packed package or in cans, it's very quick to put together. Serve with Baked Kale Chips.

Lentil, Chickpea, and Carrot Salad with Feta Cheese

PREP + COOK: 20 MINUTES • **SERVES:** 6 • **SERVING SIZE:** 1 1/2 CUPS

3 carrots, peeled and diced

2 precooked sausage links (use wheat/ gluten-free if needed), pork, chicken, or meatless, sliced (optional)

DRESSING

1/4 cup extra-virgin olive oil

1/2 lemon, juice only (about 2 tablespoons)

1 tablespoon balsamic vinegar

1 tablespoon Dijon mustard (use wheat/ gluten-free if needed)

1/2 teaspoon dried tarragon

2 1/2 cups cooked lentils (often sold in cans with other canned beans or vacuum packed), or cook your own (see directions below)

15 ounces canned chickpeas (garbanzo beans), drained and rinsed

3/4 cup crumbled reduced-fat feta or goat cheese

1/2 cup fresh flat-leaf parsley, chopped, or more to taste

DO AHEAD OR DELEGATE: Dice the carrots, slice the sausage if using, make and refrigerate the dressing, or fully prepare and refrigerate the salad.

1. In a microwave-safe bowl, steam the carrots in the microwave with 1 tablespoon of water for 2–3 minutes until they are tender. If using the sausage, brown it in a nonstick skillet with 1 tablespoon oil for 5–6 minutes.

2. Make the dressing in a measuring cup or medium bowl by whisking together the oil, lemon juice, vinegar, mustard, and tarragon.

3. In a large bowl, combine the remaining ingredients with the carrots and sausage (optional) and toss them with the dressing. Serve immediately or refrigerate for up to 4 days.

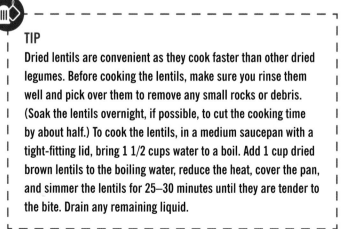

TIP

Dried lentils are convenient as they cook faster than other dried legumes. Before cooking the lentils, make sure you rinse them well and pick over them to remove any small rocks or debris. (Soak the lentils overnight, if possible, to cut the cooking time by about half.) To cook the lentils, in a medium saucepan with a tight-fitting lid, bring 1 1/2 cups water to a boil. Add 1 cup dried brown lentils to the boiling water, reduce the heat, cover the pan, and simmer the lentils for 25–30 minutes until they are tender to the bite. Drain any remaining liquid.

Baked Kale Chips

PREP + COOK: 25 MINUTES • **SERVES:** 6 • **SERVING SIZE:** 1/3 CUP

1 bunch kale (about 1 pound)

2 tablespoons extra-virgin olive oil

1/4 teaspoon kosher salt

1. Preheat the oven to 350°F. Wash and thoroughly dry the kale. Remove the widest part of the stems by grabbing hold of the bottom of the stem with one hand and sliding the thumb and forefinger of your other hand up the stem. Discard the stems.

2. Coarsely chop the kale, spread it on a baking sheet, drizzle it with the oil, and toss thoroughly (hands work best for this), then sprinkle the salt over the kale. Bake for about 20 minutes, tossing once, until the leaves are crispy, but make sure they don't turn brown and get overly crispy or they will taste burnt.

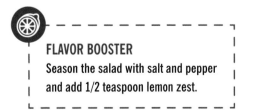

FLAVOR BOOSTER
Season the salad with salt and pepper and add 1/2 teaspoon lemon zest.

NUTRITIONAL INFORMATION | LENTIL, CHICKPEA, AND CARROT SALAD WITH FETA CHEESE (ANALYSIS FOR SALAD ONLY):

EXCHANGES / CHOICES:
2 Starch; 1 Protein, lean

Calories: 210; Calories from Fat: 30; Total Fat: 3.5 g; Saturated Fat: 1.4 g; Trans Fat: 0 g; Cholesterol: 5 mg; Sodium: 305 mg; Potassium: 565 mg; Total Carbohydrate: 32 g; Dietary Fiber: 11 g; Sugar: 5 g; Protein: 15 g; Phosphorus: 290 mg

NUTRITIONAL INFORMATION | BAKED KALE CHIPS:

EXCHANGES / CHOICES:
1 Nonstarchy Vegetable; 1 Fat

Calories: 60; Calories from Fat: 45; Total Fat: 5 g; Saturated Fat: 0.7 g; Trans Fat: 0 g; Cholesterol: 0 mg; Sodium: 95 mg; Potassium: 225 mg; Total Carbohydrate: 4 g; Dietary Fiber: 2 g; Sugar: 1 g; Protein: 2 g; Phosphorus: 40 mg

I've always loved starting a meal at a Chinese restaurant with hot and sour soup because it's a flavor and texture sensation, but I had no idea I could actually make a healthy and authentic-tasting version at home with supermarket ingredients. At least I didn't until I got this recipe from my friend Susan Levy. I love the trick of using a beaten egg to enrich the soup. Serve with Fruity Swirl Smoothies.

Hot and Sour Soup

PREP + COOK: 25 MINUTES • **SERVES:** 4 • **SERVING SIZE:** 2 CUPS

1 teaspoon sesame oil

2 ounces shiitake or oyster mushrooms, stemmed and thinly sliced (about 1/3 cup)

1 teaspoon minced garlic (about 2 cloves)

1 teaspoon fresh ginger, peeled and finely chopped

1/8 teaspoon crushed red pepper flakes (optional)

4 cups low-sodium chicken or vegetable broth

1 carrot, quartered and thinly sliced

4 teaspoons cornstarch

2 tablespoons low-sodium soy sauce (use wheat/gluten-free if needed)

1/4 cup rice vinegar

1 egg, beaten

8 ounces extra-firm tofu, cut into 1/2-inch cubes (about 1 1/2 cups), drained and wrapped in a clean towel for a few minutes

2 scallions, dark and light green parts, thinly sliced

DO AHEAD OR DELEGATE: Stem and slice the mushrooms, peel the garlic, peel and chop the ginger, quarter and slice the carrot, beat and refrigerate the egg, dice and wrap the tofu, slice the scallions, or fully prepare and refrigerate the soup.

1. In a large saucepan, heat the oil over medium-low heat. Add the mushrooms, garlic, ginger, and pepper flakes (optional) and sauté for about 2 minutes until the mushrooms start to get tender and the garlic is fragrant. Add the broth and carrots, bring to a boil, reduce the heat, and simmer until the carrots are tender, about 3 minutes.

2. Meanwhile, put the cornstarch in a small bowl and whisk in the soy sauce and vinegar. Slowly whisk the cornstarch mixture into the soup, and simmer for about 2 more minutes until the soup has thickened slightly. Pour in the egg and stir the soup rapidly until the egg cooks and thickens the soup, about 2 minutes. Add the tofu and scallions, cover, and let it stand for 1 minute. Serve immediately or refrigerate for up to 3 days.

FLAVOR BOOSTER
Add 1 tablespoon hoisin sauce or sweet Asian chili sauce for a little sweet spiciness. Drizzle a few drops of hot chili sesame oil or toasted sesame oil into the soup at the table.

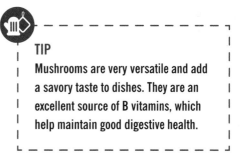

SIDE DISH

Fruity Swirl Smoothies

SERVES: 4 • **SERVING SIZE:** 1 CUP

1 cup orange juice

2/3 cup nonfat plain or vanilla yogurt

1 1/3 cups mango, fresh or frozen

1/3 cup blueberries, fresh or frozen

1 extra-small banana

1 cup ice

1. In a blender, combine the juice, yogurt, mango, blueberries, banana, and ice. Blend on high speed for 30–60 seconds until smooth.

TIP
Mushrooms are very versatile and add a savory taste to dishes. They are an excellent source of B vitamins, which help maintain good digestive health.

NUTRITIONAL INFORMATION | HOT AND SOUR SOUP:

EXCHANGES / CHOICES:
1/2 Carbohydrate; 1 Nonstarchy Vegetable; 1 Protein, lean; 1/2 Fat

Calories: 130; Calories from Fat: 55; Total Fat: 6 g;
Saturated Fat: 1.1 g; Trans Fat: 0 g; Cholesterol: 50 mg;
Sodium: 395 mg; Potassium: 415 mg; Total Carbohydrate: 9 g;
Dietary Fiber: 1 g; Sugar: 3 g; Protein: 11 g; Phosphorus: 170 mg

NUTRITIONAL INFORMATION | FRUITY SWIRL SMOOTHIES:

EXCHANGES / CHOICES:
1 1/2 Fruit

Calories: 105; Calories from Fat: 5; Total Fat: 0.5 g;
Saturated Fat: 0.1 g; Trans Fat: 0 g; Cholesterol: 0 mg;
Sodium: 20 mg; Potassium: 350 mg; Total Carbohydrate: 25 g;
Dietary Fiber: 2 g; Sugar: 19 g; Protein: 2 g; Phosphorus: 60 mg

Ever wonder what to do with leftover vegetables that didn't quite make it into your weekly plan or a bumper crop of tomatoes from your garden? Why not roast them with a little olive oil, puree, and turn them into a healthy and delicious sauce? Serve with Green Salad with Diced Orange, Walnuts, and Parmesan Cheese.

Pasta with Roasted Tomato Sauce

PREP: 15 MINUTES • **COOK:** 30 MINUTES • **SERVES:** 9 • **SERVING SIZE:** 1 1/3 CUPS

3 pounds tomatoes (8–12 tomatoes)

1 yellow onion, coarsely chopped

4 cloves garlic, peeled and halved

2 carrots, sliced

1 red bell pepper, seeded and coarsely chopped

1/4 cup extra-virgin olive oil

1/2 teaspoon salt, or more to taste

16 ounces whole-wheat radiatori pasta, or use rotini

1/2 cup grated Parmesan cheese, for serving

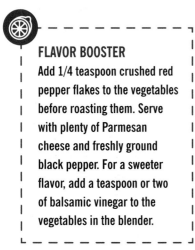

FLAVOR BOOSTER
Add 1/4 teaspoon crushed red pepper flakes to the vegetables before roasting them. Serve with plenty of Parmesan cheese and freshly ground black pepper. For a sweeter flavor, add a teaspoon or two of balsamic vinegar to the vegetables in the blender.

DO AHEAD OR DELEGATE: Cook the pasta and store tossed with a little oil to prevent sticking, chop the onion and the bell pepper, peel and halve the garlic, slice the carrots, grate the Parmesan cheese if necessary and refrigerate, or fully prepare and refrigerate or freeze the sauce.

1. Preheat the oven to 400°F and spray a large baking sheet with nonstick cooking spray.

2. In a large bowl, toss the tomatoes, onions, garlic, carrots, and bell peppers with the oil and salt. Spread them on the baking sheet and roast them for 30 minutes, tossing every 10 minutes, until the tomatoes are starting to collapse and the onions are starting to brown. Meanwhile, cook the noodles according to the package directions in salted water. (While the pasta is cooking, prepare the salad, if you are serving it.) Drain the pasta and put it in the bowl you used to toss the vegetables.

3. Puree the roasted vegetables in a standing blender or in a bowl using a stick or immersion blender (add a little water or broth if necessary to get the blender to turn), until it becomes a smooth sauce, and pour it over the noodles. If it makes more sauce than you need, refrigerate the extras for up to a week or freeze it for up to 3 months. Serve topped with plenty of Parmesan cheese.

Green Salad with Diced Orange, Walnuts, and Parmesan Cheese

SERVES: 9 • **SERVING SIZE:** 1 CUP

9 cups lettuce, any variety, torn or chopped

1 orange, peeled and diced

2 tablespoons walnuts, coarsely chopped

2 tablespoons grated Parmesan cheese

1/4 cup vinaigrette dressing

1. In a salad bowl, combine the lettuce with the orange (pour in the juice that's leftover from chopping it, too), walnuts, and Parmesan cheese. Toss with the vinaigrette or your favorite salad dressing and serve.

TIP

For a lower-carb (but equally delicious!) version of this recipe, try substituting spaghetti squash or spiralized zucchini for the pasta. To prepare spaghetti squash: Pierce the squash several times with a metal skewer or the tip of a sharp knife. Put it on a microwave-safe dish, cover with a cloth towel, and cook for 15–20 minutes on full power in the microwave, rotating and checking it after 10 minutes and then every 5 minutes, until it collapses or you can easily press in the skin with your thumb. (Alternatively, bake the squash whole at 400°F for 45–60 minutes or put it in the slow cooker with a cup of water for 8–10 hours.) Wearing oven mitts, halve the squash lengthwise, remove the seeds from the middle, and scrape the flesh into a serving bowl, using a fork to separate the strands.

NUTRITIONAL INFORMATION | PASTA WITH ROASTED TOMATO SAUCE:

EXCHANGES / CHOICES:
2 1/2 Starch; 2 Nonstarchy Vegetable; 1 Fat

Calories: 295; Calories from Fat: 70; Total Fat: 8 g;
Saturated Fat: 1.4 g; Trans Fat: 0 g; Cholesterol: 0 mg;
Sodium: 185 mg; Potassium: 495 mg; Total Carbohydrate: 46 g;
Dietary Fiber: 8 g; Sugar: 7 g; Protein: 11 g; Phosphorus: 175 mg

NUTRITIONAL INFORMATION | GREEN SALAD WITH DICED ORANGE, WALNUTS, AND PARMESAN CHEESE:

EXCHANGES / CHOICES:
1/2 Carbohydrate; 1/2 Fat

Calories: 50; Calories from Fat: 25; Total Fat: 3 g;
Saturated Fat: 0.5 g; Trans Fat: 0 g; Cholesterol: 0 mg;
Sodium: 85 mg; Potassium: 120 mg; Total Carbohydrate: 5 g;
Dietary Fiber: 1 g; Sugar: 3 g; Protein: 1 g; Phosphorus: 25 mg

FALL

WEEK 7

Turkey, Cranberry, and Wild Rice Salad (1)
SIDE DISH: Caramelized Brussels Sprouts (1a)

Penne with Smoked Salmon and Peas (2)
SIDE DISH: Green Salad with Raisins, Cashews, and Sunflower Seeds (2a)

Fried Egg and Avocado Sandwiches (3)
SIDE DISH: Seedless Grapes (3a)

Black Bean and Tomato Soup (4)
SIDE DISH: Lightly Buttered Corn (4a)

Everything Under the Tuscan Sun (Polenta with White Beans and Spinach) (5)
SIDE DISH: Fruit Kabobs (5a)

SHOPPING LIST

PRODUCE
2–4 **scallions** (1)
2 tablespoons **fresh chives** (2)
2 1/2 **yellow onions** (1a)(4)(5)
2 stalks **celery** (1)
1 **tomato** (5)
1 small head **lettuce** (2a)
6–9 ounces **baby spinach** (5)
1/4 cup **fresh dill** (2)
1 pound **brussels sprouts** (1a)
1 **avocado** (3)
1 **lemon** (2)
1/4 **lime** (4a)*
1 bunch **seedless grapes** (3a)
6–8 cups **mixed fruit** such as strawberries, blueberries, bananas, mango, grapes, and/or melon (5a)

MEAT AND FISH
5–6 ounces **smoked salmon** (2)
2–4 slices **bacon** (turkey, pork or meatless) (3)*
1 cup **cooked turkey breast** (1)

🫙 SHELVED ITEMS

8 slices **sourdough bread** (use wheat/gluten-free bread if needed) (3)

1 cup **wild rice blend**, such as Lundberg's (1)

16 ounces **whole-wheat penne pasta** (2)

12 ounces **plain prepared polenta** (sold in tubes with grains) (5)

14 1/2 ounces **no-salt-added tomato sauce** (4)

14 1/2 ounces **no-salt-added diced tomatoes** (4)

1/4 cup **julienne-cut sundried tomatoes** (5)

14 1/2 ounces **reduced-sodium chicken or vegetable broth** (4)

1/4–1/2 cup **red wine** (4)*

15 ounces **no-salt-added canned great northern beans** (5)

45 ounces **reduced-sodium canned black beans** (4)

2 tablespoons **capers** (2)*

1/2 cup **dried cranberries** (preferably naturally sweetened) (1)

1/4 cup **raisins** (2a)

1/2 cup **pecans** (1)

1/4 cup **unsalted cashews** (2a)

2 tablespoons **sunflower seeds, shelled** (2a)

15–20 colorful **toothpicks or wooden skewers** (5a)

🧂 SPICES

1/8 teaspoon **salt** (1a)

1 teaspoon **dried Italian seasoning** (5)

1/8 teaspoon **black pepper** (1a)

1 tablespoon **chili powder** (4)

🍶 STAPLES

1 teaspoon **butter** (4a)

4 tablespoons + 4 teaspoons **extra-virgin olive oil** (1a)(3)(4)(5)

2 teaspoons **balsamic vinegar** (1a)

1/2 cup **balsamic vinaigrette dressing** (1)(2a)

1 dash **hot pepper sauce**, such as Tabasco (3)*

4 **eggs** (3)

2 1/2 teaspoons **minced garlic** (1a)(4)(5)

🔒 REFRIGERATED/FROZEN

4 tablespoons **shredded Monterey Jack cheese** (3)

1/4 cup **grated Parmesan cheese** (5)*

1/2 cup **shredded part-skim mozzarella cheese** (5)

1/2 cup **shredded part-skim mozzarella or cheddar cheese** (4)*

3/4 cup **whipped cream cheese** (2)

1 cup **nonfat vanilla yogurt** (5a)*

1 cup **nonfat sour cream** (4)*

16 ounces **frozen corn kernels** (4a)

1 1/2 cups **frozen peas** (2)

Get free, printable versions of the shopping lists from this book at **TheScramble.com/diabetes**.

*optional ingredients

After our Thanksgiving feast, I find that we're eager to finish up the sweet potato pie, cornbread stuffing, and other flavorful side dishes, but the roast turkey and cranberry sauce sometimes languish at the back of the refrigerator. I invented this salad that can help you give new life to some of those leftovers. Serve with Caramelized Brussels Sprouts.

Turkey, Cranberry, and Wild Rice Salad

MARINATE: 15 MINUTES • **PREP:** 10 MINUTES • **COOK:** 60 MINUTES • **SERVES:** 6 • **SERVING SIZE:** 1 CUP

1 cup wild rice blend, such as Lundberg's

1 cup cooked turkey breast, chopped

2 stalks celery, sliced (about 1 cup)

2–4 scallions, thinly sliced (1/4–1/2 cup), to taste

1/2 cup dried cranberries (or use raisins or pomegranate seeds), or 1/2–3/4 cup cranberry sauce

1/4 cup balsamic vinaigrette dressing (or use equal parts olive oil and balsamic vinegar)

1/2 cup pecans, lightly toasted and coarsely chopped

DO AHEAD OR DELEGATE: Cook the rice, chop and refrigerate the turkey, slice the celery and the scallions, toast and chop the pecans, or fully prepare and refrigerate the salad.

1. Prepare the rice according to the package directions, using water or chicken broth. (Meanwhile, start the brussels sprouts, if you are serving them.)

2. In a medium serving bowl, combine the turkey, celery, scallions, and cranberries. When the rice is cooked, combine it with the ingredients in the bowl. Stir in the vinaigrette dressing. Refrigerate the salad for at least 15 minutes and up to 2 days. Just before serving, stir in the pecans.

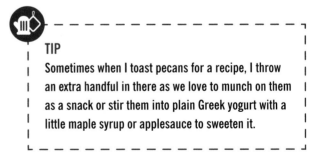

TIP
Sometimes when I toast pecans for a recipe, I throw an extra handful in there as we love to munch on them as a snack or stir them into plain Greek yogurt with a little maple syrup or applesauce to sweeten it.

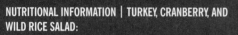

SIDE DISH

- -

Caramelized Brussels Sprouts

SERVES: 6 • **SERVING SIZE:** 1/2 CUP

2 tablespoons extra-virgin olive oil

1/2 yellow onion, finely chopped

1 pound brussels sprouts, chopped

1/2 teaspoon minced garlic (about 1 clove)

2 teaspoons balsamic vinegar

1/8 teaspoon salt

1/8 teaspoon black pepper

1. Heat the oil in a heavy skillet over medium heat. Add the onions, brussels sprouts, and garlic, and sauté them for about 10 minutes, stirring occasionally, until the sprouts are lightly browned and very tender. Add the vinegar, salt, and pepper, and continue cooking for about 5 more minutes, stirring occasionally, and reducing the heat if the sprouts are getting too deeply browned.

NUTRITIONAL INFORMATION | TURKEY, CRANBERRY, AND WILD RICE SALAD:

EXCHANGES / CHOICES:
1 1/2 Starch; 1/2 Fruit; 1 Protein, lean; 1 1/2 Fat

Calories: 250; Calories from Fat: 90; Total Fat: 10 g; Saturated Fat: 1 g; Trans Fat: 0 g; Cholesterol: 20 mg; Sodium: 130 mg; Potassium: 295 mg; Total Carbohydrate: 32 g; Dietary Fiber: 4 g; Sugar: 9 g; Protein: 10 g; Phosphorus: 200 mg

NUTRITIONAL INFORMATION | CARAMELIZED BRUSSELS SPROUTS:

EXCHANGES / CHOICES:
1 Nonstarchy Vegetable; 1 Fat

Calories: 75; Calories from Fat: 45; Total Fat: 5 g; Saturated Fat: 0.7 g; Trans Fat: 0 g; Cholesterol: 0 mg; Sodium: 65 mg; Potassium: 265 mg; Total Carbohydrate: 7 g; Dietary Fiber: 2 g; Sugar: 2 g; Protein: 2 g; Phosphorus: 45 mg

FLAVOR BOOSTER
Squeeze a little fresh lemon juice over the salad before serving.

If you like bagels and lox as much as we do, chances are that you will love this lox and cream cheese dinner. The pasta is creamy, tangy, and full of flavor like a Sunday morning New York deli special. This would also be fantastic with asparagus, cut in thirds, instead of the peas. Serve with Green Salad with Raisins, Cashews, and Sunflower Seeds.

Penne with Smoked Salmon and Peas

PREP + COOK: 30 MINUTES • **SERVES:** 8 • **SERVING SIZE:** 1 1/2 CUPS

16 ounces whole-wheat penne pasta

1 1/2 cups frozen peas

5–6 ounces smoked salmon lox, chopped (1 cup)

3/4 cup whipped cream cheese

1 lemon, use zest and cut lemon into wedges

1/4 cup fresh dill, chopped, or use 1 tablespoon dried

2 tablespoons fresh chives, finely chopped, or use 1/4 cup sliced scallions

2 tablespoons capers (optional)

DO AHEAD OR DELEGATE: Chop the salmon and refrigerate, zest and cut the lemon, chop the dill if using fresh, and chop the chives.

1. Cook the penne according to the package directions until it is al dente. (Meanwhile, prepare the salad, if you are serving it.) Before draining the pasta, add the peas to the water for the last minute of cooking and scoop out 1 cup of the cooking water and set it aside.

2. Drain the pasta, letting some water cling to the noodles, return it and the peas to the pot, stir in the salmon, cream cheese, and 1/2 cup of the water until the cream cheese evenly coats the noodles. Stir in the lemon zest, dill, chives, and capers (optional). Serve immediately with the lemon wedges.

FLAVOR BOOSTER
Double the lox, use the chives and capers.

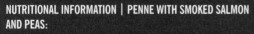

- -

Green Salad with Raisins, Cashews, and Sunflower Seeds

SERVES: 8 • **SERVING SIZE:** 1 CUP

1 small head lettuce, torn or chopped (6–8 cups)

1/4 cup raisins

1/4 cup unsalted cashews

2 tablespoons sunflower seeds, shelled

1/4 cup balsamic vinaigrette dressing

1. Combine the lettuce, raisins, cashews, and sunflower seeds and toss with the vinaigrette, or dressing of your choice.

NUTRITIONAL INFORMATION | PENNE WITH SMOKED SALMON AND PEAS:

EXCHANGES / CHOICES:
3 Starch; 1 Protein, lean

Calories: 285; Calories from Fat: 55; Total Fat: 6 g;
Saturated Fat: 2.6 g; Trans Fat: 0 g; Cholesterol: 15 mg;
Sodium: 215 mg; Potassium: 175 mg; Total Carbohydrate: 47 g;
Dietary Fiber: 7 g; Sugar: 4 g; Protein: 12 g; Phosphorus: 200 mg

NUTRITIONAL INFORMATION | GREEN SALAD WITH RAISINS, CASHEWS, AND SUNFLOWER SEEDS:

EXCHANGES / CHOICES:
1/2 Carbohydrate; 1 Fat

Calories: 75; Calories from Fat: 40; Total Fat: 4.5 g;
Saturated Fat: 0.7 g; Trans Fat: 0 g; Cholesterol: 0 mg;
Sodium: 80 mg; Potassium: 155 mg; Total Carbohydrate: 8 g;
Dietary Fiber: 1 g; Sugar: 5 g; Protein: 2 g; Phosphorus: 60 mg

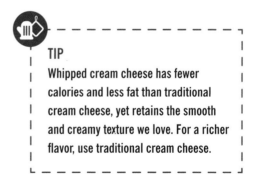

TIP
Whipped cream cheese has fewer calories and less fat than traditional cream cheese, yet retains the smooth and creamy texture we love. For a richer flavor, use traditional cream cheese.

Recently I became obsessed with making the perfect fried egg sandwich, asking everyone for their ideal recipe. Ultimately, I settled on this delectable combination but you might also enjoy adding steamed spinach, roasted peppers, mayonnaise, tapenade, or bacon. We used cheddar and jalapeño bread from the farmer's market, but assuming you can't find that, you can use sourdough, challah, French bread, even English muffins. Serve with Seedless Grapes.

Fried Egg and Avocado Sandwiches

PREP + COOK: 15 MINUTES • **SERVES:** 4 • **SERVING SIZE:** 1 SANDWICH

2–4 slices bacon (turkey, pork, or meatless) (optional)

8 slices sourdough bread, or use French bread or your favorite bread

4 eggs

4 teaspoons extra-virgin olive oil

4 tablespoons shredded Monterey Jack or cheddar cheese, or use shaved pecorino

1 avocado, thinly sliced, or use guacamole

1 dash hot pepper sauce, such as Tabasco or sriracha (optional)

DO AHEAD OR DELEGATE: Shred the cheese if necessary and refrigerate.

1. If you are including the bacon in your sandwiches, cook it according to the package directions (I like to put it on a lined baking sheet in a cold oven, heat the oven to 400°F, and let it cook for about 10 minutes until it is well browned).

2. Toast the bread until it's golden and crispy.

3. Spray a small bowl with nonstick cooking spray and gently crack an egg into it. Meanwhile, heat a large cast iron or other heavy skillet over medium-low heat. When it is hot, add the oil and swirl it around to distribute evenly. When the oil is hot, gently pour in the egg and repeat with the remaining eggs, cracking them into the bowl first, so you can add them gently to the pan (to avoid the yolks cracking and the whites spreading too much). Cover the pan for 3 minutes until the whites are opaque. Top each egg evenly with 1 tablespoon cheese.

4. Meanwhile, mash the avocado onto 4 slices of the toast, and slide an egg on top of each. Put 1/2 to 1 slice of bacon on top of each egg (optional). Sprinkle a little hot pepper sauce or sriracha on top of each egg, and top with the remaining slices of toast. Serve immediately.

Seedless Grapes

SERVES: 6 • **SERVING SIZE:** 3 OUNCES (17 SMALL GRAPES)

1 1/4 pounds seedless grapes

1. Serve either purple or green grapes (or you can serve frozen grapes for a sweet and crunchy treat). Safety note: Young children (3 and younger) should only eat halved or quartered grapes to prevent choking.

FLAVOR BOOSTER
Use the hot pepper sauce or sriracha or spread a little mustard on one of the pieces of toast.

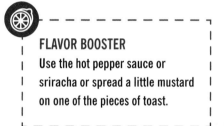

TIP
If you don't like sunny side up eggs or runny yolks, cook them a bit longer or flip them gently and cook for 1–2 more minutes so the yolks cook through. For food safety reasons (salmonella), the FDA recommends that eggs be cooked until both yolks and whites are firm. This is especially appropriate for people with diabetes who may have weakened immune systems.

NUTRITIONAL INFORMATION | FRIED EGG AND AVOCADO SANDWICHES:

EXCHANGES / CHOICES:
2 1/2 Starch; 1 Protein, medium fat; 2 Fat

Calories: 360; Calories from Fat: 160; Total Fat: 18 g;
Saturated Fat: 4.6 g; Trans Fat: 0 g; Cholesterol: 190 mg;
Sodium: 405 mg; Potassium: 330 mg; Total Carbohydrate: 36 g;
Dietary Fiber: 4 g; Sugar: 2 g; Protein: 15 g; Phosphorus: 215 mg

NUTRITIONAL INFORMATION | SEEDLESS GRAPES:

EXCHANGES / CHOICES:
1 Fruit

Calories: 60; Calories from Fat: 0; Total Fat: 0 g;
Saturated Fat: 0 g; Trans Fat: 0 g; Cholesterol: 0 mg;
Sodium: 0 mg; Potassium: 160 mg; Total Carbohydrate: 15 g;
Dietary Fiber: 1 g; Sugar: 13 g; Protein: 1 g; Phosphorus: 15 mg

This soup is a crowd-pleaser and has been a Scramble favorite in years past. Serve with Lightly Buttered Corn.

Black Bean and Tomato Soup

PREP + COOK: 30 MINUTES • **SERVES:** 6 • **SERVING SIZE:** 2 CUPS

1 tablespoon extra-virgin olive oil

1 yellow onion, chopped (about 2 cups)

1 teaspoon minced garlic (about 2 cloves)

45 ounces reduced-sodium canned black beans, drained and rinsed, return beans to cans, and fill with water to cover

14 1/2 ounces reduced-sodium chicken or vegetable broth

14 1/2 ounces no-salt-added diced tomatoes, with their liquid

14 1/2 ounces no-salt-added tomato sauce

1 tablespoon chili powder, or to taste

1/4–1/2 cup red wine (optional)

1 cup nonfat sour cream (optional)

1/2 cup shredded part-skim mozzarella or cheddar cheese (optional)

DO AHEAD OR DELEGATE: Chop the onion, peel the garlic, shred the cheese if necessary and refrigerate, or fully prepare and refrigerate or freeze the soup.

1. Heat the oil in a large pot over medium heat. Add the onions and garlic and sauté until the onions start to brown, about 5 minutes. Add the beans and water, broth, tomatoes, tomato sauce, and chili powder. Bring the soup to a boil.

2. Reduce the heat and simmer until the flavors blend and soup thickens slightly, 15–20 minutes, stirring occasionally. After the soup has been simmering for about 10 minutes, stir the red wine into the soup, if desired. (Prepare the corn now, if you are serving it.)

3. With a hand-held immersion or standing blender, puree at least 2 cups of the soup to desired consistency. Serve immediately, refrigerate for up to 3 days, or freeze for up to 3 months. Top individual bowls with the sour cream and cheese at the table, if desired.

SLOW COOKER DIRECTIONS: Omit the oil. Combine all other ingredients except the sour cream and cheese in the slow cooker. Cook on low for 8–10 hours or on high for 4–5 hours. Serve as directed. (Slow cooker cooking times may vary—get to know your slow cooker and, if necessary, adjust cooking times accordingly.)

SIDE DISH

Lightly Buttered Corn

SERVES: 6 • **SERVING SIZE:** 1/2 CUP

1 pound frozen corn kernels

1 teaspoon butter

1/4 lime (optional)

1. Cook the corn in the microwave or on the stovetop for 3–5 minutes (we like it a little undercooked so it doesn't get chewy). Toss the hot corn with the butter and fresh lime juice, if desired.

FLAVOR BOOSTER

Add 1 teaspoon cumin with the chili powder, and serve the soup with the optional toppings and/or hot pepper sauce (such as Tabasco), finely diced onion, and/or fresh cilantro.

TIP

Keeping an eye on the scale? Beans are not only an inexpensive, tasty protein-packed addition to a meal, but a recent study based on data from the National Nutrition and Health Examination Survey showed that people who eat 3/4 cup of these morsels daily, weigh, on average, over 6 pounds less than those who don't.

NUTRITIONAL INFORMATION | BLACK BEAN AND TOMATO SOUP:

EXCHANGES / CHOICES:
2 Starch; 3 Nonstarchy Vegetable; 1/2 Fat

Calories: 245; Calories from Fat: 30; Total Fat: 3.5 g;
Saturated Fat: 0.6 g; Trans Fat: 0 g; Cholesterol: 0 mg;
Sodium: 390 mg; Potassium: 940 mg; Total Carbohydrate: 43 g;
Dietary Fiber: 15 g; Sugar: 10 g; Protein: 14 g; Phosphorus: 230 mg

NUTRITIONAL INFORMATION | LIGHTLY BUTTERED CORN:

EXCHANGES / CHOICES:
1 Starch

Calories: 65; Calories from Fat: 10; Total Fat: 1 g;
Saturated Fat: 0.5 g; Trans Fat: 0 g; Cholesterol: 0 mg;
Sodium: 5 mg; Potassium: 175 mg; Total Carbohydrate: 15 g;
Dietary Fiber: 2 g; Sugar: 2 g; Protein: 2 g; Phosphorus: 60 mg

This recipe was a sleeper hit at our table. It's a one-pot wonder of Italian comfort food. Sautéing some mushrooms with the onions and garlic would also be a great addition. Serve with Fruit Kabobs.

Everything Under the Tuscan Sun
(Polenta with White Beans and Spinach)

PREP + COOK: 25 MINUTES • **SERVES:** 4 • **SERVING SIZE:** 1 1/4 CUPS

1 tablespoon extra-virgin olive oil

1 yellow onion, diced

1 teaspoon minced garlic (about 2 cloves)

1 tomato, diced

1/4 cup julienne-cut sundried tomatoes

18 ounces plain prepared polenta (sold in tubes with grains), diced

15 ounces no-salt-added canned great northern beans, or use cannellini beans, drained and rinsed

1 teaspoon dried Italian seasoning

6–9 ounces baby spinach

1/2 cup shredded part-skim mozzarella cheese

1/4 cup grated Parmesan cheese for serving (optional)

DO AHEAD OR DELEGATE: Dice the onion, tomato, and polenta, peel the garlic, shred the mozzarella cheese if necessary and refrigerate, grate the Parmesan cheese if necessary and refrigerate.

1. Heat a large heavy skillet over medium heat, and when it is hot, add the oil. When the oil is hot, add the onions and garlic and sauté until the onions are tender, about 5 minutes. (Meanwhile, assemble the fruit kabobs, if you are serving them.)

2. Add both types of tomatoes and cook for 2 more minutes. Stir in the polenta and the beans and cover for 3–4 minutes, stirring once. Stir in the Italian seasoning and the spinach, cover, and cook for about 4 more minutes until the spinach is wilted. Top with the mozzarella cheese and serve immediately, topped with the Parmesan cheese, if desired.

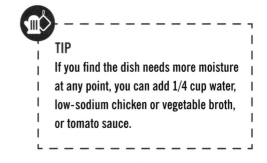

TIP
If you find the dish needs more moisture at any point, you can add 1/4 cup water, low-sodium chicken or vegetable broth, or tomato sauce.

SIDE DISH

- - - - - - - - - - - - - - - - - - - -

Fruit Kabobs

SERVES: 4 • **SERVING SIZE:** 3/4 CUP

3 cups mixed fruit such as strawberries, blueberries, bananas, mango, grapes, and/or melon

15–20 colorful toothpicks or wooden skewers

1 cup nonfat vanilla yogurt (optional)

1. Thread the fruit onto toothpicks or small skewers (kids can have fun doing this, however children under age 3 should not eat with toothpicks or skewers of any size). Serve with small bowls of yogurt for dipping (optional).

FLAVOR BOOSTER
Stir in some capers and crushed red chili flakes along with the spinach, and use freshly grated Parmesan cheese.

NUTRITIONAL INFORMATION | EVERYTHING UNDER THE TUSCAN SUN:

EXCHANGES / CHOICES:
2 Starch; 1 Nonstarchy Vegetable; 1 Protein, lean; 1/2 Fat

Calories: 245; Calories from Fat: 65; Total Fat: 7 g;
Saturated Fat: 2.1 g; Trans Fat: 0 g; Cholesterol: 10 mg;
Sodium: 425 mg; Potassium: 805 mg; Total Carbohydrate: 37 g;
Dietary Fiber: 8 g; Sugar: 5 g; Protein: 13 g; Phosphorus: 250 mg

NUTRITIONAL INFORMATION | FRUIT KABOBS:

EXCHANGES / CHOICES:
1 Fruit

Calories: 60; Calories from Fat: 0; Total Fat: 0 g;
Saturated Fat: 0.1 g; Trans Fat: 0 g; Cholesterol: 0 mg;
Sodium: 5 mg; Potassium: 230 mg; Total Carbohydrate: 15 g;
Dietary Fiber: 2 g; Sugar: 13 g; Protein: 1 g; Phosphorus: 20 mg

FALL

WEEK 8

Rosemary-Garlic Pork Roast with Whipped Sweet Potatoes (1)
SIDE DISH: Caramelized Cabbage (1a)

Baked Fish with Lemon Aioli-Panko Coating (2)
SIDE DISH: Wild Rice (2a); Simple Mixed Vegetables (2b)

Trattoria Chicken with Tomatoes and Olives (3)
SIDE DISH: Roasted Broccoli (3a)

Fettuccine with Artichokes, Roasted Peppers, and Pine Nuts (4)
SIDE DISH: Green Salad with Carrots, Hard-Boiled Egg, and Parmesan Cheese (4a)

North of the Border Veggie Chili (5)
SIDE DISH: Cornbread or Corn Muffins (5a)

SHOPPING LIST

🥕 PRODUCE

4 **carrots** (4a)(5)
1/4 **shallot** (2)
3 **yellow onions** (3)(4)(5)
1 **red bell pepper** (5)
9 cups **iceberg or romaine lettuce** (4a)
1 head **green cabbage** (1a)
1 cup **fresh basil leaves** (4)
1 tablespoon **fresh or dried rosemary** (1)
1–2 heads **broccoli** (3a)
2 1/2 pounds **sweet potatoes** (1)
1–1 1/2 cups **corn kernels, fresh, frozen, or canned** (5)
1/2 **lemon** (2)

🍖 MEAT AND FISH

2 pounds **boneless, skinless chicken breasts** (3)
1 1/2 pounds **mahi mahi, flounder, or other white fish fillets** (2)
1 1/2–2 pounds **boneless pork loin roast or pork tenderloin**, or use bone-in chicken pieces (1)

🧂 SHELVED ITEMS

3/4 cups **wild rice** (2a)

16 ounces **whole-wheat fettuccine** (4)

1 package **cornbread or corn muffin mix** (5a)

15 ounces **canned red kidney beans** (preferably unsweetened) (5)

15 ounces **canned black beans**, reduced-salt, if possible (5)

1/2 cup **pitted green olives** (3)

1/3 cup **panko breadcrumbs** (use wheat/gluten-free if needed) (2)

1 cup **roasted red peppers** (sold in jars) (4)

28 ounces **crushed tomatoes** (5)

15 ounces **diced tomatoes** (3)

1 1/2 cups water, **chicken, or vegetable broth** (2a)

1 cup **mild salsa** (5)

1 tablespoon **dried cranberries** (preferably naturally sweetened) (2a)*

1 tablespoon **pecans** (2a)*

1/4 cup **pine nuts** (4)

🧂 SPICES

1 3/8 teaspoons **salt** (1a)(2)(2b)(4)

3/4–1 teaspoon **kosher salt** (1)(3a)

1/4–1/2 teaspoon **salt-free lemon pepper seasoning** (3a)

1 teaspoon **dried oregano** (3)

1 1/2 teaspoons **dried basil** (2)(3)

7/8–1 teaspoon **black pepper** (1)(1a)

1 tablespoon **chili powder** (5)

🍶 STAPLES

3 teaspoons **butter** (1a)(2b)

1 tablespoon **trans fat-free margarine** (1)

6 tablespoons + 5 teaspoons **extra-virgin olive oil** (1)(1a) (3)(3a)(4)(5)

2 teaspoons **balsamic vinegar** (1a)

1/4 cup **mayonnaise** (2)

1/3 cup **vinaigrette dressing** (2a)(4a)

2 teaspoons **sugar** (4)

1–2 tablespoons **pure maple syrup or brown sugar** (1)

1/2 cup **nonfat or low-fat milk** (1)

1 **hard-boiled egg** (4a)

5 1/2 teaspoons **minced garlic** (1)(2)(3)(4)

🍦 REFRIGERATED/FROZEN

1 cup **shredded cheddar cheese** (5)*

1/4 cup + 2 tablespoons **grated Parmesan cheese** (4)(4a)

1 cup n**onfat plain sour cream or yogurt** (5)*

3 cups **frozen mixed vegetables** such as carrots and peas (2b)

12 ounces **frozen quartered artichoke hearts** (4)

Get free, printable versions of the shopping lists from this book at TheScramble.com/diabetes.

optional ingredients

FALL WEEK 8 • 287

My friend Kim Tilley, who is a phenomenal cook, serves this flavorful pork roast to her family. The sweet potatoes are the perfect complement to the savory pork. Serve with Caramelized Cabbage.

Rosemary-Garlic Pork Roast with Whipped Sweet Potatoes

PREP: 20 MINUTES • **COOK:** 30 MINUTES • **SERVES:** 6 • **SERVING SIZE:** 3 OUNCES MEAT + 1/2 CUP MASHED SWEET POTATOES

1 1/2–2 pounds boneless pork loin roast or pork tenderloin, or use bone-in chicken pieces

2 tablespoons extra-virgin olive oil

2 1/2 teaspoons minced garlic (about 5 cloves)

1 tablespoon fresh or dried rosemary

1/2 tablespoon kosher salt

3/4 teaspoon black pepper

2 1/2 pounds sweet potatoes (about 5 potatoes), peeled and chopped into 1-inch pieces

1 tablespoon trans fat-free margarine

1–2 tablespoons pure maple syrup or brown sugar, to taste

1/2 cup nonfat or low-fat milk

DO AHEAD OR DELEGATE: Peel the garlic, make the spice rub, peel and chop the sweet potatoes, and marinate the pork in the refrigerator for up to 24 hours.

1. Preheat the oven to 400°F. Put the meat in a large roasting pan. In a small bowl, combine the oil, garlic, rosemary, salt, and pepper. Rub the mixture over the top and sides of the meat. (If using pork tenderloin, fold the skinny piece under so you have a piece with somewhat uniform thickness.) Roast the meat for 30–40 minutes (check it after 25 minutes for pork tenderloin) until it is cooked through, or has an internal temperature of 160°F. (Meanwhile, start the cabbage, if you are serving it.)

2. While the meat is cooking, cover the sweet potatoes with water in a large saucepan and bring to a boil over high heat. Simmer the potatoes until they are fork tender, about 10–15 minutes. Drain thoroughly, and whip them in a mixing bowl with the margarine, syrup or sugar, and milk, until they are smooth. (Optional: Transfer the whipped potatoes to a small casserole dish and put them in the oven with the pork roast until the tops of the potatoes start to brown.) Cut the meat into slices and serve with warm potatoes.

SLOW COOKER DIRECTIONS: Follow the pork recipe as above, placing the pork in the slow cooker and covering with the rub mixture. Cook on low for 7–8 hours or on high for 3–4 hours. Prepare the potatoes as directed above. (Slow cooker cooking times may vary—get to know your slow cooker and, if necessary, adjust cooking times accordingly.)

FLAVOR BOOSTER
Season the pork with extra freshly ground black pepper.

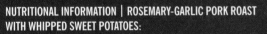

Caramelized Cabbage

SERVES: 6 • **SERVING SIZE:** 1/2 CUP

1 head green cabbage

2 teaspoons extra-virgin olive oil

2 teaspoons butter

1/2 teaspoon salt

1/8–1/4 teaspoon black pepper

2 teaspoons balsamic vinegar

1. Halve, core, and thinly slice the cabbage. In a large heavy skillet over medium heat, heat the oil and the butter. When the butter melts, add the cabbage. Cover and cook it for 3–5 minutes until it starts to cook down, then remove the lid. Cook the cabbage, turning occasionally (tongs work well), until it starts to brown, about 15 minutes. Add the salt, pepper, and vinegar and cook for about 5 more minutes until it is nicely browned.

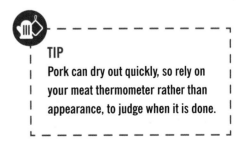

TIP

Pork can dry out quickly, so rely on your meat thermometer rather than appearance, to judge when it is done.

NUTRITIONAL INFORMATION | ROSEMARY-GARLIC PORK ROAST WITH WHIPPED SWEET POTATOES:

EXCHANGES / CHOICES:
2 Starch; 3 Protein, lean; 1 Fat

Calories: 355; Calories from Fat: 115; Total Fat: 13 g; Saturated Fat: 3.5 g; Trans Fat: 0 g; Cholesterol: 60 mg; Sodium: 260 mg; Potassium: 705 mg; Total Carbohydrate: 35 g; Dietary Fiber: 4 g; Sugar: 13 g; Protein: 24 g; Phosphorus: 235 mg

NUTRITIONAL INFORMATION | CARAMELIZED CABBAGE:

EXCHANGES / CHOICES:
2 Nonstarchy Vegetable; 1/2 Fat

Calories: 65; Calories from Fat: 25; Total Fat: 3 g; Saturated Fat: 1.1 g; Trans Fat: 0.1 g; Cholesterol: 5 mg; Sodium: 230 mg; Potassium: 260 mg; Total Carbohydrate: 9 g; Dietary Fiber: 4 g; Sugar: 5 g; Protein: 2 g; Phosphorus: 40 mg

This lemony coating keeps fish fillets ultra-moist and the panko gives it a tantalizing texture. For a gluten-free option, you can omit the panko. Serve with Wild Rice and Simple Mixed Vegetables.

Baked Fish with Lemon Aioli-Panko Coating

PREP + COOK: 25 MINUTES • **SERVES:** 4 • **SERVING SIZE:** 5 OUNCES

1 1/2 pounds mahi mahi, flounder, or other white fish fillets

1/4 cup mayonnaise

1/2 lemon, juice only (1–2 tablespoons)

1 teaspoon minced garlic (about 2 cloves)

1/4 shallot, minced (about 1 tablespoon)

1/8 teaspoon salt

1/3 cup panko breadcrumbs, or use fresh breadcrumbs

1/2 teaspoon dried basil

DO AHEAD OR DELEGATE: Prepare and refrigerate the aioli.

1. (Start the rice first, if you are serving it.) Preheat the oven to 475°F. Spray a baking sheet with nonstick cooking spray or line it with a silicone mat or foil, and lay the fish fillets on the sheet.

2. In a large measuring cup or small bowl, combine the mayonnaise, lemon juice, garlic, shallots, and salt. In another large measuring cup or bowl, combine the panko and basil.

3. Using a spatula, spread the mayonnaise mixture evenly over the fish. Top evenly with the panko mixture and gently press the panko into the coating. Bake for 10–12 minutes until the fish is cooked through and flakes easily in the thickest part. (Meanwhile, cook the vegetables, if you are serving them.)

SLOW COOKER DIRECTIONS: Omit the panko. Prepare the mayonnaise mixture as directed above but include the basil. Set each piece of fish on a piece of aluminum foil large enough to fold into a packet. Spread the mayonnaise mixture evenly over the fish, then fold the foil into a packet around the fish. Place the packets into the slow cooker, stacking as needed. Cook on low for 7–8 hours or on high for 3–4 hours. (Slow cooker cooking times may vary—get to know your slow cooker and, if necessary, adjust cooking times accordingly.)

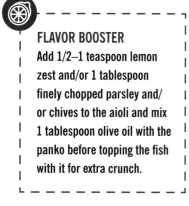

FLAVOR BOOSTER

Add 1/2–1 teaspoon lemon zest and/or 1 tablespoon finely chopped parsley and/or chives to the aioli and mix 1 tablespoon olive oil with the panko before topping the fish with it for extra crunch.

Wild Rice

SERVES: 4 • **SERVING SIZE:** 3/4 CUP

3/4 cup dry wild rice

1 1/2 cups water, chicken both, or vegetable broth

1 tablespoon dried cranberries (optional)

1 tablespoon pecans, chopped (optional)

1 tablespoon vinaigrette dressing (optional)

1. Prepare the rice, using water or broth, according to the package directions. To make it even more flavorful and colorful, stir the optional cranberries and pecans into the just-cooked rice, and add the vinaigrette dressing.

Simple Mixed Vegetables

SERVES: 4 • **SERVING SIZE:** 3/4 CUP

3 cups frozen mixed vegetables

1/4 teaspoon salt, or to taste

1 teaspoon butter

1. Defrost the vegetables in the microwave or on the stovetop until they are just hot (don't overcook). Stir in the butter and salt and serve.

TIP

In case you're not familiar with aioli, it's essentially garlic-flavored mayonnaise. As we do in this recipe, you can add other flavors like lemon juice and finely minced shallots or onions, and even a touch of Dijon mustard. Aioli is also wonderful spread on sandwiches and mixed into egg or chicken salads.

NUTRITIONAL INFORMATION | BAKED FISH WITH LEMON AIOLI-PANKO COATING:

EXCHANGES / CHOICES:
1/2 Carbohydrate; 4 Protein, lean; 1 Fat

Calories: 265; Calories from Fat: 110; Total Fat: 12 g;
Saturated Fat: 2 g; Trans Fat: 0 g; Cholesterol: 130 mg;
Sodium: 325 mg; Potassium: 730 mg; Total Carbohydrate: 5 g;
Dietary Fiber: 0 g; Sugar: 1 g; Protein: 32 g; Phosphorus: 255 mg

NUTRITIONAL INFORMATION | WILD RICE:

EXCHANGES / CHOICES:
1 1/2 Starch

Calories: 120; Calories from Fat: 0; Total Fat: 0 g;
Saturated Fat: 0.1 g; Trans Fat: 0 g; Cholesterol: 0 mg;
Sodium: 0 mg; Potassium: 120 mg; Total Carbohydrate: 25 g;
Dietary Fiber: 2 g; Sugar: 1 g; Protein: 5 g; Phosphorus: 100 mg

NUTRITIONAL INFORMATION | SIMPLE MIXED VEGETABLES:

EXCHANGES / CHOICES:
1 Nonstarchy Vegetable

Calories: 30; Calories from Fat: 10; Total Fat: 1 g;
Saturated Fat: 0.6 g; Trans Fat: 0 g; Cholesterol: 5 mg;
Sodium: 175 mg; Potassium: 115 mg; Total Carbohydrate: 4 g;
Dietary Fiber: 2 g; Sugar: 2 g; Protein: 2 g; Phosphorus: 35 mg

This chicken is impressive enough for entertaining, but easy enough for a weeknight meal. It's the kind of casual yet sophisticated meal you might find at an Italian trattoria. For a more elegant presentation, leave the chicken breasts whole and spoon the sauce over the chicken. Serve with Roasted Broccoli.

Trattoria Chicken with Tomatoes and Olives

PREP + COOK: 20 MINUTES • **SERVES:** 6 • **SERVING SIZE:** ABOUT 2 CUPS

3 teaspoons extra-virgin olive oil, divided use

2 pounds boneless, skinless chicken breasts, cut into 1-inch pieces, or use 2 pounds diced eggplant

1 yellow onion, diced

1 teaspoon minced garlic (about 2 cloves)

15 ounces diced tomatoes, with their liquid

1/2 cup pitted green olives, coarsely chopped

1 teaspoon dried oregano, or 1 tablespoon fresh

1 teaspoon dried basil, or 1 tablespoon fresh

DO AHEAD OR DELEGATE: Cut the chicken or the eggplant (and refrigerate the chicken), dice the onion, peel the garlic, chop the olives, or fully prepare and refrigerate or freeze the dish.

1. (Start the broccoli first, if you are serving it.) In a large skillet, heat 2 teaspoons oil over medium heat. Add the chicken (if you are using eggplant instead of chicken, see the Tip below for cooking instructions) and sauté until it is just cooked through, 5–7 minutes. Remove the chicken from the pan and set it aside.

2. Add the remaining oil and the onions to the skillet. Cook the onions until they are slightly softened, about 3 minutes. Add the garlic and cook for 1 more minute. Add the tomatoes, olives, oregano, and basil, and bring it to a simmer. Add the chicken (if you have picky eaters, you may want to keep some of the chicken plain or serve the sauce on the side) and stir until it is heated through. Serve immediately, refrigerate for up to 3 days, or freeze for up to 3 months.

SLOW COOKER DIRECTIONS: Add all ingredients to the slow cooker and cook on low for 6–8 hours or on high for 4–6 hours. (Slow cooker cooking times may vary—get to know your slow cooker and, if necessary, adjust cooking times accordingly.)

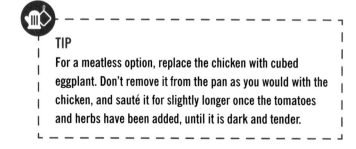

TIP

For a meatless option, replace the chicken with cubed eggplant. Don't remove it from the pan as you would with the chicken, and sauté it for slightly longer once the tomatoes and herbs have been added, until it is dark and tender.

Roasted Broccoli

SERVES: 6 • **SERVING SIZE:** 5 SPEARS

2 pounds broccoli, trim the bottom 1/2 inch of stalk, remove leaves, and cut into about 30 spears

1 tablespoon extra-virgin olive oil

1/4 teaspoon kosher salt

1/2 teaspoon salt-free lemon-pepper seasoning

1. Preheat the oven to 400°F. Cut the broccoli into spears and toss them with the oil, salt, and lemon-pepper seasoning (for a spicy taste, add some crushed red pepper flakes, too). Lay the spears flat on a baking sheet and roast for 15–20 minutes, flipping them once, until they are lightly browned in spots.

NUTRITIONAL INFORMATION | TRATTORIA CHICKEN WITH TOMATOES AND OLIVES:

EXCHANGES / CHOICES:
1 Nonstarchy Vegetable; 4 Protein, lean

Calories: 230; Calories from Fat: 70; Total Fat: 8 g; Saturated Fat: 1.6 g; Trans Fat: 0 g; Cholesterol: 90 mg; Sodium: 350 mg; Potassium: 445 mg; Total Carbohydrate: 6 g; Dietary Fiber: 2 g; Sugar: 3 g; Protein: 33 g; Phosphorus: 260 mg

NUTRITIONAL INFORMATION | ROASTED BROCCOLI:

EXCHANGES / CHOICES:
1 Nonstarchy Vegetable; 1/2 Fat

Calories: 55; Calories from Fat: 20; Total Fat: 2.5 g; Saturated Fat: 0.4 g; Trans Fat: 0 g; Cholesterol: 0 mg; Sodium: 110 mg; Potassium: 300 mg; Total Carbohydrate: 6 g; Dietary Fiber: 3 g; Sugar: 2 g; Protein: 3 g; Phosphorus: 65 mg

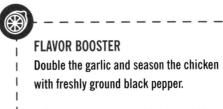

FLAVOR BOOSTER
Double the garlic and season the chicken with freshly ground black pepper.

This light and colorful pasta dish is one of my recent favorites! It's so pretty that you'd be proud to serve it to company—or make your family feel like they are special guests. Serve with Green Salad with Carrots, Hard-Boiled Egg, and Parmesan Cheese.

Fettuccine with Artichokes, Roasted Peppers, and Pine Nuts

PREP + COOK: 30 MINUTES • **SERVES:** 9 • **SERVING SIZE:** 1 1/3 CUPS

16 ounces whole-wheat fettuccine

2 tablespoons extra-virgin olive oil

1 yellow onion, diced

1 teaspoon minced garlic (1–2 cloves)

12 ounces frozen quartered artichoke hearts

1/4 cup pine nuts, toasted

1 cup roasted red peppers, drained and chopped

1 cup fresh basil leaves, loosely packed, coarsely chopped

1/2 teaspoon salt

2 teaspoon sugar

1/4 cup grated Parmesan cheese (optional)

DO AHEAD OR DELEGATE: Cook the pasta and store it tossed with a little oil to prevent sticking, dice the onion, peel the garlic, defrost the artichokes, toast the pine nuts, and chop the peppers.

1. Cook the noodles in salted water according to the package directions. Before draining them, scoop out about 1/2 cup of the pasta's cooking water and set it aside.

2. In a large heavy skillet, heat the oil over medium heat. Add the onions and garlic and sauté until the onions are tender, about 5 minutes. Meanwhile, defrost the artichokes and toast the pine nuts. Add the peppers, basil, artichokes, pine nuts, salt, and sugar to the pan and continue to cook, stirring often, until the noodles are done, about 15 minutes. Reduce the heat to medium-low or low if the mixture is getting too dry. (Meanwhile, make the salad, if you are serving it.)

3. Put the noodles in a large serving bowl, preferably a metal bowl to retain the heat, top them with the vegetable sauce, add a little of the reserved pasta cooking water to moisten the mixture, if desired, and serve immediately. Top individual servings with the cheese, if desired.

SLOW COOKER DIRECTIONS: Place all ingredients except the fettuccine and cheese in the slow cooker and stir to combine. (If you are using fresh basil, you may reserve it and add it in the last 30 minutes of cooking for a stronger flavor.) Cook on low for 6–8 hours or on high for 4–5 hours. Serve over cooked fettuccine and top with Parmesan cheese, if desired. (Slow cooker cooking times may vary—get to know your slow cooker and, if necessary, adjust cooking times accordingly.)

Green Salad with Carrots, Hard-Boiled Egg, and Parmesan Cheese

SERVES: 9 • **SERVING SIZE:** 1 CUP

1 large head iceberg or romaine lettuce, chopped (9 cups)

2 carrots, thinly sliced

1 large egg, hard-boiled and chopped

2 tablespoons grated Parmesan cheese

1/4 cup vinaigrette dressing

1. In a large bowl, combine the lettuce, carrots, egg, and Parmesan cheese and toss with the dressing.

FLAVOR BOOSTER
Serve the fettuccine with crushed red pepper flakes and freshly grated Parmesan cheese.

TIP
Nuts are an excellent source of protein and minerals. If you are trying to figure out ways to add nuts to more meals, some tasty options are salads, cereal, yogurt, and even stir-fries.

NUTRITIONAL INFORMATION | FETTUCCINE WITH ARTICHOKES, ROASTED PEPPERS, AND PINE NUTS:

EXCHANGES / CHOICES:
2 1/2 Starch; 1 Nonstarchy Vegetable; 1 Fat

Calories: 270; Calories from Fat: 65; Total Fat: 7 g;
Saturated Fat: 0.7 g; Trans Fat: 0 g; Cholesterol: 0 mg;
Sodium: 230 mg; Potassium: 315 mg; Total Carbohydrate: 44 g;
Dietary Fiber: 8 g; Sugar: 4 g; Protein: 10 g; Phosphorus: 185 mg

NUTRITIONAL INFORMATION | GREEN SALAD WITH CARROTS, HARD-BOILED EGG, AND PARMESAN CHEESE:

EXCHANGES / CHOICES:
1 Nonstarchy Vegetable; 1/2 Fat

Calories: 40; Calories from Fat: 20; Total Fat: 2.5 g;
Saturated Fat: 0.5 g; Trans Fat: 0 g; Cholesterol: 20 mg;
Sodium: 105 mg; Potassium: 130 mg; Total Carbohydrate: 4 g;
Dietary Fiber: 1 g; Sugar: 2 g; Protein: 2 g; Phosphorus: 35 mg

This is my favorite vegetarian chili yet. It's sweet, chunky, and just a little spicy. If your kids won't eat these foods mixed together, remove a couple of spoonfuls of the beans and corn to serve to them separately. Serve with Cornbread or Corn Muffins.

North of the Border Veggie Chili

PREP + COOK: 30 MINUTES • **SERVES:** 8 • **SERVING SIZE:** 1 1/2 CUPS

1 tablespoon extra-virgin olive oil

1 yellow onion, diced

1 red bell pepper, diced

2 carrots, sliced (and halved if they are large) (about 1 cup)

15 ounces canned red kidney beans, drained and rinsed, return them to the can, then add fresh water to cover

15 ounces canned black beans, reduced-salt, if possible, with their liquid

1 cup mild salsa

28 ounces crushed tomatoes

1 tablespoon chili powder, or more to taste

1–1 1/2 cup corn kernels, fresh, frozen, or canned

1 cup nonfat plain sour cream or yogurt (optional)

1 cup shredded cheddar cheese (optional)

DO AHEAD OR DELEGATE: Dice the onion, bell pepper, and carrots, thaw the corn if using frozen, or fully prepare and refrigerate or freeze the chili.

1. (Start the muffins or cornbread first, if you are serving them.) In a large heavy saucepan or stockpot, heat the oil over medium heat. Add the onions and peppers and sauté until the onions start to brown, about 5 minutes.

2. Add the carrots, both types of beans and their liquid, the salsa, tomatoes, and chili powder to the pot. Bring to a boil, lower the heat, and simmer, uncovered, for 20 minutes or up to 40 minutes, stirring occasionally. About 10 minutes before serving, stir in the corn.

3. Serve the chili topped with a dollop of sour cream or yogurt and sprinkled with cheese, if desired. The chili can also be made ahead and refrigerated for up to 3 days or frozen for up to 3 months.

SLOW COOKER DIRECTIONS: You will need at least a 5L crockpot to prepare this in its entirety. Omit the oil. Place all ingredients except the sour cream and cheese in the slow cooker and cook on low for 6–8 hours or on high for 3–4 hours. (Slow cooker cooking times may vary— get to know your slow cooker and, if necessary, adjust cooking times accordingly.)

Cornbread or Corn Muffins

SERVES: 20 • **SERVING SIZE:** 1 MUFFIN

1 (24-ounce) package cornbread or corn muffin mix

1. Prepare the corn muffins or cornbread according to package directions, using mini muffin tins, if available. Serve warm. Freeze leftover muffins for future use.

TIP
My family loves to crumble cornbread over their chili bowls and mix it all together.

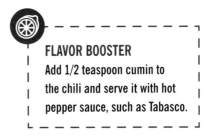

FLAVOR BOOSTER
Add 1/2 teaspoon cumin to the chili and serve it with hot pepper sauce, such as Tabasco.

NUTRITIONAL INFORMATION | NORTH OF THE BORDER VEGGIE CHILI:

EXCHANGES / CHOICES:
1 1/2 Starch; 2 Nonstarchy Vegetable; 1/2 Fat

Calories: 180; Calories from Fat: 20; Total Fat: 2.5 g;
Saturated Fat: 0.4 g; Trans Fat: 0 g; Cholesterol: 0 mg;
Sodium: 415 mg; Potassium: 900 mg; Total Carbohydrate: 35 g;
Dietary Fiber: 9 g; Sugar: 9 g; Protein: 9 g; Phosphorus: 180 mg

NUTRITIONAL INFORMATION | CORNBREAD OR CORN MUFFINS:

EXCHANGES / CHOICES:
2 Starch; 1/2 Fat

Calories: 160; Calories from Fat: 45; Total Fat: 5 g;
Saturated Fat: 0.7 g; Trans Fat: 0 g; Cholesterol: 20 mg;
Sodium: 345 mg; Potassium: 45 mg; Total Carbohydrate: 26 g;
Dietary Fiber: 4 g; Sugar: 3 g; Protein: 4 g; Phosphorus: 175 mg

QUICK AND EASY BREAKFASTS TO FUEL YOUR DAY

Fueling yourself and your family with good nutrition at the beginning of the day sets the pattern for a day of high energy and healthy eating. Don't let the fact that you're short on time stop you from filling your tank though. Here are 12 quick and easy breakfast ideas to get you going.

1. A sandwich of brown rice cakes (or a whole-wheat bagel or tortilla) with a layer of peanut butter and all-fruit jelly or sliced banana or apple in the middle.

2. A whole-grain English muffin with melted cheddar cheese (add a slice of tomato or avocado for a more sophisticated palate).

3. Hard-boiled eggs alone, or diced and mixed with cubed and lightly buttered whole-wheat toast or cheese (you can even buy hard-boiled eggs pre-made and peeled).

4. Unsweetened applesauce mixed with cottage cheese and cinnamon or granola and cinnamon.

5. Yogurt with dry whole-grain cereal (look for 100% whole grain cereal with at least 5 grams of fiber, 3 grams of protein, and no more than 8 grams of sugar per serving) or granola, and/or fruit, or instant oatmeal mixed in.

6. A banana or apple with peanut or other nut butter.

7. Bags of homemade trail mix with nuts, raisins (or other dried fruit), sunflower seeds, whole-grain cereal, or popcorn.

8. Breakfast smoothies: Store the unblended smoothie (made with yogurt, fresh or frozen fruit, or peanut butter, banana, and milk) in the refrigerator overnight, and blend it in the morning. The Fruity Swirl Smoothies on page 9 are a great option.

9. Egg Dishes that can be made ahead and frozen: You can divide these up into single servings and defrost the night before for a wholesome protein-filled breakfast. See page 180 for the Light and Fluffy Spinach and Cheese Strata. (On a more relaxed weekend morning try the Mexican Poached Eggs on page 234 or Fried Egg and Avocado Sandwiches on page 280).

10. Whole-wheat toast topped with mashed avocado and a little coarse salt.

11. Breakfast sandwiches that can be made in advance and refrigerated like the Salmon Salad Melts with Havarti on page 130.

12. Steel-cut oats (made in advance and reheated) with fresh or frozen fruit and a teaspoon of nuts.

page 280 Fried Egg and Avocado Sandwiches
SIDE DISH: Seedless Grapes

Roasted Indian Cauliflower Tossed with Chickpeas and Cashews

page 360

♈ WINTER

WINTER

Baked Chicken with Maple Butter Glaze (1)
SIDE DISH: Steamed Broccoli with Lemon-Pepper Seasoning (1a)

Succulent Salmon with Caramelized Onions (2)
SIDE DISH: Farro (2a); Green Beans with Lemon and Garlic (2b)

Pesto Vegetable Soup with Tofu or Chicken (3)
SIDE DISH: Garlic Toast (3a)

Spicy Slow-Cooked Indian Dal (4)
SIDE DISH: Fragrant Basmati Rice (4a); Curried Carrot Salad with Lime and Cilantro (4b)

Vegetarian Enchiladas Verdes (5)
SIDE DISH: Orange and Grapefruit Slices (5a)

SHOPPING LIST

🥕 PRODUCE
10 **carrots** (3)(4b)

1 small **yellow onion** (3)

1/2 large **sweet yellow onion**, such as Vidalia or Walla Walla (2)

1 **red onion** (4)

1 **jalapeño pepper** (4)

4 stalks **celery** (3)

12 ounces **baby spinach** (5)

2 cloves **garlic** (4a)*

1 1/2 teaspoon **fresh ginger** (4)

1 cup **fresh cilantro** (4)(4b)(5)

1/3 cup **fresh flat-leaf parsley** (2a)(3)

1/4 teaspoon **fresh or dried rosemary** (3a)

2 pounds **broccoli** (1a)

1 pound **green beans, fresh or frozen** (2b)

8–10 ounces **sliced button or cremini mushrooms** (5)

5/8 **lemon** (2)(2b)

1/2–1 **lime** (4b)

4 **oranges** (5a)

2 **grapefruits** (5a)

🍖 MEAT AND FISH
1 **whole chicken**, cut up (1)

1–1 1/2 pounds **salmon fillet** (use wild Alaskan salmon if possible) (2)

🧴 SHELVED ITEMS

6 slices **sourdough, French, or challah bread** (3a)

3/4 cup **brown basmati rice** (4a)

3/4 cup **farro perlato** (or use pearled barley) (2a)

8 **whole-wheat tortillas** (use wheat/gluten-free if needed) (5)

28 ounces **canned whole or diced tomatoes** (4)

28 ounces **diced tomatoes** (3)

8 1/2 cups **reduced-sodium chicken or vegetable broth** (2a)(3)(4a)

1 cup **salsa verde** (green salsa) (use a high-quality jarred salsa such as Frontera) (5)

1/4 cup **mango chutney** (4)*

1 1/2 cups **red or yellow lentils** (4)

🧂 SPICES

2 3/8 teaspoons **salt** (1)(2a)(2b)(4)(4b)

1/2 teaspoon **kosher salt** (2)(3a)

1/2 teaspoon **salt-free lemon pepper seasoning** (1a)

1/4 teaspoon **crushed red pepper flakes** (3a)*

1/4 teaspoon **black pepper** (2)(2b)

6 **whole cloves** (4a)*

1 **stick of cinnamon** (4a)*

3/4 teaspoon **ground cinnamon** (1)

1/4 teaspoon **ground ginger** (2)

1 1/4 teaspoons **ground cumin** (1)(5)

1 tablespoon **garam masala** (an Indian spice blend) (4)

1 teaspoon **turmeric** (4)

3/4 teapoon **curry powder** (4b)

1/2 teaspoon **garlic powder** (5)

1/2 teaspoon **chili powder** (5)

1 1/2 teaspoons **paprika** (1)

1/4 teaspoon **dried dill** (2)

🍶 STAPLES

1 1/2 tablespoon **trans fat-free margarine or butter** (1)

6 tablespoons + 1/2 teaspoon **extra-virgin olive oil** (2)(2a)(2b)(3a)(4b)

1 tablespoon + 1 teaspoon **canola or vegetable oil** (3)(5)

1 1/2 tablespoons **Dijon mustard** (use wheat/gluten-free if needed) (1)

2 tablespoons **pure maple syrup** (1)

4 teaspoons **minced garlic** (2b)(3a)(4)(4b)

🧊 REFRIGERATED/FROZEN

3/4 cup **shredded reduced-fat Mexican blend cheese** (5)

2 wedges **Light Laughing Cow Creamy Swiss or Garlic and Herb cheese** (5)

1 cup **nonfat sour cream** (5)*

15 ounces **extra-firm tofu** (3)

1 tablespoon **basil pesto** (3)

Get free, printable versions of the shopping lists from this book at TheScramble.com/diabetes.

optional ingredients

WINTER WEEK 1 • 303

This scrumptious chicken, adapted from a Weight Watchers recipe, has received raves from Six O'Clock Scramble members. It cooks so quickly because of the high heat and the chicken's proximity to the oven's heating element. Serve with Steamed Broccoli with Lemon-Pepper Seasoning.

Baked Chicken with Maple Butter Glaze

PREP + COOK: 30 MINUTES • **SERVES:** 6 • **SERVING SIZE:** 1 THIGH, 1 DRUMSTICK, OR 1/2 OF BREAST HALF

1 1/2 teaspoons paprika

1/2 teaspoon salt

3/4 teaspoon ground cinnamon

3/4 teaspoon ground cumin, or use chili powder

1 whole chicken, cut up (purchase it already cut up for greater ease)

2 tablespoons pure maple syrup

1 1/2 tablespoons trans fat-free margarine or butter

1 1/2 tablespoons Dijon mustard

DO AHEAD OR DELEGATE: Combine the dry spices.

1. Preheat the oven to 500°F. Line a baking sheet with aluminum foil and spray the foil with nonstick cooking spray. In a small bowl, combine the four dry spices.

2. Place the chicken pieces skin side up on the baking sheet. Sprinkle and rub the spice mixture evenly over the chicken (leave the drumsticks without spices for picky eaters, if desired). Position the sheet in the upper third of the oven, about 4 inches from the heating element, and bake it, without turning it, for 15 minutes.

3. Meanwhile, in a small saucepan combine the maple syrup, margarine, and mustard. Stir it over low heat until the butter melts. Remove it from the heat. (Start the broccoli now, if you are serving it.)

4. After the chicken has baked for 15 minutes, remove it from the oven, brush it with the maple glaze, and bake it for 5 more minutes. Brush the chicken with the glaze again and bake 5 minutes more. Remove from the oven and serve immediately, or refrigerate for up to 3 days.

SLOW COOKER DIRECTIONS: Place the chicken in the slow cooker, then sprinkle and rub the spice mixture evenly over the chicken. (Placing the chicken in the slow cooker keeps the rub contained and also eliminates mess.) Melt the butter, then combine it with the maple syrup and mustard. Brush the chicken with about half of the glaze. Cook on low for 6–8 hours, or high for 3–4 hours until the chicken is cooked through. About half an hour before serving, brush the chicken with the remainder of the glaze. (Slow cooker cooking times may vary—get to know your slow cooker and, if necessary, adjust cooking times accordingly.)

Steamed Broccoli with Lemon-Pepper Seasoning

SERVES: 6 • **SERVING SIZE:** 5 SPEARS

2 pounds broccoli, trim the bottom 1/2 inch of stalk, remove leaves, and cut into about 30 spears

1/2 teaspoon salt-free lemon-pepper seasoning, or to taste

1. Steam the broccoli florets or spears until tender, 5–8 minutes. Drain and season with the lemon-pepper seasoning.

FLAVOR BOOSTER

Substitute 1/4 teaspoon of the paprika with cayenne pepper.

TIP

In comparison to honey, maple syrup has fewer calories and a higher concentration of minerals. It's a great source of manganese and zinc. Make sure to use pure maple syrup to get the full benefit of the nutrients and best flavor.

NUTRITIONAL INFORMATION | BAKED CHICKEN WITH MAPLE BUTTER GLAZE:

EXCHANGES / CHOICES:
1/2 Carbohydrate; 3 Protein, lean; 1/2 Fat

Calories: 180; Calories from Fat: 70; Total Fat: 8 g;
Saturated Fat: 2 g; Trans Fat: 0 g; Cholesterol: 65 mg;
Sodium: 370 mg; Potassium: 215 mg; Total Carbohydrate: 6 g;
Dietary Fiber: 0 g; Sugar: 4 g; Protein: 21 g; Phosphorus: 150 mg

NUTRITIONAL INFORMATION | STEAMED BROCCOLI WITH LEMON-PEPPER SEASONING:

EXCHANGES / CHOICES:
2 Nonstarchy Vegetable

Calories: 40; Calories from Fat: 0; Total Fat: 0 g;
Saturated Fat: 0 g; Trans Fat: 0 g; Cholesterol: 0 mg;
Sodium: 40 mg; Potassium: 385 mg; Total Carbohydrate: 8 g;
Dietary Fiber: 3 g; Sugar: 2 g; Protein: 3 g; Phosphorus: 80 mg

My friend and neighbor Christine Dallaire shared this awesome recipe. You can serve it for an elegant dinner party or a special family dinner. Serve with Farro and Green Beans with Lemon and Garlic.

Succulent Salmon with Caramelized Onions

PREP: 15 MINUTES • **COOK:** 20 MINUTES • **SERVES:** 4 • **SERVING SIZE:** 3 OUNCES SALMON + 2 TABLESPOONS ONIONS

1 tablespoon extra-virgin olive oil

1/2 large sweet yellow onion, such as Vidalia or Walla Walla, halved top to bottom and thinly sliced

1/4 teaspoon ground ginger

1/4 teaspoon dried dill

1/4 teaspoon kosher salt

1/8 teaspoon black pepper

1/2 lemon, halved top to bottom and thinly sliced

1–1 1/2 pounds salmon fillet (preferably wild Alaskan)

DO AHEAD OR DELEGATE: Slice the onion and the lemon and combine the dry seasonings.

1. Preheat the oven to 350°F. Heat the oil in a large, heavy oven-proof skillet over medium heat, and add the onions. Cook for 8–10 minutes, stirring occasionally, until they are golden. (Start the farro, if you are serving it.)

2. Meanwhile, in a small bowl, combine the ginger, dill, salt, and pepper. Top the onions with the lemon slices and then the salmon, and top the salmon evenly with the spices. Transfer the skillet to the oven and cook the salmon for about 20 minutes, until it is cooked through. (Meanwhile, prepare the green beans, if you are serving them.) Remove from the oven and serve immediately.

SLOW COOKER DIRECTIONS: Cut the salmon fillet into pieces that will fit into the slow cooker, if needed. Combine the onions in the bottom of the slow cooker. Place each piece of salmon onto a separate piece of aluminum foil large enough to fold into a packet. Sprinkle the spices evenly over the salmon pieces and top with lemon slices. Fold the foil into a packet, and place the packets into the slow cooker on top of the onions, stacking as needed. Cook on low for 6–8 hours or on high for 3–4 hours (for thinner fillets check sooner). Remove the salmon from the packets, then top with the onions before serving.

FLAVOR BOOSTER
Double the dill and add 1/4 teaspoon salt-free lemon-pepper seasoning to the spice blend. Serve the salmon with fresh lemon wedges.

TIP
If you love caramelized onions, use a whole onion in this recipe instead of half.

Farro

PREP + COOK: 30 MINUTES • **SERVES:** 4 • **SERVING SIZE:** 1/2 CUP

3/4 cup farro, or use pearled barley
1 1/2 cups reduced-sodium chicken broth
1/2 teaspoon extra-virgin olive oil

1. In a medium stockpot, cook the farro or barley in broth or water according to package directions. Cook until it is tender but still chewy. Drain if necessary, toss with the oil, and serve.

Green Beans with Lemon and Garlic

SERVES: 6 • **SERVING SIZE:** 2/3 CUP

1 tablespoon extra-virgin olive oil
1 teaspoon minced garlic (about 2 cloves)
1 pound green beans, fresh or frozen
1/8 lemon, juice only (about 1 teaspoon)
1/8 teaspoon salt (optional)
1/8 teaspoon black pepper (optional)

1. Heat the oil in a large skillet over medium heat. Add the garlic and stir for about 30 seconds, until it is fragrant. Stir in the green beans. Cover the pan and steam the beans until they are tender, about 5–8 minutes. Add the lemon juice for the last minute of cooking, and season with salt and pepper, if desired.

SLOW COOKER DIRECTIONS: Put all ingredients except the lemon in the slow cooker and add 1 cup of water or broth. Cook on low for 6–8 hours or on high for 4–5 hours. Use a slotted spoon to serve.

NUTRITIONAL INFORMATION | SUCCULENT SALMON WITH CARAMELIZED ONIONS:

EXCHANGES / CHOICES:
1/2 Carbohydrate; 3 Protein, lean; 1 Fat

Calories: 215; Calories from Fat: 100; Total Fat: 11 g;
Saturated Fat: 2.2 g; Trans Fat: 0 g; Cholesterol: 65 mg;
Sodium: 200 mg; Potassium: 520 mg; Total Carbohydrate: 7 g;
Dietary Fiber: 2 g; Sugar: 3 g; Protein: 24 g; Phosphorus: 325 mg

NUTRITIONAL INFORMATION | FARRO:

EXCHANGES / CHOICES:
2 Starch

Calories: 140; Calories from Fat: 15; Total Fat: 1.5 g;
Saturated Fat: 0.2 g; Trans Fat: 0 g; Cholesterol: 0 mg;
Sodium: 195 mg; Potassium: 185 mg; Total Carbohydrate: 27 g;
Dietary Fiber: 3 g; Sugar: 0 g; Protein: 6 g; Phosphorus: 140 mg

NUTRITIONAL INFORMATION | GREEN BEANS WITH LEMON AND GARLIC:

EXCHANGES / CHOICES:
1 Nonstarchy Vegetable; 1/2 Fat

Calories: 45; Calories from Fat: 20; Total Fat: 2.5 g;
Saturated Fat: 0.4 g; Trans Fat: 0 g; Cholesterol: 0 mg;
Sodium: 0 mg; Potassium: 95 mg; Total Carbohydrate: 5 g;
Dietary Fiber: 2 g; Sugar: 1 g; Protein: 1 g; Phosphorus: 20 mg

I served this on a night that my daughter, Celia, got her braces tightened so she was glad to have something soft and flavorful she could enjoy, and I was glad she was getting nourishment beyond pudding and popsicles. Serve with Garlic Toast.

Pesto Vegetable Soup with Tofu or Chicken

PREP: 15 MINUTES • **COOK:** 20 MINUTES • **SERVES:** 6 • **SERVING SIZE:** 2 CUPS

1 tablespoon canola or vegetable oil

4 carrots, sliced

4 stalks celery, sliced

1 small yellow onion, diced

15 ounces extra-firm tofu, drained and diced, or use 1 pound chicken breast, diced

28 ounces diced tomatoes, with their liquid

4 cups reduced-sodium chicken or vegetable broth

1/4 cup fresh flat-leaf parsley, chopped

1 tablespoon basil pesto, or more to taste

DO AHEAD OR DELEGATE: Slice the carrots and the celery, dice the onion, drain and dice the tofu, or dice and refrigerate the chicken if using, chop the parsley, or fully prepare and refrigerate the soup.

1. Heat a large saucepan or stockpot over medium to medium-high heat, and add the oil. When it is hot, add the carrots, celery, and onions. Cook, stirring occasionally, until the onions are translucent, about 5 minutes.

2. Add the tofu (if using chicken, add it about 6–8 minutes before the soup is done), tomatoes, and broth, cover it, and bring it to a boil. Remove the cover and simmer the soup for 15–20 minutes until the vegetables are very tender. (Meanwhile, make the toast, if you are serving it.)

3. Stir in the parsley and pesto and let the flavors meld for about a minute before removing from the heat. Serve immediately or refrigerate for up to 3 days.

SLOW COOKER DIRECTIONS: Place all ingredients in the slow cooker, and cook on low for 6–8 hours or high for 4–6 hours, until the vegetables are softened. (Slow cooker cooking times may vary—get to know your slow cooker and, if necessary, adjust cooking times accordingly.)

FLAVOR BOOSTER
Add 1 jalapeño pepper, seeded and diced, double the parsley, and season the soup with freshly ground black pepper.

- -

Garlic Toast

SERVES: 6 • **SERVING SIZE:** 1 SLICE

3 tablespoons extra-virgin olive oil
1 teaspoon minced garlic (about 2 cloves)
1/4 teaspoon kosher salt
1/4 teaspoon fresh or dried rosemary
1/4 teaspoon crushed red pepper flakes (optional)
6 slices sourdough, French, or challah bread, about
    1/2-inch thick

1. Preheat the oven to 400°F and lay the bread on a baking sheet. In a small bowl, combine the oil, garlic, salt, rosemary, and red pepper flakes (optional). Brush the oil mixture evenly over the tops of the bread. Bake them for 7–10 minutes, until they just start to brown.

TIP

In the past, I always used the large boxes of reduced-sodium broth for soup, but recently I've found a product I like even better, Better Than Bouillon organic soup bases (I've been using the vegetable base). It dissolves easily, lasts for months when refrigerated, and is made from concentrated vegetables and other natural, flavorful ingredients, so it gives my soups a wonderful flavor and is more economical and space-efficient.

NUTRITIONAL INFORMATION | PESTO VEGETABLE SOUP WITH TOFU OR CHICKEN:

EXCHANGES / CHOICES:
3 Nonstarchy Vegetable; 1 Protein, lean; 1 Fat

Calories: 155; Calories from Fat: 70; Total Fat: 8 g;
Saturated Fat: 0.8 g; Trans Fat: 0 g; Cholesterol: 0 mg;
Sodium: 440 mg; Potassium: 740 mg; Total Carbohydrate: 14 g;
Dietary Fiber: 4 g; Sugar: 7 g; Protein: 11 g; Phosphorus: 175 mg

NUTRITIONAL INFORMATION | GARLIC TOAST:

EXCHANGES / CHOICES:
1 Starch; 1 1/2 Fat

Calories: 140; Calories from Fat: 65; Total Fat: 7 g;
Saturated Fat: 1.1 g; Trans Fat: 0 g; Cholesterol: 0 mg;
Sodium: 225 mg; Potassium: 40 mg; Total Carbohydrate: 16 g;
Dietary Fiber: 1 g; Sugar: 1 g; Protein: 3 g; Phosphorus: 35 mg

After many attempts, I finally made a delicious dal (Indian lentil stew) and the solution was so simple—just use the slow cooker! With all the fiber, vegetables, and spices, this is a pot of pure health for your family. You can also stir in a few handfuls of fresh spinach toward the end of the cooking time. Serve with Fragrant Basmati Rice and with Curried Carrot Salad with Lime and Cilantro.

Spicy Slow-Cooked Indian Dal

PREP: 15 MINUTES • **COOK:** 3 HOURS • **SERVES:** 8 • **SERVING SIZE:** 1 CUPS

1 1/2 cups red lentils, or use yellow lentils

1 red onion, peeled and diced

1 jalapeño pepper, halved lengthwise, seeded and sliced

1 1/2 teaspoons minced garlic (about 3 cloves)

1 1/2 teaspoons fresh ginger, peeled and minced

1 teaspoon turmeric, or use curry powder

1 tablespoon garam masala (an Indian spice blend)

3/4 teaspoon salt

28 ounces canned whole or diced tomatoes, with their liquid + 1 can full of water

1/2 cup fresh cilantro, chopped (optional)

1/4 cup mango chutney (optional)

DO AHEAD OR DELEGATE: Dice the onion, halve, seed, and slice the jalapeño, peel the garlic, peel and mince the ginger, chop the cilantro if using, or fully prepare and refrigerate the dish.

1. In a slow cooker, combine all the ingredients, except the cilantro and chutney. Stir and cook for 5–7 hours on low or 3–4 hours on high. (Prepare the rice during the last hour of cooking, if you are serving it.) Serve with the cilantro and chutney, if desired.

STOVETOP COOKING DIRECTIONS: In a Dutch oven or stockpot over medium heat, heat 1 tablespoon canola oil and sauté the onions, peppers, garlic, and ginger for 5–7 minutes until the onions are tender. Stir in the turmeric and garam masala for 1 minute, then add the salt, lentils, tomatoes, and water. Cover, bring to a boil, and simmer, partially covered, for about 30 minutes, stirring occasionally and breaking up the tomatoes with the spoon. Uncover and continue simmering for about 30 more minutes, stirring occasionally, until most of the liquid is absorbed and the lentils are very tender. (Meanwhile, make the rice, if you are serving it.) Serve with the cilantro and chutney, if desired.

TIP
Frozen garlic and ginger cubes, such as those made by Dorot, work beautifully in the slow cooker if you want to save time—just pop them in while still frozen.

FLAVOR BOOSTER
Use 1 1/2 jalapeño peppers (if you like a lot of spice!), use the optional cilantro and mango chutney, and put a dollop of Greek yogurt on top of each serving.

SIDE DISHES

- -

Fragrant Basmati Rice

SERVES: 8 • **SERVING SIZE:** 1/2 CUP

1 1/2 cups brown basmati rice

3 cups reduced-sodium chicken or vegetable broth (optional)

1 stick of cinnamon (optional)

6 whole cloves (optional)

2 cloves garlic (optional)

1. Cook the rice according to package directions, using broth for extra flavor, if desired. For an authentic Indian flavor, add the cinnamon, cloves, and garlic cloves to the liquid with the rice (optional). Remove the cinnamon, cloves, and garlic before serving.

Curried Carrot Salad with Lime and Cilantro

MARINATE: 30 MINUTES • **PREP:** 15 MINUTES • **COOK:** 5 MINUTES
SERVES: 8 • **SERVING SIZE:** 1/2 CUP

6 medium carrots, sliced

1 tablespoon extra-virgin olive oil

1/2–1 lime, juice only (about 2 tablespoons)

1/2 teaspoon minced garlic (about 1 clove)

3/4 teaspoon curry powder

1/4 teaspoon salt

2 tablespoons fresh cilantro, finely chopped, or use parsley or mint or a combination

1. In a microwave-safe bowl, cover the carrots and cook them in the microwave for 2–3 minutes until tender-crisp (or steam them for 5 minutes on the stovetop). Meanwhile, in a small bowl combine the remaining ingredients. Toss the carrots with the dressing and refrigerate for at least 30 minutes and up to 3 days before serving.

NUTRITIONAL INFORMATION | SPICY SLOW-COOKED INDIAN DAL:

EXCHANGES / CHOICES:
1 1/2 Starch; 1 Nonstarchy Vegetable

Calories: 150; Calories from Fat: 5; Total Fat: 0.5 g; Saturated Fat: 0.1 g; Trans Fat: 0 g; Cholesterol: 0 mg; Sodium: 365 mg; Potassium: 630 mg; Total Carbohydrate: 28 g; Dietary Fiber: 10 g; Sugar: 5 g; Protein: 10 g; Phosphorus: 215 mg

NUTRITIONAL INFORMATION | FRAGRANT BASMATI RICE:

EXCHANGES / CHOICES:
1 1/2 Starch

Calories: 120; Calories from Fat: 10; Total Fat: 1 g; Saturated Fat: 0.2 g; Trans Fat: 0 g; Cholesterol: 0 mg; Sodium: 0 mg; Potassium: 45 mg; Total Carbohydrate: 26 g; Dietary Fiber: 2 g; Sugar: 1 g; Protein: 3 g; Phosphorus: 90 mg

NUTRITIONAL INFORMATION | CURRIED CARROT SALAD WITH LIME AND CILANTRO:

EXCHANGES / CHOICES:
1 Nonstarchy Vegetable; 1/2 Fat

Calories: 35; Calories from Fat: 20; Total Fat: 2 g; Saturated Fat: 0.3 g; Trans Fat: 0 g; Cholesterol: 0 mg; Sodium: 105 mg; Potassium: 155 mg; Total Carbohydrate: 5 g; Dietary Fiber: 1 g; Sugar: 2 g; Protein: 0 g; Phosphorus: 20 mg

I love enchiladas, but traditional enchiladas can take far too long to make for a weeknight family dinner, and I often find restaurant enchiladas to be too rich and cheesy. These vegetable enchiladas, inspired by a recipe from Six O'Clock Scramble member Alison Kavanaugh, are light and full of healthy vegetables. Serve with Orange and Grapefruit Slices.

Vegetarian Enchiladas Verdes

PREP + COOK: 30 MINUTES • **SERVES:** 8 • **SERVING SIZE:** 1 ENCHILADA

1 teaspoon canola or vegetable oil

8–10 ounces sliced button or cremini mushrooms

1/2 teaspoon chili powder

1/2 teaspoon ground cumin

1/2 teaspoon garlic powder

12 ounces baby spinach

2 wedges Light Laughing Cow Creamy Swiss or Garlic and Herb cheese, cut into several pieces

1 cup salsa verde (green salsa) (use a high-quality jarred salsa such as Frontera), divided use

8 whole-wheat tortillas

3/4 cup shredded reduced-fat Mexican blend cheese

1 cup nonfat sour cream (optional)

1/4–1/2 cup fresh cilantro, chopped (optional)

DO AHEAD OR DELEGATE: Combine the dry seasonings, and chop the cilantro, if using.

1. In a large nonstick skillet, heat the oil over medium heat. Add the mushrooms, chili powder, cumin, and garlic powder, stir to combine, then cover the pan for 2 minutes. Uncover the pan and continue to sauté the mushrooms for about 2 more minutes until they are dark and tender.

2. Meanwhile, preheat the broiler, set the rack about 6 inches from the heating element, and spray a 9 × 13-inch metal baking dish with nonstick cooking spray. Add the spinach to the skillet, cover the skillet for 1–2 minutes until the spinach wilts, then uncover the pan and add the cheese wedges, stirring to distribute evenly. Remove the skillet from the heat and set it aside.

3. In a second skillet just large enough to fit a tortilla, heat 1 cup of the salsa over medium-low heat. Using tongs or your fingers, dredge both sides of a tortilla in the salsa, then place about 1/8 of the spinach and mushroom mixture on one side of the tortilla. Roll it up and place it in the baking dish. Repeat with remaining tortillas and filling. Top evenly with all the shredded cheese, and broil them for 3–4 minutes, until the cheese is melted and the edges are browned. Serve the enchiladas immediately, topped with the sour cream and cilantro, if desired.

SLOW COOKER DIRECTIONS: In a large bowl, combine the mushrooms, spices, spinach, and Laughing Cow cheese, using the tines of a fork to break up and distribute the cheese. Place a thin layer of salsa in the bottom of the slow cooker, then prepare and fill tortillas as directed, stacking filled tortillas in the slow cooker, alternating layers of tortillas with thin layers of salsa and a sprinkling of shredded cheese, reserving 1/4 of the cheese. Top with the remaining salsa, and cook on low for 3–6 hours or on high for 2–4 hours. Fifteen minutes before serving, top them with the remaining shredded cheese, and serve with the sour cream and/or cilantro at the table, if desired.

Orange and Grapefruit Slices

SERVES: 8 • **SERVING SIZE:** 3/4 CUP

4 oranges

2 grapefruit

1. Slice the fruit and serve immediately.

FLAVOR BOOSTER
Double the garlic powder
and/or use spicy salsa.

TIP
Salsa verde is composed primarily of pureed
tomatillos, onion, jalapeños, cilantro, and lime.
Like traditional salsa, you can find it in both
mild and spicy varieties. It's a tasty departure
from tomato-based salsas but can be used in
much the same way—as a dip for chips or a
simple topping for grilled meat and fish.

NUTRITIONAL INFORMATION | VEGETARIAN ENCHILADAS VERDES:

EXCHANGES / CHOICES:
1 1/2 Starch; 1 Nonstarchy Vegetable; 1 Protein, lean; 1/2 Fat

Calories: 190; Calories from Fat: 65; Total Fat: 7 g;
Saturated Fat: 2.1 g; Trans Fat: 0 g; Cholesterol: 5 mg;
Sodium: 430 mg; Potassium: 500 mg; Total Carbohydrate: 27 g;
Dietary Fiber: 6 g; Sugar: 2 g; Protein: 10 g; Phosphorus: 220 mg

NUTRITIONAL INFORMATION | ORANGE AND GRAPEFRUIT SLICES:

EXCHANGES / CHOICES:
1 Fruit

Calories: 60; Calories from Fat: 0; Total Fat: 0 g;
Saturated Fat: 0 g; Trans Fat: 0 g; Cholesterol: 0 mg;
Sodium: 0 mg; Potassium: 245 mg; Total Carbohydrate: 15 g;
Dietary Fiber: 3 g; Sugar: 13 g; Protein: 1 g; Phosphorus: 15 mg

WINTER

Crunchy Chicken Fingers (1)
SIDE DISH: Colorful Kale Salad (1a)

Quick Tilapia with Lemon, Garlic, and Capers (2)
SIDE DISH: Steamed Rice and Peas (2a)

Garlic Mashed Potato Soup (3)
SIDE DISH: Baked Breadsticks (3a); Fruit Kabobs (3b)

Orecchiette and Broccoli with Lemon Butter Sauce (4)
SIDE DISH: Roasted Parsnips or Carrots (4a)

Toasty Baked Burritos (5)
SIDE DISH: Spicy Zucchini Sticks (5a)

SHOPPING LIST

🥕 PRODUCE

4 **scallions** (3)

1/2 **yellow onion** (3)

1 pound **parsnips or carrots** (4a)

1 1/2 **red onions** (1a)(5)

1 **green or red bell pepper** (5)

1 bunch **kale** (1a)

1/4 cup **fresh basil** (4)

1 pound **broccoli** (4)

2 **zucchini** (5a)

2 large **russet (baking) potatoes** (3)

3/4 cup **corn kernels, fresh, frozen or canned** (5)

3 **lemons** (1a)(2)(4)

6–8 cups **mixed fruit** such as strawberries, blueberries, bananas, mango, grapes and/or melon (3b)

🐟 MEAT AND FISH

2 pounds **chicken tenderloins or use boneless, skinless chicken breasts** (1)

1 pound **tilapia fillets or other thin white fish** (2)

2 strips **turkey, pork, or vegetarian bacon**, preferably nitrite-free (3)*

🥫 SHELVED ITEMS

1 1/2 cups **quick-cooking brown rice** (2a)

1 pound **orecchiette noodles** (4)

8 **whole-wheat tortillas** (use wheat/gluten-free if needed) (5)

2 cups **dry stuffing mix, herb seasoned or cornbread** (1)

14 ounces **diced tomatoes with green chilies** (5)

32 ounces **low-sodium chicken or vegetable broth** (3)

1 cup **salsa** (5)*

15 ounces **low-sodium canned pinto beans** (5)

15 ounces **low-sodium canned black beans** (5)

1 tablespoon **capers** (2)

1/2 cup **dried cranberries** (preferably naturally sweetened) (1a)

1/4 cup **toasted pine nuts** (4)

15–20 colorful **toothpicks or wooden skewers** (3b)

🧂 SPICES

1 1/8–1 3/8 teaspoons **salt** (1)(1a)(2)(2a)(4)

1/4 teaspoon **kosher salt** (4a)

5/8–3/4 teaspoon **black pepper** (1)(1a)(2)(4)(4a)

3 teaspoons **ground cumin** (5)(5a)

1 teaspoon **garlic powder** (5a)

1 teaspoon **chili powder** (5)

2 teaspoons **paprika** (5a)

🧴 STAPLES

2 tablespoons **butter** (4)

1 tablespoon **trans fat-free margarine** (3)

5–7 tablespoons **extra-virgin olive oil** (1a)(2)(4a)(5a)

1 tablespoon **canola or vegetable oil** (5)

1 tablespoon **Dijon mustard** (1)

1 tablespoon **reduced-sodium soy sauce** (use wheat/gluten-free if needed) (2a)*

3 1/2–4 1/2 teaspoons **minced garlic** (2)(3)(5)

❄️ REFRIGERATED/FROZEN

1 1/3 cups **shredded reduced-fat cheddar cheese** (3)(5)

1/4 cup **grated Parmesan cheese** (4)

1 cup **guacamole** (5)*

1 cup **nonfat vanilla yogurt** (3b)*

1 1/2 cups + 2 tablespoons **nonfat sour cream** (1)(3)(5)

1 package **low-fat breadsticks (bake-at-home)**, such as Pillsbury (3a)

1 cup **frozen peas** (2a)

Get free, printable versions of the shopping lists from this book at **TheScramble.com/diabetes**.

optional ingredients

WINTER WEEK 2 • 315

These chicken strips are bound to please the kids as well as the adults in your family. You can dip them in ketchup, honey mustard, or barbecue sauce. Serve with Colorful Kale Salad.

Crunchy Chicken Fingers

PREP: 10 MINUTES • **COOK:** 20 MINUTES • **SERVES:** 6 • **SERVING SIZE:** 2 STRIPS

1/2 cup nonfat sour cream

1 tablespoon Dijon mustard

1/4 teaspoon salt, or to taste

1/8 teaspoon black pepper, or to taste

2 cups dry stuffing mix, either cornbread or herb seasoned

2 pounds chicken tenderloins or boneless, skinless chicken breasts (if using chicken breasts, cut them into 1-inch-wide strips)

DO AHEAD OR DELEGATE: Make and refrigerate the sour cream mixture, crush the stuffing, and cut and refrigerate the chicken if using boneless breasts.

1. Preheat the oven to 400°F. Spray a large baking sheet with nonstick cooking spray.

2. Put the sour cream in a shallow bowl and stir in the mustard, salt, and pepper. Put the dry stuffing in another large shallow bowl and crush it into smaller pieces, without completely pulverizing it.

3. Dip each piece of chicken in the sour cream mixture, shake off the excess, then roll and press it in the stuffing, thoroughly coating each piece. Put the coated chicken strips on the baking sheet, and spray the tops of the chicken lightly with nonstick cooking spray.

4. Bake for 20 minutes, or until strips are cooked through and lightly golden. (Meanwhile, prepare the salad, if you are serving it.)

SLOW COOKER DIRECTIONS: After dipping and coating the strips as directed, layer them in the slow cooker and cook on low for 6–8 hours or high for 3–5 hours. (Note: These don't get crunchy in the slow cooker but they still taste great.) (Slow cooker cooking times may vary—get to know your slow cooker and, if necessary, adjust cooking times accordingly.)

TIP

To make the chicken fingers extra crunchy, place them on a metal rack (sprayed with nonstick cooking spray) and put the rack on top of the baking sheet. This will allow them to get crispier on the bottom.

Colorful Kale Salad

SERVES: 6 • **SERVING SIZE:** 1 CUP

1 lemon, juice only (about 1/4 cup)

1 tablespoon extra-virgin olive oil

1 bunch kale (12 ounces), thinly sliced

1/2 red onion, thinly sliced

1/2 cup dried cranberries

1/8 teaspoon salt

1/8 teaspoon black pepper, or to taste

1. Whisk together the lemon juice and oil. In a medium to large serving bowl, pour the dressing over the kale and onions. With clean hands, gently massage the dressing into the salad to soften and flavor the kale leaves. Add the dried cranberries, salt, and pepper and serve immediately or refrigerate for up to 3 days. (Other great additions include fresh garlic, grated Parmesan cheese, and chopped walnuts.)

FLAVOR BOOSTER
Use garlic salt instead of regular salt or add 1/4 teaspoon garlic powder to the sour cream mixture. Serve the strips with spicy barbecue sauce.

NUTRITIONAL INFORMATION | CRUNCHY CHICKEN FINGERS:

EXCHANGES / CHOICES:
1 Starch; 4 Protein, lean

Calories: 255; Calories from Fat: 40; Total Fat: 4.5 g; Saturated Fat: 1.1 g; Trans Fat: 0 g; Cholesterol: 90 mg; Sodium: 430 mg; Potassium: 330 mg; Total Carbohydrate: 17 g; Dietary Fiber: 1 g; Sugar: 2 g; Protein: 35 g; Phosphorus: 275 mg

NUTRITIONAL INFORMATION | COLORFUL KALE SALAD:

EXCHANGES / CHOICES:
1/2 Fruit; 1 Nonstarchy Vegetable; 1/2 Fat

Calories: 85; Calories from Fat: 25; Total Fat: 3 g; Saturated Fat: 0.4 g; Trans Fat: 0 g; Cholesterol: 0 mg; Sodium: 70 mg; Potassium: 285 mg; Total Carbohydrate: 15 g; Dietary Fiber: 3 g; Sugar: 9 g; Protein: 2 g; Phosphorus: 50 mg

Thin fish fillets like tilapia, trout, or flounder are great for a weeknight meal. They cook quickly, and their mild taste is kid-friendly. (In fact, our son used to think tilapia was chicken!) Serve with Steamed Rice and Peas.

Quick Tilapia with Lemon, Garlic, and Capers

PREP + COOK: 15 MINUTES • **SERVES:** 4 • **SERVING SIZE:** 1 FILLET

1 tablespoon extra-virgin olive oil

1 teaspoon minced garlic (about 2 cloves)

1 pound tilapia fillets or other thin white fish fillets (about 4 fillets)

1/4 teaspoon salt, or to taste

1/8 teaspoon black pepper, or to taste

3/4 lemon, juice only (2–3 tablespoons)

1 tablespoon capers, drained, or use 1 tablespoon chopped green olives

DO AHEAD OR DELEGATE: Peel the garlic, juice the lemon.

1. (Start the rice and peas, if you are serving them.) In a large nonstick skillet, heat the oil over medium heat. Add the garlic and cook for 30 seconds until it is fragrant. Place the fillets in the pan and press them down with a spatula to ensure each fillet is completely touching the pan. Season them with a little salt and pepper. Cook the fish for 3–4 minutes, depending on the thickness of the fillets, until the bottoms start to brown.

2. Flip the fillets, pour the lemon juice over them, and season the second side with salt and pepper. Top the fish with the capers. Cook for another 3–4 minutes. When the tilapia is white throughout and flakes easily, remove it to a plate and serve immediately.

SLOW COOKER DIRECTIONS: Place each fillet on its own individual piece of aluminum foil. Drizzle each piece of fish with the oil and lemon juice, season with salt and pepper, and top with garlic and capers. Fold the foil over the fish to make a packet, and arrange the packets in the slow cooker, stacking one on top of the other as necessary. Cook on low for 5–7 hours on or on high for 3–4 hours. (Slow cooker cooking times may vary—get to know your slow cooker and, if necessary, adjust cooking times accordingly.)

FLAVOR BOOSTER
Top the fish with the zest of half a lemon when you add the lemon juice, and use extra capers and garlic.

Steamed Rice and Peas

SERVES: 4 • **SERVING SIZE:** 1 CUP

1 1/2 cups quick-cooking brown rice

1 cup frozen peas

1/4 teaspoon salt (optional)

1 tablespoon reduced-sodium soy sauce (use wheat/gluten-free if needed) (optional)

1. Cook the rice according to the package directions. Mix the frozen peas and a few shakes of salt or soy sauce (optional) into the rice while it is still hot, stir and cover for 1–2 minutes so the peas thaw.

TIP

Capers may be small, but they pack a flavorful punch. They've got a sharp, salty taste and add dimension to fish, meats, pastas, and sauces. In addition to having a lot of flavor, capers contain a number of phytonutrients and vitamins like A and K.

NUTRITIONAL INFORMATION | QUICK TILAPIA WITH LEMON, GARLIC, AND CAPERS:

EXCHANGES / CHOICES:
3 Protein, lean

Calories: 145; Calories from Fat: 55; Total Fat: 6 g; Saturated Fat: 1.3 g; Trans Fat: 0 g; Cholesterol: 50 mg; Sodium: 255 mg; Potassium: 340 mg; Total Carbohydrate: 1 g; Dietary Fiber: 0 g; Sugar: 0 g; Protein: 22 g; Phosphorus: 175 mg

NUTRITIONAL INFORMATION | STEAMED RICE AND PEAS:

EXCHANGES / CHOICES:
2 Starch

Calories: 135; Calories from Fat: 10; Total Fat: 1 g; Saturated Fat: 0.2 g; Trans Fat: 0 g; Cholesterol: 0 mg; Sodium: 30 mg; Potassium: 65 mg; Total Carbohydrate: 30 g; Dietary Fiber: 3 g; Sugar: 1 g; Protein: 4 g; Phosphorus: 105 mg

This recipe was suggested to me by 10-year-old Ames Williford, of Pennsylvania, who makes this soup for her family. It tastes like a cross between mashed and baked potatoes, so our kids love it. You can sprinkle in toppings to your liking, such as scallions, crumbled bacon, cheddar cheese, and additional sour cream. Serve with Baked Breadsticks and Fruit Kabobs.

Garlic Mashed Potato Soup

PREP: 15 MINUTES • **COOK:** 30 MINUTES • **SERVES:** 4 • **SERVING SIZE:** 2 CUPS

1 tablespoon trans fat-free margarine

1/2 yellow onion, diced

1–2 teaspoons minced garlic (3–4 cloves), to taste

2 large russet (baking) potatoes, peeled and diced

32 ounces low-sodium chicken or vegetable broth

2 tablespoons nonfat sour cream

4 scallions, thinly sliced, or use chives

1/3 cup shredded 50% reduced-fat cheddar cheese

2 strips turkey, pork, or vegetarian bacon, cooked and crumbled (optional)

DO AHEAD OR DELEGATE: Dice the onion, peel the garlic, peel and dice the potatoes and store in a bowl with enough water to cover so they don't brown, slice the scallions, shred the cheese if necessary, and refrigerate, cook, and crumble the bacon, or fully prepare and refrigerate the soup.

1. (Start the breadsticks and kabobs, if you are serving them.) In a stockpot, heat the margarine over medium heat. Add the onions and garlic and sauté for 3–5 minutes until the onions are translucent. Add the potatoes and cook, stirring frequently, for 1–2 minutes to coat them. Add the broth, bring it to a low boil, and simmer for 20–25 minutes, stirring occasionally, until the potatoes are very tender.

2. Puree the soup using a handheld immersion blender or a standing blender. Return the soup to the pot, if necessary, and stir in the sour cream until it is smooth. Serve the soup immediately, topped with the scallions, cheese, bacon, and extra sour cream, if desired, or refrigerate for up to 2 days.

SLOW COOKER DIRECTIONS: Add the onions, garlic, potatoes, and broth to the slow cooker and cook on low for 6–10 hours or on high for 3–4 hours. 30 minutes before serving, use an immersion blender or standing blender to puree the soup, then add the sour cream. Serve topped with the scallions, cheese, bacon, and extra sour cream, if desired. (Slow cooker cooking times may vary—get to know your slow cooker and, if necessary, adjust cooking times accordingly.)

FLAVOR BOOSTER
Serve with hot pepper sauce, such as Tabasco.

NUTRITIONAL INFORMATION | GARLIC MASHED POTATO SOUP:

EXCHANGES / CHOICES:
1 Starch; 1 Nonstarchy Vegetable; 1 Fat

Calories: 155; Calories from Fat: 35; Total Fat: 4 g;
Saturated Fat: 1.6 g; Trans Fat: 0 g; Cholesterol: 5 mg;
Sodium: 445 mg; Potassium: 555 mg; Total Carbohydrate: 24 g;
Dietary Fiber: 2 g; Sugar: 3 g; Protein: 7 g; Phosphorus: 135 mg

NUTRITIONAL INFORMATION | BAKED BREADSTICKS:

EXCHANGES / CHOICES:
1 Starch

Calories: 65; Calories from Fat: 10; Total Fat: 1 g;
Saturated Fat: 0.2 g; Trans Fat: 0 g; Cholesterol: 0 mg;
Sodium: 190 mg; Potassium: 15 mg; Total Carbohydrate: 13 g;
Dietary Fiber: 0 g; Sugar: 2 g; Protein: 2 g; Phosphorus: 15 mg

NUTRITIONAL INFORMATION | FRUIT KABOBS:

EXCHANGES / CHOICES:
1 Fruit

Calories: 60; Calories from Fat: 0; Total Fat: 0 g;
Saturated Fat: 0.1 g; Trans Fat: 0 g; Cholesterol: 0 mg;
Sodium: 5 mg; Potassium: 230 mg; Total Carbohydrate: 15 g;
Dietary Fiber: 2 g; Sugar: 13 g; Protein: 1 g; Phosphorus: 20 mg

SIDE DISHES

Baked Breadsticks

SERVES: 4 • **SERVING SIZE:** 1 BREADSTICK

1 package breadsticks (bake-at-home)

1. Prepare the breadsticks in the oven or toaster oven according to the package directions.

Fruit Kabobs

SERVES: 4 • **SERVING SIZE:** 3/4 CUP

6–8 cups mixed fruit such as strawberries, blueberries, bananas, mango, grapes, and/or melon
15–20 colorful toothpicks or wooden skewers
1 cup nonfat vanilla yogurt (optional)

1. Thread the fruit onto toothpicks or small skewers (kids can have fun doing this; however, children under age 3 should not eat with toothpicks or skewers of any size). Serve with small bowls of yogurt for dipping (optional).

TIP

If you don't anticipate you'll be using up the package of Cheddar cheese in a timely manner and want to keep it from spoiling, you can always freeze it. Just be sure to press out as much air as possible before re-closing the package. Keep in mind that freezing and thawing the cheese may change the texture slightly, making it more crumbly.

I bet many of us have spent hours sitting on the soccer sidelines watching our kids play. One of my favorite things to do while we're all hanging out in our folding chairs is to exchange recipes with the other parents. This one was described to me by my friend Michelle Mainelli while we watched our daughters play. After the game, my daughter Celia enjoyed eating it for dinner. Serve with Roasted Parsnips or Carrots.

Orecchiette and Broccoli with Lemon-Butter Sauce

PREP + COOK: 25 MINUTES • **SERVES:** 8 • **SERVING SIZE:** 1 1/2 CUPS

1 pound orecchiette noodles, or use
    pasta shells, whole-wheat if possible

1 pound broccoli, cut into small florets

2 tablespoons butter

1/2–1 lemon, juice only (about 1/4 cup)

1/4 cup pine nuts, toasted

1/4–1/2 teaspoon salt

1/4 cup grated Parmesan cheese

1/4 cup fresh basil, slivered

1/8 teaspoon black pepper, or to taste

DO AHEAD OR DELEGATE: Cook the pasta and store tossed with a little oil to prevent sticking, chop the broccoli, juice the lemon, toast the pine nuts, grate the Parmesan cheese, if necessary, or fully prepare and refrigerate the dish.

1. Cook the pasta in a large pot of salted water according to the package directions (leave plenty of room in the pot to add the broccoli later). (Meanwhile, start the carrots, if you are serving them.) When the pasta is 2 minutes from being cooked, add the broccoli to the pot, and cook for 2–3 more minutes. Meanwhile, remove 1/4 cup of the pasta's cooking water and set it aside.

2. In a small saucepan or skillet, heat the butter over medium heat. When it is melted, whisk in the lemon juice and set it aside. Meanwhile, lightly toast the pine nuts in a toaster oven or a dry skillet over medium-low heat and set them aside.

3. Drain the pasta and broccoli, put it in a large serving bowl, and toss with the lemon-butter sauce, the pine nuts, salt, cheese, and basil. If it is too dry, add the reserved pasta cooking water. Season the dish with salt and pepper to taste and serve immediately or refrigerate for up to 3 days.

FLAVOR BOOSTER

**For a richer sauce, use
3 tablespoons butter or
2 tablespoons butter and
1 tablespoon olive oil. Serve
with garlic salt, crushed red
pepper flakes, and lemon
wedges, and top the pasta
with lemon zest or salt-free
lemon-pepper seasoning.**

Roasted Parsnips or Carrots

SERVES: 8 • **SERVING SIZE:** 1/2 CUP

1 pound parsnips or carrots, or use a combination of both
1 tablespoon extra-virgin olive oil
1/4 teaspoon kosher salt
1/8 teaspoon black pepper

1. Preheat the oven to 450°F. Cut the parsnips and/or carrots lengthwise into halves or quarters (depending on their size) and cut those strips into 1-inch pieces. In a roasting pan, toss the pieces with the oil, salt, and pepper (add 1/2–1 teaspoon fresh thyme, if desired). Roast until they are lightly browned, 15–20 minutes, tossing once. The longer they cook, the sweeter they become.

TIP

Orecchiette can't seem to resist nesting together when you cook them. Be sure to add them to rapidly boiling water and stir vigorously several times while they are cooking to keep them separated

NUTRITIONAL INFORMATION | ORECCHIETTE AND BROCCOLI WITH LEMON-BUTTER SAUCE:

EXCHANGES / CHOICES:
3 Starch; 1 Fat

Calories: 285; Calories from Fat: 65; Total Fat: 7 g; Saturated Fat: 2.6 g; Trans Fat: 0.1 g; Cholesterol: 10 mg; Sodium: 170 mg; Potassium: 285 mg; Total Carbohydrate: 46 g; Dietary Fiber: 3 g; Sugar: 3 g; Protein: 10 g; Phosphorus: 175 mg

NUTRITIONAL INFORMATION | ROASTED PARSNIPS OR CARROTS:

EXCHANGES / CHOICES:
1 Nonstarchy Vegetable; 1/2 Fat

Calories: 40; Calories from Fat: 20; Total Fat: 2 g; Saturated Fat: 0.3 g; Trans Fat: 0 g; Cholesterol: 0 mg; Sodium: 80 mg; Potassium: 170 mg; Total Carbohydrate: 7 g; Dietary Fiber: 2 g; Sugar: 2 g; Protein: 1 g; Phosphorus: 25 mg

Burritos are one of our go-to meals for a busy night when we need quick nutrition and lots of flavor. If you are in a big hurry, you can serve the filling in warm tortillas without baking them, but if you have time, baking them gives them an extra crispness that we love. This recipe was inspired by one sent to me by my friend Marilyn Emery of Kensington, Maryland. Serve with Spicy Zucchini Sticks.

Toasty Baked Burritos

PREP: 25 MINUTES • **COOK:** 15 MINUTES • **SERVES:** 8 • **SERVING SIZE:** 1 BURRITO

1 tablespoon canola or vegetable oil

1 red onion, chopped

1 green or red bell pepper, seeded and chopped

1 1/2 teaspoons minced garlic (about 3 cloves)

1 teaspoon ground cumin

1 teaspoon chili powder

1 (15-ounce) can low-sodium pinto beans, drained and rinsed

1 (15-ounce) can low-sodium black beans, drained and rinsed

3/4 cup corn kernels, fresh, frozen, or canned

14 ounces diced tomatoes with green chilies, drained

8 whole-wheat tortillas

1 cup shredded 50% reduced-fat cheddar cheese

1 cup salsa (optional)

1 cup guacamole (optional)

1 cup nonfat sour cream (optional)

DO AHEAD OR DELEGATE: Chop the onion and the bell pepper, peel the garlic, and prepare and refrigerate the burrito mixture.

1. (Start the zucchini first, if you are making it.) Preheat the oven to 400°F.

2. Heat a large heavy skillet over medium heat and add the oil. Add the onions, peppers, garlic, cumin, and chili powder, and sauté until the vegetables soften, 5–7 minutes. Add the beans, corn, and tomatoes and continue cooking, stirring occasionally, for 5–7 more minutes until everything is hot. Remove the pan from the heat. (You can cover and set aside the mixture at this point and make the burritos later in the day.)

3. Spray a large baking sheet with nonstick cooking spray. Place 1/2–3/4 cup of the filling in the lower middle of each tortilla and top with about 1 tablespoon cheese. Fold half the tortilla up and over the filling and roll it up burrito-style to secure it. Put each burrito seam side down on the pan. Sprinkle the remaining cheese on top of the burritos, and bake for 10–15 minutes until they are heated through and lightly browned and crispy. Serve immediately with optional toppings and/or hot sauce, if desired.

SLOW COOKER DIRECTIONS: Omit the oil. Add the onions, bell peppers, garlic, cumin, chili powder, beans, corn, and tomatoes to the slow cooker and stir well to combine. Cook on low for 6–10 hours or on high for 4–5 hours. Fill and bake the tortillas in a conventional oven as directed. (Slow cooker cooking times may vary—get to know your slow cooker and, if necessary, adjust cooking times accordingly.)

Spicy Zucchini Sticks

SERVES: 8 • **SERVING SIZE:** 4 1/2 STICKS

2 zucchini
2 tablespoons extra-virgin olive oil
2 teaspoons paprika
2 teaspoons ground cumin
1 teaspoon garlic powder

1. Preheat the oven to 400°F. Halve the zucchini lengthwise, cut each of those halves lengthwise into 3 long strips, then cut each of those strips crosswise into 3 shorter strips. In a medium bowl, toss the zucchini with the oil. Combine the spices and toss them with the zucchini, until evenly distributed. Lay the strips in a single layer on a large baking sheet, and bake for 30 minutes, tossing once, until they are well browned. Remove them from the oven and serve immediately. *(Inspired by a recipe from OvertimeCook.com.)*

TIP

To make your tortillas more pliable before filling them, roll the tortillas inside a slightly damp paper or cloth towel and microwave them for about 15–30 seconds.

FLAVOR BOOSTER

Use the optional salsa and choose a spicy variety, use spicy jack cheese in place of cheddar and/or serve the burritos with hot pepper sauce.

NUTRITIONAL INFORMATION | TOASTY BAKED BURRITOS:

EXCHANGES / CHOICES:
2 1/2 Starch; 1 Nonstarchy Vegetable; 1 Protein, lean; 1/2 Fat

Calories: 295; Calories from Fat: 70; Total Fat: 8 g;
Saturated Fat: 2.1 g; Trans Fat: 0 g; Cholesterol: 5 mg;
Sodium: 415 mg; Potassium: 565 mg; Total Carbohydrate: 47 g;
Dietary Fiber: 10 g; Sugar: 5 g; Protein: 15 g; Phosphorus: 285 mg

NUTRITIONAL INFORMATION | SPICY ZUCCHINI STICKS:

EXCHANGES / CHOICES:
1 Fat

Calories: 40; Calories from Fat: 30; Total Fat: 3.5 g;
Saturated Fat: 0.5 g; Trans Fat: 0 g; Cholesterol: 0 mg;
Sodium: 5 mg; Potassium: 150 mg; Total Carbohydrate: 2 g;
Dietary Fiber: 1 g; Sugar: 1 g; Protein: 1 g; Phosphorus: 25 mg

WINTER

WEEK 3

Chicken Marsala with Mushrooms and Garlic (1)
SIDE DISH: Bulgur Wheat (1a); Sauteed Carrots with Butter and Thyme (1b)

Sesame Scallion Arctic Char or Salmon (2)
SIDE DISH: Asian Cucumber Salad (2a); Pineapple (2b)

Moroccan Farro (or Couscous) Salad with Chickpeas and Dates (3)
SIDE DISH: Hard-Boiled Eggs (3a)

Tomato-Basil and Chicken Corn Soup (4)
SIDE DISH: Apple Cheddar Cornbread (4a)

Buttery Egg Noodles with Caramelized Cabbage and Onions (5)
SIDE DISH: Arugula Salad with Diced Oranges and Avocado (5a)

SHOPPING LIST

🥕 PRODUCE
8 **carrots** (1b)(3)

4 **scallions** (2)

2 large **yellow onions** (5)

1/2 **yellow onion** (4)

9 cups **baby arugula or fresh chopped arugula** (5a)

1 1/2 pounds **white or green cabbage** (5)

2 teaspoons **fresh ginger** (2)

1 cup **fresh basil** (4)

1 tablespoon **fresh flat-leaf parsley** (1)*

1/4 cup **fresh mint** (3)

1/2 teaspoon **fresh thyme** (1b)

2 **cucumbers** (2a)

8 ounces **sliced mushrooms** (1)

1 **avocado** (5a)

1 1/2–2 **lemons** (1)(3)(5a)

1 **lime** (2)(4)

1 **orange** (5a)

1 **pineapple** (or canned pineapple rings in 100% juice) (2b)

1 **red apple**, such as Gala or Fuji (4a)

4 **dried dates** (3)

🐟 MEAT AND FISH
1 1/2 pounds **boneless, skinless chicken breasts** (1)

2 1/2 cups **cooked and diced chicken breast** (3)(4)*

1 1/4 pounds **Arctic char or salmon fillet** (2)

SHELVED ITEMS

8 ounces **farro perlato or Israeli (pearled) couscous** (3)

1 cup **bulgur wheat or use quick-cooking brown rice** (1a)

16 ounces **extra-wide egg noodles** (5)

1 package **cornbread or corn muffin mix** (4a)

28 ounces **crushed tomatoes** (4)

1/2 cup **reduced-sodium chicken broth** (1)

5 cups **low-sodium chicken or vegetable broth** (1a)(4)

2 teaspoons **rice vinegar** (2a)

1 tablespoon **apple cider vinegar** (5)

1/2 cup **Marsala wine** (1)

1/4 teaspoon **hot chili oil** (2)

15 ounces **canned chickpeas** (garbanzo beans) (3)

1/4 cup **sliced almonds** (3)

SPICES

1 3/8 teaspoons **salt** (1)(1b)(3)(5)

1/4 teaspoon **black pepper** (1)

3/4 teaspoon **ground cumin** (3)(4)

1/2 teaspoon **curry powder** (3a)*

1/2 teaspoon **paprika** (3a)*

1 teaspoon **caraway seeds** (5)*

2 teaspoons + 1 tablespoon **toasted sesame seeds** (2)(2a)

STAPLES

1 teaspoon + 2 tablespoons **butter** (1b)(5)

1 tablespoon **butter or margarine** (1)

1/2 cup **extra-virgin olive oil** (1)(1b)(3)(4)(5)(5a)

3 tablespoons **reduced-sodium soy sauce** (use wheat/gluten-free if needed) (2)(2a)

1 teaspoon **sugar** (2a)

1 tablespoon **brown sugar** (5)

2 teaspoons **honey** (3)(4)

6 **eggs** (3a)

3 1/2 teaspoons **minced garlic** (1)(2)(4)

3 tablespoons **flour** (use wheat/gluten-free if needed) (1)

REFRIGERATED/FROZEN

1/2 cup **crumbled feta cheese** (3)*

1/2 cup **reduced-fat shredded cheddar cheese** (4a)

2 cups **frozen corn kernels** (4)

Get free, printable versions of the shopping lists from this book at TheScramble.com/diabetes.

*optional ingredients

WINTER WEEK 3 • 327

This dish flooded my mind with warm memories of my grandmother, Lois Laser, who always ordered chicken or veal Marsala at her favorite Italian restaurants. The Marsala wine and lemon combination gives the chicken a sweet and tangy flavor and fills the house with a wonderful scent. Serve with Bulgur Wheat and Sautéed Carrots with Butter and Thyme.

Chicken Marsala with Mushrooms and Garlic

PREP + COOK: 30 MINUTES • **SERVES:** 6 • **SERVING SIZE:** 2/3 CUP CHICKEN, MUSHROOMS, AND SAUCE

3 tablespoons flour (use wheat/gluten-free if needed)

1/4 teaspoon salt

1/4 teaspoon black pepper

1 1/2 pounds boneless, skinless chicken breasts, cut into 1-inch pieces

4 teaspoons extra-virgin olive oil

1 tablespoon butter or margarine

8 ounces sliced mushrooms

1 1/2 teaspoons minced garlic (about 3 cloves)

1/2 cup Marsala wine

1/2 cup reduced-sodium chicken broth (freeze remaining broth for future use)

1/2 lemon, juice only (about 2 tablespoons)

1 tablespoon fresh flat-leaf parsley, chopped (optional)

DO AHEAD OR DELEGATE: Combine the flour, salt, and pepper, cut and refrigerate the chicken, peel the garlic, juice the lemon, and chop the parsley.

1. (Start the bulgur and carrots, if you are serving them.) In a medium bowl, combine the flour, salt, and pepper. Add the diced chicken and toss gently to coat it thoroughly. Heat a large heavy skillet over medium heat. Add 1 teaspoon oil and the butter and let the butter melt. Add the chicken and cook it on each side until it is browned and cooked partially through, 6–8 minutes total. Transfer the chicken to a clean plate and set it aside.

2. Add the remaining oil to the same pan without cleaning it. Sauté the mushrooms and garlic for about 1 minute, then add the wine, broth, and lemon juice. Bring the liquid to a low boil, scraping any bits of chicken from the bottom of the pan. Simmer the mixture for about 10 minutes until the mushrooms are tender and the liquid is reduced and slightly thickened.

3. Add the chicken back into the pan, spooning the sauce over it, and cook for 3–5 more minutes until the chicken is just cooked through. Season with additional salt, if desired, and sprinkle the chicken with parsley before serving (optional).

SLOW COOKER DIRECTIONS: Brown the chicken first, if desired, by following directions above; however, it is not strictly necessary. Place the chicken, mushrooms, garlic, wine, broth, lemon juice, and parsley in the slow cooker and give a quick stir to combine. Cook on low for 5–8 hours or high for 3–4 hours. Serve as directed. (Slow cooker cooking times may vary—get to know your slow cooker and, if necessary, adjust cooking times accordingly.)

FLAVOR BOOSTER

Season the chicken with a lot of freshly ground black pepper before serving.

NUTRITIONAL INFORMATION | CHICKEN MARSALA WITH MUSHROOMS AND GARLIC:

EXCHANGES / CHOICES:
1/2 Carbohydrate; 4 Protein, lean

Calories: 210; Calories from Fat: 70; Total Fat: 8 g;
Saturated Fat: 2.4 g; Trans Fat: 0.1 g; Cholesterol: 70 mg;
Sodium: 215 mg; Potassium: 355 mg; Total Carbohydrate: 6 g;
Dietary Fiber: 1 g; Sugar: 1 g; Protein: 26 g; Phosphorus: 220 mg

NUTRITIONAL INFORMATION | BULGUR WHEAT:

EXCHANGES / CHOICES:
1/2 Starch

Calories: 95; Calories from Fat: 0; Total Fat: 0 g;
Saturated Fat: 0.1 g; Trans Fat: 0 g; Cholesterol: 0 mg;
Sodium: 175 mg; Potassium: 165 mg; Total Carbohydrate: 21 g;
Dietary Fiber: 5 g; Sugar: 0 g; Protein: 4 g; Phosphorus: 90 mg

NUTRITIONAL INFORMATION | SAUTÉED CARROTS WITH BUTTER AND THYME:

EXCHANGES / CHOICES:
1 Nonstarchy Vegetable

Calories: 35; Calories from Fat: 15; Total Fat: 1.5 g;
Saturated Fat: 0.5 g; Trans Fat: 0 g; Cholesterol: 0 mg;
Sodium: 95 mg; Potassium: 195 mg; Total Carbohydrate: 6 g;
Dietary Fiber: 2 g; Sugar: 3 g; Protein: 1 g; Phosphorus: 20 mg

SIDE DISHES

Bulgur Wheat

SERVES: 6 • **SERVING SIZE:** 1/2 CUP

1 cup bulgur wheat

2 cups reduced-sodium chicken or vegetable broth, or a combination of water and broth

1. In a medium saucepan, combine the bulgur wheat and the broth or combination of broth and water. Bring it to a boil, cover, and simmer it for 15 minutes until it is tender.

Sautéed Carrots with Butter and Thyme

SERVES: 6 • **SERVING SIZE:** 1/2 CUP

1 teaspoon butter

1 teaspoon extra-virgin olive oil

6 carrots, sliced diagonally into about 1/2-inch slices

1/2 teaspoon fresh thyme, or 1/4 teaspoon dried thyme

1/8 teaspoon salt

1. Heat the butter and oil over medium heat in a heavy skillet. When the butter is melted, add the carrots and thyme. Stir the carrots to coat them, and sauté for about 1 minute. Cover the pan, and steam the carrots for 6–8 minutes to desired tenderness (you may need to reduce the heat so they don't burn). Season with salt to taste.

TIP

Because we don't use Marsala wine too often in recipes, you might want to borrow 1/2 cup from a neighbor or see if your supermarket sells very small bottles. An opened bottle stored in a cool, dark area such as your pantry can last up to a year.

I adore Arctic char because it tastes like a lighter and more delicate version of salmon, and it's a more sustainable and healthier choice than farmed salmon. This marinade gives it so much flavor that we were practically licking our plates clean. Serve with Asian Cucumber Salad and Pineapple.

Sesame Scallion Arctic Char or Salmon

MARINATE: 15 MINUTES • **PREP:** 10 MINUTES • **COOK:** 10 MINUTES • **SERVES:** 4 • **SERVING SIZE:** 4 1/2 OUNCES

2 tablespoons reduced-sodium soy sauce (use wheat/gluten-free if needed)

1/2 lime, juice only (about 1 tablespoon)

1/4 teaspoon hot chili oil

2 teaspoons fresh ginger, peeled and grated or finely chopped

1/2 teaspoon minced garlic (about 1 clove)

1 1/4 pounds Arctic char or salmon fillet

2 teaspoons toasted sesame seeds

4 scallions, green parts only, thinly sliced (about 1/4 cup)

DO AHEAD OR DELEGATE: Juice the lime, peel and grate the ginger, peel the garlic, make the marinade and marinate the fish in the refrigerator, toast the sesame seeds if necessary, and slice the scallions.

1. In a flat dish with sides just large enough to hold the fish, combine the soy sauce, lime juice, oil, ginger, and garlic. Add the fish, flesh side down, and marinate in the refrigerator for 15 minutes to 1 hour.

2. Preheat the broiler and set the oven rack about 6 inches from the heating element. (Alternatively, bake the fish at 450°F.) Spray a baking sheet with nonstick cooking spray or line it with foil for easier cleanup. Transfer the fish to the baking sheet, flesh side up, spooning some of the remaining marinade over the fish. Broil the fish for 7–10 minutes until it flakes easily with a fork. (Meanwhile, prepare the salad and chop the pineapple, if necessary.) Remove from the oven and sprinkle it evenly with the sesame seeds and scallions. Serve immediately.

SLOW COOKER DIRECTIONS: There's no need to marinate in advance. Cut the fish into pieces to fit in the slow cooker, if needed, then place each piece of fish on an individual piece of aluminum foil. Combine the marinade ingredients, and drizzle or brush over the fish, then fold the foil around the fish to form a packet. Stack the packets in the slow cooker, then cook on low for 5–8 hours or on high for 3–4 hours. Remove the fish from the foil and top it with the sesame seeds and scallions. (Slow cooker cooking times may vary—get to know your slow cooker and, if necessary, adjust cooking times accordingly.)

FLAVOR BOOSTER

Double the hot chili oil, ginger, and garlic and add 1/2 teaspoon lemon-pepper seasoning to the marinade.

NUTRITIONAL INFORMATION | SESAME SCALLION ARCTIC CHAR OR SALMON:

EXCHANGES / CHOICES:
4 Protein, lean; 1 Fat

Calories: 235; Calories from Fat: 90; Total Fat: 10 g;
Saturated Fat: 1.8 g; Trans Fat: 0 g; Cholesterol: 80 mg;
Sodium: 350 mg; Potassium: 560 mg; Total Carbohydrate: 2 g;
Dietary Fiber: 0 g; Sugar: 0 g; Protein: 31 g; Phosphorus: 370 mg

NUTRITIONAL INFORMATION | ASIAN CUCUMBER SALAD:

EXCHANGES / CHOICES:
1 Nonstarchy Vegetable

Calories: 30; Calories from Fat: 10; Total Fat: 1 g;
Saturated Fat: 0.2 g; Trans Fat: 0 g; Cholesterol: 0 mg;
Sodium: 140 mg; Potassium: 125 mg; Total Carbohydrate: 4 g;
Dietary Fiber: 1 g; Sugar: 2 g; Protein: 1 g; Phosphorus: 35 mg

NUTRITIONAL INFORMATION | PINEAPPLE:

EXCHANGES / CHOICES:
1 Fruit

Calories: 60; Calories from Fat: 0; Total Fat: 0 g;
Saturated Fat: 0 g; Trans Fat: 0 g; Cholesterol: 0 mg;
Sodium: 0 mg; Potassium: 135 mg; Total Carbohydrate: 16 g;
Dietary Fiber: 2 g; Sugar: 12 g; Protein: 1 g; Phosphorus: 10 mg

SIDE DISHES

Asian Cucumber Salad

SERVES: 4 • **SERVING SIZE:** 1 CUP

1 tablespoon reduced-sodium soy sauce (use wheat/gluten-free if needed)

2 teaspoons rice vinegar

1 teaspoon sugar

2 cucumbers, peeled, seeded, and diced

1 tablespoon toasted sesame seeds

1. In a medium bowl, whisk together the soy sauce, vinegar, and sugar. Add the cucumbers and toss thoroughly. Top with the sesame seeds. Serve immediately or refrigerate for up to 24 hours.

Pineapple

SERVES: 4 • **SERVING SIZE:** 3/4 CUP

3 cups diced fresh pineapple (or canned pineapple rings), cut into chunks

1. Peel, core, and cut the pineapple into bite-sized chunks, or use canned pineapple rings or chunks.

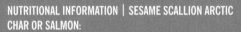

TIP

You can save time with this recipe by purchasing already toasted sesame seeds (they can often be found with the Asian foods). If you can't find toasted sesame seeds in your store, you can toast them in a skillet over medium heat or in your toaster oven on low until the seeds become light brown and fragrant, about 3 minutes. Watch them carefully, as they burn easily.

I've noticed that the food at universities is undergoing a healthy revolution. Some cafeterias feature organic and locally grown food, pasture-raised chicken, and tofu and quinoa galore. At a funky café at Johns Hopkins University we tasted a Moroccan Couscous Salad that inspired me to make my own version. Consider adding cooked chicken or shrimp, cucumbers, tomatoes, olives, red onions, or sundried tomatoes. Serve with Hard-Boiled Eggs.

Moroccan Farro (or Couscous) Salad with Chickpeas and Dates

MARINATE: 30 MINUTES • **PREP + COOK:** 20 MINUTES • **SERVES:** 6 • **SERVING SIZE:** 1 1/4 CUPS

8 ounces farro perlato or Israeli (pearled) couscous

15 ounces canned chickpeas (garbanzo beans), drained and rinsed, or 1 1/2 cups cooked chickpeas

2 carrots, quartered lengthwise and sliced

1/4 cup sliced almonds, lightly toasted

4 small dried dates, halved and chopped

1/4 cup fresh mint, coarsely chopped

1/2–1 lemon, to taste, juice only (about 1/4 cup)

2 tablespoons extra-virgin olive oil

1/4 teaspoon salt

1/4 teaspoon ground cumin

1 teaspoon honey

1 1/2 cups cooked and diced chicken breast (optional)

1/2 cup crumbled feta cheese (optional)

DO AHEAD OR DELEGATE: Cook the farro or couscous (and toss with a teaspoon of oil to prevent sticking), cook the chickpeas if using dried, quarter and slice the carrots, toast the almonds, halve and chop the dates, chop the mint, juice the lemon, prepare the salad dressing, crumble the feta cheese if using and refrigerate, or fully prepare and refrigerate the dish.

1. (Start the hard-boiled eggs first, if you are serving them.) Cook the farro according to the package directions, fluff and remove from the heat. Meanwhile, in a large bowl, combine the chickpeas, carrots, almonds, dates, and mint.

2. Make the dressing by whisking together the lemon juice, oil, salt, cumin, and honey. Add the cooked farro and chicken (optional) to the bowl, and toss everything with the dressing. Gently stir in the cheese, if desired, and refrigerate the salad for 30 minutes or up to 2 days.

FLAVOR BOOSTER
Add 1/8–1/4 teaspoon cayenne pepper and a pinch of ground cinnamon to the dressing, or add kalamata olives, finely diced red onion, or sundried tomatoes to the salad.

NUTRITIONAL INFORMATION | MOROCCAN FARRO (OR COUSCOUS) SALAD WITH CHICKPEAS AND DATES (ANALYSIS FOR SALAD ONLY):

EXCHANGES / CHOICES:
2 1/2 Starch; 1/2 Carbohydrate; 1 Protein, lean

Calories: 265; Calories from Fat: 40; Total Fat: 4.5 g;
Saturated Fat: 0.5 g; Trans Fat: 0 g; Cholesterol: 0 mg;
Sodium: 90 mg; Potassium: 410 mg; Total Carbohydrate: 45 g;
Dietary Fiber: 10 g; Sugar: 6 g; Protein: 10 g; Phosphorus: 255 mg

(ANALYSIS FOR DRESSING ONLY):

EXCHANGES / CHOICES:
1 Fat

Calories: 45; Calories from Fat: 40; Total Fat: 4.5 g;
Saturated Fat: 0.6 g; Trans Fat: 0 g; Cholesterol: 0 mg;
Sodium: 100 mg; Potassium: 10 mg; Total Carbohydrate: 2 g;
Dietary Fiber: 0 g; Sugar: 1 g; Protein: 0 g; Phosphorus: 0 mg

NUTRITIONAL INFORMATION | HARD-BOILED EGGS:

EXCHANGES / CHOICES:
1 Protein, medium fat

Calories: 70; Calories from Fat: 45; Total Fat: 5 g;
Saturated Fat: 1.6 g; Trans Fat: 0 g; Cholesterol: 185 mg;
Sodium: 70 mg; Potassium: 70 mg; Total Carbohydrate: 0 g;
Dietary Fiber: 0 g; Sugar: 0 g; Protein: 6 g; Phosphorus: 100 mg

Hard-Boiled Eggs

SERVES: 6 • **SERVING SIZE:** 1 EGG

6 eggs

1/2 teaspoon paprika (optional)

1/2 teaspoon curry powder (optional)

1. In a medium saucepan, cover the eggs in cold water and bring the water to a boil. When the water boils, turn off the heat, cover the pot, and let the eggs sit in the hot water for 15 minutes (no peeking). Transfer the eggs to a bowl of ice water, then peel them, starting by cracking the skinny pointed end and peeling down from there. Sprinkle with a bit of paprika or curry powder, if desired.

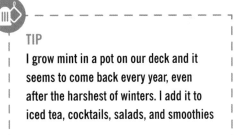

TIP

I grow mint in a pot on our deck and it seems to come back every year, even after the harshest of winters. I add it to iced tea, cocktails, salads, and smoothies

You can enjoy the fresh tastes of summer all year long with sweet and juicy canned tomatoes and crunchy and delicate frozen corn. You'll need to add fresh basil to complete the flavor trio, but because it can be grown indoors, it's still doable in the winter. I've melded the flavors of Italy and Mexico by adding a hint of cumin and lime. Serve with Apple Cheddar Cornbread.

Tomato-Basil and Chicken Corn Soup

PREP + COOK: 25 MINUTES • **SERVES:** 4 • **SERVING SIZE:** 2 CUPS

4 teaspoons extra-virgin olive oil, divided use

1/2 yellow onion, finely diced

1 1/2 teaspoons minced garlic (about 3 cloves)

1/2 teaspoon ground cumin

28 ounces crushed tomatoes

2 cups low-sodium chicken or vegetable broth

2 cups frozen corn kernels

1 cup cooked chicken breast, diced

1 cup fresh basil, chopped

1 teaspoon honey (optional)

1/2 lime, cut into wedges

DO AHEAD OR DELEGATE: Dice the onion, peel the garlic, defrost the corn, slice the lime, or fully prepare and refrigerate the soup.

1. (Start the cornbread first, if you are serving it.) In a medium stockpot, heat 1 teaspoon oil over medium heat. Add the onions and sauté until they are translucent, 3–4 minutes. Add the garlic and cumin and stir constantly for about 30 seconds, until fragrant. Add the tomatoes and broth, bring to a simmer, and continue cooking, stirring occasionally, for 5 minutes, partially covered (reduce heat if necessary to keep it at a simmer). At this point, you can puree the soup with an immersion blender or in a standing blender if you want a smoother texture.

2. Stir in the corn and chicken and cook the soup for about 5 minutes until the corn is tender. Stir in the basil, honey (optional), and remaining oil (use your highest-quality, fruitiest olive oil for drizzling in the soup). Serve with lime wedges and season with salt and black pepper to taste at the table. The soup can be enjoyed warm or cold for up to 3 days.

SLOW COOKER DIRECTIONS: Combine all ingredients except the limes and chicken in the slow cooker and cook on low for 5–10 hours or on high for 3–4 hours. Puree before serving, if desired, and stir in the chicken. (Slow cooker cooking times may vary—get to know your slow cooker and, if necessary, adjust cooking times accordingly.)

FLAVOR BOOSTER
Double the cumin and add a
pinch of cayenne pepper.

Apple Cheddar Cornbread

SERVES: 20 • **SERVING SIZE:** 1 SLICE

1 package cornbread or corn muffin mix

1 red apple, such as Gala or Fuji, peeled, cored, and diced

1/2 cup reduced-fat shredded cheddar cheese

1. Prepare the cornbread mix according to the directions, stirring in the apple and cheddar cheese. Bake according to the package directions.

TIP

While handheld immersion blenders are often associated with soup, they're also a wonderful tool for preparing dressings, sauces, smoothies, and milkshakes. Many immersion blenders come with an oversized cup that you can put ingredients into to blend. If yours does not, you can use a deep cup or bowl.

NUTRITIONAL INFORMATION | TOMATO-BASIL AND CHICKEN CORN SOUP:

EXCHANGES / CHOICES:
1 Starch; 3 Nonstarchy Vegetable; 1 Protein, lean; 1 Fat

Calories: 245; Calories from Fat: 65; Total Fat: 7 g;
Saturated Fat: 1.3 g; Trans Fat: 0 g; Cholesterol: 30 mg;
Sodium: 335 mg; Potassium: 1010 mg; Total Carbohydrate: 33 g;
Dietary Fiber: 6 g; Sugar: 12 g; Protein: 18 g; Phosphorus: 225 mg

NUTRITIONAL INFORMATION | APPLE CHEDDAR CORNBREAD:

EXCHANGES / CHOICES:
2 Starch; 1/2 Fat

Calories: 170; Calories from Fat: 55; Total Fat: 6 g;
Saturated Fat: 1 g; Trans Fat: 0 g; Cholesterol: 20 mg;
Sodium: 365 mg; Potassium: 55 mg; Total Carbohydrate: 27 g;
Dietary Fiber: 4 g; Sugar: 4 g; Protein: 4 g; Phosphorus: 190 mg

My family loves this traditional Hungarian recipe that I've adapted from The Family Dinner, *a wonderful book about how to connect with your kids at mealtime by Laurie David and Kirstin Uhrenholdt. It's very simple tasting and humble looking, yet the combination of flavors is soothing and satisfying. Serve with Arugula Salad with Diced Oranges and Avocado.*

Buttery Egg Noodles with Caramelized Cabbage and Onions

PREP + COOK: 30 MINUTES • **SERVES:** 9 • **SERVING SIZE:** 1 1/2 CUPS

1 tablespoon extra-virgin olive oil

2 tablespoons butter, divided use

2 large yellow onions, halved from top to bottom and thinly sliced

1 tablespoon brown sugar

3/4 teaspoon salt

16 ounces extra-wide egg noodles

1 1/2 pounds white or green cabbage, cored and thinly sliced

1 tablespoon apple cider vinegar

1 teaspoon caraway seeds (optional)

DO AHEAD OR DELEGATE: Slice the onions and the cabbage, cook the noodles and store, tossed with the butter to prevent sticking, or fully prepare and refrigerate the dish.

1. In a large heavy skillet, heat the oil and 1 tablespoon butter over medium heat. When the butter is bubbling, add the onions, brown sugar, and salt. Sauté, stirring occasionally, for 15–20 minutes until they are soft and golden brown (deep brown is even better if you have time). (Prepare the salad now, if you are serving it.)

2. Meanwhile, cook the noodles in salted water according to the package directions. When they are done, drain and toss them with 1 tablespoon butter.

3. When the onions are browned, add the cabbage to the skillet. Cover and sauté until the cabbage wilts, about 5 minutes, stirring occasionally. Then, remove the cover and continue to cook for about 5–10 more minutes until very tender. Add the vinegar, and cook for 1 more minute, then combine the vegetables with the noodles and let everything get hot. (Note: If you have very picky eaters you may want to keep the noodles and vegetables separate and just serve a little of the cabbage-onion mixture over their noodles.) Add the caraway seeds (optional) and serve immediately, seasoned with salt and black pepper to taste, or refrigerate for up to 3 days.

SLOW COOKER DIRECTIONS: You will need a 5L or larger slow cooker for this recipe. Combine all ingredients except the noodles and caraway seeds in the slow cooker. Stir well, and cook on low 4–6 hours or on high 2–3 hours. Top with the caraway seeds and serve over the cooked noodles. (Slow cooker cooking times may vary—get to know your slow cooker and, if necessary, adjust cooking times accordingly.)

Arugula Salad with Diced Oranges and Avocado

SERVES: 9 • **SERVING SIZE:** 1 CUP

9 cups baby arugula or fresh chopped arugula

1 avocado, peeled and diced

1 orange, peeled and diced

1/2 lemon, juice only

1 tablespoon extra-virgin olive oil

1. Combine the arugula with the avocado and the orange. (Peel and dice the orange with a paring knife over a plate and add any remaining orange juice to the salad.) Toss the salad with the lemon juice and oil.

FLAVOR BOOSTER

Top the finished dish with a sprinkle of Parmesan cheese, freshly ground black pepper, and/or a drizzle of balsamic vinegar.

TIP

Caraway seeds are a good source of fiber and minerals like iron, copper, and calcium. They have an anise-like flavor (like black licorice) and are a good addition to savory foods including soups and sauerkraut. They also add a nice flavor and aroma to breads and cakes.

NUTRITIONAL INFORMATION | BUTTERY EGG NOODLES WITH CARAMELIZED CABBAGE AND ONIONS:

EXCHANGES / CHOICES:
2 Starch; 2 Nonstarchy Vegetable; 1 Fat

Calories: 260; Calories from Fat: 65; Total Fat: 7 g;
Saturated Fat: 2.4 g; Trans Fat: 0.1 g; Cholesterol: 45 mg;
Sodium: 255 mg; Potassium: 230 mg; Total Carbohydrate: 43 g;
Dietary Fiber: 4 g; Sugar: 6 g; Protein: 7 g; Phosphorus: 130 mg

NUTRITIONAL INFORMATION | ARUGULA SALAD WITH DICED ORANGES AND AVOCADO:

EXCHANGES / CHOICES:
1 Fat

Calories: 55; Calories from Fat: 35; Total Fat: 4 g;
Saturated Fat: 0.6 g; Trans Fat: 0 g; Cholesterol: 0 mg;
Sodium: 5 mg; Potassium: 190 mg; Total Carbohydrate: 4 g;
Dietary Fiber: 2 g; Sugar: 2 g; Protein: 1 g; Phosphorus: 20 mg

WINTER

WEEK
4

Grilled Steak (or Tofu Steaks) in Chipotle Garlic Lime Marinade (1)

SIDE DISH: Guacamole with Carrots (1a)

Baked Fish with Mushrooms and Italian Herbs (2)

SIDE DISH: Farro (2a); Collard Greens with Garlic (2b)

Fiesta Tostadas (3)

SIDE DISH: Homemade Ranch Dressing with Carrots or Broccoli (3a)

Butternut Squash and Apple Soup with Crispy Sage (4)

SIDE DISH: Whole-Grain Bread (4a); Green Salad with Shredded Red Cabbage, Blue Cheese, and Walnuts (4b)

Chinese-Style Lo Mein with Vegetables (5)

SIDE DISH: Honeydew Melon or Cantaloupe (5a)

SHOPPING LIST

🥕 PRODUCE

2 pounds **baby carrots or large carrots** (1a)(3a)

1 **carrot** (5)

4 **scallions** (5)

1 tablespoon **fresh chives** (3a)

1 **sweet yellow onion** such as Vidalia or Walla Walla (4)

1/2 **red onion** (2b)

1 **red bell pepper** (5)

1 pound **collard greens** (2b)

6 cloves **garlic** (1)(2b)

1–2 tablespoons **fresh ginger** (5)

1/4 cup **fresh cilantro** (5)*

1 tablespoon **fresh flat-leaf parsley** (2a)*

1/4 cup **fresh sage leaves** (4)

3–4 pounds **butternut squash** (4)

6–8 **cremini or button mushrooms** (2)

3 **avocados** (1a)(3)

1 **lemon** (2)

2 1/2 **limes** (1)(1a)

1 **red apple**, such as Gala or Fuji (4)

1 **honeydew melon or cantaloupe** (5a)

6–8 cups **lettuce, any variety** (4b)

1 cup **red or purple cabbage** (4b)

🍖 MEAT AND FISH

1 pound **catfish or other mild white fish fillets,** such as mahi mahi, tilapia, cod, or sole (2)

2 1/4 pounds **skirt or flank steak**, trimmed of visible fat, or 2 blocks of **extra-firm tofu** (1)

SHELVED ITEMS

1 loaf **whole-grain bread** (4a)

4 cups **quick-cooking brown rice** (1)

1 1/2 cups **farro perlato** (or use pearled barley) (2a)

16 ounces **whole-wheat spaghetti or lo mein noodles** (5)

8 large **whole-wheat tortillas** (use wheat/gluten-free tortillas if needed) (3)

6 cups **reduced-sodium vegetable or chicken broth** (2a)(4)

7 ounces **chipotle peppers in adobo sauce** (1)

1/4 cup **hoisin sauce** (sold with Asian foods) (5)

1 cup **vegetarian refried beans** (Amy's is our favorite) (3)

1/2 cup **low-sodium canned black beans** (3)

1/4 cup **sliced black olives** (3)

3 tablespoons **walnut pieces** (4b)

SPICES

2 teaspoons **salt** (1)(1a)(2)(2a)(2b)(3a)

2 teaspoons **no-salt-added Italian seasoning blend** (2)

1 teaspoon **dried oregano** (1)

1/8 teaspoon **black pepper** (3a)

1/8 teaspoon **ground cinnamon** (4)

1/2 teaspoon **ground ginger** (4)

1 teaspoon **ground cumin** (1)

1 teaspoon **curry powder** (4)

3/8 teaspoon + 1/4 teaspoon **garlic powder** (1a)(2)(3a)

1/4 teaspoon **dried dill** (3a)

STAPLES

1 1/2 tablespoons **trans fat-free margarine-style spread** (2)

1 tablespoon **butter** (4)

7 1/2 tablespoons **extra-virgin olive oil** (1)(2)(2a)(2b)(4)

2 tablespoons **canola or vegetable oil** (5)

1 teaspoon **white wine vinegar** (3a)

2 tablespoons **mayonnaise** (3a)

2 tablespoons **reduced-sodium soy sauce** (use wheat/gluten-free if needed) (5)

1 1/2 teaspoons **minced garlic** (5)

1/4 cup **balsamic vinaigrette dressing** (4b)

REFRIGERATED/FROZEN

1/2 cup **shredded cheddar cheese** (3)

1/3 cup **fat-free sour cream or plain Greek yogurt** (3a)(4)

2 tablespoons **reduced-fat buttermilk** (3a)

1/2 cup **orange juice** (1)

2 tablespoons **apple cider** (4)

1/4 cup **frozen corn kernels** (3)

3 tablespoons **crumbled blue cheese or Gorgonzola** (4b)

Get free, printable versions of the shopping lists from this book at **TheScramble.com/diabetes**.

*optional ingredients

WINTER WEEK 4 • 339

Have you ever tried chipotles in adobo sauce? You can buy them in little cans in Latin markets or the international section of supermarkets. They are incredibly flavorful, but can be pretty spicy if you use too much. I love their rich, smoky flavor in marinades. If you can't find them, use chipotle chili powder, or regular chili powder will do. Serve with Guacamole with Carrots.

Grilled Steak (or Tofu Steaks) in Chipotle Garlic Lime Marinade

MARINATE: 2 HOURS • **PREP:** 15 MINUTES • **COOK:** 10 MINUTES • **SERVES:** 8 • **SERVING SIZE:** 3–4 OUNCES STEAK + 1/2 CUP RICE

2 1/4 pounds flank or skirt steak, trimmed of visible fat, or use 2 blocks of extra-firm tofu, drained and wrapped in a clean dishtowel

1/2 cup orange juice

2 limes, juice only (about 1/4 cup)

2 tablespoons extra-virgin olive oil

2 garlic cloves, coarsely chopped

7 ounces canned chipotle chilies in adobo sauce, use 3 chipotle chilies with some of their surrounding sauce, or use 3 roasted jalapeño peppers and 1 tablespoon tomato paste, or use 2 tablespoons chipotle chili powder or traditional chili powder

1 teaspoon ground cumin

1 teaspoon dried oregano

1 teaspoon salt

4 cups cooked brown rice

DO AHEAD OR DELEGATE: Drain, wrap, and slice the tofu if using, juice the limes, peel the garlic, combine the dry seasonings, make the marinade, and marinate the steak or tofu (if using steak, marinate it in the refrigerator) or prepare and refrigerate the dish.

1. Put the steak or tofu in a flat glass or ceramic dish with sides just large enough to hold it in one layer. If using steak, poke holes all over it with the tines of a fork. If using tofu, cut the tofu rectangles across the middle (so it is half of its original height for good grilling), then cut the halves into 2 pieces each.

2. In a blender (or using an immersion blender in a large measuring cup), combine all the remaining ingredients and puree.

3. Pour the marinade over the steak or tofu, flipping several times to coat. Cover and marinate for at least 2 hours and up to 12 hours, refrigerated if using the steak. If you are making both the steak and tofu, cook the tofu first, then raise the heat to make the steak (unless you have a large grill where you can do both at once).

4. **For steak:** Preheat the grill or a grill pan to medium-high heat (and start the rice). Remove the steak from the marinade, letting the excess drip back in the dish, and grill it for about 4 minutes per side. Meanwhile, in a small saucepan, bring the marinade to a boil and simmer for at least 1 minute to kill any bacteria from the meat. Transfer the steak to a cutting board and let it rest for a few minutes, before slicing it against the grain into thin strips. Serve with the (boiled) marinade.

5. **For tofu:** Preheat the grill (or grill pan brushed with oil) to medium-high heat (and start the rice). After the grill preheats,

FLAVOR BOOSTER
Add 2 –3 tablespoons fresh cilantro to the marinade.

scrub it with a grill brush and oil it well using tongs and vegetable oil rubbed on a paper towel. Remove the tofu from the marinade, letting the excess drip back in the dish, put the tofu steaks on the grill (or the grill pan), reduce the heat to low, and cover the grill. Cook for 8–10 minutes per side, rotating the tofu 90 degrees on each side halfway through cooking to create cross-hatches, if desired. Remove the tofu from the grill to a serving plate and spoon the remaining marinade over it.

6. Serve the steak or tofu immediately over rice or refrigerate for up to 3 days.

SIDE DISH

Guacamole with Carrots

SERVES: 8 • **SERVING SIZE:** 2 TABLESPOONS GUACAMOLE + 1/2 CUP CARROTS

2 avocados

1/2 lime, juice only (about 1 tablespoon)

1/4 teaspoon salt

1/4 teaspoon garlic powder

1 pound baby carrots or large carrots, cut into sticks

1. Mash the flesh of the avocados with the lime juice. Add the salt and garlic powder. Serve with the carrots.

TIP

I freeze leftover chipotle peppers and adobo sauce in a small container and break off small pieces when I need them.

NUTRITIONAL INFORMATION | GRILLED STEAK (OR TOFU STEAKS) IN CHIPOTLE GARLIC LIME MARINADE:

EXCHANGES / CHOICES:
1 1/2 Starch, 4 Protein, lean; 1/2 Fat

Calories: 325; Calories from Fat: 100; Total Fat: 11 g;
Saturated Fat: 3.4 g; Trans Fat: 0 g; Cholesterol: 70 mg;
Sodium: 370 mg; Potassium: 410 mg; Total Carbohydrate: 27 g;
Dietary Fiber: 2 g; Sugar: 2 g; Protein: 28 g; Phosphorus: 290 mg

NUTRITIONAL INFORMATION | GUACAMOLE WITH CARROTS:

EXCHANGES / CHOICES:
2 Nonstarchy Vegetable; 1 Fat

Calories: 85; Calories from Fat: 55; Total Fat: 6 g;
Saturated Fat: 0.8 g; Trans Fat: 0 g; Cholesterol: 0 mg;
Sodium: 115 mg; Potassium: 365 mg; Total Carbohydrate: 9 g;
Dietary Fiber: 4 g; Sugar: 3 g; Protein: 1 g; Phosphorus: 40 mg

Mild white fish becomes moist and succulent with these Italian flavors. Serve with Farro and Collard Greens with Garlic.

Baked Fish with Mushrooms and Italian Herbs

PREP: 10 MINUTES • **COOK:** 20 MINUTES • **SERVES:** 4 • **SERVING SIZE:** 3 OUNCES

1 1/2 teaspoons trans fat-free margarine-style spread, or use butter

1 pound catfish or other mild white fish fillets such as mahi mahi, tilapia, cod, or sole

6–8 cremini or button mushrooms, quartered

1 lemon

2 teaspoons no-salt-added Italian seasoning blend, or use a combination of dried parsley, oregano, thyme, and basil

1 teaspoon extra-virgin olive oil

1/8 teaspoon salt, or to taste

1/8 teaspoon garlic powder, or to taste

FLAVOR BOOSTER

Double the garlic powder and/or sprinkle the fish with salt-free lemon-pepper seasoning before serving.

TIP

Mushrooms are very versatile and add a rich taste to many dishes. They are an excellent source of B vitamins, which help to maintain good digestive health.

DO AHEAD OR DELEGATE: Quarter the mushrooms, zest and juice 1/2 of the lemon, and slice the remaining 1/2 lemon into wedges.

1. Preheat the oven to 375°F. (Start the farro, if you are serving it.) In a large glass or ceramic baking dish, melt the spread or butter in the microwave or conventional oven. Add the fish to the pan and turn it a couple of times to coat it lightly with the butter. Spread the mushrooms around the fish, and top everything with the zest and juice of 1/2 the lemon. (Cut the remaining 1/2 lemon into wedges to serve with the fish.) Sprinkle the Italian seasoning evenly over the fish, then drizzle the oil, salt, and garlic powder over everything.

2. Bake the fish for about 20 minutes, until it is opaque and flakes easily. (Meanwhile, prepare the Collard Greens with Garlic, if you are serving it.) Serve immediately with the reserved lemon wedges.

SLOW COOKER DIRECTIONS: Place each fillet on its own individual piece of aluminum foil. Brush them with melted spread or butter. Spread the mushrooms around the fish, and top everything with the zest and juice of 1/2 the lemon. (Cut the remaining 1/2 lemon into wedges to serve with the fish.) Sprinkle the Italian seasoning evenly over the fish, then drizzle the oil, salt, and garlic powder over everything. Fold the foil over the fish to make sealed packets, and arrange the packets in the slow cooker, stacking one on top of the other as necessary. Cook for 5–7 hours on low or 3–4 hours on high. (Slow cooker cooking times may vary—get to know your slow cooker and, if necessary, adjust cooking times accordingly.)

SIDE DISHES

Farro

SERVES: 4 • **SERVING SIZE:** 1/2 CUP

3/4 cup farro perlato (or use pearled barley), or use quinoa
for a gluten-free option

1 1/2 cups reduced-sodium chicken or vegetable broth, or
use water or combination of water and broth

1/2 teaspoon extra-virgin olive oil

1 tablespoon fresh flat-leaf parsley, chopped (optional)

1. In a medium stockpot, cook the farro
in broth or water according to package
directions. (Usually, cook it for 20–30
minutes until it is tender but still chewy.)
Drain if necessary, toss with the oil, and
top with the parsley, if desired.

Collard Greens with Garlic

SERVES: 4 • **SERVING SIZE:** 3/4 CUPS

2 tablespoons extra-virgin olive oil

1/2 red onion, chopped

4 cloves garlic, sliced

1/4 teaspoon salt

1 pound collard greens, thinly sliced

1. In a large heavy skillet over medium heat,
heat the oil and add the onions. Let them
cook for 3–4 minutes until they are tender
and starting to brown. Add the garlic and
salt and cook for 1 more minute. Add the
collard greens, toss to coat, and sauté
for 5–10 minutes to desired tenderness,
stirring occasionally. Serve immediately or
refrigerate for up to 2 days. Add a splash of
balsamic vinegar if the greens are too bitter.

This recipe, which can also be called Mexican Pizza, was inspired by an idea from my friend Jill Rabach. It marries two recipes that are kid-favorites, tacos and pizza. My family liked them so much that I had to make another batch immediately, so I doubled the recipe that I'm suggesting to you. Serve with Homemade Ranch Dressing with Carrots or Broccoli.

Fiesta Tostadas

PREP + COOK: 30 MINUTES • **SERVES:** 8 • **SERVING SIZE:** 1 TOSTADA

8 large (8-inch) whole-wheat tortillas

1 cup vegetarian refried beans (Amy's is our favorite)

1/2 cup low-sodium canned black beans, drained and rinsed

1 avocado, diced

1/4 cup frozen corn kernels, no need to thaw

1/4 cup sliced black olives, or use sausage, pepperoni, or chorizo

1/2 cup shredded cheddar cheese, or use Mexican blend, Monterey Jack, or pepper jack

DO AHEAD OR DELEGATE: Slice the olives or sausage if using, and shred the cheddar cheese if necessary, and refrigerate.

1. Preheat the oven to 425°F. Line 2 large baking sheets with silicone baking mats or nonstick cooking spray. Put the tortillas on the baking sheets, spread a thin layer of refried beans on each (about 2 tablespoon per tortilla), and top each tortilla with about 1 tablespoon beans, 1 tablespoon avocado, 1 teaspoon corn, 1 teaspoon olives, and 1 tablespoon cheese (we like them best when spread lightly with the refried beans and not overloaded with toppings).

2. Bake for about 10 minutes until the tortillas get browned and crunchy. (Meanwhile, make the ranch dressing and cut up the vegetables, if you are serving them.) Serve the tostadas immediately.

TIP

Avocados are not only heart-healthy, they're also good for your mood. They are full of monounsaturated fat, which can help provide a mood boost. There are so many ways to enjoy avocados, but one of my favorites is spread ripe avocado onto whole-grain toast with a little lemon juice and sea salt.

- -

Homemade Ranch Dressing with Carrots or Broccoli

SERVES: 8
SERVING SIZE: 3/4 TABLESPOON DRESSING + 1/2 CUP CARROT STICKS

2 tablespoons Greek yogurt or nonfat sour cream

2 tablespoons mayonnaise

2 tablespoons reduced-fat buttermilk

1 teaspoon white wine vinegar

1 tablespoon fresh chives, minced

1/4 teaspoon garlic powder

1/4 teaspoon dried dill

1/8 teaspoon salt

1/8 teaspoon black pepper

1 pound carrots, cut into sticks (or use 2 heads broccoli, cut into florets and steamed for 1–2 minutes until just bright green)

1. Whisk all ingredients, except the carrots, with a fork and serve with the vegetables. Refrigerate any leftovers in an airtight container for up to a week.

FLAVOR BOOSTER
Drizzle a little hot sauce, such as Tabasco, or fresh lime juice, or sprinkle some crushed red pepper flakes on the tostadas at the table.

NUTRITIONAL INFORMATION | FIESTA TOSTADAS:

EXCHANGES / CHOICES:
2 Starch; 1 Protein, lean; 1 Fat

Calories: 225; Calories from Fat: 80; Total Fat: 9 g;
Saturated Fat: 2.4 g; Trans Fat: 0.1 g; Cholesterol: 5 mg;
Sodium: 385 mg; Potassium: 350 mg; Total Carbohydrate: 32 g;
Dietary Fiber: 7 g; Sugar: 1 g; Protein: 9 g; Phosphorus: 180 mg

NUTRITIONAL INFORMATION | HOMEMADE RANCH DRESSING WITH CARROTS:

EXCHANGES / CHOICES:
1 Nonstarchy Vegetable; 1/2 Fat

Calories: 60; Calories from Fat: 25; Total Fat: 3 g;
Saturated Fat: 0.6 g; Trans Fat: 0 g; Cholesterol: 5 mg;
Sodium: 130 mg; Potassium: 215 mg; Total Carbohydrate: 7 g;
Dietary Fiber: 1 g; Sugar: 4 g; Protein: 2 g; Phosphorus: 50 mg

I invented this recipe as my mind wandered during one of my daughter's many soccer games. (I'm not the most devoted sports fan, so I often daydream about recipes during the games.) This combination of squash, apple, curry, and sage spoke to me on a crisp fall day. Serve with Whole-Grain Bread and Green Salad with Shredded Red Cabbage, Blue Cheese, and Walnuts.

Butternut Squash and Apple Soup with Crispy Sage

PREP: 30 MINUTES • **COOK:** 30 MINUTES • **SERVES:** 6 • **SERVING SIZE:** 1 1/2 CUPS

1 tablespoon butter, divided use

2 tablespoons extra-virgin olive oil, divided use

1 sweet yellow onion, such as Vidalia or Walla Walla, chopped

3–4 pounds butternut squash, peeled, seeded and diced

1 red apple, such as Gala or Fuji, peeled and diced

1 teaspoon curry powder

1/2 teaspoon ground ginger, or use 1 tablespoon fresh minced ginger

1/8 teaspoon ground cinnamon

3 cups reduced-sodium vegetable or chicken broth

1/4 cup fresh sage leaves

2 tablespoons apple cider, or use apple butter or apple juice

1 cup fat-free plain Greek yogurt

FLAVOR BOOSTER
Double the curry powder.

DO AHEAD OR DELEGATE: Chop the onion, peel, seed, and dice the squash, peel and dice the apple, combine the dry seasonings, or fully prepare and refrigerate or freeze the soup.

1. In a large stockpot, melt 1/2 tablespoon butter and 1/2 tablespoon oil over medium heat. When it is bubbling, add the onions. After about 3 minutes, add the squash and apples, and sauté with the onions for about 5 minutes. Add the curry powder, ginger, and cinnamon and cook for 2 more minutes. Add the broth, raise the heat to bring it to a boil, then cover and simmer for about 15 minutes, reducing the heat as needed, until the squash is tender. (Meanwhile, prepare the salad, if you are serving it.) Puree the soup in a standing blender or in the pot with an immersion blender.

2. Meanwhile, in a small skillet, heat the remaining butter and oil over medium to medium-high heat. When it is hot, add the sage leaves and cook them until they are brown and crispy, about 2 minutes. Remove them from the heat.

3. Stir the apple cider into the soup and serve it hot and topped with crumbled leaves of crispy sage (or you may enjoy it with a dollop of plain yogurt or sour cream). Alternatively, refrigerate it for up to 3 days or freeze for up to 3 months.

SLOW COOKER DIRECTIONS: Combine all the ingredients except half the butter, the oil, the sage, and the sour cream in the slow cooker. If the vegetables aren't submerged, add an extra cup of water or broth. Cook on low for 6–10 hours or on high for 4–5 hours. Puree the soup in a standing blender or in the slow cooker with an immersion blender. Make the crispy sage leaves as directed about 5 minutes before serving the soup. (Slow cooker cooking times may vary—get to know your slow cooker and, if necessary, adjust cooking times accordingly.)

Whole-Grain Bread

SERVES: 6 • **SERVING SIZE:** 1 (1-OUNCE) SLICE

1 loaf whole-grain bread

1. Warm the bread in a 300°F oven for 5–8 minutes, if desired.

Green Salad with Shredded Red Cabbage, Blue Cheese, and Walnuts

SERVES: 6 • **SERVING SIZE:** 1 1/4 CUPS

6 cups lettuce, any variety, torn or chopped

1 cup red or purple cabbage, thinly sliced

3 tablespoons crumbled blue cheese or Gorgonzola cheese

3 tablespoons walnut pieces, toasted, if desired

1/4 cup balsamic vinaigrette dressing

1. In a large bowl, combine the lettuce, cabbage, blue cheese, walnuts, and balsamic vinaigrette or salad dressing of your choice.

TIP

Want some sage advice? Adding sage, either fresh or dried, to your food has been found to improve memory and overall brain function. Sage, an earthy-tasting, fragrant herb, is delicious in savory soups, stews, and stuffings, with roasted chicken, or combined with butter to make herb butter.

NUTRITIONAL INFORMATION | BUTTERNUT SQUASH AND APPLE SOUP WITH CRISPY SAGE:

EXCHANGES / CHOICES:
1 Starch; 1 Nonstarchy Vegetable; 1 1/2 Fat

Calories: 170; Calories from Fat: 65; Total Fat: 7 g;
Saturated Fat: 1.9 g; Trans Fat: 0.1 g; Cholesterol: 5 mg;
Sodium: 295 mg; Potassium: 600 mg; Total Carbohydrate: 23 g;
Dietary Fiber: 5 g; Sugar: 9 g; Protein: 7 g; Phosphorus: 120 mg

NUTRITIONAL INFORMATION | WHOLE-GRAIN BREAD:

EXCHANGES / CHOICES:
1 Starch

Calories: 70; Calories from Fat: 10; Total Fat: 1 g;
Saturated Fat: 0.2 g; Trans Fat: 0 g; Cholesterol: 0 mg;
Sodium: 125 mg; Potassium: 70 mg; Total Carbohydrate: 12 g;
Dietary Fiber: 2 g; Sugar: 1 g; Protein: 3 g; Phosphorus: 60 mg

NUTRITIONAL INFORMATION | GREEN SALAD WITH SHREDDED RED CABBAGE, BLUE CHEESE, AND WALNUTS:

EXCHANGES / CHOICES:
1 Nonstarchy Vegetable; 1 Fat

Calories: 75; Calories from Fat: 55; Total Fat: 6 g;
Saturated Fat: 1.3 g; Trans Fat: 0 g; Cholesterol: 5 mg;
Sodium: 165 mg; Potassium: 135 mg; Total Carbohydrate: 4 g;
Dietary Fiber: 1 g; Sugar: 2 g; Protein: 2 g; Phosphorus: 45 mg

I first discovered lo mein at a Chinese food cart in Philadelphia during my freshman year of college but the noodles were bathed in oil. This healthy version, adapted from a recipe from Renegade Lunch Lady, Chef Ann Cooper, is totally guilt-free. Serve with Honeydew Melon or Cantaloupe.

Chinese-Style Lo Mein with Vegetables

PREP + COOK: 30 MINUTES • **SERVES:** 9 • **SERVING SIZE:** 1 1/3 CUPS

16 ounces whole-wheat spaghetti or lo mein noodles

2 tablespoons canola or vegetable oil, divided use

1/4 cup hoisin sauce

2 tablespoons reduced-sodium soy sauce (use wheat/gluten-free if needed), or more to taste

1–2 tablespoons fresh ginger, peeled and minced, to taste

1 1/2 teaspoons minced garlic (about 2 cloves)

4 scallions, thinly sliced

1 carrot, julienned (cut into thin strips about 1 inch long)

1 red bell pepper, julienned

1/4 cup fresh cilantro, chopped (optional)

DO AHEAD OR DELEGATE: Cook the noodles and store them tossed with a little oil to prevent sticking, peel and mince the ginger, peel the garlic, slice the scallions, julienne the carrot and the bell pepper, chop the cilantro if using, or fully prepare and refrigerate the dish.

1. Cook the noodles according to the package directions, drain, return to the pot, and toss them with 1 tablespoon oil. Meanwhile, combine the hoisin and soy sauce in a small bowl.

2. In a large nonstick skillet or wok, heat the remaining oil over medium heat. Sauté the ginger, garlic, and scallions for about 1 minute until they release their aromas. Add the carrots and peppers and sauté for about 4 minutes until they are tender crisp. (Meanwhile, cut up the melon, if you are serving it.)

3. In a large serving bowl, toss the cooked noodles with the hoisin-soy mixture and then top them with the vegetable mixture and cilantro (optional) and stir gently. Serve immediately or refrigerate for up to 3 days. Serve warm or cold.

FLAVOR BOOSTER
Drizzle hot chili oil or sesame oil on the noodles at the table.

Honeydew Melon or Cantaloupe

SERVES: 6 • **SERVING SIZE:** 1 CUP

1 honeydew melon

1. Peel and dice the melon and serve immediately or refrigerate it until ready to serve.

TIP

Clean your fruits and vegetables immediately before using or eating them. If washed before being stored, the remaining dampness can promote the growth of mold and bacteria, causing them to go bad more quickly.

NUTRITIONAL INFORMATION | CHINESE-STYLE LO MEIN WITH VEGETABLES:

EXCHANGES / CHOICES:
2 1/2 Starch; 1/2 Carbohydrate; 1/2 Fat

Calories: 235; Calories from Fat: 35; Total Fat: 4 g;
Saturated Fat: 0.4 g; Trans Fat: 0 g; Cholesterol: 0 mg;
Sodium: 250 mg; Potassium: 160 mg; Total Carbohydrate: 44 g;
Dietary Fiber: 7 g; Sugar: 4 g; Protein: 9 g; Phosphorus: 145 mg

NUTRITIONAL INFORMATION | HONEYDEW MELON OR CANTALOUPE:

EXCHANGES / CHOICES:
1 Fruit

Calories: 60; Calories from Fat: 0; Total Fat: 0 g;
Saturated Fat: 0.1 g; Trans Fat: 0 g; Cholesterol: 0 mg;
Sodium: 30 mg; Potassium: 380 mg; Total Carbohydrate: 15 g;
Dietary Fiber: 1 g; Sugar: 14 g; Protein: 1 g; Phosphorus: 20 mg

WINTER (WEEK 5)

Salsa Chicken Packets (1)
SIDE DISH: Chili-Roasted Butternut Squash (1a)

Cod and Corn Chowder Pie (2)
SIDE DISH: Steamed Green Beans with Goat or Feta Cheese (2a)

Fried Rice with Shrimp, Tofu, or Chicken (3)
SIDE DISH: Clementines (3a)

Spaghetti with Creamy Avocado Pesto and Roasted Tomatoes (4)
SIDE DISH: Roasted Brussels Sprouts (4a)

Roasted Indian Cauliflower Tossed with Chickpeas and Cashews (5)
SIDE DISH: Tropical Island Smoothies (5a)

SHOPPING LIST

🥕 PRODUCE
3–4 **scallions** (3)

2 tablespoons **fresh chives or scallions** (2)

1/2 **yellow onion** (1)

1 **red or yellow bell pepper** (1)

16 ounces **grape tomatoes** (4)

1/2 cup **fresh basil leaves** (4)

2 pounds **brussels sprouts** (4a)

1 pound **green beans** (2a)

20 ounces **peeled and cut butternut squash** (1 medium to large squash) (1a)

1 head **cauliflower** (5)

2 ripe **avocados** (4)

1 3/4 **lemons** (2)(2a)(4)

8 **clementines** (3a)

2 **bananas** (5a)

🥩 MEAT AND FISH
4 boneless, skinless **chicken breast halves** (1)

1 pound **cod or other white fish fillets** (2)

1/2 pound **peeled and deveined shrimp** (preferably U.S. or Canadian farmed or wild shrimp), or use extra-firm tofu or diced chicken breast (3)

SHELVED ITEMS

1 1/2 cups **quick-cooking brown rice** (3)

16 ounces **whole-wheat spaghetti** (4)

1 1/2 cups + 2 tablespoons **panko breadcrumbs** (2)

1/2 cup **pineapple juice** (5a)

3/4 cup **chunky salsa** (1)

1/4 cup **mango chutney** (5)*

15 ounces **canned chickpeas** (garbanzo beans) (5)

1/4 cup **raisins** (5)

1/4 cup **cashews** (5)

SPICES

1 1/8 teaspoon **salt** (2a)(4)(5)

1 teaspoon **kosher salt** (1a)(4a)

1/4 teaspoon **cayenne pepper** (5)*

3/8–5/8 teaspoon **black pepper** (2a)(3)

1 1/4 teaspoons **ground cumin** (1)(5)

1 teaspoon **curry powder** (5)

1/2 teaspoon **garlic powder** (1)

3 teaspoons **chili powder** (1)(1a)(5)

1/2 teaspoon **Old Bay seasoning** (2)

STAPLES

8–9 tablespoons **extra-virgin olive oil** (1a)(4)(4a)(5)

2 tablespoons **peanut or vegetable oil** (3)

1/4 cup **reduced-fat mayonnaise** (2)

3 tablespoons **reduced-sodium soy sauce** (use wheat/gluten-free if needed) (3)

4 **eggs** (2)(3)

1 1/2 teaspoons **minced garlic** (4)

REFRIGERATED/FROZEN

1/2 cup **shredded reduced-fat cheddar cheese** (1)

1 tablespoon **goat or feta cheese, crumbled** (2a)

1/2 cup **grated Parmesan cheese** (4)

2 cups **nonfat or low-fat plain or vanilla yogurt** (5a)

1 cup **orange juice** (5a)

1 cup **corn kernels, frozen or fresh** (2)

1 cup **frozen peas** (3)

Get free, printable versions of the shopping lists from this book at TheScramble.com/diabetes.

*optional ingredients

WINTER WEEK 5 • 351

Sometimes it's a fun change to serve the family a meal in a packet. Six O'Clock Scramble member Traci Sara shared this idea with me, and we both like how the chicken stays so moist and flavorful (don't forget to rinse and recycle the foil after dinner). Serve with Chili-Roasted Butternut Squash.

Salsa Chicken Packets

PREP: 15 MINUTES • **COOK:** 30 MINUTES • **SERVES:** 4 • **SERVING SIZE:** 1 PACKET

1 teaspoon chili powder

1/2 teaspoon garlic powder

1/4 teaspoon ground cumin

4 boneless, skinless chicken breast halves

1/2 yellow onion, thinly sliced

1 red or yellow bell pepper, seeded and cut into thin strips

3/4 cup chunky salsa

1/4 cup shredded reduced-fat cheddar cheese

DO AHEAD OR DELEGATE: Combine the dry seasonings and cut the bell pepper and the onion.

1. Preheat the oven to 350°F. In a small bowl, combine the chili powder, garlic powder, and cumin. Sprinkle and rub the mixture evenly on both sides of the chicken breasts.

2. Lay a sheet of aluminum foil that is about 1 foot long on a large baking sheet, put 1/4 of the vegetables in the center, top with one chicken breast, then 1/4 of the salsa (without too much of the liquid), and wrap it up tightly. Repeat with remaining vegetables, chicken, and salsa so you have 4 packets. Bake the packets for 30–35 minutes depending on the thickness of your chicken. (Meanwhile, prepare the squash, if you are serving it.)

3. Remove the packets from the oven, open them carefully, and sprinkle 1 tablespoon of cheese over each chicken breast. Close the packet loosely to melt the cheese, and serve the contents immediately.

SLOW COOKER DIRECTIONS: Prepare the packets as directed and place in the slow cooker, stacking as required. Cook on low for 5–8 hours or on high for 3–5 hours. At serving time, open the packets, top with the cheese, close the packets lightly, and wait a minute or so for cheese to melt. (Slow cooker cooking times may vary—get to know your slow cooker and, if necessary, adjust cooking times accordingly.)

FLAVOR BOOSTER

Double the garlic powder, use spicy salsa, and/or sprinkle the finished dish with a little hot sauce or cayenne pepper.

Chili-Roasted Butternut Squash

SERVES: 4 • **SERVING SIZE:** 2/3 CUP CUBES

20 ounces peeled and cut butternut squash (1 medium to large squash)

1 tablespoon extra-virgin olive oil

1/2 teaspoon kosher salt

1 teaspoon chili powder

1. Preheat the oven to 425°F. Spray a large baking sheet with nonstick cooking spray. In a large bowl, toss the squash, olive oil, salt, and chili powder. Spread the squash evenly on the baking sheet and cook for 25–30 minutes (or more if you like them even browner), flipping once after 15–20 minutes.

TIP

If you are trying to control your sodium intake, look for salsa that's marked "low sodium." If you have a hard time finding a low-sodium brand, you can always replace half of the salsa required in a recipe with salt-free diced tomatoes and some finely diced onion and jalapeños.

NUTRITIONAL INFORMATION | SALSA CHICKEN PACKETS:

EXCHANGES / CHOICES:
2 Nonstarchy Vegetable; 3 Protein, lean

Calories: 180; Calories from Fat: 40; Total Fat: 4.5 g;
Saturated Fat: 1.7 g; Trans Fat: 0 g; Cholesterol: 70 mg;
Sodium: 400 mg; Potassium: 465 mg; Total Carbohydrate: 8 g;
Dietary Fiber: 2 g; Sugar: 4 g; Protein: 27 g; Phosphorus: 250 mg

NUTRITIONAL INFORMATION | CHILI-ROASTED BUTTERNUT SQUASH:

EXCHANGES / CHOICES:
1 Starch; 1/2 Fat

Calories: 80; Calories from Fat: 30; Total Fat: 3.5 g;
Saturated Fat: 0.5 g; Trans Fat: 0 g; Cholesterol: 0 mg;
Sodium: 245 mg; Potassium: 355 mg; Total Carbohydrate: 13 g;
Dietary Fiber: 4 g; Sugar: 2 g; Protein: 1 g; Phosphorus: 35 mg

Loyal Scrambler and recipe contributor Jill Rabach sent me her version of this innovative take on fish cakes or chowder—it takes half the effort by putting everything in a pie plate and baking it, and the creamy texture with the crunchy topping makes a satisfying, kid-friendly meal. Serve with Steamed Green Beans with Goat or Feta Cheese.

Cod and Corn Chowder Pie

PREP: 20 MINUTES • **COOK:** 20 MINUTES • **SERVES:** 4 • **SERVING SIZE:** 1 SLICE

1 pound cod or other white fish fillets

1 lemon, use 1 teaspoon zest and juice of 1/2 lemon, or use 1/4 teaspoon salt-free lemon-pepper seasoning, divided use

1/2 teaspoon Old Bay seasoning, or use other fish or Cajun seasoning, divided use

2 large eggs

1/4 cup reduced-fat mayonnaise

1 cup corn kernels, frozen or fresh, thawed slightly, if frozen

2 tablespoons fresh chives or scallions, finely sliced

1 1/2 cup + 2 tablespoons panko breadcrumbs, preferably whole wheat, divided use

DO AHEAD OR DELEGATE: Zest and juice the lemon, prepare and refrigerate the egg mixture, thaw the corn if frozen, slice the chives, or assemble and refrigerate the pie.

1. Preheat the oven to 400°F and put the fillets on a foil-lined baking sheet coated with nonstick cooking spray (you only need a piece of foil big enough to go under the fillets). Zest the lemon, set the zest aside, and squeeze 1/2 of the lemon over the fish fillets. Season the fillets with 1/2 the Old Bay seasoning and bake for 10 minutes or until the fish just flakes easily.

2. While the fish is in the oven, spray a pie plate with nonstick cooking spray, and in a large bowl, whisk together the eggs, mayonnaise, and lemon zest until it is smooth. Stir the corn, remaining Old Bay seasoning, chives or scallions, and 1/2 cup breadcrumbs into the bowl. Using a spatula, coarsely chop the fish into bite-sized pieces and gently fold it into the egg mixture, leaving the liquid from the lemon and the fish on the pan (don't stir it into the batter).

3. Press the mixture into the pie plate and sprinkle the remaining breadcrumbs on top of the pie, pressing them lightly into the pie with the spatula. (At this point, the pie can be refrigerated for up to 12 hours.) Bake for 20 minutes or until the topping is browned slightly and the pie is firm and cooked through. (Meanwhile, prepare the green beans, if you are serving them.) Serve immediately.

SLOW COOKER DIRECTIONS: There's no need to precook the fish. In the slow cooker, whisk together the eggs, mayonnaise, and lemon zest until smooth. Stir in the corn, Old Bay seasoning, chives or scallions, and 1/2 cup breadcrumbs. Coarsely chop the fish into bite-sized pieces and gently fold it into the egg mixture. Top with the remaining breadcrumbs, and cook on low for 5–8 hours or on high for 3–5 hours. (Slow cooker cooking times may vary—get to know your slow cooker and, if necessary, adjust cooking times accordingly.)

Steamed Green Beans with Goat or Feta Cheese

SERVES: 4 • **SERVING SIZE:** 1 CUP

1 pound green beans, trimmed and halved

1 tablespoon goat or feta cheese, crumbled

1/4 lemon, juice only (about 1 tablespoon)

1/4 teaspoon salt, to taste

1/8 teaspoon black pepper

1. Steam the green beans in 1–2 inches of boiling water for 5–8 minutes, to desired tenderness. Drain and toss them immediately with the goat or feta cheese, lemon juice, salt, and pepper to taste.

FLAVOR BOOSTER

Add 1/2–1 teaspoon dried thyme to the egg mixture. Serve with hot pepper sauce, such as Tabasco, use crumbled corn flake cereal on top of the pie instead of the panko.

TIP

While you may not typically reach for the organic variety when shopping for lemons, when I know that I'm going to be using the zest of a lemon, I make sure to buy organic. Because the residue from pesticides can be found primarily on the skin of produce, I think it's worth the investment when it comes to using the most exposed part of the fruit in a recipe.

NUTRITIONAL INFORMATION | COD AND CORN CHOWDER PIE:

EXCHANGES / CHOICES:
2 Starch; 4 Protein, lean

Calories: 315; Calories from Fat: 65; Total Fat: 7 g;
Saturated Fat: 1.5 g; Trans Fat: 0 g; Cholesterol: 145 mg;
Sodium: 345 mg; Potassium: 425 mg; Total Carbohydrate: 32 g;
Dietary Fiber: 4 g; Sugar: 3 g; Protein: 29 g; Phosphorus: 275 mg

NUTRITIONAL INFORMATION | STEAMED GREEN BEANS WITH GOAT OR FETA CHEESE:

EXCHANGES / CHOICES:
2 Nonstarchy Vegetable

Calories: 45; Calories from Fat: 10; Total Fat: 1 g;
Saturated Fat: 0.6 g; Trans Fat: 0 g; Cholesterol: 0 mg;
Sodium: 155 mg; Potassium: 145 mg; Total Carbohydrate: 8 g;
Dietary Fiber: 3 g; Sugar: 2 g; Protein: 3 g; Phosphorus: 45 mg

This recipe has been one of my favorites since my mom used to make a version of it, and is now a staple in our house. It can be a side dish or main course, depending on what you choose to mix in. Serve with Clementines.

Fried Rice with Shrimp, Tofu, or Chicken

PREP + COOK: 30 MINUTES • **SERVES:** 6 • **SERVING SIZE:** 1 1/2 CUPS

1 1/2 cups quick-cooking brown rice (rice can be made up to a day ahead)

1/2 pound peeled and deveined shrimp (preferably US or Canadian farmed or wild shrimp), or use extra-firm tofu or diced chicken breast

2 tablespoons peanut or vegetable oil, divided use

2 eggs, lightly beaten

3–4 scallions, dark and light green parts, sliced (1/4 cup)

1 cup frozen peas, thawed slightly, or use water chestnuts, straw mushrooms, or diced and lightly steamed carrots

3 tablespoons reduced-sodium soy sauce or tamari (use wheat/gluten-free if needed), or more to taste

1/4–1/2 teaspoon black pepper, to taste

DO AHEAD OR DELEGATE: Cook the rice, dice the tofu or chicken if necessary and refrigerate the chicken, beat the eggs and refrigerate, slice the scallions, thaw the peas, or fully prepare and refrigerate the dish.

1. Cook the rice according to the package directions (you can cook the rice up to 24 hours in advance, and refrigerate it until ready to make the fried rice). While the rice is cooking, sauté the shrimp, tofu (see directions in Tip on next page), or chicken in 1 tablespoon oil over medium-high heat in a large nonstick frying pan or wok for several minutes until it is cooked through. (Cooked shrimp will turn pink, while cooked chicken will no longer be pink.) Remove the shrimp, tofu, or chicken from the pan and set it aside.

2. When the rice is 5 minutes from done, heat the remaining oil in the pan over medium-high heat. Add the eggs to the heated oil and cut them into small pieces with a spatula as they cook. Add the scallions and stir-fry for 1 minute. Add the rice, peas, soy sauce, and pepper, and mix thoroughly. Gently stir in the cooked shrimp, tofu, or chicken. Serve immediately or refrigerate for up to 24 hours.

FLAVOR BOOSTER
Serve with Asian chili garlic sauce, sweet chili sauce, and/or extra soy sauce.

Clementines

SERVES: 8 • **SERVING SIZE:** 1 CLEMENTINE

8 clementines

1. Peel and serve with Fried Rice with Shrimp, Tofu, or Chicken.

TIP

For perfectly cooked tofu, use extra-firm tofu packed in water. Drain the tofu, dice it into 3/4-inch pieces, and wrap it in a clean dish towel for a few minutes (or longer if time allows) to absorb extra water. In a nonstick skillet, heat 1 tablespoon peanut or vegetable oil. Sauté the tofu over medium-low heat for 10 minutes or more, tossing occasionally, until it is golden brown.

NUTRITIONAL INFORMATION | FRIED RICE WITH SHRIMP, TOFU, OR CHICKEN:

EXCHANGES / CHOICES:
1 1/2 Starch; 1 Protein, lean; 1 Fat

Calories: 195; Calories from Fat: 65; Total Fat: 7 g;
Saturated Fat: 1.6 g; Trans Fat: 0 g; Cholesterol: 115 mg;
Sodium: 430 mg; Potassium: 140 mg; Total Carbohydrate: 22 g;
Dietary Fiber: 2 g; Sugar: 1 g; Protein: 11 g; Phosphorus: 185 mg

NUTRITIONAL INFORMATION | CLEMENTINES:

EXCHANGES / CHOICES:
1/2 Fruit

Calories: 35; Calories from Fat: 0; Total Fat: 0 g;
Saturated Fat: 0 g; Trans Fat: 0 g; Cholesterol: 0 mg;
Sodium: 0 mg; Potassium: 130 mg; Total Carbohydrate: 9 g;
Dietary Fiber: 1 g; Sugar: 7 g; Protein: 1 g; Phosphorus: 15 mg

Avocados are an awesome plant-based substitute for cream, but instead of the saturated fat in cream, this rich sauce has heart-healthy monounsaturated fats. The roasted tomatoes balance the tangy and garlicky sauce with sweetness. (Thanks to Six O'Clock Scramble member and recipe tester Kathryn Howell Dalton for suggesting that addition!) Serve with Roasted Brussels Sprouts.

Spaghetti with Creamy Avocado Pesto and Roasted Tomatoes

PREP + COOK: 30 MINUTES • **SERVES:** 9 • **SERVING SIZE:** 1 1/4 CUPS

16 ounces grape tomatoes, halved

3 tablespoon extra-virgin olive oil, divided use

5/8 teaspoon salt

16 ounces whole-wheat spaghetti

1 1/2 teaspoons minced garlic (2–3 cloves)

1/2 lemon, juice only (about 2 tablespoons)

2 ripe avocados, halved, pitted, and peeled

1/2 cup fresh basil leaves

1/2 cup grated Parmesan cheese, divided use

DO AHEAD OR DELEGATE: Halve the tomatoes, cook the spaghetti, and toss with a little oil to prevent sticking, peel the garlic, juice the lemon, and grate the cheese, if necessary.

1. Preheat the oven to 400°F (and start the brussels sprouts now, if you are serving them). In a medium bowl, toss the tomatoes with 1 tablespoon oil and 1/8 teaspoon salt.

2. Spread the tomatoes on a baking sheet and roast for 20 minutes, tossing once halfway through. Cook the spaghetti according to the package directions in salted water until it is al dente.

3. Meanwhile, in a food processor or blender, puree the garlic, lemon juice, and 2 tablespoons oil until smooth. Add the avocados, basil (reserve 5 basil leaves to slice thinly and serve on top of the pasta, if desired), and 1/2 teaspoon salt, and blend until creamy.

4. In a large bowl, combine the spaghetti, the avocado sauce, and 1/2 of the cheese. Top the pasta with the tomatoes (do this at the table if you have picky eaters), and season it with freshly ground black pepper to taste. Serve immediately, topped with extra cheese, if desired.

FLAVOR BOOSTER
Serve it with crushed red pepper flakes, and top the pasta with 1/2–1 teaspoon lemon zest.

Roasted Brussels Sprouts

SERVES: 9 • **SERVING SIZE:** 3/4 CUP

2 pounds brussels sprouts

2 tablespoons extra-virgin olive oil

1/2 teaspoon kosher salt

1. Preheat the oven to 450°F. Trim the stems of the brussels sprouts a little and peel off any tough outer leaves. If the sprouts are large, cut them in half from top to bottom. Toss the sprouts with the oil and salt and roast them in the oven for 20 minutes, tossing them occasionally, until they are browned and tender. (Optional twist: Toss the roasted sprouts with 1 tablespoon dried cranberries and 1 teaspoon grated Parmesan cheese.)

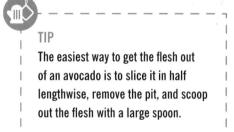

TIP

The easiest way to get the flesh out of an avocado is to slice it in half lengthwise, remove the pit, and scoop out the flesh with a large spoon.

NUTRITIONAL INFORMATION | SPAGHETTI WITH CREAMY AVOCADO PESTO AND ROASTED TOMATOES:

EXCHANGES / CHOICES:
2 1/2 Starch; 1/2 Carbohydrate; 1 1/2 Fat

Calories: 295; Calories from Fat: 100; Total Fat: 11 g;
Saturated Fat: 2.1 g; Trans Fat: 0 g; Cholesterol: 5 mg;
Sodium: 270 mg; Potassium: 365 mg; Total Carbohydrate: 43 g;
Dietary Fiber: 9 g; Sugar: 3 g; Protein: 10 g; Phosphorus: 185 mg

NUTRITIONAL INFORMATION | ROASTED BRUSSELS SPROUTS:

EXCHANGES / CHOICES:
1 Nonstarchy Vegetable; 1/2 Fat

Calories: 60; Calories from Fat: 30; Total Fat: 3.5 g;
Saturated Fat: 0.5 g; Trans Fat: 0 g; Cholesterol: 0 mg;
Sodium: 120 mg; Potassium: 285 mg; Total Carbohydrate: 6 g;
Dietary Fiber: 2 g; Sugar: 2 g; Protein: 2 g; Phosphorus: 50 mg

Six O'Clock Scramble CFO (and my good friend) Robin Thieme stopped by on a Saturday to drop off a book and was surprised to find that I was cooking a hot lunch for my husband, Andrew, and me. I confessed that I was just trying to use up some produce before it went bad. Robin joined us for lunch and we all agreed this dish is a winner. Serve with Tropical Island Smoothies.

Roasted Indian Cauliflower Tossed with Chickpeas and Cashews

PREP + COOK: 30 MINUTES • **SERVES:** 4 • **SERVING SIZE:** 2 1/2 CUPS

1 head cauliflower, cut into medium florets

3 tablespoons extra-virgin olive oil, divided use

1 teaspoon curry powder

1 teaspoon ground cumin

1 teaspoon chili powder

1/4 teaspoon cayenne pepper (optional)

1/4 teaspoon salt, or more to taste

15 ounces canned chickpeas (garbanzo beans), drained and rinsed, or use 1 1/2 cups cooked chickpeas

1/4 cup cashews

1/4 cup raisins, or more to taste (up to 1/2 cup), or use dried cranberries or currants

1/4 cup mango chutney, for serving (optional)

DO AHEAD OR DELEGATE: Chop the cauliflower, combine the spices, or fully prepare and refrigerate the dish.

1. Preheat the oven to 400°F. In a large serving bowl, toss the cauliflower with 2 tablespoons of the oil. In a small bowl, combine the spices (curry powder through salt). Toss the cauliflower with the spices, and spread the florets on a large baking sheet and roast for 15 minutes.

2. Meanwhile, in the large serving bowl, combine the chickpeas, cashews, and raisins with the remaining tablespoon of oil. Remove the cauliflower from the oven and toss in the chickpeas, cashews, and raisins. Return it to the oven for 10 more minutes until the cauliflower is well browned and tender. (Meanwhile, prepare the smoothies, if you are serving them.) Serve immediately, or refrigerate for up to 3 days.

SLOW COOKER DIRECTIONS: Add all ingredients except the chutney to the slow cooker and cook on low for 4–5 hours or on high for 2–3 hours. (Slow cooker cooking times may vary—get to know your slow cooker and, if necessary, adjust cooking times accordingly.)

Tropical Island Smoothies

SERVES: 6 • **SERVING SIZE:** 1 CUP

1/2 cup pineapple juice

1 cup orange juice

2 medium bananas

2 cups nonfat or low-fat plain or vanilla yogurt

1. In a blender, combine the pineapple juice, orange juice, bananas, yogurt, and 1 cup of ice. Blend on high speed for 30–60 seconds until smooth.

FLAVOR BOOSTER

Toss the cauliflower and spices together in a large resealable bag and let it marinate, refrigerated, for up to 24 hours. Roast some sliced red onions with the cauliflower, stir in some pomegranate seeds to the finished dish, and stir some chutney into plain nonfat Greek yogurt to make a creamy sauce.

TIP

Vegetables need to breathe, so for those veggies that you store in the refrigerator, either store them in reusable mesh bags or, if they are in plastic bags, poke holes in the bags or at least leave them open to allow air to circulate. They will last longer this way.

NUTRITIONAL INFORMATION | ROASTED INDIAN CAULIFLOWER TOSSED WITH CHICKPEAS AND CASHEWS:

EXCHANGES / CHOICES:
1 Starch; 1/2 Fruit; 2 Nonstarchy Vegetable; 1 Protein, lean; 2 1/2 Fat

Calories: 305; Calories from Fat: 145; Total Fat: 16 g;
Saturated Fat: 2.5 g; Trans Fat: 0 g; Cholesterol: 0 mg;
Sodium: 355 mg; Potassium: 705 mg; Total Carbohydrate: 34 g;
Dietary Fiber: 8 g; Sugar: 11 g; Protein: 10 g; Phosphorus: 215 mg

NUTRITIONAL INFORMATION | TROPICAL ISLAND SMOOTHIES:

EXCHANGES / CHOICES:
1 Fruit; 1/2 Milk, fat-free

Calories: 100; Calories from Fat: 0; Total Fat: 0 g;
Saturated Fat: 0.1 g; Trans Fat: 0 g; Cholesterol: 0 mg;
Sodium: 50 mg; Potassium: 430 mg; Total Carbohydrate: 22 g;
Dietary Fiber: 1 g; Sugar: 16 g; Protein: 4 g; Phosphorus: 135 mg

WINTER

Spice-Rubbed Slow-Cooked Whole Chicken (1)

SIDE DISH: Steamed Broccoli Tossed with Olive Oil and Grated Parmesan Cheese (1a)

Tortuguero Tilapia with Cilantro-Lime Sauce (2)

SIDE DISH: Quinoa (or Couscous) (2a); Simple Mixed Vegetables (2b)

Italian Shotgun Wedding Soup (3)

SIDE DISH: Tropical Fruit Salad (3a)

Rigatoni with Tomatoes and Olives (4)

SIDE DISH: Green Salad with Apples, Toasted Walnuts, and Blue Cheese (4a)

Warm Sweet Potato, Corn, and Black Bean Salad (5)

SIDE DISH: Avocado Garlic Toasts (5a)

SHOPPING LIST

PRODUCE

7 **carrots** (1)(3)
1 1/2–2 **yellow onions** (1)(3)
2 stalks **celery** (3)
8 cups **lettuce, any variety** (4a)
6 ounces **baby spinach, escarole, or arugula** (3)
3 1/2 cloves **garlic** (2)(5a)
7/8 cup **fresh cilantro** (2)(5)
1 cup **fresh parsley** (4)
3/4 pound **sweet potato(es)** (5)
2 **potatoes** (any variety) (1)
4 ears **fresh corn** (5)
1 large **avocado** (5a)
3–3 1/2 **limes** (2)(3a)(5)
2–3 **kiwis** (3a)
1 **apple** (4a)
1–2 **bananas** (3a)
2 **mangos** (3a)
1 pound **broccoli** (1a)

MEAT AND FISH

1 **whole chicken** (about 4 pounds, or use 8–10 chicken pieces) (1)
1 pound **tilapia fillets** or other thin white fish (2)
12 ounces **precooked Italian turkey, chicken or meatless sausage** (use wheat/gluten-free if needed) (3)
6 ounces **precooked lean turkey sausage** (5)

SHELVED ITEMS

1/2 **baguette** (5a)

2/3 cup **quinoa or couscous** (2a)

1 cup **orzo** (use wheat/gluten-free if needed) (3)

16 ounces **whole-wheat rigatoni noodles** (4)

6 **whole-wheat tortillas** (use wheat/gluten-free if needed)(5)*

15 ounces **diced tomatoes** (4)

10 cups **low-sodium chicken or vegetable broth** (3)

15 ounces **reduced-sodium canned black beans** (5)

6 ounces **black olives** (4)

1 teaspoon **superfine sugar** (3a)*

1/4 cup **walnuts** (4a)

SPICES

2 1/16 teaspoons **salt** (1)(2)(2b)(4)(4a)(5)

1/8 teaspoon **sea salt or other coarse salt** (5a)

1 teaspoon **Italian seasoning blend** (3)

1 teaspoon **dried thyme** (1)

1/2 teaspoon **cayenne pepper** (1)*

1 1/8 teaspoons **black pepper** (1)(2)(4a)

1/2 teaspoon **ground cumin** (5)

1 teaspoon **garlic powder** (1)

1 teaspoon **chili powder** (5)

2 teaspoons **paprika** (1)

STAPLES

1 teaspoon **butter** (2b)

6 tablespoons + 1/4 cup **extra-virgin olive oil** (1a)(2)(3)
  (4)(4a)(5a)

2 tablespoons **canola or vegetable oil** (5)

1 tablespoon **red wine vinegar** (4a)

1/2 teaspoon **honey** (4a)

2 teaspoons **minced garlic** (4)

REFRIGERATED/FROZEN

2 tablespoons **blue or Gorgonzola cheese** (4a)

2/3 cup **grated Parmesan cheese** (1a)(3)

3 cups **frozen mixed vegetables** such as carrots and peas (2b)

1 tablespoon **grated Parmesan cheese** (1a)

Get free, printable versions of the shopping lists from this book at **TheScramble.com/diabetes**.

*optional ingredients

WINTER WEEK 6 • 363

You'll love the simplicity and flexibility of this recipe, originally suggested to me by Amanda Wendt. You can customize the spices and vegetables, and it's one of those dishes that you can throw in a pot and forget about until dinnertime. You can eat the cooked chicken right away, or use the chicken in tacos, pot pie, salads, or anything else you can think of. This is a meal in itself, so no side is necessary. However, it pairs well with Steamed Broccoli Tossed with Olive Oil and Grated Parmesan Cheese.

Spice-Rubbed Slow-Cooked Whole Chicken

PREP: 15 MINUTES • **COOK:** 2–6 HOURS • **SERVES:** 6 • **SERVING SIZE:** 1 PIECE OF CHICKEN

3/4 teaspoon salt

2 teaspoons paprika

1 teaspoon dried thyme

1 teaspoon garlic powder

1 teaspoon black pepper

1/2 teaspoon cayenne pepper, or more to taste (optional)

1 whole chicken (about 4 pounds, or use 8–10 chicken pieces), skin removed, if desired

1 yellow onion, halved and sliced

4 carrots, cut into large chunks

2 potatoes (any variety), cut into large chunks

FLAVOR BOOSTER
Use 1 1/2 teaspoons garlic powder and the optional cayenne pepper. Put the rub on the chicken up to 24 hours in advance.

DO AHEAD OR DELEGATE: Combine the dry seasonings, halve and slice the onion, chop the carrots, cut the potatoes and store covered with water to prevent browning, rub the spices onto the chicken and refrigerate, or fully prepare and refrigerate or freeze the chicken.

1. In a small bowl, combine the spices. Remove any giblets from the chicken and discard. Put the vegetables in the bottom of a slow cooker. Rub the spice mixture onto the chicken and put the chicken on top of the vegetables. (Alternatively, bake the chicken in a Dutch oven or covered roasting pan at 250°F for 5 hours, or see below for faster cooking directions.)

2. Cook it on low for 5–6 hours, or on high for 2–3 hours, until the chicken is tender and falling off the bone. Transfer the chicken to a pan and put it under the broiler for 2–3 minutes if a crisper skin is desired. Serve it immediately with the vegetables and some of the pan juices, refrigerate for up to 3 days, or freeze for up to 3 months.

3. To cook the chicken faster: In a large roasting pan, cook the spiced-rubbed chicken and vegetables in the oven at 400°F for about 1 1/2 hours, covered with foil or the lid of the pan for the first 45 minutes. After 45 minutes, baste the chicken with the pan juices, stir the vegetables, and continue cooking with the pan uncovered. The chicken is done when the juices at the base of the thigh run clear or an instant-read thermometer inserted into the thickest part of the thigh measures 165°F (don't let the thermometer touch the bone). If a crisper skin is desired, put the chicken under the broiler for 2–3 minutes. If time allows, let the chicken rest for 10–15 minutes after removing from the oven before serving it.

Steamed Broccoli Tossed with Olive Oil and Grated Parmesan Cheese

SERVES: 4 • **SERVING SIZE:** 5 SPEARS

1 pound broccoli (tough bottoms cut off), cut into 20 spears
1 tablespoon extra-virgin olive oil
1 tablespoon grated Parmesan cheese

1. Steam the broccoli spears until tender, 7–10 minutes. Drain the broccoli and toss immediately with the oil and cheese.

TIP

Applying the rub to the chicken and putting it back in the refrigerator for up to 24 hours will allow the chicken to fully absorb the flavors of the rub. If you don't have time to spare, no worries—the chicken will still be delicious.

NUTRITIONAL INFORMATION | SPICE-RUBBED SLOW-COOKED WHOLE CHICKEN:

EXCHANGES / CHOICES:
1/2 Starch; 2 Nonstarchy Vegetable; 3 Protein, lean

Calories: 230; Calories from Fat: 40; Total Fat: 4.5 g;
Saturated Fat: 1.1 g; Trans Fat: 0 g; Cholesterol: 90 mg;
Sodium: 425 mg; Potassium: 690 mg; Total Carbohydrate: 17 g;
Dietary Fiber: 3 g; Sugar: 3 g; Protein: 30 g; Phosphorus: 275 mg

NUTRITIONAL INFORMATION | STEAMED BROCCOLI TOSSED WITH OLIVE OIL AND GRATED PARMESAN CHEESE:

EXCHANGES / CHOICES:
1 Nonstarchy Vegetable; 1 Fat

Calories: 65; Calories from Fat: 35; Total Fat: 4 g;
Saturated Fat: 0.7 g; Trans Fat: 0 g; Cholesterol: 0 mg;
Sodium: 50 mg; Potassium: 290 mg; Total Carbohydrate: 6 g;
Dietary Fiber: 2 g; Sugar: 2 g; Protein: 3 g; Phosphorus: 70 mg

Chef Valentin Corral at the remote Tortuguero Lodge in Costa Rica first prepared a version of this brightly flavored tilapia for us. Serve with Quinoa and Simple Mixed Vegetables.

Tortuguero Tilapia with Cilantro-Lime Sauce

PREP + COOK: 15 MINUTES • **SERVES:** 4 • **SERVING SIZE:** 1 FILLET

2 tablespoons extra-virgin olive oil, divided use

1 pound tilapia fillets or other thin white fish fillets (4 fillets)

1/4 teaspoon salt, or to taste

1/8 teaspoon black pepper, or to taste

1/3 cup fresh cilantro, or use basil or flat-leaf parsley

3 whole cloves garlic

1 lime

DO AHEAD OR DELEGATE: Juice half the lime and cut the other half into 4 wedges, and make and refrigerate the sauce for the fish.

1. (If you are making the quinoa, start it first.) In a large nonstick skillet, heat 1 tablespoon oil over medium-high heat. Place the tilapia fillets in the pan and press them down with a spatula to ensure each fillet is completely touching the pan. Cook the fillets on each side until they are lightly browned, about 3–4 minutes per side. After flipping the fish, season it with salt and pepper. (Meanwhile, prepare the vegetables, if you are serving them.)

2. While the fish is cooking, make the sauce one of two ways: Puree the cilantro, garlic, 1 tablespoon olive oil, and the juice of half the lime in a food processor or blender. Or, by hand, finely chop the cilantro and garlic, put it in a small serving bowl, and stir in 1 tablespoon olive oil and the juice of half a lime. Season with salt and pepper to taste.

3. When the fish is done cooking, put it on a serving plate and top it with the sauce (or serve the sauce on the side). Cut the remaining half lime into 4 wedges for serving.

FLAVOR BOOSTER
Add some of the zest of the lime to the cilantro-lime mixture.

SIDE DISHES

Quinoa (or Couscous)

SERVES: 4 • **SERVING SIZE:** 1/2 CUP

2/3 cup quinoa or couscous

1. Prepare the quinoa according to the package directions, making sure to rinse the quinoa with cold water before cooking. (I use a fine metal strainer to rinse it.)

Simple Mixed Vegetables

SERVES: 4 • **SERVING SIZE:** 3/4 CUP

3 cups frozen mixed vegetables, such as carrots and peas

1 teaspoon butter

1/4 teaspoon salt, or to taste

1. Defrost the vegetables in the microwave or on the stovetop until they are just hot (don't overcook). Stir in the butter and salt and serve.

TIP

Try to purchase tilapia that has been raised in the United States. If possible, avoid farmed tilapia from China and Taiwan, where pollution is a widespread problem. This and other important information about making healthy choices for our bodies and our oceans is available on Monterey Bay Aquarium's Seafood Watch website (www.seafoodwatch.org).

NUTRITIONAL INFORMATION | TORTUGUERO TILAPIA WITH CILANTRO-LIME SAUCE:

EXCHANGES / CHOICES:
3 Protein, lean; 1 Fat

Calories: 175; Calories from Fat: 80; Total Fat: 9 g;
Saturated Fat: 1.7 g; Trans Fat: 0 g; Cholesterol: 50 mg;
Sodium: 125 mg; Potassium: 350 mg; Total Carbohydrate: 1 g;
Dietary Fiber: 0 g; Sugar: 0 g; Protein: 22 g; Phosphorus: 180 mg

NUTRITIONAL INFORMATION | QUINOA:

EXCHANGES / CHOICES:
1 1/2 Starch

Calories: 110; Calories from Fat: 20; Total Fat: 2 g;
Saturated Fat: 0.3 g; Trans Fat: 0 g; Cholesterol: 0 mg;
Sodium: 5 mg; Potassium: 160 mg; Total Carbohydrate: 20 g;
Dietary Fiber: 3 g; Sugar: 2 g; Protein: 4 g; Phosphorus: 140 mg

NUTRITIONAL INFORMATION | SIMPLE MIXED VEGETABLES:

EXCHANGES / CHOICES:
1/2 Starch; 1 Nonstarchy Vegetable

Calories: 75; Calories from Fat: 15; Total Fat: 1.5 g;
Saturated Fat: 0.7 g; Trans Fat: 0 g; Cholesterol: 5 mg;
Sodium: 235 mg; Potassium: 190 mg; Total Carbohydrate: 10 g;
Dietary Fiber: 3 g; Sugar: 6 g; Protein: 3 g; Phosphorus: 60 mg

Everyone loves Italian Wedding Soup, but the thought of making both the meatballs and the soup on a harried weeknight is a little daunting. So I love this shortcut of using flavorful sausage instead of the meatballs, while still using the fresh vegetables that make this soup so nourishing. Serve with Tropical Fruit Salad.

Italian Shotgun Wedding Soup

PREP + COOK: 30 MINUTES • **SERVES:** 8 • **SERVING SIZE:** 1 1/3 CUPS

1 tablespoon extra-virgin olive oil

1/2 yellow onion, finely chopped (1 cup)

3 carrots, halved (or quartered if large) and finely chopped (about 1 cup)

2 stalks celery, thinly sliced (about 1 cup)

12 ounces precooked Italian turkey, chicken, or meatless sausage (use wheat/gluten-free if needed), sliced into 1/2-inch slices

1 teaspoon Italian seasoning blend, or more to taste

10 cups low-sodium chicken or vegetable broth

1 cup orzo, whole wheat if available, or use ditalini or other small pasta shape

6 ounces baby spinach, escarole, or arugula (or use 1 cup frozen spinach)

1/3 cup grated Parmesan cheese

DO AHEAD OR DELEGATE: Chop the onion and the carrots, slice the celery, slice and refrigerate the sausage, defrost the spinach if using frozen, grate the cheese if necessary and refrigerate, or fully prepare and refrigerate or freeze the soup.

1. Heat a large stockpot or Dutch oven over medium heat, add the oil, and when it is hot, add the onions, carrots, celery, and sausage, and sauté until the vegetables start to soften and the sausage starts to brown, 5–7 minutes. Stir in the Italian seasoning, then add the broth, cover, and bring to a boil.

2. When it is boiling, stir in the orzo, cover to bring it back to a boil, then uncover and simmer for about 8 minutes, until the orzo is al dente. Stir in the spinach to wilt for 1 minute. Season with salt and pepper to taste, and serve immediately, topped with the cheese, if desired, or refrigerate for up to 3 days or freeze for up to 3 months.

SLOW COOKER DIRECTIONS: You will need a slow cooker that is 4 quarts or larger for this meal. Omit the oil. Add all ingredients except the orzo and the cheese to the slow cooker, and cook on low for 6–10 hours or on high for 4–5 hours. Add the orzo to the slow cooker for the last 30 minutes of cooking. Serve topped with the cheese. (Slow cooker cooking times may vary—get to know your slow cooker and, if necessary, adjust cooking times accordingly.)

Tropical Fruit Salad

SERVES: 8 • **SERVING SIZE:** 1/2 CUP

2–3 kiwis, diced, or use sliced grapes

2 mangos, or use 2 cups frozen, diced

1–2 banana(s), sliced

1 teaspoon superfine sugar (optional)

1/2–1 lime, juice only (1–2 tablespoons) (optional)

1. Combine the kiwis or grapes, mangos, and bananas (or fruit of your choice). For an optional dressing, dissolve the sugar in the lime juice, and toss the mixture gently with the fruit.

FLAVOR BOOSTER

Sauté 2–3 cloves garlic with the vegetables, add 1/2 cup dry white wine with the broth, and serve with crushed red pepper flakes.

TIP

We love grating fresh Parmesan cheese over our soup with a Microplane grater. If you have a wedge of Parmesan, throw the rind into the soup with the Italian seasoning to flavor the soup, and remove it before serving.

NUTRITIONAL INFORMATION | ITALIAN SHOTGUN WEDDING SOUP:

EXCHANGES / CHOICES:
1 Starch; 1 Nonstarchy Vegetable; 2 Protein, lean

Calories: 190; Calories from Fat: 65; Total Fat: 7 g;
Saturated Fat: 2.1 g; Trans Fat: 0 g; Cholesterol: 40 mg;
Sodium: 440 mg; Potassium: 625 mg; Total Carbohydrate: 19 g;
Dietary Fiber: 3 g; Sugar: 3 g; Protein: 15 g; Phosphorus: 210 mg

NUTRITIONAL INFORMATION | TROPICAL FRUIT SALAD:

EXCHANGES / CHOICES:
1 Fruit

Calories: 60; Calories from Fat: 0; Total Fat: 0 g;
Saturated Fat: 0.1 g; Trans Fat: 0 g; Cholesterol: 0 mg;
Sodium: 0 mg; Potassium: 210 mg; Total Carbohydrate: 15 g;
Dietary Fiber: 2 g; Sugar: 12 g; Protein: 1 g; Phosphorus: 20 mg

This is a delicious, simple recipe for a weeknight dinner. Serve with Green Salad with Apples, Toasted Walnuts, and Blue Cheese.

Rigatoni with Tomatoes and Olives

PREP + COOK: 25 MINUTES • **SERVES:** 8 • **SERVING SIZE:** 1 3/4 CUPS

16 ounces whole-wheat rigatoni noodles

1 tablespoon extra-virgin olive oil

2 teaspoons minced garlic (about 4 cloves)

15 ounces diced tomatoes, with their liquid

6 ounces black olives, canned, whole, or sliced, and drained and rinsed

1/4 teaspoon salt (optional)

1/8 teaspoon pepper

1 cup fresh flat-leaf parsley, minced

1/4 cup grated Parmesan cheese

DO AHEAD OR DELEGATE: Cook the noodles and toss them with a little oil to keep them from sticking, peel and mince the garlic, slice the olives, if desired, and mince the parsley.

1. Cook the noodles according to the package directions.

2. Meanwhile, heat the oil in a large heavy skillet over medium heat. Cook the garlic for about 1 minute until it becomes fragrant and golden. Add the tomatoes and olives, salt (optional), and pepper and simmer until the pasta is finished. (Meanwhile, make the salad if you are serving it.)

3. In a large metal bowl, combine the rigatoni with the sauce and parsley. Top with the cheese before serving.

TIP

I love using a large metal bowl for serving pasta, as it keeps the food warm and makes it look so appetizing!

Green Salad with Apples, Toasted Walnuts, and Blue Cheese

SERVES: 8 • **SERVING SIZE:** 1 CUP

2 tablespoons extra-virgin olive oil

1 tablespoon red wine vinegar

1/2 teaspoon honey

1/16 teaspoon salt

1/16 teaspoon black pepper

8 cups lettuce, any variety, torn or chopped

1 apple, diced

1/4 cup walnuts, lightly toasted

2 tablespoons blue cheese or Gorgonzola cheese, crumbled

1. To make the dressing, whisk together the oil, vinegar, honey, salt, and pepper. Toss the lettuce with the apples, walnuts, blue cheese, and the dressing.

NUTRITIONAL INFORMATION | RIGATONI WITH TOMATOES AND OLIVES:

EXCHANGES / CHOICES:
3 Starch; 1 Nonstarchy Vegetable; 1/2 Fat

Calories: 270; Calories from Fat: 65; Total Fat: 7 g;
Saturated Fat: 1.1 g; Trans Fat: 0 g; Cholesterol: 0 mg;
Sodium: 285 mg; Potassium: 270 mg; Total Carbohydrate: 47 g;
Dietary Fiber: 6 g; Sugar: 3 g; Protein: 10 g; Phosphorus: 180 mg

NUTRITIONAL INFORMATION | GREEN SALAD WITH APPLES, TOASTED WALNUTS, AND BLUE CHEESE:

EXCHANGES / CHOICES:
1/2 Carbohydrate; 1 Fat

Calories: 80; Calories from Fat: 65; Total Fat: 7 g;
Saturated Fat: 1.1 g; Trans Fat: 0 g; Cholesterol: 0 mg;
Sodium: 55 mg; Potassium: 125 mg; Total Carbohydrate: 5 g;
Dietary Fiber: 1 g; Sugar: 4 g; Protein: 2 g; Phosphorus: 35 mg

This salad is a looker, and it's full of flavor and good nutrition, too. You could get creative with ingredients and add some cherry tomatoes or avocado, and swap the cilantro for basil. Serve with Avocado Garlic Toasts.

Warm Sweet Potato, Corn, and Black Bean Salad

PREP + COOK: 25 MINUTES • **SERVES:** 6 • **SERVING SIZE:** 1 1/4 CUPS SALAD + 1 OUNCE TURKEY SAUSAGE

3/4 pound sweet potatoes, peeled, and cut into 1/2-inch cubes

1 1/2 cups frozen corn kernels, or 3–4 ears corn, kernels sliced off cob

15 ounces reduced-sodium canned black beans, drained and rinsed

1/2 cup fresh cilantro, chopped, loosely packed, or use basil

2 tablespoons canola or vegetable oil

1 1/2 limes, juice only (about 3 tablespoons)

1/2 teaspoon salt

1/2 teaspoon ground cumin

1 teaspoon chili powder

6 whole-wheat tortillas (optional)

6 ounces precooked lean turkey sausage

DO AHEAD OR DELEGATE: Peel and dice the sweet potato(es), cut the kernels off the corn if using fresh, juice the limes, combine the dry seasonings, or fully prepare and refrigerate the salad.

1. (Start the toasts first, if you are serving them.) In a medium stockpot, bring 2 inches of water to a boil over high heat. Add the sweet potatoes, cook them for 4–5 minutes until they are fork tender, then add the corn kernels for 1 minute. Drain and transfer to a serving bowl, and add the beans and cilantro.

2. While the potatoes are cooking, make a dressing with the oil, lime juice, salt, cumin, and chili powder, toss it with everything in the serving bowl, and heat the sausage. Serve immediately with the sausage, wrapped in warm tortillas, if desired, or refrigerate for up to 3 days and serve it warm or cold.

TIP

My husband, Andrew, thinks everything tastes better in a tortilla. When choosing tortillas, I look for whole-grain brands that don't contain any partially hydrogenated oils, also known as trans fats. Making your own tortillas is also a fun family activity when you have the time.

SIDE DISHES

Avocado Garlic Toasts

SERVES: 6 • **SERVING SIZE:** 2 SLICES

2 tablespoons extra-virgin olive oil

1/2 baguette (8 ounces), whole grain or white, thinly sliced
   in 12 pieces

1/2 clove garlic, peeled and halved

1 large avocado, peeled and very thinly sliced

1/8 teaspoon sea salt or other coarse salt, or to taste

1. Preheat the oven to 400°F. Pour the oil into a small bowl. Lay the baguette slices on a baking sheet and, using a pastry brush, brush the tops lightly with the oil. Bake them for 5–7 minutes, until they just start to brown on the edges. Remove from the oven, transfer to a serving plate, and allow them to cool. Rub the top of each baguette slice firmly with the cut side of the garlic clove. Fan the avocado slices over the toasted baguette slices and season them lightly with the salt. Serve immediately. (These are also delicious topped with chopped toasted pistachios.)

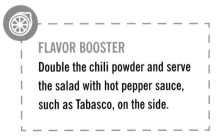

FLAVOR BOOSTER
Double the chili powder and serve the salad with hot pepper sauce, such as Tabasco, on the side.

WINTER (WEEK 7)

Irresistible Honey-Curry Chicken (1)
SIDE DISH: Punjabi-Style Potatoes (1a)

Salmon (or Tofu) Tacos (2)
SIDE DISH: Chopped Cucumber and Avocado Salad (2a)

Penne Rigate with Garden Vegetables (3)
SIDE DISH: Baby Greens with Sliced Pear and Pecans (3a)

Winter Rainbow Soup (4)
SIDE DISH: Whole-Grain Baguette (4a)

Lovely Lentils with Spinach and Tomatoes (5)
SIDE DISH: Seedless Grapes (5a)

SHOPPING LIST

PRODUCE
1 **yellow onion** (5)
2 **small yellow onions** (1a)(4)
1 small **red onion** (3)
1 **yellow bell pepper** (3)
1 **jalapeño pepper** (1a)
1/2 **tomato** (1a)
6–9 ounces **baby spinach** (5)
14 ounces **baby salad greens** (3a)
1/4 head **purple cabbage** (4)
1 tablespoon **fresh ginger** (1a)
1 **zucchini** (3)
1 **cucumber** (2a)
1 small **sweet potato** (4)
1 1/2 pounds **red potatoes** (1a)
8 ounces **sliced mushrooms** (3)
2 **avocados** (2a)
5/8 **lemon** (1)(2a)
2 **pears** (3a)
2 cups **seedless grapes** (5a)

MEAT AND FISH
6–8 pieces **bone-in chicken, any variety** (1)
1 pound **salmon fillet** (2)
1 pound **hot Italian sausage** (use wheat/gluten-free if needed) (3)*

🫙 SHELVED ITEMS

1 **whole-grain baguette** (4a)

16 ounces **whole-wheat penne rigate** (3)

12 **corn tortillas** (2)

24 ounces **red pasta sauce** (3)

14 ounces **diced tomatoes** (5)

2 1/2 cups **reduced-sodium vegetable broth** (4)

2 cups **low-sodium chicken or vegetable broth** (5)

1–3 teaspoons **apple cider vinegar** (4)

3/4 cup **dried green/brown lentils** (5)

1/4 cup **dried currants or raisins** (5)

3 tablespoons **pecans** (3a)

🧂 SPICES

1 5/8 teaspoons **salt** (1)(1a)(2)(5)

1/2 teaspoon **dried rosemary** (4)

1/4 teaspoon **cayenne pepper** (2)*

1 teaspoon **ground cinnamon** (5)

2 1/2 teaspoons **ground cumin** (2)(5)

1 teaspoon **garam masala** (an Indian spice blend) (1a)

1 tablespoon + 1 teaspoon **curry powder** (1)(1a)

1/4 teaspoon **garlic powder** (2)

1/2 teaspoon **paprika** (2)

🫙 STAPLES

2 tablespoons **trans fat-free margarine** (1)

5 tablespoons **extra-virgin olive oil** (2)(3)(4)(5)

2 tablespoons **canola or vegetable oil** (1a)

1/2 teaspoon **balsamic vinegar** (2a)

1/2 cup **vinaigrette dressing** (3a)

1 tablespoon **Dijon or yellow mustard** (use wheat/
gluten-free if needed) (1)

2 tablespoons **Worcestershire sauce** (3)

1 1/2 tablespoons **honey** (1)

3 1/2 teaspoons **minced garlic** (1a)(3)(4)

1 teaspoon **cornstarch** (1)*

🧊 REFRIGERATED/FROZEN

1 tablespoon **crumbled Gorgonzola or blue cheese** (2a)

1/4 cup **grated Parmesan cheese** (4)

8 ounces **guacamole** (2)

1/2 cup **pico de gallo** (fresh chopped) salsa (2)

1/4–1/2 cup **nonfat sour cream** (3)

1/4 cup **orange juice** (1)

1 cup **frozen shelled edamame** (4)

Get free, printable versions of the shopping lists from this book at **TheScramble.com/diabetes**.

*optional ingredients

WINTER WEEK 7 • 375

This is a wonderful chicken recipe, from Six O'Clock Scramble member and recipe tester Nancy Bolen. Both Nancy's and my sometimes-picky children gobbled it up! Serve with Punjabi-Style Potatoes.

Irresistible Honey-Curry Chicken

PREP: 10 MINUTES • **COOK:** 50 MINUTES • **SERVES:** 6 • **SERVING SIZE:** 1 THIGH OR 1 DRUMSTICK

2 tablespoons trans fat-free margarine, or use butter

1/4 cup orange juice

1/2 lemon, juice only (about 2 tablespoons)

1 1/2 tablespoons honey

1 tablespoon Dijon or yellow mustard (use wheat/gluten-free if needed)

1 tablespoon curry powder

1/2 teaspoon salt

6–8 pieces bone-in chicken (3 medium thighs and 3 drumsticks), skin removed

1 teaspoon cornstarch (optional)

DO AHEAD OR DELEGATE: Make and refrigerate the sauce and remove the skin from the chicken, if desired.

1. Preheat the oven to 375°F. In a small saucepan, melt the margarine or butter over medium heat. Once it's melted, add the next six ingredients (orange juice through salt) to the pot and whisk them together. Remove from heat.

2. Place the chicken in a 9 × 13-inch baking pan. Pour the sauce evenly over the chicken, reserving the unwashed saucepan. Bake for 45–50 minutes, basting occasionally, until the chicken is cooked through. (Meanwhile, prepare the potatoes, if you are serving them.)

3. When the chicken is fully cooked, remove it from the oven and put it on a serving plate. Pour the sauce from the bottom of the baking pan into a serving bowl to serve with the chicken and potatoes. (Optional step for a richer sauce: In the saucepan, whisk together the cornstarch and 1/3 cup cold water. Add the sauce from the chicken to the cornstarch mixture and set it over medium-high heat. Bring to a boil, and cook, stirring often, until it thickens, about 2 minutes.)

SLOW COOKER DIRECTIONS: Omit the margarine. Place all ingredients except the chicken into the slow cooker and whisk until smooth. Add the chicken, turning to coat, then cook on low for 6–8 hours or on high for 3–4 hours. (Slow cooker cooking times may vary—get to know your slow cooker and, if necessary, adjust cooking times accordingly.)

TIP

Most of the fat and calories in poultry resides in its skin. For easy skin trimming, use a kitchen scissors (wash the scissors in hot sudsy water when you are done) or pull the skin off with a paper towel (it helps you get a good grip).

Punjabi-Style Potatoes

SERVES: 6 • **SERVING SIZE:** 1 CUP

2 tablespoons canola or vegetable oil

1 small yellow onion, finely diced

1 tablespoon fresh ginger

1 1/2 teaspoons minced garlic

1 jalapeño pepper, seeded and finely diced

1 teaspoon curry powder

1 teaspoon garam masala (an Indian spice blend)

1/2 tomato, chopped

1 1/2 pounds red potatoes, chopped

1/2 teaspoon salt

1. Heat a large heavy skillet over medium heat and add the oil. When it is hot, add the onions. When they start to brown after about 5 minutes, add the ginger, garlic, jalapeño, curry powder, and garam masala, covered. Cook for 2 more minutes, then stir in the tomatoes. Add the potatoes and salt and stir to coat them. Add 1 cup warm water, bring it to a boil, cover, and reduce the heat to simmer for 15 minutes, stirring occasionally. Uncover and simmer for 10 more minutes or until most of the liquid is absorbed and the potatoes are very tender. Serve immediately.

FLAVOR BOOSTER
Add 1/8 teaspoon black pepper to the sauce.

NUTRITIONAL INFORMATION | IRRESISTIBLE HONEY-CURRY CHICKEN:

EXCHANGES / CHOICES:
1/2 Carbohydrate; 2 Protein, lean; 1/2 Fat

Calories: 150; Calories from Fat: 65; Total Fat: 7 g;
Saturated Fat: 1.7 g; Trans Fat: 0 g; Cholesterol: 65 mg;
Sodium: 335 mg; Potassium: 200 mg; Total Carbohydrate: 7 g;
Dietary Fiber: 0 g; Sugar: 5 g; Protein: 15 g; Phosphorus: 120 mg

NUTRITIONAL INFORMATION | PUNJABI-STYLE POTATOES:

EXCHANGES / CHOICES:
1 1/2 Starch; 1 Fat

Calories: 150; Calories from Fat: 45; Total Fat: 5 g;
Saturated Fat: 0.4 g; Trans Fat: 0 g; Cholesterol: 0 mg;
Sodium: 200 mg; Potassium: 515 mg; Total Carbohydrate: 25 g;
Dietary Fiber: 3 g; Sugar: 2 g; Protein: 3 g; Phosphorus: 65 mg

Can we ever have enough variations on tacos? This version was suggested by longtime Scramble member Jen Grosman. I made both the tofu and salmon versions for dinner, and to my surprise, the tofu version was even more popular with my family, but both fillings were demolished by the time dinner was done. Serve with Chopped Cucumber and Avocado Salad.

Salmon (or Tofu) Tacos

PREP + COOK: 20 MINUTES • **SERVES:** 6 • **SERVING SIZE:** 2 TACOS

1/2 teaspoon paprika

1/2 teaspoon ground cumin

1/4 teaspoon cayenne pepper (optional)

1/4 teaspoon garlic powder

1/4 teaspoon salt

1 pound salmon fillet (preferably wild Alaskan), cut into 2 pieces, or use 15 ounces extra-firm tofu, cut into 8 long pieces, drained and pressed dry (use a clean dish towel)

1 tablespoon extra-virgin olive oil, or use 2 tablespoons canola or vegetable oil for the tofu

1/2 cup pico de gallo (fresh chopped salsa), plus extra for serving

12 corn tortillas, warmed

8 ounces guacamole (store-bought or make your own with 2–3 mashed avocados, 1 tablespoon fresh lime or lemon juice, and 1/4 teaspoon salt)

DO AHEAD OR DELEGATE: Cut the salmon and refrigerate, or cut and drain the tofu, make the spice rub and put it on the salmon or the tofu (and refrigerate the salmon if using), and make the guacamole, if preparing your own (and refrigerate tightly covered to prevent browning).

1. In a small bowl, combine the dry spices and salt. Sprinkle and rub them all over the flesh of the salmon (or all over the tofu). (This can be done up to 12 hours in advance.)

2. To cook the salmon: Heat the oil in a large heavy skillet over medium-high heat. When it is hot, add the salmon flesh-side down, and sear (cook without moving it) for about 4 minutes until it is crisp and browned. (Meanwhile, make the salad, if you are serving it.) Flip and cook it on the other side for about 4 minutes.

3. When it is about 2/3 of the way cooked through on the second side, use a metal spatula to chop up the salmon, skin and all, and add 1/2 cup of the salsa (you may want to reserve the salsa to serve on the side for picky eaters). Continue cooking for 1–2 more minutes until the salmon is just cooked through. Transfer the salmon to a serving bowl, and serve it in the tortillas over a thin layer of guacamole and topped with a little extra salsa, if desired.

4. To cook the tofu: Use a large nonstick skillet and heat the vegetable oil over medium-high heat. Sauté the well-dried tofu for 15 minutes total, or until it is browned and crispy on all sides, turning it occasionally and chopping it a bit as it nears the end of the cooking time. Add the salsa to the pan as above and proceed with the recipe.

Chopped Cucumber and Avocado Salad

SERVES: 6 • **SERVING SIZE:** 2/3 CUP

1 cucumber, peeled, seeded, and chopped

2 avocados, peeled and chopped

1 tablespoon crumbled Gorgonzola or blue cheese

1/8 lemon, juice only (about 1 teaspoon)

1/2 teaspoon balsamic vinegar, or more to taste

1. In a medium bowl, combine the cucumbers, avocados, and cheese. Top everything with the lemon juice and vinegar. Toss gently and serve it immediately.

FLAVOR BOOSTER
Add some fresh cilantro to the tacos.

To make your own pico de gallo (fresh salsa) combine 2 large tomatoes, diced (about 3 cups), 1/4 yellow onion, finely diced (3/4 cup), 1 jalapeño pepper, seeds removed, minced, 2 tablespoons fresh flat-leaf parsley or cilantro, chopped, 1/2 lime, juice only, about 1 tablespoon, 1 teaspoon extra-virgin olive oil, and 1/4 teaspoon salt. Serve immediately or refrigerate for up to a week.

NUTRITIONAL INFORMATION | SALMON (OR TOFU) TACOS:

EXCHANGES / CHOICES:
2 Starch; 2 Protein, lean; 2 Fat

Calories: 330; Calories from Fat: 135; Total Fat: 15 g; Saturated Fat: 2.5 g; Trans Fat: 0 g; Cholesterol: 40 mg; Sodium: 370 mg; Potassium: 575 mg; Total Carbohydrate: 28 g; Dietary Fiber: 6 g; Sugar: 1 g; Protein: 19 g; Phosphorus: 385 mg

NUTRITIONAL INFORMATION | CHOPPED CUCUMBER AND AVOCADO SALAD:

EXCHANGES / CHOICES:
1/2 Carbohydrate; 1 1/2 Fat

Calories: 90; Calories from Fat: 70; Total Fat: 8 g; Saturated Fat: 1.3 g; Trans Fat: 0 g; Cholesterol: 0 mg; Sodium: 25 mg; Potassium: 285 mg; Total Carbohydrate: 5 g; Dietary Fiber: 4 g; Sugar: 1 g; Protein: 1 g; Phosphorus: 35 mg

This satisfying meal, suggested by Six O'Clock Scramble member Megan Miller, brings your garden or farmer's market bounty to your dinner table. Meat lovers can brown a pound of hot Italian sausage in the pan before adding the vegetables. Serve with Baby Greens with Sliced Pear and Pecans.

Penne Rigate with Garden Vegetables

PREP: 20 MINUTES • **COOK:** 15 MINUTES • **SERVES:** 10 • **SERVING SIZE:** 2 CUPS

1 tablespoon extra-virgin olive oil

1 pound hot Italian sausage (use wheat/gluten-free if needed) (optional)

1 small red onion, diced

1 teaspoon minced garlic (about 2 cloves)

16 ounces whole-wheat penne rigate

8 ounces sliced mushrooms

1 yellow bell pepper, seeded and diced

1 zucchini, quartered lengthwise and sliced

24 ounces red pasta sauce, any variety

2 tablespoons Worcestershire sauce

1/4–1/2 cup nonfat sour cream, to taste

DO AHEAD OR DELEGATE: Cook the pasta and store tossed with a little oil to prevent sticking, dice the onion, peel the garlic, seed and dice the yellow pepper, quarter and slice the zucchini, or fully prepare and refrigerate the dish.

1. In a Dutch oven or large heavy skillet, heat the oil over medium heat. (If you are using the sausage, brown it now, then proceed with the recipe.) Add the onions and garlic and sauté it for 2–3 minutes until fragrant.

2. Meanwhile, cook the pasta according to the package directions until it is al dente.

3. Add the mushrooms, peppers, and zucchini to the pot with the onions and garlic, cover partially, and sauté for about 15 minutes, stirring occasionally, until the vegetables are tender. (Meanwhile, make the salad, if you are serving it.) Add the pasta sauce and Worcestershire sauce and cook for 5–10 more minutes until the pasta is done.

4. Remove the sauce from the heat and stir in the sour cream and the pasta. Serve immediately or refrigerate for up to 2 days (the sauce gets even better with age).

SLOW COOKER DIRECTIONS: Omit the oil. Mix all ingredients except the penne and sour cream in the slow cooker and cook on low for 6–8 hours or on high for 3–4 hours. Turn the slow cooker off, then stir in the sour cream and cooked penne. (Slow cooker cooking times may vary—get to know your slow cooker and, if necessary, adjust cooking times accordingly.)

Baby Greens with Sliced Pear and Pecans

SERVES: 10 • **SERVING SIZE:** 1 1/2 CUPS

14 ounces baby salad greens

2 medium pears, sliced

3 tablespoons pecans, coarsely chopped or broken and lightly toasted

1/2 cup vinaigrette dressing

1. Toss the greens with the pears, pecans, and dressing.

FLAVOR BOOSTER
Stir in 1/4–1/2 teaspoon black pepper when combining the pasta and sauce.

TIP
You can substitute the equivalent amount of nonfat Greek yogurt for the sour cream. This will give the meal some additional protein.

NUTRITIONAL INFORMATION | PENNE RIGATE WITH GARDEN VEGETABLES:

EXCHANGES / CHOICES:
2 1/2 Starch; 1 Nonstarchy Vegetable; 1 Fat

Calories: 255; Calories from Fat: 45; Total Fat: 5 g;
Saturated Fat: 0.6 g; Trans Fat: 0 g; Cholesterol: 0 mg;
Sodium: 230 mg; Potassium: 475 mg; Total Carbohydrate: 46 g;
Dietary Fiber: 7 g; Sugar: 7 g; Protein: 8 g; Phosphorus: 145 mg

NUTRITIONAL INFORMATION | BABY GREENS WITH SLICED PEAR AND PECANS:

EXCHANGES / CHOICES:
1/2 Carbohydrate; 1 Fat

Calories: 75; Calories from Fat: 35; Total Fat: 4 g;
Saturated Fat: 0.5 g; Trans Fat: 0 g; Cholesterol: 0 mg;
Sodium: 150 mg; Potassium: 130 mg; Total Carbohydrate: 9 g;
Dietary Fiber: 2 g; Sugar: 5 g; Protein: 1 g; Phosphorus: 20 mg

These colorful cool weather vegetables keep you warm and healthy and fill you up with fiber and soothing liquid without loading you up with calories. We think this soup tastes even better on day two, so it's a good one to make ahead and enjoy on an extra busy night. Serve with Whole-Grain Baguette.

Winter Rainbow Soup

PREP + COOK: 30 MINUTES • **SERVES:** 4 • **SERVING SIZE:** 2 CUPS

1 tablespoon extra-virgin olive oil

1/2 teaspoon dried rosemary

1 small yellow onion, diced (about 1 cup)

1/4 head purple cabbage, thinly sliced, then cut the slices in half (about 2 cups)

1 teaspoon minced garlic (about 2 cloves)

1 small sweet potato, peeled and diced (about 2 cups)

1 cup frozen shelled edamame, thawed

2 1/2 cups reduced-sodium vegetable broth

1 1/2 cups water

1–3 teaspoons apple cider vinegar, to taste

1/4 cup grated Parmesan cheese, for serving

DO AHEAD OR DELEGATE: Dice the onion, slice the cabbage, peel the garlic, peel and dice the sweet potato, grate the cheese if necessary, or fully prepare and refrigerate or freeze the soup.

1. Heat a large saucepan over medium heat, and when it is hot, add the oil. When the oil is hot, add the rosemary, onions, and cabbage and sauté, stirring occasionally, until softened, 5–7 minutes.

2. Add the garlic and sweet potatoes and sauté for 2 more minutes, then stir in the edamame, broth, and water. Bring it to a boil and reduce the heat to simmer for about 8 minutes until the sweet potatoes are fork tender. (Meanwhile, warm the bread, if you are serving it.) Stir in the vinegar, and season with salt and pepper, if desired.

3. Serve immediately topped with the cheese, or refrigerate for up to 3 days, or freeze for up to 3 months.

SLOW COOKER DIRECTIONS: Omit the oil. Combine all remaining ingredients except the vinegar and cheese in the slow cooker. Cook on low for 8–10 hours or on high for 4–5 hours. Stir in the vinegar and serve topped with the cheese, as directed. (Slow cooker cooking times may vary—get to know your slow cooker and, if necessary, adjust cooking times accordingly.)

Whole-Grain Baguette

SERVES: 6 • **SERVING SIZE:** 1 (1-OUNCE) SLICE

1 whole-grain baguette

1. Warm the baguette in a 300°F oven for about 5 minutes if desired, and slice it.

FLAVOR BOOSTER
Double the garlic and serve the soup with plenty of freshly ground pepper.

TIP
The purple cabbage in this recipe gives the soup some colorful appeal. If you happen to already have green cabbage, that would work in this soup as well. Regardless of the color, cabbage is high in fiber and nutrients and low in calories.

NUTRITIONAL INFORMATION | WINTER RAINBOW SOUP:

EXCHANGES / CHOICES:
1 Starch; 2 Nonstarchy Vegetable; 1 Fat

Calories: 185; Calories from Fat: 65; Total Fat: 7 g;
Saturated Fat: 1.5 g; Trans Fat: 0 g; Cholesterol: 5 mg;
Sodium: 425 mg; Potassium: 580 mg; Total Carbohydrate: 23 g;
Dietary Fiber: 5 g; Sugar: 8 g; Protein: 9 g; Phosphorus: 160 mg

NUTRITIONAL INFORMATION | WHOLE-GRAIN BAGUETTE:

EXCHANGES / CHOICES:
1 Starch

Calories: 70; Calories from Fat: 10; Total Fat: 1 g;
Saturated Fat: 0.2 g; Trans Fat: 0 g; Cholesterol: 0 mg;
Sodium: 125 mg; Potassium: 70 mg; Total Carbohydrate: 12 g;
Dietary Fiber: 2 g; Sugar: 1 g; Protein: 3 g; Phosphorus: 60 mg

This sweet and fragrant combination, suggested by Jennifer Gross, hits just the right notes for my family, and is healthy vegetarian food at its best. Our young dinner guest Sophie Martel enjoyed three helpings of the stew! Serve with Seedless Grapes.

Lovely Lentils with Spinach and Tomatoes

PREP: 25 MINUTES • **COOK:** 30 MINUTES • **SERVES:** 4 • **SERVING SIZE:** 1 1/2 CUPS

3/4 cup dried green/brown lentils, soaked in water overnight, if possible

2 tablespoons extra-virgin olive oil

1 yellow onion, finely diced

2 teaspoons ground cumin

1 teaspoon ground cinnamon

1/3 teaspoon salt

2 cups low-sodium chicken or vegetable broth

14 ounces diced tomatoes

1/4 cup dried currants or raisins

6–9 ounces baby spinach (or use 1 pound regular spinach, ends trimmed)

DO AHEAD OR DELEGATE: Soak the lentils, dice the onion, combine the dry seasonings, add 1/2–1 teapoon curry powder, or fully prepare and refrigerate the dish.

1. (If you have soaked the lentils for faster cooking, drain them before proceeding with the recipe.) In a large heavy skillet, heat the oil over medium heat. Add the onions, cumin, cinnamon, and salt, and cook until the onions are very soft, about 10 minutes.

2. Add the lentils and broth and bring it to a boil. Cover, reduce the heat, and simmer for 30 minutes (15 minutes for pre-soaked lentils). Add the tomatoes, currants or raisins, and spinach. Bring it back to a boil, cover, and reduce the heat to simmer for 10 more minutes or until the lentils are tender. Serve immediately or refrigerate it for up to 3 days.

SLOW COOKER DIRECTIONS: Omit the oil. Put the remaining ingredients except the spinach into the slow cooker. Cook on low for 5–6 hours or on high for 2 1/2 hours. Turn off the slow cooker, stir in the spinach, and put the cover back on. Allow the spinach to cook using the residual heat of the pot for 10–15 minutes. (Slow cooker cooking times may vary—get to know your slow cooker and, if necessary, adjust cooking times accordingly.)

FLAVOR BOOSTER
Add 1/4–1/2 teaspoon cayenne pepper with the other spices.

Seedless Grapes

SERVES: 6 • **SERVING SIZE:** 3 OUNCES (17 SMALL GRAPES)

1 1/4 pounds seedless grapes

1. Serve alongside Lovely Lentils with Spinach and Tomatoes.

TIP

A 2012 study published by the American Heart Association associates high-fiber diets with decreased risk of stroke. Foods generally containing generous amounts of fiber are fruits, vegetables, whole grains, and beans like lentils, so make sure to incorporate plenty of these into your diet.

NUTRITIONAL INFORMATION | LOVELY LENTILS WITH SPINACH AND TOMATOES:

EXCHANGES / CHOICES:
1 1/2 Starch; 1/2 Fruit; 2 Nonstarchy Vegetable; 1 Protein, lean; 1/2 Fat

Calories: 260; Calories from Fat: 70; Total Fat: 8 g; Saturated Fat: 1.2 g; Trans Fat: 0 g; Cholesterol: 0 mg; Sodium: 415 mg; Potassium: 1055 mg; Total Carbohydrate: 38 g; Dietary Fiber: 12 g; Sugar: 13 g; Protein: 13 g; Phosphorus: 265 mg

NUTRITIONAL INFORMATION | SEEDLESS GRAPES:

EXCHANGES / CHOICES:
1 Fruit

Calories: 60; Calories from Fat: 0; Total Fat: 0 g; Saturated Fat: 0 g; Trans Fat: 0 g; Cholesterol: 0 mg; Sodium: 0 mg; Potassium: 160 mg; Total Carbohydrate: 15 g; Dietary Fiber: 1 g; Sugar: 13 g; Protein: 1 g; Phosphorus: 15 mg

WINTER
WEEK 8

Sizzling Korean Beef (1)
SIDE DISH: Green Salad with Asian Pear, Crumbled Gorgonzola Cheese, and Fresh Mint (1a)

Breaded Tilapia with Garlic-Lime Sauce (2)
SIDE DISH: Buckwheat (Kasha) (2a); Roasted Asparagus (2b)

Slow-Cooker Sweet and Smoky Corn and Pinto Bean Stew (3)
SIDE DISH: Sliced Apples (3a)

Fusilli with Pistachio-Arugula Pesto (4)
SIDE DISH: Honey-Glazed Carrots (4a)

Broccoli and Chickpea Salad with Lemon Vinaigrette (5)
SIDE DISH: Whole-Grain Bread (5a)

SHOPPING LIST

🥕 PRODUCE
1 pound **carrots** (4a)
6 **scallions** (2)(5)
2 **yellow onions** (1)(3)
1 **red bell pepper** (5)
2 heads **butter lettuce or other soft lettuce** (1a)
5 ounces **baby arugula** (4)
1–2 cloves **garlic** (4)
1 tablespoon **fresh ginger** (1)
1 cup **fresh flat-leaf parsley** (5)
2 tablespoons **fresh mint leaves** (1a)
1 large head **broccoli** (5)
1 1/2 pounds **asparagus** (2b)
2 medium **white or sweet potatoes** (3)
1 1/2 **lemons** (4)(5)
1/2 **lime** (2)
4 **apples** (3a)
2 **Asian pears** (1)(1a)

🐟 MEAT AND FISH
4 **tilapia fillets** (2)
1 1/4 pounds **skirt steak** (1)
1/2 pound **smoked ham or soy chorizo** (3)

SHELVED ITEMS

1 cup **quick-cooking brown rice** (1)

8 slices **whole-grain bread** (5a)

1 cup **buckwheat** (kasha) (2a)

16 ounces **whole-wheat fusilli noodles** (use wheat/ gluten-free if needed) (4)

1 cup **tortilla chips** (3)*

16 ounces **medium or spicy salsa** (3)

1 **chipotle pepper in adobo sauce** (3)*

1/2 cup **white wine** (2)

16 ounces **dry pinto beans** (3)

15 ounces canned **chickpeas** (garbanzo beans) (5)

1/4 cup **dried cranberries** (preferably naturally sweetened) (5)

1/2 cup **shelled unsalted pistachio nuts** (4)

1/4 cup **chopped walnuts** (5)

3 cups **cooked brown rice** (1)

SPICES

1 1/8–1 1/4 teaspoons **salt** (2)(3)(4a)(5)

1/4 teaspoon **kosher salt** (2b)

3/8 teaspoon **black pepper** (2)(2b)(5)

1 tablespoon **smoked paprika** (3)

1 tablespoon **sesame seeds** (1)

STAPLES

1 tablespoon **butter** (4a)

4 teaspoon **trans fat-free margarine** (2)

1 tablespoon + 1/2 cup **extra-virgin olive oil** (2b)(4)(5)

1 tablespoon **sesame oil** (1)

2 tablespoons **balsamic vinegar** (5)

1/4 cup **vinaigrette dressing** (1a)

1/4 cup **reduced-sodium soy sauce** (use wheat/gluten-free if needed) (1)

1/4 cup + 1–2 teaspoons **honey** (3a)(4a)

3 teaspoons **minced garlic** (1)(2)(3)

1/2 cup **flour** (use wheat/gluten-free if needed) (2)

REFRIGERATED/FROZEN

2 tablespoons **crumbled Gorgonzola or blue cheese** (1a)

1 cup **shredded sharp cheddar cheese** (3)*

1 cup **crumbled reduced-fat feta cheese** (5)

1/4 cup **grated Parmesan cheese** (4)

16 ounces **frozen roasted corn** (3)

Get free, printable versions of the shopping lists from this book at **TheScramble.com/diabetes**.

*optional ingredients

WINTER WEEK 8 • **387**

The ingredients in this dish are based on the Korean dish beef bulgogi, which would traditionally be cooked on a hibachi grill, then wrapped in lettuce leaves. Serve with Green Salad with Asian Pear, Crumbled Gorgonzola Cheese, and Fresh Mint.

Sizzling Korean Beef

MARINATE: 10 MINUTES • **PREP:** 20 MINUTES • **COOK:** 10 MINUTES • **SERVES:** 6 • **SERVING SIZE:** 3 OUNCES STEAK + 1/2 CUP RICE

1 1/4 pounds skirt steak

1/4 cup reduced-sodium soy sauce (use wheat/gluten-free if needed)

1 tablespoon sesame seeds

1 tablespoon sesame oil

1 tablespoon fresh ginger, grated

1 1/2 teaspoons minced garlic (about 2–3 cloves)

1/2 Asian pear, peeled and grated

1 yellow onion, halved top to bottom and thinly sliced

3 cups cooked brown rice

DO AHEAD OR DELEGATE: Slice the steak, make the marinade and marinate the steak in the refrigerator, slice the onion.

1. If time allows, freeze the raw steak for 15–20 minutes, so it's easier to thinly slice. Meanwhile, in a medium to large bowl, combine the remaining ingredients, except the rice. (Prepare the rice now.)

2. Thinly slice the steak across the grain, and add it to the bowl with the marinade. Let it stand at least 10 minutes, or refrigerate and marinate for up to 24 hours.

3. (Make the salad if you are serving it.) Heat a large nonstick skillet over high heat. Add about 1/2 the steak, onions, and marinade, and cook, turning the meat often, for 3–4 minutes until it is browned. Transfer it to a serving bowl. Repeat with the remaining steak, onions, and marinade until it is all cooked through. Serve immediately over the rice, or refrigerate for up to 3 days.

SLOW COOKER DIRECTIONS: Combine the sauce ingredients in the slow cooker. Add the sliced beef and pear and stir well to combine. Cook on low for 5–6 hours or on high for 2 1/2–3 hours. Optional: Stir once or twice during cooking time to prevent beef slices from sticking together. (Slow cooker cooking times may vary—get to know your slow cooker and, if necessary, adjust cooking times accordingly.)

FLAVOR BOOSTER

Add 1/2–1 teaspoon Asian chili garlic sauce to the marinade, or serve it on the side.

Green Salad with Asian Pear, Crumbled Gorgonzola Cheese, and Fresh Mint

SERVES: 6 • **SERVING SIZE:** 1 CUP

2 heads butter lettuce or other soft lettuce, torn or chopped

1 Asian pear, diced

2 tablespoons crumbled Gorgonzola or blue cheese

2 tablespoons fresh mint leaves, chopped

1/4 cup vinaigrette dressing (see page 98 for salad dressing recipes)

1. Toss the lettuce with the pear, Gorgonzola or blue cheese, mint, and the vinaigrette dressing or dressing of your choice.

TIP

Rubs and marinades not only add extra flavor to meat, but some marinades, like this one, can also help tenderize the beef.

NUTRITIONAL INFORMATION | SIZZLING KOREAN BEEF:

EXCHANGES / CHOICES:
1 1/2 Starch; 1 Nonstarchy Vegetable; 3 Protein, lean; 1 Fat

Calories: 315; Calories from Fat: 110; Total Fat: 12 g;
Saturated Fat: 3.5 g; Trans Fat: 0.3 g; Cholesterol: 60 mg;
Sodium: 415 mg; Potassium: 325 mg; Total Carbohydrate: 28 g;
Dietary Fiber: 3 g; Sugar: 2 g; Protein: 24 g; Phosphorus: 225 mg

NUTRITIONAL INFORMATION | GREEN SALAD WITH ASIAN PEAR, CRUMBLED GORGONZOLA CHEESE, AND FRESH MINT:

EXCHANGES / CHOICES:
1/2 Carbohydrate; 1/2 Fat

Calories: 50; Calories from Fat: 25; Total Fat: 3 g;
Saturated Fat: 0.8 g; Trans Fat: 0 g; Cholesterol: 0 mg;
Sodium: 140 mg; Potassium: 170 mg; Total Carbohydrate: 5 g;
Dietary Fiber: 1 g; Sugar: 3 g; Protein: 1 g; Phosphorus: 30 mg

This light and delicate fish is terrific with Buckwheat (Kasha) and Roasted Asparagus.

Breaded Tilapia with Garlic-Lime Sauce

PREP + COOK: 15 MINUTES • **SERVES:** 4 • **SERVING SIZE:** 1 FILLET

1/2 teaspoon minced garlic (about 1 clove)

1/2 cup white wine, or use a scant 1/2 cup vegetable broth mixed with 1 teaspoon vinegar

1/2 lime, juice only (about 1 tablespoon)

1/2 cup flour (use wheat/gluten-free if needed)

4 teaspoons trans fat-free margarine, divided use, or use butter

4 tilapia fillets (about 1 pound)

1/4 teaspoon salt, divided use

1/8 teaspoon black pepper, divided use

2 scallions, green parts only, thinly sliced

FLAVOR BOOSTER
Serve the fish with fresh lime wedges and sprinkle it with fresh cilantro or parsley.

DO AHEAD OR DELEGATE: Peel the garlic, juice the lime, slice the scallions, and combine the garlic, wine, and lime juice.

1. (Start the buckwheat and asparagus first, if you are serving them.) In a small bowl, combine the garlic, wine, and lime juice. Set it aside. Put the flour on a shallow plate. Melt 3 teaspoons margarine or butter in a large nonstick skillet over medium-high heat.

2. Dredge the fillets in the flour, and add them to the skillet, pressing them with a spatula to make sure the fish makes good contact with the pan. Season the tops of the fish with 1/2 of the salt and pepper. Cook the fish for 3–4 minutes per side, until it is lightly browned. After flipping it, season the second side with salt and pepper. Transfer the fish to a clean plate and cover it lightly to keep it warm.

3. In the skillet that held the fish, melt the remaining 1 teaspoon margarine or butter over medium heat. Add the wine mixture to the skillet and cook it at a low boil until it is thickened and reduced by half, about 2 minutes. Stir in the scallions after about 1 minute. Pour the sauce over the fish (you may want to leave some fish plain for picky eaters) and serve immediately.

SLOW COOKER DIRECTIONS: Combine the garlic, wine, lime juice, and margarine or butter in the slow cooker (omit the flour). Sprinkle the fish with salt and pepper and add to the slow cooker, turning it over a few times in the sauce. Cook it on low for 6–8 hours or on high for 3 1/2–4 hours. Add the scallions 10 minutes before serving the fish. (Slow cooker cooking times may vary—get to know your slow cooker and, if necessary, adjust cooking times accordingly.)

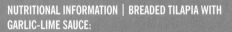

SIDE DISHES

Buckwheat (Kasha)

SERVES: 4 • **SERVING SIZE:** 2/3 CUP

1 cup buckwheat (kasha)

1. Prepare the buckwheat (kasha) according to the package directions, using 2 cups of water or reduced-sodium vegetable or chicken broth.

Roasted Asparagus

SERVES: 4 • **SERVING SIZE:** 3–5 SPEARS (1/4 OF SPEARS)

1 1/2 pounds asparagus, ends trimmed

1 tablespoon extra-virgin olive oil

1/4 teaspoon kosher salt

1/8 teaspoon black pepper

1. Toss the asparagus spears with the oil, salt, and pepper. Roast them in a flat baking dish in a single layer at 450°F until they are tender and starting to brown, 15–20 minutes. For a delicious alternative, top the asparagus with fresh lemon juice or a splash of balsamic vinegar and grated Parmesan cheese after removing it from the oven.

TIP

When sautéing something delicate like fish, I use the largest spatula I can get away with. It makes it easier to flip the fish without running the risk of it falling apart.

NUTRITIONAL INFORMATION | BREADED TILAPIA WITH GARLIC-LIME SAUCE:

EXCHANGES / CHOICES:
1/2 Starch; 3 Protein, lean

Calories: 195; Calories from Fat: 45; Total Fat: 5 g;
Saturated Fat: 1.4 g; Trans Fat: 0 g; Cholesterol: 50 mg;
Sodium: 225 mg; Potassium: 375 mg; Total Carbohydrate: 11 g;
Dietary Fiber: 1 g; Sugar: 0 g; Protein: 24 g; Phosphorus: 195 mg

NUTRITIONAL INFORMATION | BUCKWHEAT:

EXCHANGES / CHOICES:
1 1/2 Starch

Calories: 95; Calories from Fat: 5; Total Fat: 0.5 g;
Saturated Fat: 0.1 g; Trans Fat: 0 g; Cholesterol: 0 mg;
Sodium: 0 mg; Potassium: 90 mg; Total Carbohydrate: 21 g;
Dietary Fiber: 3 g; Sugar: 1 g; Protein: 4 g; Phosphorus: 75 mg

NUTRITIONAL INFORMATION | ROASTED ASPARAGUS:

EXCHANGES / CHOICES:
1 Nonstarchy Vegetable; 1/2 Fat

Calories: 50; Calories from Fat: 30; Total Fat: 3.5 g;
Saturated Fat: 0.5 g; Trans Fat: 0 g; Cholesterol: 0 mg;
Sodium: 130 mg; Potassium: 190 mg; Total Carbohydrate: 3 g;
Dietary Fiber: 2 g; Sugar: 1 g; Protein: 2 g; Phosphorus: 45 mg

This smoky, sweet stew has endless variations. It can be served over rice, inside a tortilla, or simply in a bowl topped with cheddar cheese or crushed tortilla chips. Since learning that there's no real need to soak dry beans before cooking them, I've been making them a lot more often instead of using canned beans. Serve with Sliced Apples.

Slow-Cooker Sweet and Smoky Corn and Pinto Bean Stew

PREP: 10 MINUTES • **COOK:** 6 HOURS • **SERVES:** 11 • **SERVING SIZE:** ABOUT 1 1/3 CUPS

16 ounces dry pinto beans, rinsed

16 ounces frozen roasted corn, or use regular frozen corn kernels

1 yellow onion, diced

2 medium white or sweet potatoes, peeled and chopped into 1-inch pieces (about 3 cups)

1/2 pound lean smoked ham or soy chorizo, chopped

16 ounces medium or spicy salsa

6 cups water

1 tablespoon smoked paprika

1 teaspoon minced garlic, (about 2 cloves)

1 chipotle pepper in adobo sauce, with a little of the sauce (optional)

1/16 teaspoon salt

1 cup shredded sharp cheddar cheese (optional)

1 cup tortilla chips, crushed (optional)

DO AHEAD OR DELEGATE: Dice the onion, peel and chop the potatoes (if using white potatoes, store them covered with water to prevent browning), chop the ham or chorizo and refrigerate, peel the garlic, shred the cheese if necessary and refrigerate, and crush the tortilla chips if using.

1. Combine all of the ingredients except the cheese and chips in the slow cooker and stir. Cover and cook on low for 6–8 hours. Serve immediately topped with the cheese and chips, if desired, or refrigerate for up to 4 days.

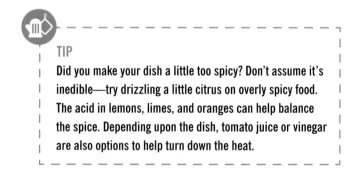

TIP

Did you make your dish a little too spicy? Don't assume it's inedible—try drizzling a little citrus on overly spicy food. The acid in lemons, limes, and oranges can help balance the spice. Depending upon the dish, tomato juice or vinegar are also options to help turn down the heat.

- -

Sliced Apples

SERVES: 4 • **SERVING SIZE:** 1 SMALL APPLE

4 apples (about 4 ounces each), cored and sliced
1/4 cup honey (optional)

1. Slice the apples. For a simple dessert, serve with the honey for dipping.

FLAVOR BOOSTER
Add 2–3 chopped fresh sage leaves to the stew, use the optional chipotle pepper, or serve the stew with hot pepper sauce, such as Tabasco.

NUTRITIONAL INFORMATION | SLOW-COOKER SWEET AND
SMOKY CORN AND PINTO BEAN STEW:

EXCHANGES / CHOICES:
2 1/2 Starch; 1 Nonstarchy Vegetable; 1 Protein, lean

Calories: 255; Calories from Fat: 20; Total Fat: 2.5 g;
Saturated Fat: 0.6 g; Trans Fat: 0 g; Cholesterol: 10 mg;
Sodium: 455 mg; Potassium: 855 mg; Total Carbohydrate: 46 g;
Dietary Fiber: 11 g; Sugar: 4 g; Protein: 16 g; Phosphorus: 245 mg

NUTRITIONAL INFORMATION | SLICED APPLES:

EXCHANGES / CHOICES:
1 Fruit

Calories: 55; Calories from Fat: 0; Total Fat: 0 g;
Saturated Fat: 0 g; Trans Fat: 0 g; Cholesterol: 0 mg;
Sodium: 0 mg; Potassium: 110 mg; Total Carbohydrate: 14 g;
Dietary Fiber: 2 g; Sugar: 11 g; Protein: 0 g; Phosphorus: 10 mg

I admit it, I'm a bit of a pesto fanatic. While I think classic basil pesto is one of the most ingenious food creations of all time, I like to experiment with other nuts and flavors in pesto, like this version with pistachios, arugula, and lemon. Arugula can be a little peppery, but baby arugula is milder. If it is still too peppery for your family, substitute baby spinach. Serve with Honey-Glazed Carrots.

Fusilli with Pistachio-Arugula Pesto

PREP + COOK: 25 MINUTES • **SERVES:** 8 • **SERVING SIZE:** 1 1/4 CUPS

16 ounces whole-wheat fusilli noodles (use brown rice or quinoa pasta for a gluten-free option)

1/2 cup shelled unsalted pistachio nuts, or use sunflower seeds, cashews, or other nut or seed of your choice

5 ounces baby arugula or spinach

1/4 cup grated Parmesan cheese

1/4 cup extra-virgin olive oil

1/2 lemon, juice only (about 2 tablespoons)

1–2 cloves garlic, to taste

DO AHEAD OR DELEGATE: Cook the pasta and store tossed with a little oil to prevent sticking, grate the Parmesan cheese if necessary and refrigerate, juice the lemon, peel the garlic, prepare the pesto, or fully prepare and refrigerate the dish.

1. (Start the carrots first, if you are serving them.) Cook the noodles in salted water according to the package directions until they are al dente, and reserve about 1/2 cup of their cooking water before draining.

2. Meanwhile, in a food processor or blender, pulse the pistachios and 2 packed cups of the arugula until they are finely chopped. Add the remaining ingredients and pulse until it is well blended but not too smooth (unless you prefer it that way).

3. Drain the noodles and toss them immediately with the remaining arugula and the arugula pesto, adding some of the reserved pasta water to thin the sauce as needed. Serve immediately or refrigerate for up to 2 days.

FLAVOR BOOSTER
Add 1/4–1/2 teaspoon lemon zest to the pesto and/or serve the dish with freshly ground pepper.

Honey-Glazed Carrots

SERVES: 8 • **SERVING SIZE:** 1/2 CUP

1 tablespoon butter

1 pound carrots, sliced

1–2 teaspoons honey

1/8 teaspoon salt, or to taste (optional)

1. Heat the butter in a large heavy skillet over medium heat. Add the carrots and honey, and stir to coat the carrots. Sauté, stirring occasionally, for 8–10 minutes until the carrots are tender and slightly browned. (If they are getting too browned, reduce the heat.) Season with salt before serving, if desired.

TIP

If you're drawn to foods that are labeled "sugar-free," be aware that this doesn't necessarily translate to healthy and low-calorie. The item could still be high in fat and carbohydrates. Your best bet is to stick to whole foods like fruits, veggies, and whole grains where you know exactly what you're getting and your body is getting what it needs.

NUTRITIONAL INFORMATION | FUSILLI WITH PISTACHIO-ARUGULA PESTO:

EXCHANGES / CHOICES:
3 Starch; 1 Protein, lean; 1 1/2 Fat

Calories: 315; Calories from Fat: 110; Total Fat: 12 g; Saturated Fat: 1.9 g; Trans Fat: 0 g; Cholesterol: 0 mg; Sodium: 70 mg; Potassium: 270 mg; Total Carbohydrate: 46 g; Dietary Fiber: 6 g; Sugar: 3 g; Protein: 11 g; Phosphorus: 210 mg

NUTRITIONAL INFORMATION | HONEY-GLAZED CARROTS:

EXCHANGES / CHOICES:
1 Nonstarchy Vegetable; 1/2 Fat

Calories: 35; Calories from Fat: 15; Total Fat: 1.5 g; Saturated Fat: 0.9 g; Trans Fat: 0.1 g; Cholesterol: 5 mg; Sodium: 45 mg; Potassium: 160 mg; Total Carbohydrate: 6 g; Dietary Fiber: 1 g; Sugar: 3 g; Protein: 0 g; Phosphorus: 20 mg

This colorful salad, suggested by Six O'Clock Scramble member Anne O'Neill, is perfect to make a day or two ahead of time. Its Mediterranean ingredients are flexible—you can add sliced kalamata olives, a finely chopped shallot, 1/4 of a red onion, farro (an Italian grain), or even tuna. Serve with Whole-Grain Bread.

Broccoli and Chickpea Salad with Lemon Vinaigrette

PREP + COOK: 20 MINUTES • **SERVES:** 8 • **SERVING SIZE:** 1 1/2 CUPS

1 large head broccoli, cut into florets

1 red bell pepper, chopped into 1/4-inch pieces, or use 1/2 cup chopped jarred red peppers

15 ounces canned chickpeas (garbanzo beans), drained and rinsed, or use 1 1/2 cups cooked

1 cup flat-leaf parsley, chopped

1/4 cup chopped walnuts, lightly toasted, or use toasted pine nuts

4 scallions, dark and light green parts, thinly sliced (about 1/2 cup), or use red onion

1/4 cup extra-virgin olive oil

2 tablespoons balsamic vinegar

1 lemon, juice only (about 1/4 cup)

1/4–1/2 teaspoon salt, to taste

1/8 teaspoon black pepper

1 cup crumbled reduced-fat feta cheese

1/4 cup dried cranberries

DO AHEAD OR DELEGATE: Cut and cook the broccoli, chop the bell pepper if using fresh, cook the chickpeas if necessary (see instructions for cooking beans in a slow cooker on page 121), chop the parsley, toast the nuts, slice the scallions, juice the lemon, prepare the salad dressing, crumble the feta cheese if necessary and refrigerate, or fully prepare and refrigerate the salad.

1. Steam the broccoli in the microwave or on the stovetop for 3 minutes until it is bright green. Let it cool for a few minutes and chop the broccoli into bite-sized pieces. In a large bowl, combine the broccoli, bell pepper, chickpeas, parsley, nuts, and scallions.

2. Meanwhile, in a large measuring cup, whisk together the oil, vinegar, lemon juice, salt, and pepper. Toss the dressing with the ingredients in the bowl, then gently stir in the cheese and cranberries. Serve immediately or refrigerate for up to 3 days.

FLAVOR BOOSTER
Add the zest of the lemon, 1 minced garlic clove, and/or 1 teaspoon Dijon mustard, anchovy paste, or horseradish sauce to the dressing.

Whole-Grain Bread

SERVES: 8 • **SERVING SIZE:** 1 SLICE

8 slices whole-grain bread

1. Warm the bread in a 300°F oven for 5–8 minutes, if desired.

TIP

While some fresh herbs are not as readily available (and are often pricier) during the winter, parsley is generally available year-round. While thought of by many as a garnish, parsley, especially flat-leaf parsley, is a flavorful and nutritious addition for everything from salads to seafood to smoothies. Parsley has a light clean flavor that can be used liberally in recipes, whereas some other stronger-tasting herbs (like thyme, sage and rosemary) require more restraint.

NUTRITIONAL INFORMATION | BROCCOLI AND CHICKPEA SALAD WITH LEMON VINAIGRETTE:

EXCHANGES / CHOICES:
1 Carbohydrate; 1 Protein, lean; 1/2 Fat

Calories: 135; Calories from Fat: 55; Total Fat: 6 g;
Saturated Fat: 1.6 g; Trans Fat: 0 g; Cholesterol: 5 mg;
Sodium: 280 mg; Potassium: 365 mg; Total Carbohydrate: 17 g;
Dietary Fiber: 5 g; Sugar: 6 g; Protein: 9 g; Phosphorus: 160 mg

NUTRITIONAL INFORMATION | WHOLE-GRAIN BREAD:

EXCHANGES / CHOICES:
1 Starch

Calories: 70; Calories from Fat: 10; Total Fat: 1 g;
Saturated Fat: 0.2 g; Trans Fat: 0 g; Cholesterol: 0 mg;
Sodium: 125 mg; Potassium: 70 mg; Total Carbohydrate: 12 g;
Dietary Fiber: 2 g; Sugar: 1 g; Protein: 3 g; Phosphorus: 60 mg

Fiesta Tostadas | page 344

page 320   Garlic Mashed Potato Soup
SIDE DISH: Baked Breadsticks

Index

Asian Edamame and Brown Rice Salad
SIDE DISH: Hard-Boiled Egg

page
48

Previous Cookbooks by Aviva Goldfarb